You Won't
Believe It's
Gluten-Free!

Also by ROBEN RYBERG

The Gluten-Free Kitchen

You Won't Believe It's Gluten-Free!

500 Delicious, Foolproof
Recipes for Healthy Living

ROBEN RYBERG

Da Capo
LIFE
LONG

A MEMBER OF THE PERSEUS BOOKS GROUP

Design and composition by Trish Wilkinson
Set in 11-point Goudy

Library of Congress Cataloging-in-Publication Data

Ryberg, Roben.
    You won't believe it's gluten-free! : 500 delicious, foolproof recipes for healthy living / Roben Ryberg.
        p.   cm.
    Includes bibliographical references and index.
    ISBN 978-1-56924-252-0 (alk. paper)
    1. Gluten-free diet—Recipes. I. Title.
RM237.86.R933 2008
641.5'638—dc22   2008017440

First Da Capo Press edition 2008
ISBN: 978-1-56924-252-0

Published by Da Capo Press
A Member of the Perseus Books Group
www.dacapopress.com

Recipes for Chocolate Velvet Icing and Vanilla Velvet Icing were adapted from *The Gluten-Free Kitchen* by Roben Ryberg, copyright Prima Health, a division of Random House, ISBN 0-7615-2272-7. Used with permission.

Da Capo Press books are available at special discounts for bulk purchases in the United States by corporations, institutions, and other organizations. For more information, please contact the Special Markets Department at the Perseus Books Group, 2300 Chestnut Street, Suite 200, Philadelphia, PA 19103, or call (800) 810-4145, extension 5000, or e-mail special.markets@ perseusbooks.com.

9

To Dad.

Contents

CHAPTER 11 197
Beef, Pork, and Lamb

CHAPTER 10 169
Chicken and Turkey

CHAPTER 16
Cakes

CHAPTER 17
Icings

Foreword

Roben Ryberg's cookbook, *You Won't Believe It's Gluten-Free,* is a follow-up to her first book, *The Gluten-Free Kitchen.* In it, she has increased the diversity of recipes for all occasions, as well as diversity of the ingredients for these recipes. While there are increasing numbers of books that cater to people with gluten intolerance, there are only a few books on the market that can provide information of the quality and range found in this book.

Gluten intolerance is manifested in several forms, as gluten sensitive enteropathy or celiac disease, dermatitis herpetiformis, or DH, or gluten intolerance without celiac disease. Gluten is the term for the storage protein of wheat. There are similar proteins, to which people with celiac disease react, found in rye and barley. As a result the latter two grains are included in the grains to be avoided when an individual is on a gluten-free diet. All other grains are tolerated by over 99 percent of those with celiac disease.

The human digestive system does not fully digest gluten, none of us! We did not evolve to eat wheat. This compares to meats in which the proteins are fully digested into single amino acids or small molecules made up of two or three amino acids. When gluten is digested by our digestive system large amino acid fragments remain. Amino acids are the small fragments that are the building blocks of proteins. Celiac disease is thought to occur when these larger, undigested gluten fragments enter the lining of the small intestine and in genetically predisposed people cause an inflammatory response that causes villous atrophy. This mechanism is fully described in the book I coauthored with Rory Jones, *Celiac Disease: A Hidden Epidemic*, published by HarperCollins.

Gluten sensitive enteropathy or celiac disease is a lifelong, unique autoimmune illness. It occurs in about 1 percent of the population worldwide. There is little knowledge among physicians about the subtle clinical presentations, use of serologic testing, and long-term management. Not only is a gluten-free diet needed. Those with celiac disease require advice and counseling about nutritious and varied substitutes for gluten, similar to the ingredients described in this book, assessment and monitoring of their health and nutrition status, and good medical follow-up for their disease for those with celiac disease, have an increased burden of disease compared to the general population. Patients often get no or inadequate medical follow-up. This compares dramatically with the healthcare systems in most European countries, where celiac disease is regarded as a common and important condition.

In contrast to the general prevalence of this disease there is little medical support for those with celiac disease in the United States. Over the last few years only a few university medical centers have developed specific celiac disease centers like the Celiac Disease Center at Columbia University in New York City.

The Celiac Disease Center at Columbia University provides comprehensive medical care for adults and pediatric patients with celiac disease, including nutrition and attention to the multiple associated conditions that occur in celiac disease. The center is diagnosing and treating more than 2,400 patients annually from around the world and providing better access to proper testing, diagnosis, treatment, and follow-up care.

All of the center's research is directed toward celiac disease and reflects its multisystem nature, including cardiovascular disease, cancer, thyroid disease, infertility, and psychiatric and behavior problems in childhood. Additional information is available online at www.celiacdiseasecenter.org.

It is only with good, ongoing medical care and great attention to a varied and nutritious diet that an adequate quality of life can be maintained.

The entity of gluten intolerance in the absence of celiac disease is more problematic for physicians to deal with. Surprising that something could be more difficult than celiac disease itself! It is more problematic than celiac disease because there is nothing a physician can measure or quantitate in order to assess the patient's disease burden. This compares to celiac disease where we measure antibody levels, assess intestinal biopsy status, and measure vitamin and mineral levels as well as bone density. Gluten intolerance is the reporting of patients that they feel better or symptoms resolve when gluten is withdrawn from the diet.

Dermatitis herpetiformis, or DH, is a manifestation of gluten intolerance that can be assessed. It is diagnosed by skin biopsy, though special studies are required for the biopsy. It is an intensely itchy, usually blistering rash. A very strict gluten-free diet is the mainstay of treatment. While the drug dapsone may be used to control the lesions it is the diet that prevents the disease and reduces the risk of the development of lymphoma, a known risk of the disease.

Celiac disease and gluten intolerance is a great example of how we need to know what we are eating. This is something that is increasingly difficult in this day and age of food being grown far from where we live, processed foods, fast foods and food additives the names of which continue to baffle. Roben's book helps, though more support is needed from the government, industry and individuals for celiac disease research.

Peter H. R. Green, M.D.

Professor of Clinical Medicine
College of Physicians and Surgeons
Columbia University Medical Center

Director, Celiac Disease Center
at Columbia University

SEPTEMBER, 2007

■ ■ ■

Acknowledgments

Thank you to everyone who wrote comments about my first book, *The Gluten-Free Kitchen*. Improvements in food theory and dietary approach would be impossible without your insights. Each and every comment that crossed my desk was considered when working on this text. This book is better because of you.

THOSE THAT TEST

The taste testers are a very special and diverse group of family, friends, colleagues, teachers, school staff, celiac support groups, and friends of friends, young, old, and in between. Some have dietary restrictions but most do not.

The scrutiny of food by this small army of volunteers was invaluable in making food not just good for gluten-free, but just plain good.

OTHER IMPORTANT PEOPLE

A book of this nature is a group effort. A giant thank-you to my husband, my teenage children, and their friends. To my dear friends George and Eileen. To fellow foodies Mireille, Colleen, Diane, Cassandra, and Stacie. To the special professionals I call my friends, Katie, Lee, and Harriet. And to others unnamed, but very much appreciated.

■ ■ ■

Introduction

In 2000, I published my first cookbook, *The Gluten-Free Kitchen*. Since then, the diagnosis and awareness of gluten sensitivity has skyrocketed. Several years ago, I began to write a new, more expansive cookbook for people who have been diagnosed with a wheat allergy, gluten intolerance, or celiac disease. Immediately, I realized certain guiding principles were essential to the project: the food must be even better, the scope broader, and the process simpler.

Many of you have spent years feeling ill and searching for a diagnosis. And, while finally uncovering the nature of your problem can be an enormous relief, some may feel that the old expression, "The cure is worse than the ailment," applies. You recognize that embracing the treatment—careful avoidance of all wheat, rye, barley, and contaminated oats—is a challenging undertaking that must be taken seriously. And ultimately, you're left wondering if you'll ever eat anything besides broiled chicken and steamed vegetables.

When I first began working with gluten-free foods over fifteen years ago, wheat-alternatives were limited and didn't taste very good. Over time, gluten-free baking became more sophisticated. Alternative grains, such as millet and sorghum, were discovered. (Actually, they were rediscovered, as alternative grains have long been dietary staples for both people and animals, here and abroad.) Today, the gluten-free industry has embraced blends that often contain four or more different flours. Dough enhancers and additives have also entered the picture. Unfortunately, many of these blends contain grains that rank among the top food allergens in the United States. The irony of introducing so many grains to those with sensitive immune systems is difficult to miss.

My work is the result of daring to think differently, to think simpler. What if individual flours were embraced for their own properties? And therein the theory for this book was born: use just *one* gluten-free flour to create delicious food. But would it be possible? Could "real" textures and tastes be achieved with just one flour? Food science and countless hours in the kitchen would provide the answer. Yes. Joyfully, simply, yes!

This book contains recipes for almost any occasion, from quick snacks to formal dinners, for dishes that are appealing to the eye and to the taste buds. In addition to appetizers, salads, soups, entrées, and desserts, you will also find numerous breads, cakes, and cookies. Most recipes use a single flour—rice, corn, potato, or oat—and I've included multiple versions of many recipes for those sensitive to one or more of these flours. For taste and nutrition, two grains have been combined in some bread recipes.

Xanthan gum is my preferred binder, but guar gum can often be substituted. Otherwise, everyday ingredients are used extensively. Simply put, a little xanthan gum and a package of any single flour will have you creating delicious gluten-free food.

These recipes have been tested by hundreds of individuals, from family and friends to those living with special diets. Their opinions prove beyond any doubt that gluten-free foods can and should be every bit as good as traditional foods.

The recipes in this cookbook don't require that you be an expert, although I do dive into food analysis on occasion. Being a little adventurous and a lover of food are the only prerequisites for using this book with great success.

So, clean out your kitchen (yes, I tell you how to do that, too), do a little shopping, and then jump in! Join me in the fun of cooking and talking food. Embrace feeling better by eating safely. And welcome back to eating well.

■ ■ ■

KITCHEN AND BAKING

There are thousands of nuances to living a gluten-free life that you pick up over time. You learn which grocery store or health food store has the best selection of gluten-free flours and foods. You learn which restaurants understand the seriousness of your dietary condition and strive to provide you with safe meals.

This chapter will help you through some of the early adjustments in living gluten-free, beginning with creating a safe cooking environment. I hope this chapter will help you avoid a few slip-ups. Some of these steps will seem obvious; others may surprise you.

This chapter also includes menu suggestions, a handy analysis of gluten-free flours, and a discussion on converting "regular" baking recipes to gluten-free ones.

CREATING A SAFE GLUTEN-FREE KITCHEN

Many gluten-free individuals live with others who do not have restricted diets. Changes in your environment will naturally affect their environment as well. You need a plan! I've seen these plans take two major directions. Generally speaking, the first is to designate safe areas within the kitchen, including a separate cabinet, a separate countertop, and a separate shelf in the refrigerator. The second is to designate the entire kitchen as a gluten-free zone.

The latter, choosing to make all foods in the home gluten-free, simplifies life considerably—and prevents any likelihood of cross-contamination. Cross-contamination is rampant in a nonsegregated kitchen: crumbs remain in a toaster or silverware drawer (I still wonder how they get there), a knife is dipped into a jar of jam after it is used to spread peanut butter, flour floats in the air after a bag of it has been opened, or someone grabs a handful of chips after picking up a slice of pizza. The list is endless, but you get the idea.

Plain soap and water and a lot of common sense will make your kitchen safer. Wash every surface from high to low. Wipe counters frequently. And keep forbidden food away from your safe area! If you have roommates who are a little messy, grab a roll of waxed paper or a clean dish, and prepare your food on that. If you choose to use a microwave, be sure your food is covered. Do not share a toaster, waffle iron, or other appliance that is hard to clean.

Now that you have the general exterior of your kitchen clean, we have to venture to what is inside the cabinets: dishes and glassware. All dishes and glasses should be fine as long as they are well washed and are not so worn that they have cracks or damaged areas that may hide miniscule amounts of gluten. Really, it is so much better to have three safe bowls than a whole pile of suspect ones.

Silverware must be kept clean and, once washed, away from forbidden foods. Those wayward crumbs matter.

Pots, pans, and bakeware can be difficult to evaluate. As of this writing, there has been no definite evidence that nonstick coatings on pans and bakeware are a source of cross-contamination. You must make your own common-sense determination, but if there are pits and scratches on the surface of your existing nonstick cookware, I suggest buying just one or two nonstick ones for gluten-free cooking. Stainless (and aluminum) pans and bakeware are thought to be safe. Scrub these items well before using for gluten-free cooking and baking.

Mixing bowls are similarly evaluated. If a plastic bowl is in good shape, without nicks, consider using it. If you want to be 100 percent safe, consider using glass or stainless-steel bowls.

Other cooking items: Wooden spoons that have been used for traditional cooking should be considered unsafe for gluten-free cooking, because they can retain microscopic fragments of food in their grain. A colander or strainer that has been used for non-gluten-free foods? Good question. I would personally opt for a new one dedicated to gluten-free draining, as little bits of food can be difficult to remove from those tiny holes.

Getting your kitchen environment clean is really not too difficult. Keeping your designated area safe is another matter. Once again, you'll need a plan of action. Here are a few ideas that have worked for others:

1. Use a clean plate or piece of waxed paper as your food preparation area.
2. Do not share condiments; segregate in the fridge or somehow mark the containers.
3. Be first to fix your plate of food, to avoid accidental cross-contamination; or, better yet, fix your plate before any other food is put into serving dishes.
4. Place a serving utensil in each dish to avoid cross-contamination.
5. Place unsafe foods on a separate table, or in a different room (seriously).

ROBEN'S PANTRY

Before we start with basic baking ingredients, I would like to point out that the FDA has instituted regulations requiring disclosure of certain major allergens in the ingredient listings of foods. This makes label reading easier. Often, you will see dairy, soy, and wheat labeled separately in boldface. But barley, oats (when cross-contaminated), rye, spelt, and kamut can be harder to see. Look closely when you read labels and use online resources (listed in the appendix) to make the job easier.

On to basic baking ingredients in my pantry:

Flours

Cornstarch and/or Cornmeal. Any brand. The primary difference among cornstarch brands is Rumford's use of genetically unmodified corn. No baking differences among brands were noted during recipe testing. Cornstarch is widely available in any grocery store.

Please note that some major brands of cornmeal are not manufactured in dedicated facilities. Cross-contamination is often limited by good manufacturing processes, but you must personally evaluate your comfort level in using products from such companies.

I've used cornstarch because it is widely available, affordable, and works well. Cornmeal is a nice whole-grain addition to a number of recipes.

Potato Starch. Any brand, including Bob's Red Mill and various potato starches from Asian markets. You may also find potato starch in the kosher section of your grocery store, although I've found it to be a little more expensive there. No baking differences among brands were noted during recipe testing. Note that potato starch and potato flour are not the same. Potato starch is white in color. Potato flour is creamy beige. Potato starch is often available in larger grocery stores, health food stores, and Asian markets.

I've used potato starch because it is widely available, affordable, and works well. It is a good option for individuals who cannot tolerate corn.

Rice Flour. Any brand, including Bob's Red Mill and various rice flours from Asian markets. I've also found "enriched" rice flour in the Mexican section of several grocery stores. In testing, I found Bob's Red Mill to be a little grittier than some of the others. However, the small amount of grit is barely noticeable in most recipes. If you use other brands, weight measurement will be more accurate than cup measurement. Brown rice flour may be substituted for white rice flour and should also be measured by weight for best results. Rice flour is often available in larger grocery stores, health food stores, and Asian markets.

As with cornstarch, I've used rice flour because it is widely available, affordable, and works well. It is sometimes available "enriched," which helps boost its nutritional value and is a good first step for individuals who want to eventually use brown rice flour (which may be substituted in these recipes).

Oat Flour. Manufacturers of gluten-free oats are listed in the appendix of this book. Do not use oats that are not clearly labeled gluten-free, as they may be contaminated with other unaccept-able grains. (Many mills combine grains, then separate them later through a number of sieves. Farm trucks also transport a variety of grains.)

I've used oat flour because it tastes good, works well, and is whole grain. I believe that safe gluten-free oat flour (and oats) will soon become mainstream in grocery stores because uncontaminated oats are now accepted as safe for a gluten-free diet (although acceptable quantities are still under evaluation), and they are a widely appreciated whole grain. In the meantime, you may need to search for them in health food stores and from online suppliers.

Other Flours. Sorghum (white, not gray), millet (yellow, not gray), and brown rice flours are sometimes used in my bread-type recipes for additional flavor and nutrition. Although not necessary to make most recipes in this book, they are available in many grocery stores, health food stores, and online sources.

Other Preferred Ingredients

Baking Powder. Rumford is my favorite brand of baking powder. All recipes utilizing baking powder have been tested with Rumford. A detailed discussion of baking powder is included at the beginning of chapter 16. In fact, using certain other brands will change baking results.

Baking Soda. Arm & Hammer is my baking soda of choice and is widely available.

Butter. Any brand. Annatto (a yellow coloring derived from achiote seeds) is sometimes used in butter and is not tolerated by all, but it is gluten-free.

Cocoa Powder. Hershey's. Other brands used in testing did not perform as flavorfully.

Cream Cheese. Philadelphia is my favorite brand.

Eggs. Any brand. Size large.

Milk. 2% milk was utilized in recipe testing.

Oil. Canola oil was used unless otherwise indicated. Olive oil was used on occasion.

Salt. Any brand. (Some individuals with the DH presentation of celiac disease avoid iodized salt during the healing process.)

Spices, Flavorings, Extracts. McCormick brand.

Sugar. White, brown, and confectioners' sugars are all used. Confectioners' sugar may contain cornstarch. I've even heard of one having wheat starch as an ingredient (how unusual!). Double-check ingredient listings.

Xanthan Gum. Bob's Red Mill preferred. Recipes were tested using a variety of brands, including Bob's Red Mill and the Gluten-Free Pantry. (Some people are under the impression that xanthan gum is corn-based. Verification with the manufacturer may show their process uses sugarcane, not corn.) Prior to a meeting and working in an out-of-state kitchen, I was stunned to find the available xanthan gum was approximately 30 percent less effective than Bob's Red Mill. If needed for dietary reasons, guar gum may be successfully substituted at $1\frac{1}{4}$ teaspoon for each teaspoon of xanthan gum. Use of guar gum makes for thinner batters and doughs, which may be fine for some recipes but can pose difficulties with cookies and shaped breads.

Yogurt. Any brand plain yogurt. I believe lowfat performs better than nonfat.

NAVIGATING THE SUPERMARKET

Now that major baking items have been addressed, let's walk through the market together!

Fresh Fruits and Vegetables. This section of the grocery store may be your new best friend, especially when first starting the gluten-free diet. In addition to the main ingredients needed for a recipe, such as squash or pears, I always keep the following on hand: garlic, onions, red or white potatoes, and bagged salad.

Note that salad bars, even in grocery or health food stores, can be risky. Wayward croutons or pasta salad could be a real setback. If you choose to use a salad bar, you should limit your risk. First, make friends with people in that department. Ask about their procedures for setting up the bar. And try to be an early visitor after setup to avoid any accidental movement of ingredients from one area to another. Each different salad bar has an element of risk that you must evaluate to your own comfort level.

Bakery. Alas, this department is not for you. Airborne flour is not a good thing. Unless you really must have a traditional baked good for someone else because you ran out of time for gluten-free baking, just walk past it.

Deli. The deli is another area to watch for cross-contamination. If you choose to buy meats from the deli department, ask the attendant to change his or her gloves before working on your order. To someone behind the counter, a little glob of macaroni or potato salad wiped with a gloved finger may be no big deal, but to you it is cross-contamination. Those same hands (in those same gloves) may have also been handling the fried chicken. You must be kindly insistent and make allies in this department, too. Check ingredients on deli meats for potential sources of gluten as well. Online sources (see appendix) have lists of gluten-free deli meats.

Seafood. When you don't know what to cook, seafood offers a quick solution! Again, you must watch for cross-contamination. Ask for fresh gloves. Those crab cakes sitting in the same display case shouldn't come anywhere near what you're purchasing. You may even wish to ask for your selection to come straight from the shipping package. Tilapia, salmon, and shrimp are all among my favorite super-quick dinners.

Meats. Chicken, beef, pork, and turkey are all used in this book. The "added solutions" in chicken and turkey could make one nervous. Fortunately, I have yet to see a prohibited ingredient in these products. And, under the new federal guidelines, an ingredient with nutritional value (such as wheat) should be listed. That said, you must be diligent and careful. Read the label anyway. And never use an accompanying gravy packet.

Dairy. Milk, cheese, yogurt. Except for annatto coloring in cheese (which is gluten-free) bothering some people, this is a pretty safe choice for food. Note that blue cheese can have distant bread origins, so you'll have to proceed with those varieties as you think reasonable. Again, online resources are great for background information to make such determinations. Or, you can make it easy and choose among the hundreds of other cheeses.

Baking Products. The baking aisle has some great foods for the gluten-free diet: chocolate, nuts, olive oil, cornmeal, cornstarch, sugar, and so on. Just avoid any mixes in this aisle. Most if not all mixes will contain wheat. Among spices and blends, McCormick is my choice, as they clearly label any wheat in their blends. McCormick also makes fine vanilla flavoring and extract.

I also use nonstick cooking oil spray extensively. Read the labels on these as well. Pam is a good brand. You will also find bouillon cubes in most baking aisles, near the spices. Herb-Ox clearly labels theirs as gluten-free. And, they are affordable.

Condiments. La Choy brand soy sauce is my first choice for soy sauce. San-J has a gluten-free version of soy sauce and is less widely available; look for it in health food stores. Most other brands are made with wheat and are unsafe for the gluten-free diet. Read labels and check online resources for current listings of safe condiments. Happily, you will find many are safe for the gluten-free diet. Kraft is known to clearly label.

Canned Items. Generally, plain canned fruits and vegetables are gluten-free, but frozen usually have far less sodium and brighter flavor. Any canned item in a sauce requires a closer look; read the label. Many soups also contain gluten. But, at this writing, Dinty Moore Beef Stew is gluten-free.

There are treasures in your grocery store; you just need to look for them. The recipes in this book use the simplest of staples—tomato paste (use one that has only tomatoes in the ingredient list), evaporated milk, and so on. Start safely within these pages, then branch out.

Dried Grains and Beans. Rice, brown rice, lentils, split peas, beans, and plain instant potatoes, and so on. They are all gluten-free and good for you! But be careful of mixes. Some are fine, but you must check labels each and every time you purchase an item. It would be a shame to get needlessly sick.

Snacks. Rice crackers are available in many grocery stores. And some taste great. Some brands of potato chips appear safe, but the manufacturer may make unsafe snacks in the same facility, so you need to be informed. In the short term, a visit to a health food store for your gluten-free snacks may be easier. Otherwise, you need to spend a little time researching online resources. Or, better yet, grab an apple or a banana to munch on. Many components of a healthy diet are gluten-free.

Cereals and Breakfast Items. Fortunately, this aisle is easy—avoid it! Fruity Pebbles and one Disney cereal were gluten-free at this printing, but labels must always be rechecked. Also, some mainstream manufacturers have facilities that process unsafe foods. You need to know how they clean between runs of product. Over time, you will learn which companies have embraced allergy-friendly procedures. A health food store (or special section at larger grocery stores) should have an affordable assort-ment of safe cereals. Cream of Rice cereal is gluten-free. At this time, Quaker oats and store-brand oats must be considered unsafe because of potential cross-contamination in the manufacturing process.

TOOLS IN ROBEN'S KITCHEN

I thought it would be helpful for you to know exactly what I use in my kitchen to prepare these recipes every day. Few items are fancy, and not all items are essential. If you're new to cooking, this would be a nice list to share with family and friends who are hoping to support your new gluten-free lifestyle. Sometimes it is the little things that make cooking so much easier.

Baking Pans. I use a variety of baking pans. I prefer metal pans purchased from the local kitchen supply store and/or Wilton cake pans, available in craft

---

▪ ▪ ▪ NOTE ▪ ▪ ▪

Although not the entire list of unsafe ingredients, certain words should jump out at you like red flags when reading labels. They are: wheat, rye, oats (because of possible cross-contamination), barley, kamut, spelt, and malt. Avoid all products listing any of these ingredients.

stores. I use nonstick spray as needed to avoid sticking food. But I avoid using nonstick baking pans as they may be suspect for cross-contamination if also used for baking traditional foods. (Debate of this topic continues, but I have not yet seen a conclusive study. So I suggest being careful and erring on the side of caution.) A nice selection of baking pans would be: a 9 x 5-inch loaf pan, one or two 9-inch round baking pans, a 9-inch square baking pan, a 9 x 13-inch rectangular baking pan, a twelve-cup muffin pan, and two cookie sheets. I also use a French bread pan for making baguettes.

Bowls. I use nonreactive metal bowls. They are easy to clean and nearly indestructible. I also use a bowl-type strainer. It is especially helpful when draining pasta. Several glass bowls are nice to have on hand for microwaving when the need arises.

Blender. I have two blenders in my kitchen. The first is a traditional blender that I use to cream soups (such as Cream of Broccoli Soup) or to make Corn-Free Confectioners' Sugar. Although it doesn't have the power of a traditional blender, I like a stick (handheld) blender. A stick blender looks like it sounds, with the power button and motor at one end and a little blending blade at the other. That little blade can easily cream soups, rescue lumpy gravy, and even make a milkshake. Mine is a modest home model made by Farberware.

Bread Machine. Totally unnecessary for recipes in this book. I don't use one, although there is one tucked away in the corner of my basement. With the exception of one or two recipes in this book that use yeast, there is simply no need for rising time. Nearly all of the doughs in these pages would be damaged by the heavy, repeated mixings of a bread machine. Buy one only if you wish to make bread recipes outside of those in this book; many accomplished gluten-free cooks use bread machines to great advantage.

Cooling Racks. I have several cooling racks. They are especially handy when making cookies.

Crock Pot. Crock Pots are wonderful for preparing soup stock, slow-cooked meals, and tender meats. I recommend a standard 4-quart model.

Cutting Boards. I have several (okay, more than several) gel-type cutting boards. They can be tossed in the dishwasher and are easy on my knives. I change boards frequently, and always after cutting meats of any kind.

Deep Fryer. I own a little nonstick deep fryer that is perfect for frying appetizers, corn dogs, fish and chips, and so on. It has a temperature gauge on the electrical plug. You can certainly eat well, and healthy, without this tool, but it sure is nice to have when you want chicken wings or onion rings. Until a study is done to conclude if a nonstick surface is a source of cross-contamination, it would be best to dedicate this appliance for just gluten-free foods.

Food Processor. I own one but rarely use it. A good knife or handheld grater (stainless steel) will do nearly all the jobs needed in this book. The only exception is grinding nuts for the nut cake recipe. I would forgo the food processor and buy nuts already ground.

Grater. If you like cheese, this hand tool is irreplaceable. Freshly grated cheese tastes better than pregrated cheese, although I do use both. I use a little one-sided handheld grater that cost just a dollar or two. Also, pregrated cheeses may have a dusting of starch (often corn) to prevent clumping. This may be important if you have multiple food restrictions.

Knives. As I seldom use a food processor, I cut almost everything by hand. Over time, I have invested in good knives. It is better to have a few good knives (a chef's knife and paring knife) than a number of mediocre ones. A small sharpening device is helpful, too.

Measuring Spoons and Cups. You need a good set of measuring spoons. They need not be expensive, but should be manufactured by a well-known kitchen company, such as KitchenAid or Farberware. Accuracy is very important. A clear glass (Pyrex) measuring cup and a standard set of metal measuring cups should handle all your needs.

Microwave Oven. Used often in my kitchen. It is also great for reheating leftovers. A stash of gluten-free foods in the freezer can be a treasure when you don't feel like cooking.

Mixer. I own a KitchenAid stand mixer, but a high-quality hand mixer should be able to tackle any recipe in this book, with the exception of pie crusts and biscuits. The difficulty in mixing pie crusts and biscuits is in cutting the cold butter or cream cheese into the flour. This can be done by hand, if needed. You may have heard that a heavy-duty mixer is necessary for making gluten-free breads and the like. This is true for many gluten-free bread recipes, but not for those in this book.

Plastic Containers. Used for storing flours and xanthan gum.

Pots and Pans. I have a number of triple-clad pots and pans hanging from my pot rack. I also have one nonstick pan. There are two important features of my pots and pans. The steel pans have a thick bottom and the nonstick pan is used exclusively for gluten-free cooking, as nonstick pans are a suspected source for cross-contamination. I also have one omelet pan that I use nearly every day, although rarely for omelets.

Resealable Plastic Bags. I often use these bags to shape bagels and other breads.

Rolling Pin. I have a French rolling pin. It looks like a slender cylinder of wood that tapers toward each end. Any rolling pin should be fine. Please note that wooden items can trap little particles of gluten. Keep this item (and other wood items) exclusively for gluten-free baking. In this book, you will find a rolling pin used only for pie crusts. If you don't care to make pies, I wouldn't bother purchasing one.

Scale. One of my most important kitchen items! I use a digital Pelouze postage scale purchased from Staples. It allows weight by ounces or grams. It also permits a bowl to be placed on the scale, then "zeroed out" by pushing a button. One of the greatest difficulties in gluten-free baking is the accuracy of flour measurements. (For example, one person may scoop more lightly, or a package may simply have settled.) If you have difficulty in making baked goods, get a scale and measure ingredients by weight.

School Supplies. A few school supplies are so helpful! A ruler (clear plastic) and a pair of scissors (dedicated to food preparation) come in handy when first measuring the size of flat breads, flour tortillas, and individual pizza crusts.

Spray Bottle. I have a little spray bottle for the sole purpose of spraying breads. It is very easy to mist a loaf of French bread or tray of bagels with this handy little tool. Although technically not of "food grade" plastic, I purchased mine for just a dollar.

Spoons and Other Utensils. I use metal spoons. Wooden spoons are easily a source of cross-contamination, so it is easiest just to avoid them. I also use plastic spatulas (silicone to avoid melting) and wire whisks. And, if you're being extravagant, an offset spatula for spreading icing is very nice.

Toaster. Any toaster would be just fine, but it should not be shared with traditional bread. This is often a point of cross-contamination.

Waffle Iron. Any good brand is fine. A Belgian style (makes deeper pockets in the waffle) will give you exceptionally nice results. Again, use only for gluten-free.

Wooden Skewers and Popsicle Sticks. I use wooden skewers for cooking outside on the grill. I use wooden Popsicle sticks for making corn dogs. I also use them in making cheese sticks because they allow me to more evenly coat the cheese with batter. (They can be removed before serving if desired.)

MENU SUGGESTIONS

Until you have mastered the gluten-free diet, it is better to eat safely at home. With good company and a few willing hands, you and your guests will have a great time! Here are a few ideas to get you started: (Recipes found in this book Look Like This, general suggestions are lowercased.)

Brunch. Coffee Cake, Waffles, Oven-Baked Eggs in Tomato Cups, sausages, and fresh fruit

Football Party. cheese and Crackers, Chicken Wings, Fried Cheese Sticks and Potato Wedges, and salsa and tortilla chips

Thanksgiving Dinner. Roasted Turkey, Mashed Potatoes, Green Bean Casserole, Rolls, Cranberry Salad, Fruit and Green Salad, and Pumpkin Custard

Barbecue. Especially Good Hamburgers, Rolls, Potato Salad, Coleslaw, vegetable tray, and Blueberry Cobbler

Barbecue at Friend's House (if you must). Bring salmon packet and Veggie Packet to be placed (sealed the whole time!) on their grill for 15 to 20 minutes. Bring brownies for sharing.

Kid's Birthday Sleepover. Pizza, Fruit Salad, Soft Chocolate Cake, and ice cream

Friends in from Snow Activities. Black Bean Soup, Cream of Broccoli Soup, and Applesauce Quick Bread

Homey Dinner. Spicy Roadside Chicken, Oven-Roasted Potatoes, Summer Vegetables, and Scalloped Apples

Chinese Dinner. Beef and Broccoli Stir-Fry, Orange Chicken, rice, Green

Beans with Heat, Fortune Cookies, and orange wedges

A Romantic Dinner. Red Snapper with Tomato and Capers, Sugar Snap Peas, and Vanilla Crème with Strawberry Sauce

Holiday Cookie Exchange. Sugar Cookies, Chocolate Chip Cookies, Lebkuchen, and/or Pecan Cookies

BAKING WITH GLUTEN-FREE FLOURS

Here's some honest feedback on gluten-free bread—a lot of it is awful, but it *doesn't* have to be! In the chart that follows, I review the properties of many of the gluten-free flours used today.

Wheat gluten is a natural binder; it traditionally gives breads and baked goods their stretchy, springy texture. Using this book's gluten-free recipes, you'll get real bread texture and pleasant flavor. My descriptions are honest and straightforward. Soon, you will find which flours you like and which ones you can leave at the market.

The most important common factor among the flours used in this book is taste. Affordability and nutrition follow closely. In my recipes, cornstarch, potato starch, and rice flour are the "white" flours of gluten-free flour. You

have eaten traditional "white" flour for years. It is a blank sheet on which to design food. It is the same in gluten-free cooking, although I wish all three could at least be found "enriched."

We know that American diets have too many processed foods, devoid of nutritional value. All highly refined grains should be eaten in moderation. One of the most promising whole-grain options for the gluten-free diet is oat flour. It tastes good! And, that's all by itself— this is proven in recipe after recipe in this book! (Just like cornstarch and rice flour, I expect safe oats to be mainstream in the not-too-distant future.)

The other whole grains included in this book do not always taste best alone. However, sorghum, millet, and brown rice add good flavor to breads. (And brown rice flour may be substituted for white rice flour in other recipes). Using multiple flours requires some general guidelines:

For a tight, moist crumb and springy texture, use (by weight):

⅓ gritty flour
⅔ powdery flour

For a lighter texture, use (by weight):

¼ gritty flour
¾ powdery flour

Analysis of Gluten-Free Flours

Please note that I am not gluten intolerant. I do not have a wheat allergy. I am a bona fide food junkie! I eat traditional breads and rolls often. My palate is not influenced by years of eating a restricted diet. I tell it as I taste it and bake accordingly. Flours used in this book are boldface. All analysis completed using same simple bread recipe to allow meaningful comparisons.

WEIGHT PER CUP

Ounces	Grams	Flours	Description/Observations	Use This Flour?	Class
4.8	130	All-purpose white flour*	bleached wheat flour, bran removed (often enriched) excellent leavening – 6 excellent when transformed with yeast (the magic of gluten formation); surprising "gna" flavor when made without benefit of rising times	*n/a for gluten-free for comparison only	
3.9	110	Amaranth	high-protein grain, spicy/nutty flavor modest leavening – 3 unpleasant flavor; springy texture, needs less liquid	No. Flavor does not merit use.	
4.1	118	Arrowroot starch	good leavening – 4 nice crust, collapses like tapioca starch (requires much less water), metallic taste	No. Flavor does not merit use.	
4.4	125	Brown rice flour	whole grain of rice milled, gritty	Substitute for rice flour. Used sparsely in this book.	gritty
4.5	130	Buckwheat flour	high protein modest leavening – 3 short-dense loaf, strong flavor	Yes. In small quantity. Not used in this book.	powdery
4	110	Chickpea flour	ground chickpeas; powdery good leavening – 4 nice texture, loaf is a little short (requires more leavening) pretty loaf; tastes like hummus	Yes. With other flours in breads.	powdery
2.9	82	Cocoa	ground cocoa bean, fat removed	Yes. In non-bread baking.	powdery
4.5	128	Corn flour	whole-grain corn, ground well; gritty modest leavening – 3 very short-dense loaf	Substitute for cornmeal. Not used in this book.	gritty
5	140	**Cornmeal**	whole-grain corn, ground; gritty modest leavening – 3 short-dense loaf, nice corn flavor	Yes. Alone in cornbread. With other flours in breads.	gritty
4.4	125	**Cornstarch**	starch from corn; powdery strong leavening – 10 tastes like less than nothing light and fluffy in baking	Yes. Alone and in combination With other flours in breads.	powdery
4.8	135	**Millet flour**	whole-grain millet; gritty modest leavening – 3 dense pretty loaf, tastes like wheat-corn combined can have bitter aftertaste after reheating or storage	Yes. Alone in "cornbread." With other flours in breads.	gritty
3.8	105	Montina flour	whole-grain Indian ricegrass; dried grass texture high protein and high fiber manfacturer says it tastes nutty; but I think it tastes like bland, dry grass; would be good to add textures to gluten-free breads; overwhelming texture used alone	Yes. In small quantities. With other flours in breads.	gritty

Analysis of Gluten-Free Flours

WEIGHT PER CUP					
Ounces	Grams	Flours	Description/Observations	Use This Flour?	Class
4.3	122	**Oat flour***	whole-grain oats, ground; powdery modest leavening – 3 dense, heavy loaf, nice oat flavor	Yes. Alone and in combination with other flours in breads. *use only safe g/f oats	gritty
		Potato flour	dehydrated potatoes; powdery not tested alone, adds moisture to breads not the same as potato starch!	Yes. In tiny quantities. Not used in this book.	
5.5	155	**Potato starch**	starch from potatoes; powdery modest leavening – 5, can become rubbery (use less binder) very mild flavor	Yes. Alone and in combination With other flours in breads.	powdery
4.4	125	Quinoa flour	ground whole-grain flour modest leavening – 3; expensive grain short, dense loaf; terrible grassy taste I do not use	No. Flavor does not merit use.	
5.3	150	**Rice flour**	rice flour, bran removed (sometimes enriched); powdery modest leavening – 3; but better leavening achievable very dense, short loaf, bad "gna" flavor when used with yeast	Yes. Alone and in combination with other flours.	gritty
4.6	132	**Sorghum flour**	ground whole-grain flour modest leavening – 4 tight, dense loaf, taste is not bad when used with other flours flour seems powdery, but has behavior of gritty flours in baking	Yes. With other flours in breads.	gritty
	85	Soy flour	ground soybeans, high in fat; powdery sometimes used as egg replacer shorter shelf-life than other flours	No. Flavor does not merit use.	
5	140	Sweet rice flour	ground rice, bran removed more gelatinous	Yes. Sometimes used as thickener. Not used in this book.	
4.4	125	Tapioca starch	starch from tapioca root, also known as tapioca flour; powdery strong leavening – 10++, very gummy, no flavor (use less binder)	Yes. Use in combination with other flours. Not used in this book.	powdery
5	140	Teft flour	modest leavening – 4 very tight, dense loaf earthy, grassy taste	No. Flavor does not merit use.	

There are two methods for substituting flours in recipes. The first is to use equal amounts of flours with similar leavening or a combination of flours that would equal similar leavening. For example, use ½ tapioca starch (10) plus ½ sorghum (4) for potato starch (5).

The other method is to substitute one powdery flour for another powdery flour. For example, bean flour for sorghum.

In order to maintain light, fluffy texture, our light sandwich bread recipe contains no more than 25 percent of gritty flour with the remaining 75 percent powdery.

In order to maintain gluten-like structure, our medium-textured bread recipe contains no more than 50 percent gritty flour, with the remaining 50 percent powdery.

Adhering to these guidelines will get you in the ballpark of producing a nice loaf of bread, but you should also look to the other properties of the flours. For example, tapioca can be gummy and you may need to reduce the liquid and/or xanthan gum in the recipe.

CONVERTING RECIPES

When I first started writing this book, I thought it would be great to teach people how to convert traditional recipes into gluten-free recipes. By the time I finished developing so many formulations, it was obvious that to do so would require writing another book, which would be incredibly boring to read. Instead, we can do something else wonderful. We can duplicate the taste, texture, and moistness of that favorite recipe!

The underlying problem with converting a traditional recipe to gluten-free begins with wheat flour itself. This is because wheat-based recipes are amazing. Let me give you a few examples:

Say you want to make a traditional prepackaged muffin mix. You measure your liquid with a coffee cup because you can't find your measuring cup. Although it is unlikely you have exactly 8 ounces in your coffee-cup measurement, your results will be totally edible. This is because wheat-based formulations accommodate broad liquid/flour ratios.

Similarly, imagine that you and your friend are making traditional, identical recipes for banana bread. You're by the book, measuring ingredients carefully, making sure you level the top of the measuring cup filled with flour. Your friend is free-wheeling and measures by digging in the bag and shaking off the excess flour. It is very likely that both of your banana breads will be very good. This is because wheat-based formulations have large tolerances for inexactness.

However, inexactness in measuring ingredients is probably the foremost factor in failed gluten-free recipes.

Imagine your mom's special cake recipe uses 2 cups of flour and your grandma's similar special cake recipe uses $2\frac{1}{2}$ cups of flour. A gluten-free recipe might use $1\frac{1}{4}$ cups of gluten-free flour. So, do I tell you to replace each 1 cup of wheat flour with $\frac{1}{2}$ cup of gluten-free flour? Or do I tell you to replace each $1\frac{1}{4}$ cups of flour with $\frac{1}{4}$ cup of gluten-free flour? That small amount of gluten-free flour matters to the success of the finished cake!

Gluten-free flours also require many different formulations: one for bread, one for pizza crust, one for soft cake, one for pound cake, one for cookies, one for waffles, and so on. We can't make our flours act like wheat flour, so we must create new formulations for each subtlety in our foods. A little more binder, a little less raising agent, a little more liquid, and so on. It is always something! Even something as simple as wanting a chocolate cake instead of vanilla makes for a whole new formulation. It's enough to make your head spin. But, never fear, you have hundreds of successful recipe formulations right in the pages of this book.

There is an easier way to duplicate and honor an heirloom recipe than to struggle to convert it. We just need to approach it differently.

First, think about that special recipe. Let's say your mom made the best eggnog pound cake ever! (I've never had one, but it sounds awfully good!) You remember that it is moist, slightly sweeter than most pound cakes, and has a hint of nutmeg—it says so on your copy of her recipe.

Now that you know what you want to make, let's pick a flour your body tolerates. You say no to corn, which maybe you're a little allergic to, and choose potato. Okay. Now, turn to my recipe for Vanilla Pound Cake. Substitute eggnog for the milk and ponder whether to increase the sugar just a little. . . you may decide not to because eggnog is a little sweeter than milk. Then add a little nutmeg and maybe reduce the vanilla flavoring just a little. Finally, you bake it. . . and voilà—Eggnog Pound Cake.

Isn't that a lot simpler than trying to convert Mom's wheat-based recipe? Using this approach will give you so many more successes.

Happy baking!

■ ■ ■

METRIC CONVERSIONS

- The recipes in this book have not been tested with metric measurements, so some variations might occur.
- Remember that the weight of dry ingredients varies according to the volume or density factor: 1 cup of flour weighs far less than 1 cup of sugar, and 1 tablespoon doesn't necessarily hold 3 teaspoons.

— General Formulas for Metric Conversion

Ounces to grams	$\Rightarrow$ ounces × 28.35 = grams
Grams to ounces	$\Rightarrow$ grams × 0.035 = ounces
Pounds to grams	$\Rightarrow$ pounds × 453.5 = grams
Pounds to kilograms	$\Rightarrow$ pounds × 0.45 = kilograms
Cups to liters	$\Rightarrow$ cups × 0.24 = liters
Fahrenheit to Celsius	$\Rightarrow$ (°F – 32) × 5 ÷ 9 = °C
Celsius to Fahrenheit	$\Rightarrow$ (°C × 9) ÷ 5 + 32 = °F

— Linear Measurements

½ inch = 1½ cm
1 inch = 2½ cm
6 inches = 15 cm
8 inches = 20 cm
10 inches = 25 cm
12 inches = 30 cm
20 inches = 50 cm

— Volume (Dry) Measurements

¼ teaspoon = 1 milliliter
½ teaspoon = 2 milliliters
¾ teaspoon = 4 milliliters
1 teaspoon = 5 milliliters
1 tablespoon = 15 milliliters
¼ cup = 59 milliliters
⅓ cup = 79 milliliters
½ cup = 118 milliliters
⅔ cup = 158 milliliters
¾ cup = 177 milliliters
1 cup = 225 milliliters
4 cups or 1 quart = 1 liter
½ gallon = 2 liters
1 gallon = 4 liters

— Volume (Liquid) Measurements

1 teaspoon = ⅙ fluid ounce = 5 milliliters
1 tablespoon = ½ fluid ounce = 15 milliliters
2 tablespoons = 1 fluid ounce = 30 milliliters
¼ cup = 2 fluid ounces = 60 milliliters
⅓ cup = 2⅔ fluid ounces = 79 milliliters
½ cup = 4 fluid ounces = 118 milliliters
1 cup or ½ pint = 8 fluid ounces = 250 milliliters
2 cups or 1 pint = 16 fluid ounces = 500 milliliters
4 cups or 1 quart = 32 fluid ounces = 1,000 milliliters
1 gallon = 4 liters

— Oven Temperature Equivalents, Fahrenheit (F) and Celsius (C)

100°F = 38°C
200°F = 95°C
250°F = 120°C
300°F = 150°C
350°F = 180°C
400°F = 205°C
450°F = 230°C

— Weight (Mass) Measurements

1 ounce = 30 grams
2 ounces = 55 grams
3 ounces = 85 grams
4 ounces = ¼ pound = 125 grams
8 ounces = ½ pound = 240 grams
12 ounces = ¾ pound = 375 grams
16 ounces = 1 pound = 454 grams

2

APPETIZERS

Bar foods and social finger foods are the inspiration for this chapter. Whether you're kicking back to watch a ball game with friends or spending a quiet evening at home, you'll find good things in these pages.

With the slightest bit of hesitation, I've included your favorite fried munchies. (You must deal with your own food conscience!) From cheese sticks to calamari, I've tried to cover your cravings and keep you from cheating.

Note that making appetizers at home is much safer than eating the restaurant versions. Though many finger foods from some restaurants would appear safe at first glance, unfortunately, they are often fried in the same oil as gluten-containing foods. This makes anything prepared in that oil cross-contaminated and unsafe.

I hope this chapter introduces you to how fun and rewarding cooking appetizers can be. Surprisingly, crackers take only a few minutes to make. Steamed clams are a cinch. And your egg rolls may be better than those at your local carry-out!

Asian Meatballs

These meatballs have a subtle Asian flavor, much like you would taste in a wonton. Unfortunately, I cannot make a viable wonton, as rice wrappers do not do well in boiling broth. However, these meatballs, with a little Asian Dipping Sauce, should fill the void nicely.

- In a medium-size bowl, combine all the ingredients. Shape into meatballs, using approximately 1 rounded teaspoon per meatball. Place in a lightly greased pan over medium heat. Cook until no pink remains, 3 to 5 minutes.

■ Makes 20 to 25 meatballs ■

$1/2$ pound ground pork

$1/4$ pound shrimp, peeled and chopped small

1 teaspoon sugar

1 teaspoon soy sauce (check that it is gluten-free)

2 green onions, chopped finely

$1/4$ teaspoon salt

Asian Dipping Sauce

- Combine all the ingredients in a cup or small bowl. Stir.

■ Makes $1/4$ cup sauce ■

2 tablespoons soy sauce (check that it is gluten-free)

2 tablespoons distilled white vinegar

$1/2$ teaspoon sugar

WHAT ABOUT BEER?

Should you choose to enjoy a beer with your finger foods, it must be one of the gluten-free varieties. Any theory that the fermentation process in making beer would somehow make it gluten-free is not true. And, finally, despite their names, wine coolers are often malt-based and are highly suspect for the gluten-free diet. Currently, I've heard of just one manufacturer that has a highly refined manufacturing process that makes their suspect beverage safe. Until this process is recognized by a national celiac support group, I cannot in good conscience suggest using such a product.

Calamari is another word for squid. Prepared well, it is simply delicious. If you can find it fresh, ask your seafood salesperson to clean it for you. If you purchase it frozen, it should be ready to use.

Please note that I have made xanthan gum optional in the rice version, but it makes the coating lighter. The difference is subtle, but worthwhile if you have xanthan gum on hand. The use of xanthan gum in the corn and potato versions is more essential, as the coating seems "dusty" without it.

The baking soda is utilized in this recipe solely to add a little browning to the crust. Otherwise, the crust is quite pale.

The use of Old Bay Seasoning and sometimes ground red pepper enhances the flavor of the squid. You can easily double the amount of spice to good advantage if you prefer a more robust flavor. A super-fast light tomato sauce for dipping is included at the end of the calamari recipes.

Calamari ■ *Corn-based*

Among our testers, all recipes for calamari were well received. I place this one second, just after the rice version. This recipe produces a more uniform coating, whereas the rice coating is a little sparse.

■ Thaw the squid. Preheat the oil to 370°F.

■ Drain and slice the squid tubes into ¼-inch rings. Cut the tentacles as desired.

■ In a small bowl, combine all the dry ingredients and stir well. Toss the squid in the flour mixture and drop into the hot oil.

■ Cook for approximately 45 seconds, until the batter just begins to brown. Remove from the oil. Drain and serve hot.

1 (1-pound) package frozen, prepared raw squid

⅔ cup cornstarch, 85 grams

½ teaspoon salt

½ teaspoon baking soda

½ teaspoon xanthan gum

1 teaspoon Old Bay Seasoning (or other favorite seasoning)

¼ teaspoon ground red pepper

Oil, for frying

■ Serves 4 to 6 ■

Calamari ▪ *Oat-based*

Like the rice version of calamari, this one has a crispy crust. It should be noted that oat flour tends to muddy the oil.

- ▪ Thaw the squid. Preheat the oil to 370°F.
- ▪ Drain and slice the squid tubes into ¼-inch rings. Cut the tentacles as desired.
- ▪ In a small bowl, combine all the dry ingredients and stir well. Toss the squid in the flour mixture and drop into the hot oil.
- ▪ Cook for approximately 45 seconds, until the batter just begins to brown. Remove from the oil. Drain and serve hot.

▪ Serves 4 to 6 ▪

1 (1-pound) package frozen, prepared raw squid

²/₃ cup oat flour, 80 grams

½ teaspoon salt

½ teaspoon baking soda

⅛ teaspoon xanthan gum (optional)

1 teaspoon Old Bay Seasoning (or other favorite seasoning)

Oil, for frying

Calamari ▪ *Potato-based*

The crust on this version is a little more substantial, making the calamari seem a little heavier.

- ▪ Thaw the squid. Preheat the oil to 370°F.
- ▪ Drain and slice the squid tubes into ¼-inch rings. Cut the tentacles as desired.
- ▪ In a small bowl, combine all the dry ingredients and stir well. Toss the squid in the flour mixture and drop into the hot oil.
- ▪ Cook for approximately 45 seconds, until the batter just begins to brown. Remove from the oil. Drain and serve hot.

▪ Serves 4 to 6 ▪

1 (1-pound) package frozen, prepared raw squid

½ cup potato starch, 80 grams

½ teaspoon salt

½ teaspoon baking soda

½ teaspoon xanthan gum

1 teaspoon Old Bay Seasoning (or other favorite seasoning)

¼ teaspoon ground red pepper

Oil, for frying

Calamari ▪ *Rice-based*

This version of calamari has a light, crisp crust that adds a light crunch. Hot from the oil, they are addictive. No sauce is needed.

- ▪ Thaw the squid. Preheat the oil to 370°F.
- ▪ Drain and slice the squid tubes into ¼-inch rings. Cut the tentacles as desired. The calamari should be barely damp to the touch. Excess moisture will prevent crisping during the frying process.
- ▪ In a small bowl, combine all the dry ingredients and stir well. Toss the squid in the flour mixture and drop into the hot oil.
- ▪ Cook for approximately 45 seconds, until the batter just begins to brown. Remove from the oil. Drain and serve hot.

▪ Serves 4 to 6 ▪

1 (1-pound) package frozen, prepared raw squid

½ cup rice flour, 75 grams

½ teaspoon salt

½ teaspoon baking soda

½ teaspoon xanthan gum (optional)

1 teaspoon Old Bay Seasoning (or other favorite seasoning)

Oil, for frying

Calamari Dipping Sauce

Although calamari is good all by itself, this super-fast dipping sauce is nice to serve on the side. It is a little sweet, a little spicy, a little Italian. The intriguing flavor belies the simple ingredients.

- ▪ Combine all the ingredients in a microwave-safe bowl. Mix well. Microwave on high for approximately 2 minutes, or bring to a boil in a small saucepan over medium heat.

▪ Makes ¾ cup sauce ▪

½ cup tomato ketchup

1 teaspoon dried oregano

⅛ teaspoon crushed red pepper

⅛ teaspoon garlic powder

1 tablespoon sugar

¼ cup water

Chicken Wings

Truthfully, the best chicken wings are deep-fried, then spiced or sauced. Avoiding gluten often means avoiding the oil in which foods are fried. Cross-contamination via shared oil is a very serious matter. However, you don't have to miss out. I have styled these after the best chicken wings I've ever eaten—from the Old Pike Inn in my hometown.

- Cut the tips (smallest section) off the wings at the joint. Discard. Cut the wings at the remaining joint to form traditional "wings." Set aside.
- Heat the oil to 370°F. Add the wings and fry until cooked through and the chicken skin is quite crispy, approximately 15 minutes. The wings will be golden in color. Remove from the oil and drain on paper towels.
- In a medium-size bowl, combine the wings and hot sauce. Toss to coat. Transfer the wings to a serving plate. Sprinkle with the thyme, oregano, and crushed red pepper.

■ Makes approximately 12 wings ■

1 1/2 pounds whole chicken wings
1/2 cup hot sauce
1/4 teaspoon dried thyme
1/4 teaspoon dried oregano
1/4 teaspoon crushed red pepper
Canola or peanut oil, for frying

> **NOTE:** If you don't care for very spicy wings, simply toss the cooked wings in 1/2 cup of your favorite barbecue sauce and serve.

Clams and Mussels on the Shell

This is a super-fast way to present lightly steamed clams or mussels. They are steamed in the shallowest amount of water, then topped with a little garlic cream right in the shell.

12 small clams, or 24 mussels

$^1\!/_4$ cup cream

1 teaspoon garlic salt

$^1\!/_4$ teaspoon garlic powder

- Wash and place the clams in a skillet in a single layer. Add $^1\!/_2$ to $^3\!/_4$ cup of water and cover the pan with a lid. Place the pan over high heat and cook just until the clams open, 3 to 5 minutes. You may actually hear the shells pop open and hit the lid of your pan. Remove from the heat.

- While the clams are cooking, combine the cream, garlic salt, and garlic powder in a bowl. Stir well. The sauce will thicken in just a minute or two. Set aside.

- Using a small knife, disconnect the muscle from each clamshell if still attached. Remove the top half of each shell, if desired. Place $^1\!/_4$ to $^1\!/_2$ teaspoon of sauce on top of each clam. Serve right away.

■ Serves 2 to 3 ■

Corn Dogs ▪ *Corn-based*

This recipe provides for a relatively light corn coating on the hot dogs. I use Popsicle sticks to hold the hot dogs.

- Heat the oil, in a saucepan or dedicated deep fryer (see note), to 370°F.
- Place a Popsicle stick lengthwise into each hot dog. Pat the hot dogs dry to remove excess moisture from their surface. Set aside.
- Mix together the ingredients for the batter in a medium-size bowl.
- One by one, coat the hot dogs with the batter (a rolling motion works well). Place in the hot oil and fry until golden, 3 to 4 minutes.
- Serve hot.

▪ Serves 10 ▪

1 pound hot dogs

Peanut or canola oil, for frying

Batter:

3/4 cup cornmeal, 105 grams

1/2 cup cornstarch, 65 grams

1 teaspoon salt

1 teaspoon baking powder

1 tablespoon sugar

1/2 teaspoon xanthan gum

1/8 teaspoon baking soda

1 egg

1 cup milk

Corn Dogs ▪ *Rice-based*

The coating on this corn dog is very comparable to those made with corn. Crispy on the outside, a little tender breading on the inside. Yum.

- Heat the oil, in a saucepan or dedicated deep fryer, to 370°F.
- Place a Popsicle stick lengthwise into each hot dog. Pat the hot dogs dry to remove excess moisture from their surface. Set aside.
- Mix together the ingredients for the batter in a medium-size bowl.
- One by one, coat the hot dogs with the batter (a rolling motion works well). Place in the hot oil and fry until golden, 3 to 4 minutes.
- Serve hot.

▪ Serves 10 ▪

1 pound hot dogs

Peanut or canola oil, for frying

Batter:

3/4 cup rice flour, 115 grams

1/2 teaspoon salt

1/4 teaspoon black pepper

1 1/4 teaspoons baking powder

1/8 teaspoon baking soda

1 teaspoon sugar

1/2 teaspoon xanthan gum

1 egg

3/4 cup milk

Crab Egg Rolls

Sometimes a delicate touch produces an unexpected surprise.

- Combine all but the last two ingredients in a medium-size bowl. Mix well.

- Place several spring roll wrappers at a time in a shallow bowl of cool water to soften them. This takes just 2 or 3 minutes.

- Place the mixture by the tablespoon in the lower third of a wrapper, leaving at least a 1-inch margin on each side. Fold the short end up and over the mixture, then fold the sides over the mixture. Roll up toward the far end. Place in a single layer in a baking pan.

- Cover with a damp cloth if not frying right away.

- Heat the oil in large skillet over medium heat. Add the egg rolls and cook for approximately 5 minutes on each side, until nicely browned and cooked through. Please know that you will surely have at least one broken egg roll, and using a spatula is much less likely to tear the wrappers. Too much filling will also make the egg rolls more likely to break during the frying process.

■ Makes 12 egg rolls ■

8 ounces pasteurized claw crabmeat

3 ounces cabbage, finely chopped (about 1 cup)

3 spring onions, sliced finely

1 tablespoon toasted sesame seeds

1 teaspoon soy sauce (check that it is gluten-free)

1 egg white

1/4 teaspoon salt

12 spring roll wrappers

2 tablespoons oil, for frying

NOTE: If you use a deep fryer, be sure that it is dedicated to gluten-free cooking only, otherwise cross-contamination could occur.

Crackers, Cheese ■ *Corn-based*

These poofy little crackers are rolled and cut. Miniature cookie cutters are available in cooking supply stores if you wish to mimic the tiny crackers loved by children.

- Preheat the oven to 400°F. Lightly grease a baking sheet.

- Combine all the ingredients, except the milk, in a medium-size bowl. Mix until the mixture resembles a fine crumb. Add the milk and beat well.

- On a lightly greased surface, pat or roll the dough to $1/8$-inch thickness. Cut into $3/4$-inch squares or another small shape that you like. You can also cut the dough into larger round or square cracker shapes, if desired (just extend the baking time).

- Prick the tops of the crackers with a fork and sprinkle lightly with your desired topping.

- Bake on the prepared baking sheet until golden brown and crisp, approximately 10 minutes. The crackers will be light and crispy, although barely browning at the edges. The bottom of the crackers will have a bit more color.

■ Makes approximately 5 dozen small crackers ■

4 ounces cheddar cheese, shredded

4 tablespoons ($1/4$ cup) butter, softened

$3/4$ cup cornstarch, 95 grams

$1/4$ teaspoon salt

$1/4$ teaspoon xanthan gum

$1/2$ teaspoon baking powder

$1/4$ teaspoon baking soda

2 tablespoons milk

Topping:

Salt, dried herbs, or spices, as desired

Crackers, Cheese ■ *Oat-based*

These crackers are little puffs. They are crisp, light, and bright in flavor.

- Preheat the oven to 400°F. Lightly grease a baking sheet.
- Combine all the ingredients, except the milk, in a medium-size bowl. Mix until the mixture resembles a fine crumb. Add the milk and beat well.
- On a lightly greased surface, pat or roll the dough to 1/8-inch thickness. Cut into 3/4-inch squares or another small shape that you like. You can also cut the dough into larger round or square cracker shapes, if desired (just extend the baking time).
- Pierce the tops of the crackers with a fork and sprinkle lightly with your desired topping.
- Bake on the prepared baking sheet until golden brown and crisp, 9 to 10 minutes. The crackers will be light and crispy, although barely browning at the edges. Similarly, the bottom of the crackers will have little color. Be careful not to underbake.

■ Makes approximately 5 dozen small crackers ■

4 ounces cheddar cheese, shredded

4 tablespoons (1/4 cup) butter, softened

3/4 cup oat flour, 90 grams

1/4 teaspoon salt

1/2 teaspoon xanthan gum

1/4 teaspoon baking soda

3 tablespoons milk

Topping:

Salt, dried herbs, or spices, as desired

Crackers, Cheese ■ *Potato-based*

When testing this recipe, I just couldn't resist adding $1/4$ teaspoon of cayenne. This makes for a more "adult" cracker. Omit the cayenne if you want a milder cracker.

- Preheat the oven to 400°F. Lightly grease a baking sheet.
- Combine all the ingredients, except the milk, in a medium-size bowl. Mix until the mixture resembles a fine crumb. Add the milk and beat well.
- On a lightly greased surface, pat or roll the dough to $1/8$-inch thickness. Cut into $3/4$-inch squares or another small shape that you like. You can also cut the dough into larger round or square cracker shapes, if desired (just extend the baking time).
- Prick the tops of the crackers with a fork and sprinkle lightly with your desired topping.
- Bake on the prepared baking sheet until golden brown and crisp, 10 to 12 minutes. The crackers will be light and crispy, although barely browning at the edges. The bottom of the crackers will have a bit more color.

■ **Makes approximately 5 dozen small crackers** ■

4 ounces cheddar cheese, shredded

4 tablespoons ($1/4$ cup) butter, softened

$2/3$ cup potato starch, 100 grams

$1/4$ teaspoon salt

$1/4$ teaspoon xanthan gum

$1/2$ teaspoon baking powder

$1/4$ teaspoon baking soda

$1/4$ teaspoon ground cayenne (optional)

2 tablespoons milk

Topping:

Salt, dried herbs, or spices, as desired

Crackers, Cheese ▪ *Rice-based*

This might be my favorite rice-based cracker. Simply addictive. If the crackers lose their crispness, refresh in a hot oven for a few minutes.

- Preheat the oven to 400°F. Lightly grease a baking sheet.
- Combine all the ingredients, except the milk, in a medium-size bowl. Mix until the mixture resembles a fine crumb. Add the milk and beat well.
- On a lightly greased surface, pat or roll the dough to $1/8$-inch thickness. Cut into $3/4$-inch squares or other small shape that you like. You can also cut the dough into larger round or square cracker shapes, if desired (just extend the baking time).
- Prick the tops of the crackers with a fork and sprinkle lightly with your desired topping.
- Bake on the prepared baking sheet until golden brown and crisp, 9 to 10 minutes. The crackers will be light and crispy, although barely browning at the edges. The bottom of the crackers will have a bit more color.

▪ Makes approximately 5 dozen small crackers ▪

4 ounces cheddar cheese, shredded

4 tablespoons ($1/4$ cup) butter, softened

$2/3$ cup rice flour, 100 grams

$1/4$ teaspoon salt

$1/2$ teaspoon xanthan gum

$1/2$ teaspoon baking powder

$1/4$ teaspoon baking soda

3 tablespoons milk

Topping:

Salt, dried herbs, or spices, as desired

Crackers, Cream Cheese ▪ *Corn-based*

Crackers are very easy to make. Who would have guessed that? It's like playing with Play-Doh! Get the kids to join in.

- Preheat the oven to 400°F. Lightly grease a baking sheet.
- Combine all the ingredients, except the milk, in a medium-size bowl. Mix until the mixture resembles a fine crumb. Add the milk and beat well.
- By teaspoonfuls, roll the dough into balls and place on the prepared baking sheet. Press the dough flat with the heel of your hand. The crackers should be so thin that you can see the baking sheet through the dough.
- Prick the tops of crackers with a fork and sprinkle liberally with your desired topping.
- Bake until golden brown and crisp, 6 to 8 minutes.

▪ Makes approximately 4 dozen crackers ▪

4 ounces cream cheese

4 tablespoons (¼ cup) butter

¾ cup cornstarch, 95 grams

¼ teaspoon salt

¼ teaspoon xanthan gum

¼ teaspoon baking soda

1 tablespoon milk

Topping:

Salt, dried herbs, or spices, as desired

Crackers, Cream Cheese ▪ *Oat-based*

These crackers may surprise you. While made from a whole-grain flour, they are surprisingly delicate.

- Preheat the oven to 400°F. Lightly grease a baking sheet.
- Combine all the ingredients, except the milk, in a medium-size bowl. Mix until the mixture resembles a fine crumb. Add the milk and beat well.
- By teaspoonfuls, roll the dough into balls and place on the prepared baking sheet. Press the dough flat with the heel of your hand. The crackers should be so thin that you can see the baking sheet through the dough.
- This cracker likes to poof in the middle, so be sure to prick very well with a fork. Sprinkle liberally with your desired topping.
- Bake until the crackers begin to color at edges, 6 to 8 minutes. Unlike the other cream cheese crackers, these will not be crisp when first removed from the oven.

▪ Makes approximately 4 dozen crackers ▪

4 ounces cream cheese

4 tablespoons (¼ cup) butter

¾ cup oat flour, 90 grams

¼ teaspoon salt

½ teaspoon xanthan gum

¼ teaspoon baking soda

1 tablespoon milk

Topping:

Salt, dried herbs, or spices, as desired

Crackers, Cream Cheese ■ *Potato-based*

These crackers are very mild in flavor.

- Preheat the oven to 400°F. Lightly grease a baking sheet.
- Combine all the ingredients, except the milk, in a medium-size bowl. Mix until the mixture resembles a fine crumb. Add the milk and beat well.
- By teaspoonfuls, roll the dough into balls and place on the prepared baking sheet. Press the dough flat with the heel of your hand. The crackers should be so thin that you can see the baking sheet through the dough.
- Prick the tops of crackers with a fork and sprinkle liberally with your desired topping.
- Bake until golden brown and crisp, 6 to 8 minutes.

■ Makes approximately 4 dozen crackers ■

4 ounces cream cheese

4 tablespoons ($^1/_4$ cup) butter

$^2/_3$ cup potato starch, 100 grams

$^1/_4$ teaspoon salt

$^1/_4$ teaspoon xanthan gum

$^1/_4$ teaspoon baking soda

1 tablespoon milk

Topping:

Salt, dried herbs, or spices, as desired

Crackers, Cream Cheese ■ *Rice-based*

Rice flour makes this cracker dough reasonably easy to handle. There is a bit of "grit" in these soft, buttery crackers. They are much better cooled than fresh from the oven.

- Preheat the oven to 400°F. Lightly grease a baking sheet.
- Combine all the ingredients, except the milk, in a medium-size bowl. Mix until the mixture resembles a fine crumb. Add the milk and beat well.
- By teaspoonfuls, roll the dough into balls and place on the prepared baking sheet. Press the dough flat with the heel of your hand. The crackers should be so thin that you can see the baking sheet through the dough.
- Prick the tops of the crackers with a fork and sprinkle liberally with your desired topping.
- Bake until golden brown and crisp, 6 to 8 minutes.

■ Makes approximately 4 dozen crackers ■

4 ounces cream cheese

4 tablespoons ($^1/_4$ cup) butter

$^2/_3$ cup rice flour, 100 grams

$^1/_4$ teaspoon salt

$^1/_2$ teaspoon xanthan gum

$^1/_4$ teaspoon baking soda

2 tablespoons milk

Topping:

Salt, dried herbs, or spices, as desired

Crackers, Saltine ▪ *Corn-based*

These crackers are a little darker in color than commercially produced saltine crackers. But the flavor is nearly identical.

- Preheat the oven to 400°F.
- Combine the butter, cornstarch, salt, xanthan gum, and baking soda in a medium-size bowl. Beat until the mixture forms a fine crumb. Add the remaining ingredients and beat well.
- Press the dough as thinly as possible on an ungreased baking sheet, to $1/8$-inch thickness or less. Moistened fingertips are helpful in pressing the dough. Do not be concerned if some spots are paper thin and others are a little thicker. Cut into $1\frac{1}{2}$-inch squares or another size of your liking.
- Prick the tops of the crackers with a fork and sprinkle with salt.
- Bake until golden brown and crisp, 10 to 12 minutes. The crackers will be light and crispy, with a bit of color on the surface and more browning on the bottom. Do not underbake. If a cracker seems bendable, put it back in the oven for a few more minutes.

▪ Makes approximately 2 dozen crackers ▪

6 tablespoons butter

$3/4$ cup cornstarch, 95 grams

$1/4$ teaspoon salt

$1/2$ teaspoon xanthan gum

$1/4$ teaspoon baking soda

1 egg white

1 teaspoon apple cider vinegar

2 tablespoons plain yogurt

Topping:

Salt

> **NOTE:** When making cream cheese or saltine crackers, it is very important that the dough be spread extremely thin. This helps ensure crispness across the entire cracker. If your crackers are a little thick, increase the baking time a bit. The cracker's crispness should be apparent, even when testing warm from the oven. If the slightly tacky texture of the dough is bothersome to you, it may be placed in the refrigerator for an hour before baking.

Crackers, Saltine ▪ *Oat-based*

This cracker tastes like a cross between a flat wheat cracker and a saltine. It is light in texture and pretty substantial in flavor.

- Preheat the oven to 400°F.

- Combine the butter, oat flour, salt, xanthan gum, baking soda, and baking powder in a medium-size bowl. Beat until the mixture forms a fine crumb. Add the remaining ingredients and beat well.

- Press the dough as thinly as possible on an ungreased baking sheet, to $1/8$-inch thickness or less. Moistened fingertips are helpful in pressing the dough. Do not be concerned if some spots are paper thin and others are a little thicker. Cut into $1\frac{1}{2}$-inch squares or another size of your liking.

- Prick the tops of the crackers with a fork and sprinkle with salt.

- Bake until golden brown and crisp, 8 to 10 minutes. The crackers will be lightly browned with a tender, crisp texture (even while hot).

> ▪ Makes approximately 2 dozen crackers ▪

6 tablespoons butter

$3/4$ cup oat flour, 90 grams

$1/4$ teaspoon salt

$3/4$ teaspoon xanthan gum

$1/4$ teaspoon baking soda

$1/2$ teaspoon baking powder

1 egg white

1 teaspoon apple cider vinegar

$1/4$ cup plain yogurt

Topping:

Salt

Crackers, Saltine ▪ *Potato-based*

This version of the saltine cracker is probably the most sensitive to thorough baking. If it is underbaked, it will have a gummy edge to it. But baked to crisp texture, it is a pretty amazing saltine.

- Preheat the oven to 400°F.

- Combine the butter, potato starch, salt, xanthan gum, and baking soda in a medium-size bowl. Beat until the mixture forms a fine crumb. Add the remaining ingredients and beat well.

- Press the dough as thinly as possible on an ungreased baking sheet, to $1/8$-inch thickness or less. Moistened fingertips are helpful in pressing the dough. Do not be concerned if some spots are paper thin and others are a little thicker. Cut into $1^1/2$-inch squares or another size of your liking.

- Prick the tops of the crackers with a fork and sprinkle with salt.

- Bake until golden brown and crisp, 12 to 18 minutes. The crackers will be light and crispy, with a bit of color on the surface and more browning on the bottom. Do not underbake. If a cracker seems bendable, put it back in the oven for a few more minutes.

▪ Makes approximately 2 dozen crackers ▪

---

6 tablespoons butter

$2/3$ cup potato starch, 100 grams

$1/4$ teaspoon salt

Scant $1/2$ teaspoon xanthan gum

$1/4$ teaspoon baking soda

1 egg white

1 teaspoon apple cider vinegar

2 tablespoons plain yogurt

Topping:

Salt

Crackers, Saltine ▪ *Rice-based*

This is a rice cracker made in the saltine style. It looks and tastes quite good. I won't kid you—the texture is more delicate when compared to a traditional saltine cracker. I would describe it as a cousin to a saltine.

- Preheat the oven to 400°F.
- Combine the butter, rice flour, salt, xanthan gum, baking soda, and baking powder in a medium-size bowl. Beat until the mixture forms a fine crumb. Add the remaining ingredients and beat well.
- Press the dough as thinly as possible on an ungreased baking sheet, to $1/8$-inch thickness or less. Moistened fingertips are helpful in pressing the dough. Do not be concerned if some spots are paper thin and others are a little thicker. Cut into $1\frac{1}{2}$-inch squares or another size of your liking.
- Prick the tops of the crackers with a fork and sprinkle with salt.
- Bake until golden brown and crisp, 10 to 12 minutes. The crackers will be light golden brown, with some spots just a little darker. The crackers should not be bendable but have a tender, crisp texture (even while hot). Do not underbake.

▪ Makes approximately 2 dozen crackers ▪

6 tablespoons butter
$2/3$ cup rice flour, 100 grams
$1/4$ teaspoon salt
$3/4$ teaspoon xanthan gum
$1/4$ teaspoon baking soda
$1/2$ teaspoon baking powder
1 egg white
1 teaspoon apple cider vinegar
$1/4$ cup plain yogurt

Topping:
Salt

Fried Cheese Sticks ▪ *Corn-based*

Crispy outside, gooey inside. Good.

- Heat the oil, in a saucepan or dedicated deep fryer, to a temperature of 370° to 375°F.
- In a small bowl, beat together the batter ingredients.
- Dip the cheese sticks into the batter and place in the hot oil. It is important to fully coat the cheese with the batter so that it doesn't seep out into the oil.
- Fry for approximately 2 minutes, until the coating is golden brown. Drain on paper towels and sprinkle liberally with salt.

▪ Makes 12 sticks ▪

1 (12-ounce package) mozzarella cheese sticks

Peanut or canola oil, for frying

Batter:

3/4 cup cornmeal, 105 grams

1 teaspoon salt

1/2 teaspoon cayenne

1/4 teaspoon black pepper

1/4 teaspoon baking powder

1 teaspoon sugar

1/2 teaspoon xanthan gum

1/8 teaspoon baking soda

1 egg

1/2 cup milk

Topping:

Salt

Fried Cheese Sticks ▪ *Rice-based*

These deep-fried sticks are crispy on the outside and gooey inside. Although $1/2$ teaspoon of cayenne might seem excessive, the flavor is really quite mild.

- Heat the oil, in a saucepan or dedicated deep fryer, to a temperature of 370° to 375°F.
- In a small bowl, beat together the batter ingredients.
- Dip the cheese sticks into the batter and place in the hot oil. It is important to fully coat the cheese with the batter so that it doesn't seep out into the oil.
- Fry for approximately 2 minutes, until the coating is golden brown. Drain on paper towels and sprinkle liberally with salt.

▪ Makes 12 sticks ▪

1 (12-ounce) package mozzarella cheese sticks
Peanut or canola oil, for frying

Batter:
$3/4$ cup rice flour, 115 grams
$1/2$ teaspoon salt
$1/4$ teaspoon black pepper
$1/2$ teaspoon cayenne
$1/4$ teaspoon baking powder
$1/8$ teaspoon baking soda
$1/2$ teaspoon xanthan gum
1 egg
$3/4$ cup milk

Topping:
Salt

Garlic Spread

This simple spread is a nice base for smoked salmon, capers, caviar, or other strongly flavored toppings. Our taste testers wouldn't stop eating it. It is reminiscent of Boursin cheese, the black pepper version. When first made, it has a hint of soft garlic flavor. Wait a few hours and you'll discover a longer, mellower garlic flavor.

- Place the head of garlic in a small, microwave-safe bowl. Add 1 tablespoon of water to the bowl. Microwave on high until the garlic is very tender, approximately 1 minute.
- Remove the cloves from the skin. Cut off the tough bottom end. Puree in a blender with the milk. Place in a medium-size bowl.
- Add the other ingredients. Blend until smooth and creamy.

▪ Makes $2/3$ cup ▪

1 head garlic, approximately $2 1/2$ ounces
2 tablespoons milk
4 ounces cream cheese
$1/2$ teaspoon salt
$1/4$ teaspoon freshly ground black pepper
Hot sauce

Mini Quiche

These mini quiches would be delightful for a wedding, brunch, or other special gathering. They are easy to make. I like to use pepper Jack cheese.

- Prepare the crust. Set aside. Lightly grease a mini muffin tin.
- Preheat the oven to 375°F. In a medium-size bowl, beat the eggs, milk, and salt until nearly uniform in color. Set aside.
- Press approximately 1 rounded teaspoonful of dough into each section of the prepared muffin tin. Press as thinly as possible with moistened fingertips.
- Divide the cheese among the unbaked shells. Divide the green onion among the shells. Cover with the egg mixture.
- Bake for 20 to 25 minutes, until the egg is fully cooked and begins to brown, and the crust begins to brown.

■ Makes 24 to 30 mini quiches ■

Recommended crust:

Any version of cream cheese cracker dough, chilled if time permits

Filling:

4 eggs

1/2 cup milk

Pinch of salt

2 ounces Monterey Jack cheese, grated

1 green onion, sliced finely

1/4 teaspoon salt

Pinch of cayenne (optional)

NOTE: If you need an even faster version, cut thin slices of prosciutto to line the muffin cups, then fill with the filling and bake.

Onion Rings ▪ *Corn-based*

These are very good onion rings. If you share them, no one will know they are gluten-free. I'll never tell!

- Heat the oil, in a saucepan or dedicated deep fryer, to 370°F.
- In a small bowl, combine the batter ingredients. Add the sliced onion.
- Remove the onion slices from the batter and place in the hot oil. Fry for approximately 2 minutes, until the coating is golden brown. Drain on paper towels and sprinkle liberally with salt.

▪ Serves 4 ▪

1 large onion, preferably sweet, peeled and sliced 1/4 inch thick

Peanut or canola oil, for frying

Batter:
3/4 cup cornstarch, 95 grams
1/2 teaspoon salt
1/4 teaspoon baking powder
1/8 teaspoon baking soda
1/2 teaspoon xanthan gum
1/2 cup milk

Topping:
Salt

NOTE: If making fried onions to use in green bean casserole, cut the slices 1/8 inch thick and barely coat with batter. These thin slices will fry in approximately 1 minute. No additional salt is needed after frying.

Onion Rings ▪ *Potato-based*

These traditional onion rings have a very crispy coating. Be careful not to apply too much coating or a bit of gumminess will occur closest to the onion. With just one or two test rings, you can master the desired level of battering.

- Heat the oil, in a saucepan or dedicated deep fryer, to 370°F.
- In a small bowl, combine the batter ingredients. Add the onion.
- Remove the onion slices from the batter and place in the hot oil. Fry for approximately 2 minutes, until the coating is golden brown. Drain on paper towels and sprinkle liberally with salt.

▪ Serves 4 ▪

1 large onion, preferably sweet, peeled and sliced ¼ inch thick

Peanut or canola oil, for frying

Batter:

⅔ cup potato starch, 100 grams

½ teaspoon salt

¼ teaspoon pepper

¼ teaspoon paprika

¼ teaspoon baking powder

⅛ teaspoon baking soda

⅛ teaspoon xanthan gum

½ cup milk

Topping:

Salt

NOTE: The batter may be thinned with a few tablespoons of milk as needed. The batter does thicken a bit if allowed to sit for a while.

Onion Rings ▪ *Rice-based*

The coating on these rings is similar to bread crumbs, as opposed to a very smooth batter texture. Fry these to a deep golden brown to get a very crispy exterior.

- Heat the oil, in a saucepan or dedicated deep fryer, to 370°F.
- In a small bowl, combine the batter ingredients. Add the onion.
- Remove the onion slices from the batter and place in the hot oil. Fry for approximately 2 minutes, until the coating is golden brown. Drain on paper towels and sprinkle liberally with salt.

▪ Serves 4 ▪

1 large onion, preferably sweet, peeled and sliced 1/4 inch thick

Peanut or canola oil, for frying

Batter:

3/4 cup rice flour, 115 grams

1/2 teaspoon salt

1/4 teaspoon black pepper

1/4 teaspoon baking powder

1/8 teaspoon baking soda

1/2 teaspoon xanthan gum

1 egg

3/4 cup milk

Topping:

Salt

Potato Wedges

Potato wedges are cousin to twice-baked potatoes. I personally like these better. If you don't care for bacon, a little shredded chicken is a nice alternative. These and a salad would make a great dinner. Admittedly, this is not the most low-fat dish in this book, but it's very satisfying!

- Pierce the potatoes several times with a fork. Microwave on high for 10 to 12 minutes, until the potatoes are cooked through.

- Cook the bacon in the microwave oven until crispy (see note). Break into bits. Set aside.

- Cut the potatoes into quarters. Scoop out the center of each potato, leaving a margin of about $1/4$ inch of potato next to the skin. Discard the center of the potatoes (or save for dinner another night).

- Spray the top of each potato wedge with nonstick spray or brush lightly with oil. Top each potato wedge with cheddar cheese and bacon bits. Place under the broiler for 3 to 5 minutes. The cheese should be melted and bubbly, and the edges of the potatoes will just begin to brown. Sprinkle generously with hot sauce. Top with sour cream and/or salsa, as desired.

■ Serves 8 ■

4 russet potatoes (about
   1 $3/4$ pounds), scrubbed

4 slices bacon

4 ounces cheddar cheese,
   shredded

$1/4$ teaspoon salt

Nonstick spray, or 1
   tablespoon oil

2 tablespoons hot sauce

$1/2$ cup low-fat sour cream
   (optional)

$1/2$ cup salsa (optional)

NOTE: Cooking four slices of thick bacon in the microwave oven (between paper towels) takes about 3 $1/2$ minutes on high.

Puffed Spring Roll Wrappers

These are essentially instant snacks, inspired by a posting on my favorite celiac discussion board. Little strips of dry spring roll wrappers are quickly fried to a crisp, much like a pappadam (a crackerlike Indian flatbread), but are lighter and melt in your mouth, like a Taco Bell cinnamon treat. We'll make ours both sweet and savory to enjoy. Don't worry if the wrappers break unevenly; it doesn't matter. If you come across very wide, clear rice noodles that are thicker than spring roll wrappers, you'll have even better results.

■ In a medium-size to large skillet, heat the oil to approximately 370°F. Place pieces of the spring roll wrappers in the oil, without crowding. They will expand during frying. As soon as they puff up (3 to 5 seconds), transfer to paper towels to drain. While they are still hot, either sprinkle with salt and pepper or place in large bowl with cinnamon-sugar, and toss to coat.

■ Continue with the remaining pieces of the wrappers.

■ Serves 4 ■

Savory rolls:

4 spring roll wrappers, cut into 8 pieces

1/4 teaspoon salt

1/4 teaspoon black pepper

(or other favorite spice blend)

Sweet rolls:

4 spring roll wrappers, cut into 16 pieces

1/4 cup sugar

1 teaspoon ground cinnamon

2 cups oil, for frying

NOTE: Pappadams are usually gluten-free, because they are made with lentil flour. They are delicious and flavorful. You may find them at larger grocery stores and Indian markets.

Shauna's Egg Rolls

While visiting my friend Shauna, I watched as she made egg rolls. She didn't measure any of the ingredients, but her end results were outstanding. If you prefer to deep-fry your egg rolls, you do not need to precook the ingredients. I have substituted spring roll wrappers (rice) for traditional egg roll wrappers (wheat). The brief pan-frying helps to avoid the pitfalls of deep-frying a rice wrapper—they like to open.

- Place the ground chicken in a large skillet. Cook over medium heat until cooked through. Add the remaining ingredients except for the wrappers and oil, and stir well. Lower the heat to medium-low. Cover and cook until the cabbage is tender-crisp, 5 to 7 minutes. Remove the pan from the heat. Remove the lid to speed cooling.

- Place several spring roll wrappers at a time in a shallow bowl of cool water to soften them. This takes just 2 or 3 minutes.

- Once the cabbage mixture is cool enough to handle, place a slightly rounded tablespoonful into a wrapper. Here's the procedure: Place the mixture in the lower third of the wrapper, leaving at least 1 inch on each side. Fold the short end up and over the mixture, then fold the sides over the mixture. Roll toward the far end. Place in a single layer in a baking pan.

- Cover with a damp cloth if not frying right away.

- Heat the oil in a large skillet over medium heat. Add the egg rolls and cook for approximately 5 minutes on each side. Please know that you will surely have at least one broken egg roll, and using a spatula is much less likely to tear the wrappers. Too much filling will also make the egg rolls more likely to break during the frying process.

■ Makes 15 egg rolls ■

½ pound ground chicken or turkey

¼ pound raw shrimp, peeled, deveined, and chopped

½ pound cabbage, chopped finely

1 stalk celery, chopped finely

1 small onion, chopped finely

1 clove garlic, minced

2 teaspoons soy sauce (check that it is gluten-free)

¼ teaspoon salt

¼ teaspoon pepper

1 (15-ounce) package spring roll wrappers

2 tablespoons oil, for frying

Steamed Clams and Mussels with Garlic Dipping Butter

A little wine, a little garlic, a little butter. That's all you need for a nice pot of steamed clams and mussels. Let me tell you in advance to remove the clams and mussels from the pot, not drain them in a colander. You'll want to reduce the broth and pour it over the finished dish.

- Wash and sort the mussels and clams. Any clam or mussel that does not close tightly when tapped, or that has a broken shell or has an unpleasant smell, should be discarded.

- Place half of the garlic in a large pot with the white wine and thyme. Bring to a rapid boil.

- Add the clams and mussels. Keeping the heat high, cover the pot with a lid and steam until the clams and mussels open, 5 to 7 minutes. Again, discard any that do not open. Drain.*

- In a small saucepan, combine the butter, remaining garlic, and the salt. Simmer until the garlic is just fragrant.

- Serve alongside the clams and mussels, for dipping.

- Serves 8 to 10 as an appetizer -

*The tasty liquid that remains from the steaming may be reduced over high heat until approximately $1/2$ cup remains and poured over the cooked clams and mussels, if desired.

2 pounds mussels

30 small littleneck clams

2 cloves garlic, diced finely

1 $1/2$ cups white wine

1 teaspoon dried thyme (optional)

8 tablespoons butter

$1/4$ teaspoon salt

NOTE: If you do not care for wine, substitute $3/4$ cup of apple juice and $3/4$ cup of water.

Stuffed Mushrooms

Much of the flavor for this dish comes from the sausage. I use Jimmy Dean's hot sausage. I've used large white stuffing mushrooms (with a cap size ranging from $1^{1}/4$ to $2^{1}/2$ inches) but, really, any size would be just fine. If you are a true mushroom lover, you might consider using a darker mushroom for more flavor. Either way, enjoy.

12–14 ounces fresh mushrooms
$^{1}/4$ pound sausage
1 small onion, peeled and diced finely
$^{1}/4$ teaspoon salt
$^{1}/4$ teaspoon black pepper
$^{1}/4$ teaspoon dried sage
1 egg
1 teaspoon cornstarch or potato starch

- Wash the mushrooms. Remove and save the stems. Place the mushroom caps upside down in a single layer in a baking pan.
- Remove and discard the very end of the mushroom stems (that once rooted in the dirt). Finely chop the remaining mushroom stems. Place in a medium-size skillet with the sausage (crumbled) and onion and cook over medium-high heat until the sausage is fully cooked, 3 to 4 minutes. Transfer to a large bowl. Allow to cool.
- Once the filling mixture is at room temperature, add the egg and starch.
- Preheat the oven to 375°F.
- Scoop by spoonfuls into the mushroom caps. The filling will thicken while it bakes.
- Bake, covered, until the mushrooms are very tender, approximately 20 minutes. Remove the cover and bake for 5 more minutes. Less time will be needed for smaller mushrooms.

■ Makes 16 large stuffed mushrooms ■

NOTE: Some of you will be thinking that the filling must contain crushed crackers. That is simply not true. We tested the mushrooms, using gluten-free crackers (crushed into fine crumbs) to bind the filling, and the only difference was ease in handling the filling. The flavor was virtually the same. So, save those expensive gluten-free crackers to enjoy with your cheese tray.

Sweet-and-Sour Meatballs

Most meatballs seem to be made with beef. But I believe poultry, or even pork, combines much better with a sweet-and-sour sauce. (Have you ever heard of sweet-and-sour beef? I didn't think so.) You may certainly substitute ground beef if you prefer, but I'm sticking with ground turkey.

- Prepare the meatballs: In a medium-size bowl, combine the turkey and onion. Shape by tablespoonfuls into balls. Pour the oil into a skillet to prevent sticking, and add the meatballs. Cook, covered, over medium heat until cooked through, approximately 10 minutes. No pink should remain. Remove from the heat and set aside.

- Prepare the sauce: In a small saucepan, cook the onion in the oil until it begins to soften. Add the drained pineapple chunks, 1/4 cup of the retained juice, the chile sauce, and the sugar. Cook over medium heat until the flavors blend and the sugar is completely dissolved.

■ Serves 6 to 8 ■

Meatballs:

1 pound ground turkey or pork

1 medium-size onion, diced finely

1 tablespoon oil

Sweet-and-sour sauce:

1 small onion, cut into large chunks

1/2 tablespoon oil

1 (8-ounce) can pineapple chunks in own juice, drained, juice reserved

1 (7.5-ounce) jar sweet chile sauce

4 teaspoons sugar

Tomato and Olive Tapenade

Do you ever get tired of traditional salsa? Me, neither. But I do like variety. This tapenade came about when my young friend Owen and I were cooking. We enjoyed it with traditional corn tortilla chips, but this would also be great on sandwiches, focaccia, and so on.

- In a medium-size bowl, combine all the ingredients. Mix well.

■ Makes approximately 4 cups; serves 12 to 15 ■

1 pint cherry or grape tomatoes, diced finely

1 small yellow or orange bell pepper, seeded and diced finely (about 5 ounces)

1 small onion, diced finely

1 (5.75-ounce) jar green olives, drained and chopped finely

1 tablespoon olive oil

1/2 ounce fresh basil, chopped finely (optional)

White Bean Dip

This dip is very similar to hummus and is brightened by the lemon juice. It is milder in flavor than hummus. For bolder flavor, substitute black beans and add a little cayenne.

- Place 3 tablespoons of the olive oil and the garlic in a skillet. Cook over medium heat. As soon as the garlic is fragrant, add the beans and salt. Heat through.
- Puree in a blender with the water, to make a smooth paste. Place in a serving bowl and pour the remaining 1 tablespoon of olive oil over the top.

■ Serves 4 ■

$1/4$ cup olive oil

1 clove garlic, chopped finely

1 (15.5-ounce) can white beans or great northern beans, drained

$1/2$ teaspoon salt

2 tablespoons water

Juice of 1 small lemon

White Beans with Garlic

My friend Bob and I would go to a great little Italian restaurant in Washington, D.C., several times a year for white beans, pizza, and red wine. Naturally, I find this a great first dish, followed by pizza.

- Heat the olive oil and garlic in a skillet over medium heat. As soon as the garlic is fragrant, add the beans and heat through.
- Add the salt and the parsley for color, if desired.

■ Serves 4 ■

3 tablespoons olive oil

1 clove garlic, chopped

1 (15.5-ounce) can white beans or great northern beans, drained

$1/4$ teaspoon salt

Pinch of fresh parsley, to garnish (if desired)

■■■ BREAKFAST

Breakfast is a great meal to have any time of the day. Insecure about your cooking ability? Breakfast is a great place to start!

Pancakes and waffles take just a few minutes to make and are really hard to mess up. Waffles are also easily reheated in a toaster. However, please note that waffle irons and toasters are sources for cross-contamination if shared with wheat-containing foods; please use dedicated equipment for your breakfast treats.

If you want a great breakfast gravy, try the Tomato Gravy recipe. It is very, very good. And, if you want something sweet in the morning, the doughnuts, cinnamon rolls, and coffee cake will surely make you happy.

■ ■ ■

Bagels ▪ *Corn- and rice-based*

No pot of boiling water is needed to achieve a thick, crisp crust! Just a little bottle of water does the job. This bagel has a thick, crisp crust and a chewy but not too heavy middle, much like the lighter versions commercially available in the bread aisle of a grocery store. When first made, the texture is quite pleasing, but it is even better a few hours later. Freeze extras!

- Preheat the oven to 350°F. Lightly grease a baking sheet.
- Mix the warm water and salt in a small spray bottle. Set aside.
- Place the egg whites in a medium-size bowl. Beat until very frothy, with big and little bubbles. Add the remaining ingredients. Mix well until thick.
  The dough will appear soft, with many very small air bubbles. Place the dough in a resealable plastic bag. Cut 1 inch diagonally off one lower corner of the bag.
- Pipe the dough into three large or four small circles onto the prepared baking sheet.
- Spray liberally with the salt water. Bake for 5 minutes. Spray again with salt water.
- Continue baking for 15 to 20 more minutes, until nicely browned.

▪ Makes 3 or 4 bagels ▪

Water Spray:

1/2 cup warm water

1/2 teaspoon salt

Bagels:

3 egg whites

1 teaspoon sugar

2 tablespoons oil

1/3 cup plain yogurt

1 cup cornstarch, 125 grams

1/3 cup rice flour, 50 grams

1 teaspoon baking powder

1/4 teaspoon baking soda

1/2 teaspoon salt

3/4 teaspoon xanthan gum

1 tablespoon apple cider vinegar

Bagels ▪ *Potato- and sorghum-based*

This bagel needs to sit for at least 30 minutes after baking for the texture to develop correctly; please do not skip this step. The texture of the corn and rice bagel recipe is slightly different, but this bagel has a light and chewy multigrain texture.

- Preheat the oven to 350°F. Lightly grease a baking sheet.
- Mix the warm water and salt in a small spray bottle. Set aside.
- Place the egg whites in a medium-size bowl. Beat until very frothy, with big and little bubbles. Add the remaining ingredients. Mix well until thick. The dough will appear soft, with many very small air bubbles. Place the dough in a resealable plastic bag. Cut 1 inch diagonally off one lower corner of the bag.
- Pipe the dough into three large or four small circles onto the prepared baking sheet.
- Spray liberally with the salt water. Bake for 5 minutes. Spray again with salt water.
- Continue baking for 15 to 20 more minutes, until nicely browned.

▪ Makes 3 or 4 bagels ▪

Water Spray:
1/2 cup warm water
1/2 teaspoon salt

Bagels:
3 egg whites
1 1/2 tablespoons oil
1/3 cup plain yogurt
3/4 cup potato starch, 115 grams
1/4 cup sorghum flour, 35 grams
1 1/2 teaspoons baking powder
1/4 teaspoon baking soda
1/2 teaspoon salt
3/4 teaspoon xanthan gum
1 tablespoon apple cider vinegar

Cinnamon Rolls ▪ *Corn-based*

These are some of the fastest and tastiest cinnamon rolls you may ever have that are gluten-free! They are light and fluffy. This recipe makes nine large rolls, so you'll need to share or put some in the freezer. The dough is very soft, making the rolling and lifting technique difficult to master on your first attempt, but don't let that discourage you from trying these.

- Preheat the oven to 350°F. Grease a 9-inch square baking pan.

- Make the dough: Cream the butter and sugar in a medium-size bowl. Add the egg whites and beat until very frothy. Add the remaining dough ingredients. Mix well.

- Place two large pieces of plastic wrap or aluminum foil, overlapping their edges, on a counter. Spray with nonstick spray. Place the dough on the plastic wrap or foil and press out (moistened fingertips help) as thinly as possible; 14 x 12 inches is a nice size, but a thinner, broader dough will give you more layers.

- In a small bowl, combine the filling ingredients. Mix well. Sprinkle over the dough as evenly as possible. Use the edge of the paper to roll the dough very gently into a long cylinder. Pull away the paper as you go. This will be awkward.

- Cut into nine even slices. With moistened hands, gently place the slices into the prepared baking pan. This, too, will seem quite difficult at first. For the prettiest results, smooth the tops of the rolls with moistened fingertips as well.

- Bake for 40 to 45 minutes, until golden brown. The rolls should test cleanly with a toothpick. Flip the pan over onto a serving plate so the filling (now quite liquid) will ooze over the top of the rolls.

▪ Makes 9 very large rolls ▪

4 tablespoons (¹/₄ cup) butter, softened

¹/₃ cup sugar

5 egg whites

³/₄ cup plain yogurt

2 cups cornstarch, 250 grams

2¹/₂ teaspoons baking powder

1 teaspoon baking soda

¹/₂ teaspoon salt

2 teaspoons xanthan gum

¹/₂ teaspoon vanilla extract

1 tablespoon apple cider vinegar

Filling:

4 tablespoons (¹/₄ cup) butter, very softened

1 cup brown sugar

1¹/₂ teaspoons ground cinnamon

NOTE: If you press the dough more thinly into a longer rectangle, it may be cut and placed into twelve sections of a greased muffin tin.

Coffee Cake ▪ *Corn-based*

Here is a not-too-sweet coffee cake. The topping melts into the batter while it bakes, to form swirls of sweet cinnamon flavor in the cake. It is best enjoyed at room temperature, as it will seem too moist when hot from the oven.

- Preheat the oven to 350°F. Lightly grease a 9-inch round or square baking pan.
- Combine the oil with the sugar in a medium-size bowl. Add the eggs. Beat with an electric mixer until light yellow and a little thicker. This will take a minute or two. Add the other dough ingredients. Beat well. Spread the batter in the prepared baking pan.
- Mix all the topping ingredients together in a bowl, until they crumble. Sprinkle evenly on top of the dough.
- Bake for 25 to 30 minutes, until a toothpick inserted in the middle tests cleanly.

▪ Serves 9 ▪

1/4 cup oil

1/3 cup sugar, 65 grams

2 eggs

1/2 cup plain yogurt

1 1/4 cups cornstarch, 155 grams

2 teaspoons baking powder

1/4 teaspoon baking soda

1/4 teaspoon salt

2 teaspoons vanilla extract

1 1/4 teaspoons xanthan gum

Topping:

1/2 teaspoon ground cinnamon

1/4 cup brown sugar

3 tablespoons butter

Coffee Cake ▪ *Potato-based*

This not-too-sweet coffee cake is best enjoyed at room temperature, as it will seem too moist when hot from the oven.

- Preheat the oven to 350°F. Lightly grease a 9-inch round or square baking pan.
- Combine the oil with the sugar in a medium-size bowl. Add the eggs. Beat with an electric mixer until light yellow and a little thicker. This will take a minute or two. Add the other dough ingredients. Beat well. The batter will thicken a little. Pour into the prepared baking pan.
- Mix all the topping ingredients together in a bowl, until they crumble. Sprinkle evenly on top of the dough.
- Bake for 30 minutes, until a toothpick inserted in the middle tests cleanly.

▪ Serves 9 ▪

1/4 cup oil

1/2 cup sugar, 100 grams

2 eggs

1/2 cup plain yogurt

1 cup potato starch, 155 grams

2 teaspoons baking powder

1/4 teaspoon baking soda

1/4 teaspoon salt

1 1/4 teaspoons vanilla extract

1 teaspoon xanthan gum

Topping:

1/2 teaspoon ground cinnamon

1/4 cup brown sugar

3 tablespoons butter

Coffee Cake ▪ *Rice-based*

This is a rich, buttery coffee cake. It tastes like it has far more butter in it than it actually does. The flavor of the cake is reminiscent of a good vanilla rice pudding, but the texture of the cake is springy, not too light, and not too heavy.

▪ Preheat the oven to 350°F. Lightly grease a 9-inch round or square baking pan.

▪ Combine the butter with the sugar in a medium-size bowl. Add the eggs and egg white. Beat with an electric mixer until light yellow and a little thicker. This will take a minute or two. Add the other dough ingredients. Beat well. The batter will be soft and billowy. Spread in the prepared baking pan.

▪ Mix all the topping ingredients together, until they crumble. Sprinkle evenly on top of the dough.

▪ Bake for 25 to 35 minutes, until a toothpick inserted in the middle tests cleanly.

▪ Serves 9 ▪

4 tablespoons (¼ cup) butter

½ cup sugar, 100 grams

2 eggs

1 egg white

½ cup plain yogurt

¾ cup rice flour, 115 grams

1 tablespoon baking powder

1 teaspoon baking soda

½ teaspoon salt

1 teaspoon vanilla extract

¾ teaspoon xanthan gum

2 teaspoons apple cider vinegar

Topping:

½ teaspoon ground cinnamon

¼ cup brown sugar

3 tablespoons butter

Danish ▪ *Corn-based*

My youngest son tested this Danish for me. He walked out of the kitchen with the whole Danish and wouldn't share. This is rich, buttery, and soft. A small, thick puddle of jam bakes prettier than a thin layer of jam.

- ▪ Preheat the oven to 350°F. Lightly grease a baking sheet.

- ▪ Combine all the dough ingredients, except the milk and egg white, in a medium-size bowl. Stir until the mixture resembles a fine crumb. Beat the egg white in a separate cup until frothy. Add the egg white and milk to the crumb mixture. Beat well.

- ▪ With moistened hands, shape approximately 1/4 cup of dough into an oval approximately 1/3 inch thick. Place on the prepared baking sheet. Depress the center of the dough slightly. Place 1 tablespoon of jam in the depression. Repeat until all the dough is used.

- ▪ Bake for approximately 20 minutes, until the Danish is browned and tests cleanly with a toothpick.

- ▪ Prepare the glaze and drizzle over the tops of the Danish.

▪ Makes 6 Danish ▪

4 ounces cream cheese

4 tablespoons (1/4 cup) butter

3/4 cup cornstarch, 95 grams

1/4 cup sugar, 50 grams

1/4 teaspoon salt

2 teaspoons baking powder

1/2 teaspoon xanthan gum

1/4 teaspoon baking soda

1/4 cup milk

1 egg white

Topping:

1/3 cup seedless jam

Confectioners' Glaze (page 323)

Doughnuts, Cake ■ *Corn-based*

For ease of making, the batters for this and the following doughnuts are dropped from a spoon into hot oil. You will end up with the "hole" of the doughnut. The texture of this corn-based doughnut is very similar to that of a traditional cake doughnut, just a little lighter. You may also notice that no fat is added to the batter. We tried the recipe with and without fat. Fat-free was better.

- Combine all the doughnut ingredients except the oil in a medium-size bowl. Beat until light and fluffy. Heat the oil to 375°F.
- Drop the dough by rounded teaspoonfuls into the hot oil. Cook until light golden brown and cooked through, 2 to 3 minutes. Drain. Roll in confectioners' sugar.

■ Makes 20 to 25 holes; serves 5 ■

1 cup cornstarch, 125 grams

2 tablespoons sugar

1/2 teaspoon baking soda

1/2 teaspoon baking powder

1 egg

1/2 cup plain yogurt

1/2 teaspoon xanthan gum

1/2 teaspoon vanilla extract

1 tablespoon apple cider vinegar

Canola or peanut oil, for frying

Topping:

1/2 cup confectioners' sugar

Doughnuts, Cake ■ *Rice-based*

Although the corn version of cake doughnuts is my favorite among those in this book, this rice version has a tight cake texture, a light vanilla flavor, and a soft exterior.

■ Combine all the doughnut ingredients except the oil in a medium-size bowl. Beat until light and fluffy. Heat the oil to 375°F.

■ Drop the dough by rounded teaspoonfuls into hot oil. Cook until light golden brown and cooked through, 2 to 3 minutes. Drain. Roll in confectioners' sugar.

■ Makes 20 to 25 holes; serves 5 ■

3/4 cup rice flour, 115 grams

3 tablespoons sugar

1/2 teaspoon baking soda

1/2 teaspoon baking powder

2 eggs

1/2 cup plain yogurt

3/4 teaspoon xanthan gum

1 teaspoon vanilla extract

1 tablespoon oil

1 tablespoon apple cider vinegar

Canola or peanut oil, for frying

Topping:

1/2 cup confectioners' sugar

Doughnuts, Chocolate Cake ■ *Oat-based*

I am a traditionalist when it comes to doughnuts. Oats by themselves in a doughnut are fine, better with a little spice (see note), but even better with chocolate.

■ Combine all the doughnut ingredients except the oil in a medium-size bowl. Beat until light and fluffy. Heat the oil to 375°F.

■ Drop the dough by rounded teaspoonfuls into the hot oil. Cook until light golden brown and cooked through, approximately 2 minutes. Drain. Roll in confectioners' sugar.

■ Makes 25 to 30 holes; serves 6 ■

1 cup oat flour, 120 grams

1/2 cup unsweetened cocoa powder, 40 grams

1/2 cup sugar

1/2 teaspoon baking soda

1 teaspoon baking powder

2 eggs

1/2 cup plain yogurt

1/2 teaspoon xanthan gum

1 1/2 teaspoons vanilla extract

1 tablespoon oil

Canola or peanut oil, for frying

Topping:

1/2 cup confectioners' sugar

NOTE: If you want to do a nonchocolate oat cake-style doughnut, omit the cocoa, increase the oat flour to 1 1/4 cups (150 grams), and add 1 tablespoon of apple cider vinegar and 1/2 teaspoon of ground cinnamon. Cook for approximately 3 minutes.

English Muffins ∎ *Corn- and rice-based*

English muffins are easy to make. No special equipment needed! And they have lots of nooks and crannies, too! This is my favorite of the two English muffin recipes I'm giving here; they're light, airy, and a little crispy/crunchy.

- Preheat the oven to 350°F. Lightly grease a baking sheet.

- Place the egg whites in a medium-size bowl. Beat until very frothy, with big and little bubbles. Add the remaining ingredients except the 2 tablespoons of rice flour. Mix well until the batter thickens. The dough will have lots of little air bubbles.

- Sprinkle 1 tablespoon of the remaining rice flour on the prepared baking sheet.

- Drop the dough by ½ cupfuls onto the sheet. Remembering that every lost bubble is a lost nook or cranny, gently shape the dough with wet fingertips into a flat disk approximately ½ inch thick and 3 inches in diameter. For the nicest presentation, it is important to make the top and sides smooth and to slightly depress the center of each muffin to avoid a dome shape. Sprinkle the tops with the remaining tablespoon of rice flour.

- Bake for approximately 15 minutes, until just golden brown. Test with a toothpick if you are uncertain of doneness. Let cool well before splitting each muffin in half.

∎ Makes 5 English muffins ∎

3 egg whites

1 teaspoon sugar

2 tablespoons oil

⅓ cup apple juice

1 cup cornstarch, 125 grams

⅓ cup, 50 grams, plus 2 tablespoons rice flour

1 tablespoon baking powder

1 teaspoon baking soda

½ teaspoon salt

¾ teaspoon xanthan gum

1 tablespoon apple cider vinegar

English Muffins ■ *Potato- and sorghum-based*

With not as many nooks and crannies as the corn and rice version, this is a tasty English muffin with a heavier texture.

- Preheat the oven to 350°F. Lightly grease a baking sheet.

- Place the egg whites in a medium-size bowl. Beat until very frothy, with big and little bubbles. Add the remaining ingredients except the 2 tablespoons of sorghum flour. Mix well until the batter thickens. The dough will have lots of little air bubbles.

- On the prepared baking sheet, sprinkle 1 tablespoon of the remaining sorghum flour.

- Drop the dough by $1/2$ cupfuls onto the sheet. Remembering that every lost bubble is a lost nook or cranny, gently shape the dough with wet fingertips into a flat disk approximately $1/2$ inch thick and 3 inches in diameter. For the nicest presentation, it is important to make the top and sides smooth and to slightly depress the center of each muffin to avoid a dome shape. Sprinkle the tops with the remaining tablespoon of sorghum flour.

- Bake for approximately 15 minutes, until just golden brown. Test with a toothpick if you are uncertain of doneness. Let cool well before splitting each muffin in half.

■ Makes 5 English muffins ■

3 egg whites

$1 1/2$ tablespoons oil

$1/3$ cup apple juice

$3/4$ cup potato starch, 115 grams

$1/4$ cup, 35 grams, plus 2 tablespoons sorghum flour

1 tablespoon baking powder

1 teaspoon baking soda

$1/2$ teaspoon salt

$3/4$ teaspoon xanthan gum

1 tablespoon apple cider vinegar

> **NOTE:** The use of two grains produced superior results for the English muffins.

Oven-Baked Eggs in Tomato Cups

This makes a nice luncheon presentation that tastes just like it sounds, only better. The Parmesan cheese and hot sauce are a simple yet perfect accompaniment to the fresh tomato and egg.

- Preheat the oven to 350°F. Lightly grease a shallow baking dish.

- Wash tomatoes and cut in half. Scoop out the centers and discard. If needed, slice a very small piece off the bottom of each tomato to form a stable base. Place the tomatoes cut side up in the prepared baking dish.

- Crack and place one egg into each tomato half. Top each tomato half with $1/2$ teaspoon of Parmesan cheese and a light sprinkling of salt.

- Bake for 30 to 40 minutes (depending upon the shape of the tomatoes), until the egg whites are cooked through. Top with several drops of hot sauce and garnish with fresh herbs, if desired.

■ Serves 8 ■

4 medium-size, firm tomatoes

8 eggs

4 teaspoons grated Parmesan cheese

$1/4$ teaspoon salt

Hot sauce (optional)

Fresh herbs, to garnish (optional)

Pancakes ■ *Corn-based*

Soft, light, and yummy—a classic breakfast dish.

- Place all the ingredients in a medium-size bowl. Mix very well. The batter will seem quite thin, but will thicken considerably. Heat a pan or griddle to medium heat. (A drop of water should "dance" on the surface.) Pour the batter into the pan to your desired size of pancakes. Cook until small bubbles appear on the surface and the bottom becomes lightly browned. Flip and continue to cook until lightly browned on both sides.

■ Makes eight to ten 4-inch pancakes ■

1 egg

$1 1/2$ cups cornstarch, 190 grams

1 tablespoon baking powder

$1/4$ cup oil

$1/4$ teaspoon salt

2 tablespoons sugar

1 cup milk

$1/4$ teaspoon xanthan gum

$1/2$ teaspoon vanilla extract (optional)

Pancakes ■ *Oat-based*

These pancakes taste slightly of whole grain.

■ Place all the ingredients in a medium-size bowl. Mix very well. The batter will thicken a bit as it is mixed. Heat a pan or griddle to medium heat. (A drop of water should "dance" on the surface.) Pour the batter into the pan to your desired size of pancakes. Cook until small bubbles appear on surface and the bottom is lightly browned. Flip and continue to cook until lightly browned on both sides.

■ Makes ten to twelve 4-inch pancakes ■

2 eggs

1 1/2 cups oat flour, 185 grams

1 tablespoon plus 1 teaspoon baking powder

1/4 cup oil

1/4 teaspoon salt

2 tablespoons sugar

1 1/2 cups milk

1/2 teaspoon xanthan gum

1/4 teaspoon vanilla extract (optional)

Pancakes ■ *Potato-based*

While I often find potato outstanding in many gluten-free applications, I personally prefer the other pancake recipes I've included. However, if potato is your flour of choice, these will pleasantly satisfy your morning pancake craving.

■ In a medium-size bowl, mix the potato starch and oil. Stir very well to evenly coat the starch with the oil. (This prevents the pancake from tasting gummy.) Add all the other ingredients and mix well. The batter will thicken a bit as it is stirred. Heat a pan or griddle to medium heat. (A drop of water should "dance" on the surface.) Pour the batter into the pan to your desired size of pancakes. Cook until small bubbles appear on the surface and the bottom is lightly browned. Flip and continue to cook until lightly browned on both sides.

■ Makes eight 4-inch pancakes ■

3/4 cup potato starch, 115 grams

2 tablespoons oil

1 egg

1/2 cup milk

1/2 teaspoon vanilla extract

2 teaspoons baking powder

1/4 teaspoon salt

2 tablespoons sugar

1/2 teaspoon xanthan gum

Pinch of baking soda

Pancakes ■ *Rice-based*

This is a good pancake; the only precaution is to be sure it is cooked all the way through. I asked the three testers to describe how these pancakes tasted. "Like pancakes," was their repeated response while polishing off the whole batch.

- Place all the ingredients in medium-size bowl. (I like to add the milk last, as the batter will thicken upon sitting.) Mix very well. The batter will become quite thick. Heat a pan or griddle to medium heat. (A drop of water should "dance" on the surface.) Pour the batter in the pan to your desired size of pancakes. Spread with a spoon if necessary. Cook until small bubbles appear on the surface and the bottom is lightly browned. Flip and continue to cook until lightly browned on both sides.

■ Makes eight to ten 4-inch pancakes ■

2 eggs

$^3/_4$ cup rice flour, 110 grams

1 tablespoon baking powder

$^1/_4$ cup oil

$^1/_4$ teaspoon salt

2 tablespoons sugar

$^3/_4$ teaspoon xanthan gum

$^1/_2$ teaspoon vanilla extract

1 cup milk

Tomato Gravy

Can you imagine such a thing? I couldn't either, but I met a Southern gentleman while traveling through Georgia who assured me it was wonderful. He graciously shared his recipe with me, which utilizes a traditional roux (blend of flour and fat), so I've had to tweak it for the gluten-free diet. And, true to his word, it is delicious. Thank you, Mike. If you use a spicy sausage, omit the salt and pepper.

1/2 medium-size onion, peeled and diced

1/4 pound sausage

1 (15.5-ounce) can chopped tomatoes

1 tablespoon cornstarch or potato starch

1/4 teaspoon salt

1/4 teaspoon freshly ground black pepper

- Place the onion and sausage in a medium-size saucepan. Break up the sausage into crumbles. If the meat renders a lot of fat, drain and discard fat. Combine the tomatoes and starch in small bowl (I actually combine it in the can!). Stir well to dissolve the starch. Add to the pan with the salt and pepper.
- Cook and stir gently until thick. Avoid overcooking. Serve over biscuits or toast.

■ Serves 2 ■

> NOTE: If you have never tried tomato gravy, please know that it is a little humble in appearance. A few slices of orange or a wedge of cantaloupe will make the presentation much prettier. If you already love this gravy, I'm sure you'll be enjoying it on rice, pasta, pizza, and who knows what else.

Waffles ▪ *Corn-based*

Light, airy, delicious. If you're unsure of which waffle recipe to try first, make this one.

▪ Preheat your waffle iron.

▪ Place all the ingredients in medium-size bowl. Mix very well. The batter will seem thin but will thicken considerably if allowed to sit for a minute or two. It will better fill the waffle iron when the batter is thicker. Place a large $1/2$ cup of batter into the waffle iron. Cook to your desired level of browning, about $1^{1/2}$ minutes.

▪ Makes four 8-inch waffles ▪

2 eggs

1 $^{1/2}$ cups cornstarch, 190 grams

1 tablespoon baking powder

$^{1/3}$ cup oil

$^{1/4}$ teaspoon salt

2 tablespoons sugar

$^{3/4}$ cup milk

$^{1/4}$ teaspoon xanthan gum

$^{1/2}$ teaspoon vanilla extract (optional)

> **NOTE:** Have a newly diagnosed wheat- or gluten-intolerant friend? Why not buy a new waffle iron and include a favorite recipe from this book? You can explain that cross-contamination is a serious issue and give your friend something yummy to look forward to.

Waffles ▪ *Oat-based*

These waffles are light, yet filling. There's something about vanilla with oats that softens the whole-grain taste.

▪ Preheat your waffle iron.

▪ Place all the ingredients in a medium-size bowl. Mix very well. The batter will become thicker and thicker from the xanthan gum. Place a large $1/2$ cup of batter into the waffle iron. Cook to your desired level of browning, about $1^{1/2}$ minutes. Allow to cool for just a minute or so before serving; otherwise, these waffles will seem too moist.

▪ Makes five 8-inch waffles ▪

3 eggs

1 $^{1/2}$ cups oat flour, 185 grams

1 tablespoon plus 1 teaspoon baking powder

$^{1/3}$ cup oil

$^{1/4}$ teaspoon salt

2 tablespoons sugar

$^{3/4}$ cup milk

$^{3/4}$ teaspoon xanthan gum

$^{1/2}$ teaspoon vanilla extract

Waffles ■ *Potato-based*

Potato could just be my favorite stand-alone flour. It is not perfect since it is a starch but, boy, does it taste good.

- Preheat your waffle iron.
- Place all the ingredients in a medium-size bowl. Mix very well. The batter will seem quite thin but will thicken considerably if allowed to sit for a minute or two. It will better fill the waffle iron when the batter is thicker. Place a large $1/2$ cup of batter into the waffle iron. Cook to your desired level of browning, about $1^1/2$ minutes. Allow to cool for just a minute or so, for the best texture.

■ Makes four 8-inch waffles ■

2 eggs

1 cup potato starch, 155 grams

1 tablespoon baking powder

$1/3$ cup oil

$1/4$ teaspoon salt

2 tablespoons sugar

$3/4$ cup milk

$1/4$ teaspoon xanthan gum

$1/2$ teaspoon vanilla extract (optional)

Waffles ■ *Rice-based*

These waffles are medium-textured. They have a very slight hint of grit, as if a small amount of cornmeal was added to the batter.

- Preheat your waffle iron.
- Place all the ingredients in a medium-size bowl. Mix well. The batter will be very thick; it will become even thicker as it sits—like fluffy mayonnaise. Place a large $1/2$ cup of batter into the waffle iron. Cook to your desired level of browning, $1^1/2$ to 2 minutes.

■ Makes four 8-inch waffles ■

3 eggs

$1^1/3$ cups rice flour, 200 grams

1 tablespoon plus 1 teaspoon baking powder

$1/3$ cup oil

$1/4$ teaspoon salt

2 tablespoons sugar

1 cup milk

1 teaspoon xanthan gum

$1/2$ teaspoon vanilla extract

4

BREADS— BAGUETTES, LOAVES, ROLLS, AND MORE

I am so very happy to be able to share these favorite bread recipes with you. These breads taste very similar to traditional breads. They have great "real" bread texture. And, they are easy to make.

This chapter contains recipes for breads made with single grains as well as those made with two grains. Quite a few recipes are dairy-free.

Single-grain breads are nice while you (and your health provider) are evaluating what you can and cannot tolerate, especially if you have multiple food sensitivities. Multigrain breads provide good variety and the added nutrition of whole grains. And dairy-free breads are nice for those who cannot tolerate dairy, which is especially common dur-

ing the early months after diagnosis, when your gut is beginning to heal.

For the record, with the exception of recipes using rice flour alone, dairy does not necessarily improve the taste of gluten-free breads. Yeast doesn't guarantee better flavor, either. Very few recipes in this book use yeast.

You may have eaten bread that "tastes" gluten-free. Depending upon the recipe, yeast and/or egg yolks are the likely culprits. Certain kinds of gluten-free breads can have a "gna" taste. Yes, that is my word for that funky, lingering, earthy (but not in a good way) taste so often associated with gluten-free breads. You won't find that characteristic in these recipes— instead, real bread textures and flavors will have you baking these breads again and again.

If you look at the ingredients used in my gluten-free breads, you might think I've spent one too many hours in the kitchen. But I haven't.

At first glance, you may consider it odd that egg whites are used in the bread recipes. Really, this makes a lot of sense. If you mix an egg white in a bowl, you'll notice thousands of little air bubbles of various sizes and shapes. And if you squint (work with me here), you will notice that they look like the inside of a nice slice of bread (only clear).

Also to their advantage, egg whites are readily available and are a good source of protein. By now, you may be wondering why I don't use egg yolk in these breads. That's simple: it does not enhance the flavor or texture of the bread.

Finally, I need to mention that not all gluten-free rolls will stand up to that juicy burger. Put a slice of lettuce between the burger and the bun to ensure the best overall texture. Alternatively, a light toasting of the bun will also help delay any premature moistness of your roll.

Baguette, French ▪ *Corn-based*

So, you're missing this classic French bread and wonder if this recipe can really produce a genuine baguette? Our taste testers were pleasantly surprised by the taste and texture. You should really try this recipe.

- Preheat the oven to 400°F. Lightly grease a French bread pan. (You may also use a disposable foil pan bent into a curved shape.)

- Place the egg whites in a medium-size bowl. Beat until very frothy, with big and little bubbles. Add the remaining ingredients. Mix well until the mixture thickens. It should seem soft and thick. Place the dough in a large, square plastic bag. Snip a corner off the bottom edge of the bag, no more than 1½ inches across.

- Pipe large, thick strips or smaller roll-size strips of dough into the prepared pan. Moisten the entire top of the dough with very moist fingertips or spritz well with water and smooth with your fingertips.

- If you can remember to, spritz with water 10 minutes into the baking time. (This helps to crisp the crust.) Bake for a total of 15 to 20 minutes, until the bread is golden and no wet spots are visible.

▪ Makes 2 baguettes ▪

3 egg whites

1 tablespoon oil

½ cup apple juice

1¼ cups cornstarch, 155 grams

2 teaspoons baking powder

1 teaspoon baking soda

½ teaspoon salt

1⅛ teaspoons xanthan gum

1 tablespoon apple cider vinegar

> **NOTE:** When dairy is replaced with water or apple juice in a bread or roll recipe, the amount of xanthan gum required is reduced.

Baguette ▪ *Oat-based*

I used a little honey to sweeten this baguette, as honey and oats go so well together. Because oat flour has some binding ability, less xanthan gum is needed as compared with the baguette made with rice. This loaf is better at room temperature and has a definite whole-grain taste.

- Preheat the oven to 375°F. Lightly grease a French bread pan. (You may also use a disposable foil pan bent into a curved shape.)

- Place the egg whites in a medium-size bowl. Beat until very frothy, with big and little bubbles. Add the remaining ingredients. Mix well until the mixture thickens. It should seem soft and thick, like softly whipped cream. Place the dough in a large, square plastic bag. Snip a corner off the bottom edge of the bag, approximately 2 inches across.

- Pipe large, thick strips or smaller roll-size strips of dough into the prepared pan. Spritz lightly with water.

- If you can remember to, spritz with water 10 minutes into the baking time. (This helps to crisp the crust.) Bake for an additional 15 minutes, until the bread is nicely browned and tests cleanly with a toothpick.

▪ Makes 2 small baguettes ▪

3 egg whites

1 tablespoon oil

1/4 cup apple juice

3/4 cup oat flour, 90 grams

2 teaspoons baking powder

1/2 teaspoon baking soda

1 tablespoon honey

1/4 teaspoon salt

1 1/4 teaspoons xanthan gum

1 tablespoon apple cider vinegar

Baguette ▪ *Potato-based*

This is a pretty baguette with a nice chewiness and a very mild flavor. Eat this bread when cooled, as it may taste slightly gummy if eaten warm (a typical characteristic of some potato-based recipes).

- Preheat the oven to 400°F. Lightly grease a French bread pan. (You may also use a disposable foil pan bent into a curved shape.)

- Place the egg whites in a medium-size bowl. Beat until very frothy, with big and little bubbles. Add the remaining ingredients. Mix well until the mixture thickens. It should seem soft and thick. Place the dough in a large, square plastic bag. Snip a corner off the bottom edge of the bag, no more than $1^{1}/_{2}$ inches across.

- Pipe large, thick strips or smaller roll-sized strips of dough into the prepared pan. Moisten the entire top of the dough with very moist fingertips or spritz well with water and smooth with your fingertips.

- If you can remember to, spritz with water 10 minutes into the baking time. (This helps to crisp the crust.) Bake for a total of 15 to 20 minutes, until the bread is golden and no wet spots are visible.

▪ Makes 2 baguettes ▪

3 egg whites

1 tablespoon oil

$^{1}/_{2}$ cup plain yogurt

$1^{1}/_{4}$ cups potato starch, 195 grams

2 teaspoons baking powder

1 teaspoon baking soda

$^{1}/_{2}$ teaspoon salt

1 teaspoon xanthan gum

1 tablespoon apple cider vinegar

Baguette ▪ *Rice-based*

This bread is very soft in the middle and has lots of air pockets. The crust (my favorite part) is soft and chewy. Please note that, when hot from the oven, the bread melts in your mouth but not in a good way, so enjoy this baguette at room temperature. It softens considerably overnight. Crisp the outside of the bread in an oven for 5 minutes, if serving the next day.

3 egg whites

1 tablespoon oil

1/2 cup milk

1/2 cup rice flour, 75 grams

2 teaspoons baking powder

1/2 teaspoon baking soda

1 1/2 teaspoons sugar

1/4 teaspoon salt

1 3/4 teaspoons xanthan gum

1 tablespoon apple cider vinegar

- Preheat the oven to 375°F. Lightly grease a French bread pan. (You may also use a disposable foil pan bent into a curved shape.)

- Place the egg whites in a medium-size bowl. Beat until very frothy, with big and little bubbles. Add the remaining ingredients. Mix well until the mixture thickens. It should seem soft and thick, like softly whipped cream. Place the dough in a large, square plastic bag. Snip a corner off the bottom edge of the bag, approximately 2 inches across.

- Pipe large, thick strips or smaller roll-sized strips of dough into the prepared pan. Spritz lightly with water.

- If you can remember to, spritz with water 10 minutes into the baking time. (This helps to crisp the crust.) Bake for an additional 20 minutes, until the bread is nicely browned and tests cleanly with a toothpick.

▪ Makes 2 small baguettes ▪

> NOTE: When using rice alone in a recipe, a dairy liquid provides a better end-taste than does water or apple juice.

Croutons

For those times when you just want a little extra something on top of your salad, try these. You can add a little Parmesan cheese in addition to the garlic salt, if you want extra flavor.

2 slices gluten-free bread
(preferably thinly sliced)
Nonstick cooking spray
1/4 teaspoon garlic salt

- Toast the bread as you would for breakfast. Allow it to cool. Toast for a second time (and third if needed), but watch closely to avoid burning. You want the bread to dry out but not burn. While it is still hot, spray both sides of the toast with nonstick spray. Sprinkle both sides with garlic salt. Cut into small cubes.

■ Serves 4 ■

Everyday Loaf ■ *Corn-based*

This bread has great real-bread texture and mild flavor. It is my favorite single-grain loaf.

1/4 cup oil
2 tablespoons sugar
4 egg whites
3/4 cup plain yogurt
2 cups cornstarch, 250 grams
1 1/4 teaspoons baking soda
1/2 teaspoon salt
1 1/2 teaspoons xanthan gum
1 tablespoon apple cider vinegar

- Preheat the oven to 350°F. Lightly grease a medium-size loaf pan.
- Cream the oil and sugar in a medium-size bowl. Add the egg whites and beat until very frothy. Add the remaining ingredients. Mix well.
- Pour into the prepared loaf pan. Bake for approximately 60 minutes, until golden brown. The bread should test cleanly with a toothpick.

■ Serves 12 ■

Everyday Loaf ▪ *Potato-based*

This is a mild loaf of medium texture. Sliced too thickly, it will have an impression of slight gumminess. However, sliced thinly, it is quite nice—soft and springy. If potato is your flour of choice, this loaf may be ideal.

- Preheat the oven to 350°F. Lightly grease a medium-size loaf pan.
- Cream the oil and sugar in a medium-size bowl. Add the egg whites and beat until very frothy. Add the remaining ingredients. Mix well.
- Pour into the prepared loaf pan. Bake for approximately 50 minutes, until golden brown. The bread should test cleanly with a toothpick.

▪ Serves 12 ▪

1/4 cup oil

2 tablespoons sugar

4 egg whites

3/4 cup plain yogurt

1 2/3 cups potato starch, 255 grams

1 1/4 teaspoons baking soda

1/2 teaspoon salt

1 teaspoon xanthan gum

1 tablespoon apple cider vinegar

Everyday Loaf ▪ *Rice-based*

Yes, you really can make a pleasant loaf of rice-only bread. This loaf is mild in flavor, light in texture, and tight in crumb. The small ratio of flour to other ingredients makes for a nongritty loaf. Although other breads in this chapter do a better job of mimicking the taste of traditional wheat-based breads, this is certainly a lovely gluten-free loaf.

- Preheat the oven to 350°F. Lightly grease a medium-size loaf pan.
- Cream the oil and sugar. Add the egg whites and beat until very frothy. Add the remaining ingredients. Mix well until the batter looks like softly whipped cream.
- Pour into the prepared loaf pan. Bake for approximately 50 minutes, until golden brown. The bread should test cleanly with a toothpick.

▪ Serves 12 ▪

2 tablespoons oil

1 tablespoon sugar

6 egg whites

1 cup milk

1 cup rice flour, 150 grams

1 tablespoon plus 1 teaspoon baking powder

1 teaspoon baking soda

3/4 teaspoon salt

1 tablespoon plus 1 teaspoon xanthan gum

1 1/2 tablespoons apple cider vinegar

Garlic Bread or Texas Toast

Garlic bread is so delicious, but to be gluten-free it does need to be made just a tiny bit differently than traditional garlic bread. And, yes, that is garlic salt, not garlic powder. If you were to try using garlic powder, you would be disappointed in the results.

- If using baguette or rolls, cut in half horizontally. Place cut side up on a baking tin.
- Place under the broiler until lightly toasted. Remove from the broiler. Brush the tops with the olive oil and sprinkle lightly with the garlic salt.
- Return to the broiler and toast until the bread is your desired level of darkness.

1 baguette, several rolls, or thick slices of bread

2 teaspoons olive oil

1/4 teaspoon garlic salt

NOTE: Butter may be more traditional in the making of garlic bread, but I think you will enjoy the olive oil. It is a healthier fat and tastes great, especially in this application. If you must, though, a tablespoon or two of butter may be substituted for the oil.

Multigrain Loaf ▪ *Corn- and rice-based*

This loaf is not as light as traditional, squishy loaves of bread, yet not quite as dense as a heavy white bread. It has an understated, mild flavor. This is a good everyday loaf. Try it for French toast.

- Preheat the oven to 350°F. Lightly grease a medium-size loaf pan.
- Cream the butter and sugar in a medium-size bowl. Add the egg whites and beat until very frothy. Add the remaining ingredients. Mix well. Gently place the dough in the prepared loaf pan. Smooth the top of the loaf with moistened fingertips. The dough may settle a little during baking.
- Bake for 50 to 60 minutes, until golden. The loaf should test cleanly with a toothpick.

4 tablespoons (1/4 cup) butter, softened

1/4 cup brown sugar

5 egg whites

1 cup plain yogurt

2 cups cornstarch, 250 grams

1/3 cup rice flour, 50 grams

1 tablespoon baking powder

1 teaspoon baking soda

1 teaspoon salt

1 tablespoon xanthan gum

1 1/2 tablespoons apple cider vinegar

▪ Serves 14 ▪

Multigrain Loaf ■ *Corn- and sorghum-based*

This is a medium-textured loaf with great bread flavor and real-bread texture. Except for the slightly bumpy top, it's pretty hard to identify this as a gluten-free—no kidding!

- Preheat the oven to 350°F. Lightly grease a medium-size loaf pan.

- In a medium-size bowl, beat the egg whites until very frothy. Add the remaining ingredients. Mix well. Gently place the dough in the prepared loaf pan. Smooth the top of the loaf with moistened fingertips.

- Bake for 40 to 50 minutes, until golden. The loaf should test cleanly with a toothpick.

■ Serves 14 ■

5 egg whites

2 tablespoons oil

3/4 cup apple juice

2 cups cornstarch, 250 grams

1/2 cup sorghum, 60 grams

1 tablespoon baking powder

1 teaspoon baking soda

1 teaspoon salt

1 tablespoon xanthan gum

1 1/2 tablespoons apple cider vinegar

Multigrain Loaf ■ *Potato- and brown rice–based*

Most rice flour is more finely milled today than it was when originally considered a staple flour for gluten-free baking. This loaf is very white in color and has a soft, springy texture—not too light and not too heavy. It has a hint of rice flavor and is better served at room temperature.

- Preheat the oven to 350°F. Lightly grease a medium-size loaf pan.

- Cream the sugar and butter in a medium-size bowl. Add the egg whites and beat until very frothy. Add the remaining ingredients. Mix well. Gently place the dough in the prepared loaf pan. Smooth the top of the loaf with moistened fingertips. The dough may settle a little during baking.

- Bake for 40 to 45 minutes, until golden. The loaf should test cleanly with a toothpick.

■ Serves 12 ■

4 tablespoons (1/4 cup) butter, softened

1/4 cup brown sugar

5 egg whites

1 cup plain yogurt

1 3/4 cups potato starch, 270 grams

1/3 cup brown rice flour, 40 grams

1 tablespoon baking powder

1 teaspoon baking soda

1 teaspoon salt

1 tablespoon xanthan gum

1 1/2 tablespoons apple cider vinegar

Multigrain Loaf ▪ *Potato- and cornmeal-based*

If you were to cross traditional corn bread with a home-style white bread, you would end up with this loaf. It is moist, with a nice springy texture and tight structure; the corn bread crumbliness is gone. You might find using two slices of this bread for a sandwich a little too heavy in corn bread flavor. However, a nice open-faced sandwich would be delicious.

▪ Preheat the oven to 350°F. Lightly grease a medium-size loaf pan.

▪ Cream the butter and sugar in a medium-size bowl. Add the egg whites and beat until very frothy. Add the remaining ingredients. Mix well. Gently place the dough in the prepared loaf pan. Smooth the top of the dough with moistened fingertips.

▪ Bake for 40 to 45 minutes, until golden. The loaf should test cleanly with a toothpick.

▪ Serves 12 ▪

4 tablespoons (1/4 cup) butter, softened

1/4 cup sugar

5 egg whites

3/4 cup plain yogurt

1 1/4 cups potato starch, 195 grams

3/4 cup cornmeal, 105 grams

1 tablespoon baking powder

1 1/2 teaspoons baking soda

1 teaspoon salt

1 tablespoon xanthan gum

1 1/2 tablespoons apple cider vinegar

Multigrain Loaf ▪ *Potato- and sorghum-based*

This loaf has a crisp, almost crinkled top crust and a medium texture. It tastes like a mild traditional white bread with a little more flavor—pleasant and familiar. My youngest son simply said, "It tastes like bread." As a traditional bread eater, I wouldn't hesitate to use it anytime. For this recipe, I used Bob's Red Mill brand of white sorghum flour.

- Preheat the oven to 350°F. Lightly grease a medium-size loaf pan.

- Cream the butter and sugar in a medium-size bowl. Add the egg whites and beat until very frothy. Add the remaining ingredients. Mix well to remove all lumps. Gently place the dough in the prepared loaf pan. Smooth the top of the loaf with moistened fingertips. The dough may settle a little during baking.

- Bake for 40 to 50 minutes, until golden. The loaf should test cleanly with a toothpick.

▪ Serves 12 ▪

4 tablespoons (1/4 cup) butter, softened

1/4 cup sugar

5 egg whites

1 cup plain yogurt

1 3/4 cups potato starch, 270 grams

1/3 cup sorghum flour, 45 grams

1 tablespoon baking powder

1 teaspoon baking soda

1 teaspoon salt

2 3/4 teaspoons xanthan gum

1 1/2 tablespoons apple cider vinegar

Multigrain Loaf, Light Texture ■ *Potato- and millet-based*

If you're new to the gluten-free diet and are looking to fill that almost fluffy wheat-based white bread spot, this should be the first bread you try. As far as gluten-free breads go, it bakes tall in the pan and makes for pretty slices that have real-bread texture.

- ■ Preheat the oven to 350°F. Lightly grease a medium-size loaf pan.

- ■ Cream the butter and sugar in a medium-size bowl. Add the egg whites and beat until very frothy. Add the remaining ingredients. Mix well. Gently place the dough in the prepared loaf pan. Smooth the top of the loaf with moistened fingertips. The dough may settle a little during baking.

- ■ Bake for 40 to 45 minutes, until golden. The loaf should test cleanly with a toothpick.

■ Serves 12 ■

4 tablespoons (¹/4 cup) butter, softened

¹/4 cup brown sugar

5 egg whites

1 cup plain yogurt

1³/4 cups potato starch, 270 grams

¹/3 cup millet flour, 45 grams

1 tablespoon baking powder

1 teaspoon baking soda

1 teaspoon salt

2³/4 teaspoons xanthan gum

1¹/2 tablespoons apple cider vinegar

Multigrain Loaf, Medium Texture ■ *Potato- and millet-based*

As far as flavor and texture go, this may be my very favorite gluten-free loaf of bread. Medium in texture, it tastes like "real" homemade bread, although it is not the prettiest loaf. It has a tight springy texture but is not heavy in flavor. I suggest thin slices for sandwiches.

- Preheat the oven to 350°F. Lightly grease a medium-size loaf pan.

- Cream the butter and sugar in a medium-size bowl. Add the egg whites and beat until very frothy. Add the remaining ingredients. Mix well. Gently place the dough in the prepared loaf pan. Smooth the top of the loaf with moistened fingertips. The dough may settle a little during baking.

- Bake for 40 to 45 minutes, until golden. The loaf should test cleanly with a toothpick.

■ Serves 12 ■

4 tablespoons ($^1/_4$ cup) butter, softened

$^1/_4$ cup brown sugar

5 egg whites

1 cup plain yogurt

1 $^1/_4$ cups potato starch, 195 grams

$^3/_4$ cup millet flour, 100 grams

1 tablespoon baking powder

1 teaspoon baking soda

1 teaspoon salt

1 tablespoon xanthan gum

1 $^1/_2$ tablespoons apple cider vinegar

Rolls ▪ *Corn-based*

This recipe has real "roll" texture. The taste is incredibly mild, so don't hesitate to add a little onion powder, garlic salt, or other flavor you like!

- Preheat the oven to 350°F. Grease an 8-inch square baking pan.
- Combine the sugar and butter in a medium-size bowl. Add the egg whites and beat until very frothy. Add the remaining ingredients. Mix well. Place the dough in a large, square plastic bag. Snip one corner off the bottom edge of the bag, no more than 1 1/2 inches wide.
- Pipe two large sub rolls or gently shape six dinner-size rolls in the prepared baking pan. Bake for 20 minutes, until golden.

   ▪ Makes 2 large sub rolls or 6 dinner-size rolls. ▪

2 tablespoons butter, softened

1 1/2 tablespoons sugar

3 egg whites

1/2 cup plain yogurt

1 1/4 cups cornstarch, 155 grams

2 teaspoons baking powder

1 teaspoon baking soda

1/2 teaspoon salt

1 1/4 teaspoons xanthan gum

1 tablespoon apple cider vinegar

Rolls ▪ *Corn- and cornmeal-based*

This recipe produces a batch of large, fluffy, soft-textured rolls. They have a faint taste of cornbread. If you can imagine a commercial-style potato roll made a little fluffier, you would have this roll. These are especially nice for sandwiches. It is ironic to me that the roll most structurally like a potato roll is made of corn.

- Preheat the oven to 350°F. Grease an 8-inch square baking pan.
- In a medium-size bowl, beat the egg whites until very frothy. Add the remaining ingredients. Mix well. Place the dough in a large, square plastic bag. Snip one corner off the bottom edge of the bag, no more than $1\frac{1}{2}$ inches wide.
- Pipe two large sub rolls or gently shape six to nine dinner-size rolls in the prepared baking pan. Bake for 20 to 25 minutes, until the rolls are golden and test cleanly with a toothpick.

▪ Makes 2 large sub rolls or 6 to 9 dinner-size rolls ▪

3 egg whites
$1\frac{1}{2}$ tablespoons sugar
2 tablespoons oil
$\frac{1}{2}$ cup apple juice
1 cup cornstarch, 125 grams
$\frac{1}{3}$ cup cornmeal, 40 grams
2 teaspoons baking powder
1 teaspoon baking soda
$\frac{1}{2}$ teaspoon salt
$\frac{3}{4}$ teaspoon xanthan gum
1 tablespoon apple cider vinegar

Rolls ▪ *Corn- and oat-based*

This is a nice dinner-type roll reminiscent of a whole-wheat roll.

- Preheat the oven to 350°F. Grease nine sections of a muffin tin.
- In a medium-size bowl, beat the egg whites until very frothy. Add the remaining ingredients. Mix well. Divide the dough among the sections of the prepared muffin tin. Bake for 20 minutes, until the rolls are golden and test cleanly with a toothpick.

▪ Makes 9 rolls ▪

3 egg whites
2 tablespoons oil
$\frac{1}{2}$ cup apple juice
1 cup cornstarch, 125 grams
$\frac{1}{3}$ cup oat flour, 40 grams
2 teaspoons baking powder
1 teaspoon baking soda
$\frac{1}{2}$ teaspoon salt
$\frac{3}{4}$ teaspoon xanthan gum
1 tablespoon apple cider vinegar

Rolls ■ *Corn- and rice-based*

This is a light, soft-textured roll. It has a nice, light, slightly sweet flavor. This roll would be good for almost any use.

- Preheat the oven to 350°F. Grease an 8-inch square baking pan.

- In a medium-size bowl, beat egg whites until very frothy. Add the remaining ingredients. Mix well. Place the dough in a large, square plastic bag. Snip one corner off the bottom edge of the bag, no more than 1^1/2 inches wide.

- Pipe two large sub rolls or gently shape into six to nine dinner-size rolls in the prepared baking pan. Bake for 20 to 25 minutes, until the rolls are golden and test cleanly with a toothpick.

■ Makes 2 large sub rolls or 6 to 9 dinner-size rolls ■

3 egg whites

1 tablespoon sugar

2 tablespoons oil

^{1}/2 cup apple juice

1 cup cornstarch, 125 grams

^{1}/3 cup rice flour, 50 grams

2 teaspoons baking powder

1 teaspoon baking soda

^{1}/2 teaspoon salt

^{3}/4 teaspoon xanthan gum

1 tablespoon apple cider vinegar

NOTE: At this point, you may have noticed that there is no roll made with rice alone. This is because rice flour will not take on that characteristic bread texture all by itself, no matter how many food science rules I pull out of my hat. I could give you what looks like a roll made of rice, but it would have the taste and texture of a light, pleasant unsweetened muffin. You deserve a real roll, not a bad imitation. So please enjoy the recipes here that combine rice with corn or potato or try the rice-only baguette.

Rolls ■ *Potato-based*

Making rolls or bread with only potato is nearly impossible. If you bake these rolls in a muffin tin and allow them to cool fully before removing them from the pan, you will have success. If you remove them from the pan while still hot, they will collapse.

- Preheat the oven to 350°F. Grease nine sections of a muffin tin.

- Place the egg whites in a medium-size bowl. Beat until very frothy, with big and little bubbles. Add the remaining ingredients. Mix well until the mixture thickens. The dough will be too soft to hold a shape by itself. Place the dough by large spoonfuls into the prepared sections of the muffin tin.

- Bake for approximately 20 minutes, until the rolls are golden and test cleanly with a toothpick. Allow to cool fully before removing from the tin.

■ Makes 9 rolls ■

3 egg whites

2 tablespoons oil

1 tablespoon sugar

$1/2$ cup apple juice

1 cup potato starch, 155 grams

2 teaspoons baking powder

1 teaspoon baking soda

$1/2$ teaspoon salt

$1/4$ teaspoon xanthan gum

1 tablespoon apple cider vinegar

NOTE: Potato starch has a more binding nature than do most other gluten-free flours (except tapioca starch). This binding nature is offset by using less xanthan gum. However, using less xanthan gum makes for a weaker batter, often thinner than batters or doughs made with other grains. Accordingly, most of our rolls that use potato starch will be baked in a muffin tin. Fortunately, pouring batter into a muffin tin is even easier than shaping rolls. These rolls have the taste and texture of traditional rolls.

Rolls ▪ *Potato- and millet-based*

For those who cannot tolerate corn, millet provides a very nice corn/wheat taste alternative. This dinner-type roll is probably the most likely to be mistaken for a traditional roll. Note, however, that as with other millet uses, a slight bitter taste may surface if extras are frozen or stored overnight in the fridge.

- Preheat the oven to 350°F. Lightly grease nine sections of a muffin tin.
- Place the egg whites in a medium-size bowl. Beat until very frothy, with big and little bubbles. Add the remaining ingredients. Mix well until the mixture thickens. The dough will be too soft to hold a shape by itself. Place the dough by large spoonfuls into the prepared sections of the muffin tin.
- Bake for approximately 20 minutes, until the rolls are golden and test cleanly with a toothpick.

▪ Makes 9 rolls ▪

3 egg whites
2 tablespoons oil
1/2 cup apple juice
3/4 cup potato starch, 115 grams
1/4 cup millet flour, 40 grams
2 teaspoons baking powder
1 teaspoon baking soda
1/2 teaspoon salt
1/2 teaspoon xanthan gum
1 tablespoon apple cider vinegar

Rolls ▪ *Potato- and oat-based*

This is a nice dinner roll that tastes lightly of oats.

- Preheat the oven to 350°F. Lightly grease nine sections of a muffin tin.
- Place the egg whites in a medium-size bowl. Beat until very frothy, with big and little bubbles. Add the remaining ingredients. Mix well until the mixture thickens. The dough will be too soft to hold a shape by itself. Place the dough by large spoonfuls into the prepared sections of the muffin tin.
- Bake for approximately 20 minutes, until the rolls are golden and test cleanly with a toothpick.

▪ Makes 9 rolls ▪

3 egg whites
2 tablespoons oil
1/2 cup apple juice
3/4 cup potato starch, 115 grams
1/3 cup oat flour, 40 grams
2 teaspoons baking powder
1 teaspoon baking soda
1/2 teaspoon salt
1/2 teaspoon xanthan gum
1 tablespoon apple cider vinegar

Rolls ■ *Potato- and rice-based*

This is a mild, white roll with a hint of rice flavor.

- Preheat the oven to 350°F. Lightly grease nine sections of a muffin tin.
- Place the egg whites in a medium-size bowl. Beat until very frothy, with big and little bubbles. Add the remaining ingredients. Mix well until the mixture thickens. The dough will be too soft to hold a shape by itself. Place the dough by large spoonfuls into the prepared sections of the muffin tin.
- Bake for approximately 20 minutes, until the rolls are golden and test cleanly with a toothpick.

■ Makes 9 rolls ■

3 egg whites
2 tablespoons oil
1/2 cup apple juice
1 teaspoon sugar
3/4 cup potato starch, 115 grams
1/4 cup rice flour, 40 grams
2 teaspoons baking powder
1 teaspoon baking soda
1/2 teaspoon salt
1/2 teaspoon xanthan gum
1 tablespoon apple cider vinegar

Rolls ■ *Potato- and sorghum-based*

While this roll is baked in a muffin tin, it has taste and texture similar to a wheat roll. It is relatively light in texture but not squishy. It has a little breadlike stretch when you pull it apart.

- Preheat the oven to 350°F. Grease nine sections of a muffin tin.
- Place the egg whites in a medium-size bowl. Beat until very frothy, with big and little bubbles. Add the remaining ingredients. Mix well until the mixture thickens. The dough will be too soft to hold a shape by itself. Place the dough by large spoonfuls into the prepared sections of the muffin tin.
- Bake for approximately 20 minutes, until the rolls are golden and no wet spots are visible.

■ Makes 9 rolls ■

3 egg whites
2 tablespoons oil
1/2 cup apple juice
3/4 cup potato starch, 115 grams
1/4 cup sorghum flour, 35 grams
2 teaspoons baking powder
1 teaspoon baking soda
1/2 teaspoon salt
1/2 teaspoon xanthan gum
1 tablespoon apple cider vinegar

Single-Grain Loaf ▪ *Corn-based*

Quick, pleasant, plain white bread. Imagine a Pepperidge Farm–style, heavier white bread.

- Preheat the oven to 350°F. Lightly grease a medium-size loaf pan.
- Cream the butter and sugar in a medium-size bowl. Add the egg whites and beat until very frothy. Add the remaining ingredients. Mix well. Place the dough in the prepared loaf pan. Smooth the top of the loaf with moistened fingertips.
- Bake for 40 minutes, until golden. The loaf should test cleanly with a toothpick.

▪ Serves 12 ▪

4 tablespoons (¹/4 cup) butter, softened

¹/4 cup sugar

5 egg whites

³/4 cup plain yogurt

2 cups cornstarch, 250 grams

2¹/2 teaspoons baking powder

1¹/2 teaspoons baking soda

³/4 teaspoon salt

2 teaspoons xanthan gum

1¹/2 tablespoons apple cider vinegar

Single-Grain Loaf ▪ *Corn- and cornmeal-based*

This is a tall, fluffy loaf. When it cools, the sides begin to pull in ever so slightly. Sliced, it looks a lot like a commercial loaf of bread. The taste is faintly reminiscent of corn, yet very mild. The familiar flavor, pleasant texture, and readily available ingredients put this at or near the top of my favorites.

- Preheat the oven to 350°F. Lightly grease a medium-size loaf pan.
- Cream the butter and sugar in a medium-size bowl. Add the egg whites and beat until very frothy. Add the remaining ingredients. Mix well. Gently place the dough in the prepared loaf pan. Smooth the top of the loaf with moistened fingertips.
- Bake for 45 to 55 minutes, until golden. The loaf should test cleanly with a toothpick.

▪ Serves 14 ▪

4 tablespoons (¹/4 cup) butter, softened

¹/4 cup brown sugar

5 egg whites

1 cup plain yogurt

2 cups cornstarch, 250 grams

¹/3 cup cornmeal, 45 grams

1 tablespoon baking powder

1 teaspoon baking soda

1 teaspoon salt

1 tablespoon xanthan gum

1¹/2 tablespoons apple cider vinegar

5

BREADS—
CORN BREADS
AND BISCUITS

Have you enjoyed those biscuits from a refrigerated cardboard tube? Do you think the best biscuits are made by a chicken joint? Has your grandmother refused to share her secret recipe? Take heart! You have the opportunity to become a great biscuit maker. The recipes in this chapter are very easy and will please the most avid biscuit fans.

This chapter also holds a few surprises when it comes to corn bread. While there is a corn-only corn bread recipe, I have also formulated two corn bread–style breads that contain no corn. After all, you may have multiple intolerances or you might just like variety. Once you try these versions, you may wonder why corn bread has always been made from corn.

Angel Biscuits ▪ *Oat-based*

Not quite a biscuit, not quite a roll.

- Preheat the oven to 350°F. Lightly grease an 8-inch square baking pan.
- Combine the butter and sugar in a bowl. Add the egg whites and beat until very frothy. Add the remaining ingredients. Mix well.
- Place the dough in the prepared baking pan. Gently shape into nine small biscuits.
- Bake for approximately 20 minutes, until golden on top and a biscuit tests cleanly with a toothpick.

▪ Makes 9 biscuits ▪

3 tablespoons butter, softened

2 tablespoons sugar

3 egg whites

1/2 cup plain yogurt

1 1/4 cups oat flour, 155 grams

2 teaspoons baking powder

1 teaspoon baking soda

1/2 teaspoon salt

1 1/2 teaspoons xanthan gum

1 tablespoon apple cider vinegar

Angel Biscuits ▪ *Rice-based*

- Preheat the oven to 350°F. Lightly grease an 8-inch square baking pan.
- Combine the butter and sugar in a bowl. Add the egg whites and beat until very frothy. Add the remaining ingredients. Mix well.
- Place the dough in the prepared baking pan. Gently shape into nine small biscuits.
- Bake for approximately 20 minutes, until golden on top and a biscuit tests cleanly with a toothpick.

▪ Makes 9 biscuits ▪

3 tablespoons butter, softened

2 tablespoons sugar

3 egg whites

1/2 cup plain yogurt

1 cup rice flour, 150 grams

2 teaspoons baking powder

1 teaspoon baking soda

1/2 teaspoon salt

1 1/2 teaspoons xanthan gum

1 tablespoon apple cider vinegar

Biscuits ▪ *Corn-based*

For flavor, I've opted to use butter in our biscuit recipes. A slightly smaller amount of shortening may be substituted for the butter, if desired. These biscuits are tender and have real biscuit taste. Please note that because the dough is very soft to handle, the biscuits are most easily shaped by simple cutting of the dough with a knife. This small sacrifice in appearance is more than offset by the correct taste and texture.

- Preheat the oven to 375°F. Grease a baking sheet.
- In a medium-size bowl, blend all the ingredients except the milk and vinegar. Add the milk and vinegar. Mix well. The dough will be quite fragile. Pat out the dough on the prepared baking sheet to $1/2$- to $3/4$-inch thickness. Cut into square biscuits and separate with the side of the knife.
- Bake for 15 to 20 minutes, until the biscuits begin to brown. Brush with melted butter, if desired.

▪ Makes 6 to 8 biscuits ▪

4 tablespoons ($1/4$ cup) butter

$1 1/3$ cups cornstarch, 165 grams

$1 1/4$ teaspoons xanthan gum

1 tablespoon baking powder

$1/2$ teaspoon baking soda

2 teaspoons sugar

$1/2$ teaspoon salt

$3/4$ cup milk

1 teaspoon vinegar

Topping (optional):

1 tablespoon butter, melted

Biscuits ▪ *Oat-based*

These biscuits are moist, tender, and have true biscuit texture. The whole-grain flavor is a nice change of pace from a traditional white biscuit.

- Preheat the oven to 375°F. Grease a baking sheet.
- In a medium-size bowl, blend all the ingredients except the milk and vinegar. Add the milk and vinegar. Mix well. The dough will be quite fragile. Pat out the dough on the prepared baking sheet to $1/2$-inch thickness. Cut into square biscuits and separate with the side of the knife.
- Bake for 15 to 20 minutes, until the biscuits begin to brown. Brush with melted butter, if desired.

▪ Makes 6 to 8 biscuits ▪

$1/4$ pound butter

$1 1/3$ cups oat flour, 165 grams

1 teaspoon xanthan gum

1 tablespoon baking powder

$1/2$ teaspoon baking soda

$1 1/2$ tablespoons sugar

$1/2$ teaspoon salt

$3/4$ cup milk

1 teaspoon vinegar

Topping (optional):

1 tablespoon butter, melted

Biscuits ▪ *Potato-based*

Are you ready for some big, fluffy, beautiful biscuits? These biscuits should be enjoyed at room temperature. Otherwise, there is a gummy edge, which tends to be the nature of potato starch when used alone.

- Preheat the oven to 375°F. Grease a baking sheet.
- In a medium-size bowl, blend all the ingredients except the milk and vinegar. Add the milk and vinegar. Mix well. The dough will be quite fragile. Pat out the dough on the prepared baking sheet to $1/2$- to $3/4$-inch thickness. Cut into square biscuits and separate with the side of the knife.
- Bake for 20 minutes, until the biscuits begin to brown. Do not underbake. Brush with melted butter, if desired. Remove from the baking sheet with a spatula (handling by hand will cause the structure to partially collapse) and leave on a cooling rack until room temperature.

▪ Makes 6 to 8 biscuits ▪

$1/4$ pound ($1/2$ cup) butter
1 cup plus 2 tablespoons potato starch, 175 grams
$1 1/8$ teaspoons xanthan gum
1 tablespoon baking powder
$1/2$ teaspoon baking soda
1 tablespoon sugar
$1/2$ teaspoon salt
$3/4$ cup milk
1 teaspoon vinegar

Topping (optional):
1 tablespoon butter, melted

Biscuits ▪ *Rice-based*

This recipe creates tender, soft biscuits. They are light, with a faint rice flavor. The buttery taste is also subtle. Certainly, enjoyable to all.

- Preheat the oven to 375°F. Grease a baking sheet.
- In a medium-size bowl, blend all the ingredients, except milk and vinegar, to a fine crumb. Add the milk and vinegar. Mix well until combined into a pasty, soft dough. It will be quite fragile. Pat out the dough on the prepared baking sheet to $1/2$-inch thickness. Cut into square biscuits and separate with the side of the knife.
- Bake for 15 to 20 minutes, until the biscuits begin to brown. Brush with melted butter, if desired.

▪ Makes 6 to 8 biscuits ▪

$1/4$ pound ($1/2$ cup) butter
1 cup rice flour, 150 grams
$1 1/4$ teaspoons xanthan gum
1 tablespoon baking powder
$1/2$ teaspoon baking soda
$1 1/2$ tablespoons sugar
$1/2$ teaspoon salt
$3/4$ cup milk
1 teaspoon vinegar

Topping (optional):
1 tablespoon butter, melted

Cheesy Corn Bread ▪ *Corn-based*

This is a very moist corn bread. The use of creamed corn and pepper Jack cheese makes for a great corn bread. The cheese and pepper flavors are very subtle.

- Preheat the oven to 375°F. Grease an 8-inch square baking pan.
- In a medium-size bowl, combine all the ingredients. Mix well, being sure to remove any lumps. The batter will be thick. You will begin to notice air bubbles from the baking powder.
- Pour the batter into the prepared pan. Bake for 25 to 30 minutes, until the corn bread tests cleanly with a toothpick and the top is lightly browned.

▪ Makes 9 servings ▪

1 (8-ounce) can cream-style corn

2 tablespoons milk

1 egg

1/4 cup oil

1/2 cup cornstarch, 60 grams

1/2 teaspoon salt

1 tablespoon plus 1 teaspoon baking powder

1 cup cornmeal, 140 grams

1/3 cup sugar

1/2 teaspoon xanthan gum

2 ounces pepper Jack cheese, grated

Corn Bread ▪ *Corn-based*

I received lots of nice comments on the corn bread in my first book. I've modified that recipe to use just corn in this recipe.

- Preheat the oven to 375°F. Grease an 8-inch square baking pan.
- In a medium-size bowl, combine all the ingredients. Mix well, being sure to remove any lumps. The batter will be thick. You will begin to notice air bubbles from the baking powder.
- Pour the batter into the prepared pan. Bake for 25 to 30 minutes, until the corn bread tests cleanly with a toothpick and the top is lightly browned.

▪ Makes 9 servings ▪

1 cup milk

1 egg

1/4 cup oil

1/2 cup cornstarch, 60 grams

1/2 teaspoon salt

1 tablespoon plus 1 teaspoon baking powder

1 cup cornmeal, 140 grams

1/3 cup sugar

1/2 teaspoon xanthan gum

Corn Bread ▪ *Millet-based*

Millet has a pleasant taste, sort of a cross between wheat and corn in flavor. If you can't eat corn or want to vary your diet with other whole grains, this is a good alternative. Please keep in mind that the flavor of millet can become a little bitter if the bread is served a day or later after baking.

▪ Preheat the oven to 375°F. Grease an 8-inch square baking pan.

▪ Combine all the ingredients in medium-size bowl. Stir well to remove any lumps.

▪ Immediately pour the batter into the prepared pan. (You want to retain as many baking powder bubbles as possible.)

▪ Bake for 30 minutes, until the bread tests cleanly with a toothpick and the top is lightly browned.

▪ Makes 9 servings ▪

1 cup milk

1 1/4 cups millet flour, 170 grams

1 egg

1/4 cup oil

1/2 teaspoon salt

2 tablespoons baking powder

1/4 cup brown sugar

3/4 teaspoon xanthan gum

Corn Bread ▪ *Rice-based*

This corn-free corn bread is quite mild, making it ideal to serve alongside chili or with your favorite jam. By itself, it is rather plain. (I developed this recipe for those who cannot tolerate corn but might wish to fill that corn bread craving.)

▪ Preheat the oven to 375°F. Grease an 8-inch square baking pan.

▪ Combine all the ingredients in a medium-size bowl. Stir well to remove any lumps.

▪ Immediately pour the batter into the prepared pan. (You want to retain as many baking powder bubbles as possible.) Jiggle the pan to level the batter.

▪ Bake for 30 minutes, until the bread tests cleanly with a toothpick and the top is lightly browned.

▪ Makes 9 servings ▪

1 cup milk

1 1/4 cups rice flour, 190 grams

1 egg

1/4 cup oil

1/2 teaspoon salt

2 tablespoons baking powder

1/3 cup sugar, 70 grams

1/2 teaspoon xanthan gum

BREADS—
PIZZA, FLATBREADS,
FOCACCIA, AND MORE

Can I tempt you with a great flat-bread to wrap as a gyro? How about a pizza crust that is oven-ready in less than five minutes? Or how about a perfect flour tortilla?

Oh, you want them to taste good, too? No problem—got you covered.

Some of the recipes in this chapter use just one grain, where others use two grains to offer more taste options. With a minimal amount of time and effort, there is absolutely no reason not to enjoy pizza. I've included a great pizza sauce to get you started with topping your pizza as well.

Flatbread ■ *Corn-based*

This flatbread is quite flat, pliable, and airy. Fold it like a taco and stuff it with your favorite sandwich fillings. This bread also makes for a pretty great gyro.

- Preheat the oven to 350°F. Lightly grease a baking sheet.
- Combine the oil and sugar. Add the egg whites and beat until very frothy. Add the remaining ingredients. Mix well. The dough will at first seem quite thin, but keep beating until thickened.
- Drop by $^1/_2$ cupfuls onto the prepared baking sheet. With wet fingertips, press the dough to approximately $^1/_8$-inch thickness and an 8-inch diameter.
- Bake for 10 to 15 minutes, until golden brown.

■ Makes four 8-inch flatbreads ■

2 tablespoons olive oil

1 $^1/_2$ tablespoons sugar

3 egg whites

$^1/_2$ cup plain yogurt

1 $^1/_4$ cups cornstarch, 155 grams

1 tablespoon baking powder

1 teaspoon baking soda

$^3/_4$ teaspoon salt

1 $^1/_4$ teaspoons xanthan gum

1 tablespoon apple cider vinegar

NOTE: If the dough is not spread thinly enough, a puffier bread disk is formed, which is not necessarily a bad thing. Thinner was the preference in our home, however.

Flatbread ▪ *Corn- and rice-based*

- Preheat the oven to 350°F. Lightly grease a baking sheet.
- Place the egg whites in a medium-size bowl. Beat until very frothy, with big and little bubbles. Add the remaining ingredients. Mix well until the mixture thickens. The dough will have lots of little air bubbles.
- Drop by ¹⁄₂ cupfuls onto the prepared baking sheet. With wet fingertips, press the dough to approximately ¹⁄₈-inch thickness and a 7-inch diameter.
- Bake for 10 to 15 minutes, until just browned at the edges and golden brown on the bottom.

▪ Makes four 7-inch flatbreads ▪

3 egg whites
1 teaspoon sugar
2 tablespoons oil
¹⁄₃ cup apple juice
1 cup cornstarch, 125 grams
¹⁄₃ cup rice flour, 50 grams
1 tablespoon baking powder
1 teaspoon baking soda
¹⁄₂ teaspoon salt
³⁄₄ teaspoon xanthan gum
1 tablespoon apple cider vinegar

Flatbread ▪ *Potato- and rice-based*

Patting out this dough into the flatbread shape is a little difficult. You will be pressing lots of air bubbles flat. Your efforts will be rewarded with a light, tasty flatbread, light colored on one side and golden on the other. This flatbread is best at room temperature.

- Preheat the oven to 350°F. Lightly grease a baking sheet.
- Place the egg whites in a medium-size bowl. Beat until very frothy, with big and little bubbles. Add the remaining ingredients. Mix well until the mixture thickens. The dough will have lots of little air bubbles.
- Drop by ¹⁄₂ cupfuls onto the prepared baking sheet. With wet fingertips, press the dough to approximately ¹⁄₈-inch thickness and a 7-inch diameter.
- Bake for 10 to 15 minutes, until just browned at the edges and golden brown on the bottom.

▪ Makes four 7-inch flatbreads ▪

3 egg whites
2 tablespoons oil
¹⁄₃ cup apple juice
1 teaspoon sugar
³⁄₄ cup potato starch, 115 grams
¹⁄₄ cup rice flour, 40 grams
1 tablespoon baking powder
1 teaspoon baking soda
¹⁄₂ teaspoon salt
¹⁄₂ teaspoon xanthan gum
1 tablespoon apple cider vinegar

Flatbread ■ *Potato- and sorghum-based*

This ranks among my favorite flatbread recipes. I prefer the corn versions, but this one comes in a close second. It's very pliable, with a slight whole-grain taste. It has an amazing, real-bread texture if you tear off a piece. Good warm or cool.

■ Preheat the oven to 350°F. Lightly grease a baking sheet.

■ Place the egg whites in a medium-size bowl. Beat until very frothy, with big and little bubbles. Add the remaining ingredients. Mix well until the mixture thickens. The dough will have lots of little air bubbles.

■ Drop by $1/2$ cupfuls onto the prepared baking sheet. With wet fingertips, press the dough to approximately $1/8$-inch thickness and a 7-inch diameter.

■ Bake for 10 to 15 minutes, until just browned at the edges and golden brown on the bottom.

■ Makes four 7-inch flatbreads ■

3 egg whites

1 $1/2$ tablespoons oil

$1/3$ cup apple juice

$3/4$ cup potato starch, 115 grams

$1/4$ cup sorghum flour, 35 grams

1 tablespoon baking powder

1 teaspoon baking soda

$1/2$ teaspoon salt

$3/4$ teaspoon xanthan gum

1 tablespoon apple cider vinegar

Flour Tortillas ■ *Corn-based*

Gluten-free flour tortillas are pretty easy to make, though shaping them into a perfect circle can be tricky. Like traditional flour tortillas, they tear, fold, and taste much the same. Try to press these as thin as possible, otherwise, they will be just a little thicker than traditional flour tortillas.

- Preheat the oven to 350°F. Lightly grease a baking sheet.
- Combine the oil and sugar in a medium-size bowl. Add the egg whites and beat until very frothy. Add the remaining ingredients. Mix well. The dough will at first seem quite thin, but keep beating. The batter should still look rather thin, like gloppy, too-thick gravy.
- Drop by $1/4$ cupfuls onto the prepared baking sheet. With wet fingertips, press the dough to approximately $1/16$-inch thickness (almost translucent) and a 6-inch diameter.
- Bake for approximately 15 minutes, until the edges begin to brown and the bottom has golden brown spots.

■ Makes six 6-inch flour tortillas ■

2 tablespoons olive oil

1 $1/2$ tablespoons sugar

3 egg whites

$1/2$ cup milk

1 $1/4$ cups cornstarch, 155 grams

$1/4$ teaspoon baking soda

$3/4$ teaspoon salt

1 $1/4$ teaspoons xanthan gum

1 tablespoon apple cider vinegar

Flour Tortillas ▪ *Corn- and rice-based*

- Preheat the oven to 350°F. Lightly grease a baking sheet.
- Combine the sugar and oil in a medium-size bowl. Add the egg whites and beat until very frothy. Add the remaining ingredients. Mix well. The dough will at first seem quite thin, but keep beating. The batter should still look rather thin, like gloppy, too-thick gravy.
- Drop by ¼ cupfuls onto the prepared baking sheet. With wet fingertips, press the dough to approximately ¹⁄₁₆-inch thickness (almost translucent) and a 6-inch diameter.
- Bake for approximately 15 minutes, until the edges begin to brown and the bottom has golden brown spots.

1 teaspoon sugar

2 tablespoons oil

3 egg whites

⅓ cup apple juice

1 cup cornstarch, 125 grams

⅓ cup rice flour, 50 grams

¼ teaspoon baking soda

½ teaspoon salt

¾ teaspoon xanthan gum

1 tablespoon apple cider vinegar

▪ Makes six 6-inch flour tortillas ▪

Flour Tortillas ▪ *Potato- and rice-based*

This flour tortilla is for those with corn sensitivity. It really should be eaten at room temperature rather than warm or hot.

- Preheat the oven to 350°F. Lightly grease a baking sheet.
- Combine the sugar and oil in a medium-size bowl. Add the egg whites and beat until very frothy. Add the remaining ingredients. Mix well. The dough will at first seem quite thin. Keep beating. The batter should still look rather thin, like gloppy, too-thick gravy.
- Drop by ¼ cupfuls onto the prepared baking sheet. With wet fingertips, press dough to approximately ¹⁄₁₆-inch thickness (almost translucent) and a 6-inch diameter.
- Bake for approximately 15 minutes, until the edges begin to brown and the bottom has golden brown spots.

1 teaspoon sugar

2 tablespoons oil

3 egg whites

⅓ cup apple juice

¾ cup potato starch, 115 grams

¼ cup rice flour, 40 grams

¼ teaspoon baking soda

½ teaspoon salt

½ teaspoon xanthan gum

1 tablespoon apple cider vinegar

▪ Makes six 6-inch flour tortillas ▪

Flour Tortillas ■ *Potato- and sorghum-based*

This tortilla has a good multigrain flavor. When torn apart, it also has perhaps the best traditional texture.

- Preheat the oven to 350°F. Lightly grease a baking sheet.
- Combine the sugar and oil in a medium-size bowl. Add the egg whites and beat until very frothy. Add the remaining ingredients. Mix well. The dough will at first seem quite thin, but keep beating. The batter should still look rather thin, like gloppy, too-thick gravy.
- Drop by 1/4 cupfuls onto the prepared baking sheet. With wet fingertips, press the dough to approximately 1/16-inch thickness (almost translucent) and a 6-inch diameter.
- Bake for approximately 15 minutes, until the edges begin to brown and the bottom has golden brown spots.

■ Makes six 6-inch flour tortillas ■

1 1/2 tablespoons oil

3 egg whites

1/3 cup apple juice

3/4 cup potato starch, 115 grams

1/4 cup sorghum flour, 35 grams

1/4 teaspoon baking soda

1/2 teaspoon salt

3/4 teaspoon xanthan gum

1 tablespoon apple cider vinegar

Flour Tortillas ■ *Oat-based*

If you miss "real" dough, you'll appreciate this recipe.

- Place the yeast and warm water in a medium-size bowl. Stir to dissolve the yeast. Add all the other ingredients and mix well. Allow the dough to rest for about an hour. This gives the yeast a bit of time to develop flavor. You won't see much, if any, rise in the dough. Divide the dough into eight pieces (approximately 1/3 cup each).
- Shape each piece of dough into a ball. You cannot overhandle this dough. As a matter of fact, I believe the tortillas benefit from a little extra kneading.
- On a floured (with oat flour) surface, roll the dough into an 8-inch circle. Lightly grease and heat a skillet, preferably nonstick, until hot. Place the circle of dough in the hot pan. Cook until lightly browned on each side—just a minute or two. Repeat with the remaining pieces of dough.

■ Makes eight 8-inch flour tortillas ■

1 envelope (or 1 tablespoon) active dry yeast

1 1/4 cups warm water

3 cups oat flour

2 tablespoons oil

2 teaspoons sugar

1 teaspoon salt

2 teaspoons xanthan gum

Focaccia ■ *Corn-based*

Focaccia is great for entertaining. Guests enjoy the home-made treat while sharing conversation and a little dipping dish of olive oil and spices.

- Preheat the oven to 350°F. Lightly grease a baking sheet.
- Combine the oil and sugar in a medium-size bowl. Add the egg whites and beat until very frothy. Add the remaining ingredients. Mix well. Press the dough to approximately ¼-inch thickness on the prepared baking sheet. Dimple the dough with your fingertips. Add a topping as desired. Bake for 15 to 20 minutes, until lightly browned.

■ Makes one 12-inch circle; serves 6 ■

Dough:
2 tablespoons olive oil
1 ½ tablespoons sugar
2 egg whites
½ cup plain yogurt
1 ¼ cups cornstarch, 155 grams
2 teaspoons baking powder
1 teaspoon baking soda
½ teaspoon salt
1 ½ teaspoons xanthan gum
1 tablespoon apple cider vinegar

Topping suggestions:
Drizzle with
1–2 teaspoons olive oil, ¼ teaspoon salt, 1 teaspoon dried rosemary, and ¼ teaspoon cayenne
OR
1–2 teaspoons olive oil, ¼ teaspoon salt, slivered onions, and ¼ teaspoon black pepper

Pizza Crust ▪ *Corn-based*

A pizza crust ready to go in the oven in five minutes! This crust is too mild in flavor on its own, so I've added a little garlic salt. Use this recipe for bread sticks, too!

- Preheat the oven to 350°F. Lightly grease a baking sheet.
- Combine the oil and sugar in a medium-size bowl. Add the egg whites and beat until very frothy. Add the remaining ingredients. Mix well. The dough will at first seem quite thin, but keep beating until thickened. Place the dough on the middle of the prepared baking sheet. With wet fingertips, press the dough to approximately 1/4-inch thickness for a thick crust. Press thinner as desired for a thinner crust. Add your desired topping.
- Bake for 20 to 25 minutes, until golden brown.

▪ Makes one 12-inch crust ▪

Dough:

2 tablespoons olive oil

1 1/2 tablespoons sugar

3 egg whites

1/2 cup plain yogurt

1 1/4 cups cornstarch, 155 grams

1 teaspoon baking powder

1 teaspoon baking soda

3/4 teaspoon garlic salt

1 1/4 teaspoons xanthan gum

1 tablespoon apple cider vinegar

Topping suggestions:

Drizzle of olive oil

1 recipe Pizza Sauce (page 112)

1/2 cup shredded mozzarella cheese and 1/2 cup shredded Monterey Jack cheese

Pizza Crust ▪ *Corn- and rice-based*

When this pizza crust is finished baking, it looks a little bumpy. As my nonceliac, pizza-loving teenage son said, "They're not pretty, but they're pretty good." The crust is crisp on the outside and a little chewy on the inside. It was the preferred crust during our taste tests.

- Preheat the oven to 350°F. Lightly grease a baking sheet.

- Place the egg whites in a medium-size bowl. Beat until very frothy, with big and little bubbles. Add the remaining ingredients. Mix well until the mixture thickens.

- For individual pizza crusts, drop approximately ⅓ cup of dough onto the prepared baking sheet. Press out to a 6-inch diameter, slightly thicker at the sides. (The bottom will appear very, very thin.) Moist fingertips help a lot with this process. Bake without any topping for 8 to 9 minutes, until the bottom of the dough is lightly browned.

- Raise the oven temperature to 400°F.

- Add your desired topping. Bake until the crust is golden and any cheese is melted, approximately 5 minutes. The crust will be a little thinner after the final baking.

- For one large pizza, drop the dough onto a greased cookie sheet. Spread to nearly the edges, with the dough a bit thicker at the sides. Follow the baking directions above.

▪ Makes 1 extra-large or 5 individual crusts ▪

3 egg whites

1 teaspoon sugar

2 tablespoons oil

⅓ cup apple juice

1 cup cornstarch, 125 grams

⅓ cup rice flour, 50 grams

2 teaspoons baking powder

1 teaspoon baking soda

½ teaspoon salt

¾ teaspoon xanthan gum

1 tablespoon apple cider vinegar

Pizza Crust ▪ *Potato- and rice-based*

This is a mild pizza crust. It has a good texture with a traditional crust appearance. Allow it to cool for several minutes after baking, for the best texture.

- Preheat the oven to 350°F. Lightly grease a baking sheet.

- Place the egg whites in a medium-size bowl. Beat until very frothy, with big and little bubbles. Add the remaining ingredients. Mix well until the mixture thickens.

- For individual pizza crusts, drop approximately 1/3 cup of dough onto the prepared baking sheet. Press out to a 6-inch diameter, slightly thicker at the sides. (The bottom will appear very, very thin.) Moist fingertips help a lot with this process. Bake without any topping for 10 to 13 minutes, until the bottom of the dough is lightly browned.

- Raise the oven temperature to 400°F.

- Add your desired topping. Bake until the crust is golden and any cheese is melted, approximately 5 minutes. The crust will be a little thinner after the final baking.

- For one large pizza, drop the dough onto a greased cookie sheet. Spread to nearly the edges, with the dough a bit thicker at the sides. Follow the baking directions above.

▪ Makes 1 extra-large or 5 individual crusts ▪

3 egg whites

2 tablespoons oil

1/3 cup apple juice

1 teaspoon sugar

3/4 cup potato starch, 115 grams

1/4 cup rice flour, 40 grams

2 teaspoons baking powder

1 teaspoon baking soda

1/2 teaspoon salt

1/2 teaspoon xanthan gum

1 tablespoon apple cider vinegar

> **NOTE:** For the famous New York pizza with the "red oil" dripping down your arm, start your toppings with a little olive oil, then pizza sauce, and finally the cheese.

Pizza Crust ■ *Potato- and sorghum-based*

This is a soft, thin-crusted pizza crust. Pat dough thicker for a thicker crust. Bake longer or on a pizza stone for a crispy crust. This crust came in second in our taste test.

- Preheat the oven to 350°F. Lightly grease a baking sheet.

- Place the egg whites in a medium-size bowl. Beat until very frothy, with big and little bubbles. Add the remaining ingredients. Mix well until the mixture thickens.

- For individual pizza crusts, drop approximately 1/3 cup of dough onto the prepared baking sheet. Press out to a 6-inch diameter, slightly thicker at the sides. (The bottom will appear very, very thin.) Moist fingertips help a lot with this process. Bake without any topping for 9 to 10 minutes, until the bottom of the dough is lightly browned.

- Raise the oven temperature to 400°F.

- Add your desired topping. Bake until the crust is golden and any cheese is melted, approximately 5 minutes. The crust will be a little thinner after the final baking.

- For one large pizza, drop the dough onto a greased cookie sheet. Spread to nearly the edges, with the dough a bit thicker at the sides. Follow the baking directions above.

■ Makes 1 extra-large or 5 individual crusts ■

3 egg whites

1 1/2 tablespoons oil

1/3 cup apple juice

3/4 cup potato starch, 115 grams

1/4 cup sorghum flour, 35 grams

2 teaspoons baking powder

1 teaspoon baking soda

1/2 teaspoon salt

3/4 teaspoon xanthan gum

1 tablespoon apple cider vinegar

Pizza Crust ▪ *Rice-based*

For the longest time, even through writing most of this book, I felt rice-only pizza crust was impossible. It isn't. This is not my favorite pizza crust, but it has a pleasant taste and is quick to make. The texture improves as the pizza cools.

3 egg whites

1 tablespoon oil

$^1/_2$ cup milk

$^1/_2$ cup rice flour, 75 grams

1 teaspoon baking powder

$^1/_2$ teaspoon baking soda

$^1/_2$ teaspoon sugar

$^1/_4$ teaspoon salt

2 teaspoons xanthan gum

1 tablespoon apple cider vinegar

- Preheat the oven to 350°F. Lightly grease a baking sheet.

- Place the egg whites in a medium-size bowl. Beat until very frothy, with big and little bubbles. Add the remaining ingredients. Mix well until the mixture thickens to a pasty dough. This will take a minute or two.

- For individual pizza crusts, drop $^1/_3$ to $^1/_2$ cup of dough onto the prepared baking sheet. Press out to a 6-inch diameter, slightly thicker at the sides. (The bottom will appear very, very thin.) Moist fingertips help a lot with this process. Bake without adding any topping for 10 to 15 minutes, until the bottom of the dough is lightly browned and the edges of the crust begin to color slightly.

- Raise the oven temperature to 400°F.

- Add your desired topping. Bake until the crust is golden and any cheese is melted, approximately 5 minutes. The crust will be a little thinner after the final baking.

- For one large pizza, drop the dough onto a greased cookie sheet. Spread to nearly the edges, with the dough a bit thicker at the sides. Follow the baking directions above.

▪ Makes 1 large or 4 individual crusts ▪

Pizza Sauce

You may notice that this sauce has a strong flavor. It's the perfect choice to elevate the flavor of homemade pizza or to use as a dipping sauce for bread sticks.

■ In a medium-size saucepan, over medium heat, sauté the olive oil and minced garlic, allowing the flavors to blend. Add all the other ingredients and mix well. Bring to almost a boil, then lower the heat to low and simmer for approximately 5 minutes. It takes a few minutes for the flavor of the dried spices to reawaken.

■ Makes approximately 15 ounces pizza sauce, ■
enough for two 12-inch pizzas

1 tablespoon olive oil

1 clove garlic, minced

1 (6-ounce) can tomato paste

9 ounces water

1 teaspoon dried oregano

1 teaspoon dried basil

1/2 teaspoon red pepper flakes

1 teaspoon salt

Stuffing

I'll admit it, if you will—that handy little box of stuffing mix is really not too bad. Like the box kind, our version will be made on top of the stove. Any gluten-free bread should do fine.

■ Toast the bread and cut into small cubes. Set aside. Place the onion and celery in a medium-size saucepan with the butter. Cook over medium heat until the onion begins to wilt. Add the remaining ingredients except the bread. Bring to a boil, being sure the bouillon cube is fully dissolved. Turn off the heat.

■ Add the bread and gently toss to mix well. Cover for a minute or two for the flavors to blend. Fluff with a fork before serving.

6 slices gluten-free bread, 300 grams

1/2 small onion, diced finely, or 1 tablespoon dried, chopped onions

1/2 stalk celery, diced finely

2 tablespoons butter

1 teaspoon ground sage

1 teaspoon dried parsley

1/4 teaspoon dried thyme

1/4 teaspoon black pepper

1 chicken bouillon cube

1/4 teaspoon salt

3/4 cup water

> NOTE: Two teaspoons of poultry seasoning can be substituted for the sage, parsley, and thyme in this recipe. Please use whatever is easiest for you.

White Pizza

This makes a great appetizer!

- Preheat the oven to 350°F. Lightly grease a baking sheet.
- Place the pizza dough on the prepared baking sheet. Spread to nearly the edges, with the dough a bit thicker on the sides. The bottom of the dough should appear very, very thin. Bake for 9 to 10 minutes, until the bottom of dough is lightly browned.
- Raise the oven temperature to 400°F.
- Spread the olive oil over the crust. Finely chop the garlic and sprinkle over the top of the pizza. Sprinkle the salt and oregano over the top of the pizza. Sprinkle the shredded cheese over the top of the pizza. Bake until the crust is golden and the cheese is melted, approximately 5 minutes.

■ Serves 5 ■

1 pizza crust recipe, mixed and ready to bake

3 tablespoons olive oil

2 cloves garlic

1/4 teaspoon salt

1 teaspoon oregano

1/2 cup shredded mozzarella cheese

7

SWEET YEAST-STYLE BREADS

Like so many breads in this book, none of the recipes in this chapter use yeast—it is simply not needed. Yeast sometimes does funky, undesirable things to flavor in gluten-free baking. However, here apple juice or apple cider vinegar does a wonderful job of mimicking that yeasty flavor.

Unconventional use of other ingredients helps to achieve great texture and flavor as well. Bread stretch is mimicked by egg whites, and subtle fruit essence is heightened with Grand Marnier. But the rich, buttery taste is genuine, thanks to cream cheese or butter.

So, which recipes to try first? How about Monkey Bread or Candied Yeast Bread? The Monkey Bread is a super-easy pile of sticky rolls in a pan, while the Candied Yeast Bread is in the same neighborhood as German stollen or Italian panettone.

Be aware that taste and texture were of primary importance in formulating these recipes—fat and calories were secondary!

Candied Sweet Bread ▪ *Corn-based*

This is a sweet, yeasty bread specked with candied fruit and raisins. It is baked in a round cake pan, as the dough is too soft to shape. It has very nice bread structure.

- Preheat the oven to 350°F. Grease an 8- or 9-inch round cake pan.

- Cream the oil and sugar in a medium-size bowl. Add the egg whites and beat until very frothy. Add the remaining ingredients. Mix well.

- Pour into the prepared cake pan. Bake for approximately 40 minutes, until golden brown. The bread should test cleanly with a toothpick.

- Stir the glaze ingredients in a small cup until well blended. Pour over the almost-cooled loaf.

▪ Serves 14 ▪

NOTE: The dough is slow to pick up on the citrus flavors of the candied fruit. I've used Grand Marnier to do the job. If you prefer to not use the liqueur, lemon extract will be fine.

¼ cup oil

½ cup sugar

4 egg whites

¾ cup plain yogurt

2 cups cornstarch, 250 grams

1¼ teaspoons baking soda

½ teaspoon salt

1½ teaspoons xanthan gum

2 teaspoons Grand Marnier, or ½ teaspoon lemon extract

1 tablespoon apple cider vinegar

½ cup candied fruit

2 tablespoons raisins

Glaze (optional):

1 cup confectioners' sugar

2 tablespoons milk

½ teaspoon Grand Marnier, or ¼ teaspoon lemon extract

Candied Sweet Bread ▪ *Potato-based*

This bread has quite a bit of texture; it is not heavy, but does have real substance. It would be especially nice with coffee or tea for a not-too-sweet treat.

- Preheat the oven to 350°F. Grease an 8- or 9-inch round cake pan.
- Cream the oil and sugar in a medium-size bowl. Add the egg whites and beat until very frothy. Add the remaining ingredients. Mix well.
- Pour into the prepared cake pan. Bake for approximately 40 minutes, until golden brown. The bread should test cleanly with a toothpick.
- Stir the glaze ingredients in a small cup until well blended. Pour over the almost-cooled loaf.

▪ Serves 14 ▪

$\frac{1}{4}$ cup oil

$\frac{1}{2}$ cup sugar

4 egg whites

$\frac{3}{4}$ cup plain yogurt

1 $\frac{2}{3}$ cups potato starch, 255 grams

1 $\frac{1}{4}$ teaspoons baking soda

$\frac{1}{2}$ teaspoon salt

1 $\frac{1}{4}$ teaspoons xanthan gum

2 teaspoons Grand Marnier, or $\frac{1}{2}$ teaspoon lemon extract

1 tablespoon apple cider vinegar

$\frac{1}{2}$ cup candied fruit

2 tablespoons raisins

Glaze (optional):

1 cup confectioners' sugar

2 tablespoons milk

$\frac{1}{2}$ teaspoon Grand Marnier, or $\frac{1}{4}$ teaspoon lemon extract

Candied Sweet Bread ■ *Rice-based*

This is a very moist, lightly sweet bread. It is dense enough to stand up to a pat of butter and would certainly be nice lightly toasted. There is no grittiness to this bread.

- Preheat the oven to 350°F. Grease an 8- or 9-inch round cake pan.
- Cream the oil and sugar in a medium-size bowl. Add the egg whites and beat until very frothy. Add the remaining ingredients. Mix well.
- Pour into the prepared cake pan. Bake for approximately 40 minutes, until golden brown. The bread should test cleanly with a toothpick.
- Stir the glaze ingredients in a small cup until well blended. Pour over the almost-cooled loaf.

■ Serves 14 ■

$1/4$ cup oil

$1/2$ cup sugar

4 egg whites

$3/4$ cup plain yogurt

1 cup rice flour, 150 grams

$1 1/4$ teaspoons baking soda

$1/2$ teaspoon salt

$1 1/2$ teaspoons xanthan gum

2 teaspoons Grand Marnier, or $1/2$ teaspoon lemon extract

1 tablespoon apple cider vinegar

$1/2$ cup candied fruit

2 tablespoons raisins

Glaze (optional):

1 cup confectioners' sugar

2 tablespoons milk

$1/2$ teaspoon Grand Marnier, or $1/4$ teaspoon lemon extract

Cinnamon Bread ▪ *Corn-based*

This bread is medium-textured with a light cinnamon flavor and would make excellent French toast.

- Preheat the oven to 350°F. Lightly grease a medium-size loaf pan.
- Cream the oil and sugar in a medium-size bowl. Add the egg whites and beat until very frothy. Add the remaining ingredients. Mix well.
- Pour into the prepared loaf pan. Bake for approximately 60 minutes, until golden brown. The bread should test cleanly with a toothpick.

▪ Serves 12 ▪

1/4 cup oil

1/2 cup sugar

4 egg whites

3/4 cup plain yogurt

2 cups cornstarch, 250 grams

1 1/4 teaspoons baking soda

1/2 teaspoon salt

1 1/2 teaspoons xanthan gum

1 teaspoon vanilla extract

1 teaspoon ground cinnamon

1 tablespoon apple cider vinegar

1/2 cup raisins (optional)

Cinnamon Bread ▪ *Oat-based*

This loaf of oat bread has a tight crumb and is not very sweet. The whole-grain taste competes with the cinnamon flavor. I kept finding myself wanting just one more nibble. Perhaps it was the fine aroma that called me back for more.

- Preheat the oven to 350°F. Lightly grease a medium-size loaf pan.
- Cream the oil and sugar in a medium-size bowl. Add the egg whites and beat until very frothy. Add the remaining ingredients. Mix well.
- Pour into the prepared loaf pan. Bake for approximately 40 minutes, until golden brown. The bread should test cleanly with a toothpick.

▪ Serves 12 ▪

1/4 cup oil

1/2 cup sugar

4 egg whites

3/4 cup plain yogurt

1 2/3 cups oat flour, 200 grams

1 1/4 teaspoons baking soda

1/2 teaspoon salt

1 1/4 teaspoons xanthan gum

1 1/2 teaspoons vanilla extract

1 1/2 teaspoons ground cinnamon

1 tablespoon apple cider vinegar

1/2 cup raisins (optional)

Cinnamon Bread ▪ *Potato-based*

This bread slices more easily after it cools a bit. It is moist and has a breadlike chewiness. It also has a notable cinnamon flavor and is quite good with the optional raisins.

- ▪ Preheat the oven to 350°F. Lightly grease a medium-size loaf pan.
- ▪ Cream the oil and sugar in a medium-size bowl. Add the egg whites and beat until very frothy. Add the remaining ingredients. Mix well.
- ▪ Pour into the prepared loaf pan. Bake for approximately 50 minutes, until golden brown. The bread should test cleanly with a toothpick.

▪ Serves 12 ▪

$1/4$ cup oil

$1/2$ cup sugar

4 egg whites

$3/4$ cup plain yogurt

$1 2/3$ cups potato starch, 255 grams

Scant $1 1/4$ teaspoons baking soda

$1/2$ teaspoon salt

$1 1/4$ teaspoons xanthan gum

1 teaspoon vanilla extract

1 teaspoon ground cinnamon

1 tablespoon apple cider vinegar

$1/2$ cup raisins (optional)

Cinnamon Bread ▪ *Rice-based*

This loaf of bread is pretty and petite. It has a tight, moist crumb, almost a quick bread texture, but is not quite as sweet. Bake in a smaller loaf pan and extend the baking time if you want a taller loaf. There is no grittiness, and the taste and texture are very pleasant.

- ▪ Preheat the oven to 350°F. Lightly grease a medium-size loaf pan.
- ▪ Cream the oil and sugar in a medium-size bowl. Add the egg whites and beat until very frothy. Add the remaining ingredients. Mix well.
- ▪ Pour into the prepared loaf pan. Bake for approximately 50 minutes, until golden brown. The bread should test cleanly with a toothpick.

▪ Serves 12 ▪

$1/4$ cup oil

$1/2$ cup sugar

4 egg whites

$3/4$ cup plain yogurt

1 cup rice flour, 150 grams

$1 1/4$ teaspoons baking soda

$1/2$ teaspoon salt

$1 1/2$ teaspoons xanthan gum

1 teaspoon vanilla extract

1 teaspoon ground cinnamon

1 tablespoon apple cider vinegar

$1/2$ cup raisins (optional)

Monkey Bread ■ *Corn-based*

Monkey bread is the lazy man's cinnamon roll (count me in!): little pieces of dough surrounded by sweet goodness, all piled together in one pan. Eating this bread involves picking it apart lump by lump.

- Preheat the oven to 350°F. Grease a medium-size loaf pan.

- Combine the butter and sugar in a medium-size bowl. Add the egg whites and beat until very frothy. Add the remaining ingredients. Mix well. Set aside.

- In a small bowl, combine the filling ingredients. It is easy to cut the ingredients together with a fork, until small crumbles remain.

- Drop rounded tablespoons of the dough into the bottom of the prepared pan. Sprinkle with the filling and continue layering until the dough and filling are used.

- Bake for 30 to 35 minutes, until the bread is lightly browned and tests cleanly with a toothpick. Cut around the edge of the pan with a butter knife and coax the bread from the sides if it appears to stick. Invert onto a serving plate.

■ Serves 6 ■

Dough:

2 tablespoons butter, softened

3 tablespoons sugar

3 egg whites

1/2 cup plain yogurt

1 1/4 cups cornstarch, 155 grams

2 teaspoons baking powder

1 teaspoon baking soda

1/2 teaspoon salt

1 1/4 teaspoons xanthan gum

1 tablespoon apple cider vinegar

1/2 teaspoon vanilla extract

Filling:

1/2 cup brown sugar

1/2 teaspoon ground cinnamon

4 tablespoons (1/4 cup) butter

Monkey Bread ▪ *Potato-based*

In this recipe, during the last few minutes of baking, the nuggets of bread collide and trap the cinnamon mixture. If you eat these while hot, they will seem slightly gummy. If you allow the bread to cool a bit, this stickiness disappears. Waiting may be difficult!

- Preheat the oven to 350°F. Grease a medium-size loaf pan.

- Combine the butter and sugar in a medium-size bowl. Add the egg whites and beat until very frothy. Add the remaining ingredients. Mix well. Set aside.

- In a small bowl, combine the filling ingredients. It is easy to cut the ingredients together with a fork, until small crumbles remain.

- Drop rounded tablespoons of the dough into the bottom of the prepared pan. Sprinkle with the filling and continue layering until the dough and filling are used.

- Bake for 30 to 40 minutes, until the bread is lightly browned and tests cleanly with a toothpick. Cut around the edge of the pan with a butter knife and coax the bread from the sides if it appears to stick. Invert onto a serving plate.

▪ Serves 6 ▪

Dough:

2 tablespoons butter, softened

1/4 cup sugar

3 egg whites

1/2 cup plain yogurt

1 cup potato starch, 155 grams

2 teaspoons baking powder

1 teaspoon baking soda

1/2 teaspoon salt

1 teaspoon xanthan gum

1 tablespoon apple cider vinegar

1/2 teaspoon vanilla extract

Filling:

1/2 cup brown sugar

1/2 teaspoon ground cinnamon

4 tablespoons (1/4 cup) butter

Monkey Bread ■ *Rice-based*

Although monkey bread is not known for its visual appearance, this version might be a little less attractive. Its beauty lies in satisfying that craving for a tasty, moist, yeasty breakfast treat.

- Preheat the oven to 350°F. Grease a medium-size loaf pan.

- Beat the egg whites in a medium-size bowl until frothy. Add the remaining ingredients. Mix well until the mixture becomes quite thick. (This takes a few minutes.) Set aside.

- In a small bowl, combine the filling ingredients. It is easy to cut the ingredients together with a fork, until small crumbles remain.

- Drop rounded tablespoons of the dough into the bottom of the prepared pan. Sprinkle with the filling and continue layering until the dough and filling are used.

- Bake for 30 to 35 minutes, until the bread is lightly browned and tests cleanly with a toothpick. Cut around the edge of the pan with a butter knife and coax the bread from the sides if it appears to stick. Invert onto a serving plate.

■ Serves 6 ■

Dough:
3 egg whites
1 tablespoon oil
1/4 cup milk
1/2 cup rice flour, 75 grams
2 teaspoons baking powder
1/2 teaspoon baking soda
1 tablespoon sugar
1/4 teaspoon salt
1 3/4 teaspoons xanthan gum
1 tablespoon apple cider vinegar
1 teaspoon vanilla extract

Filling:
1/2 cup brown sugar
1/2 teaspoon ground cinnamon
4 tablespoons (1/4 cup) butter

Nut Braid ▪ *Corn-based*

This bread would be perfect to serve with afternoon tea or coffee. It is rich, soft, and slightly sweet. My husband called it "delicious."

- Preheat the oven to 350°F. Lightly grease a baking sheet.

- Combine all the ingredients, except the egg whites and milk, in a medium-size bowl. Mix until the dough resembles a fine crumb. Beat the egg whites in a separate cup until frothy. Add the egg whites and milk to the crumb mixture. Beat well.

- Divide the dough into three long strips. Carefully braid into one long loaf, or simply lay the three strips side by side (so much easier and almost as pretty) on the prepared baking sheet.

- In a small bowl, combine the pecans, sugar, butter, and vanilla. Mix well. Apply liberally over the dough.

- Bake for 20 to 25 minutes, until nicely browned. (Bake a little longer if making a braid.) Prepare the Confectioners' Glaze and drizzle over the top of the bread, as desired.

▪ Serves 6 ▪

4 ounces cream cheese

4 tablespoons (¹/4 cup) butter

³/4 cup cornstarch, 95 grams

¹/4 cup sugar, 40 grams

¹/4 teaspoon salt

1 tablespoon baking powder

³/4 teaspoon xanthan gum

¹/4 teaspoon baking soda

2 egg whites

2 tablespoons milk

Nut mixture:

¹/2 cup chopped pecans

¹/4 cup brown sugar

1 tablespoon butter

¹/2 teaspoon vanilla extract

Confectioners' Glaze (page 323) (optional)

8

QUICK BREADS AND MUFFINS

You will find some wonderful treasures in this chapter. If you're nervous about using rice flour as a stand-alone flour, these recipes will calm your fears.

Yogurt, pureed fruit, or pureed vegetables add great moistness to many of the breads and muffins. Dairy is not used in every recipe. If you must avoid it, you need quick breads as well.

If you love chocolate, try some of the chocolate chip or chocolate–chocolate chip muffin recipes. If you're avoiding dairy, try Applesauce Quick Bread or Pumpkin Bread, being sure to use a version that doesn't utilize yogurt, milk, or butter.

■ ■ ■

Applesauce Quick Bread ■ *Corn-based*

This is a very soft quick bread. The top of the loaf will flatten a bit, but that is the tradeoff for an incredibly moist loaf.

- ■ Preheat the oven to 350°F. Grease a 9 x 4-inch loaf pan.
- ■ In a large bowl, combine all the ingredients. Mix well. The batter will be thin.
- ■ Pour into the prepared pan. Bake for 40 to 45 minutes, until a toothpick inserted in the middle tests cleanly.

■ Serves 10 ■

3/4 cup applesauce, or 1 (6-ounce) jar baby food applesauce

1 teaspoon vinegar

1/2 cup sugar, 100 grams

1/4 cup oil

1/2 teaspoon vanilla extract

1/2 teaspoon ground cinnamon

2 eggs

3/4 cup plus 2 tablespoons cornstarch, 110 grams

1 teaspoon baking soda

1/4 teaspoon xanthan gum

1/2 teaspoon salt

Applesauce Quick Bread ■ *Oat-based*

My family was divided over favorites for quick breads made with fruits. The men in the house had a strong preference for this applesauce variety.

- ■ Preheat the oven to 350°F. Lightly grease an 8-inch square baking pan.
- ■ In a large bowl, combine all the ingredients. Mix well. The batter will thicken as it is mixed.
- ■ Pour into the prepared pan. Bake for approximately 30 minutes, until a toothpick inserted in the middle tests cleanly.

■ Serves 9 ■

3/4 cup applesauce, or 1 (6-ounce) jar baby food applesauce

1/2 cup sugar, 100 grams

1/4 cup oil

1/2 teaspoon vanilla extract

1 teaspoon ground cinnamon

2 eggs

1 1/4 cups oat flour, 155 grams

1 1/2 tablespoons baking powder

1/2 teaspoon xanthan gum

1/2 teaspoon salt

Applesauce Quick Bread ▪ *Potato-based*

This is a very pretty, moist loaf. Our taste testers preferred it over the corn version, but couldn't really say why. The breads are very similar.

▪ Preheat the oven to 350°F. Grease a 9 x 4-inch loaf pan.

▪ In a medium-size bowl, combine all the ingredients and mix well. The batter will thicken as it is mixed.

▪ Pour into the prepared pan. Bake for 40 to 50 minutes, until a toothpick inserted in the middle tests cleanly.

▪ Serves 10 ▪

³/4 cup applesauce, or
   1 (6-ounce) jar baby food
   applesauce

1 teaspoon vinegar

¹/2 cup sugar, 100 grams

¹/4 cup oil

1 egg

¹/4 cup milk

¹/2 teaspoon vanilla extract

¹/2 teaspoon ground
   cinnamon

1 cup potato starch,
   155 grams

1 teaspoon baking soda

¹/4 teaspoon xanthan gum

¹/2 teaspoon salt

Applesauce Quick Bread ▪ *Rice-based*

This quick bread is pleasant all around: moist, light, and with a mild apple flavor.

- Preheat the oven to 350°F. Lightly grease an 8-inch square baking pan.
- In a large bowl, mix the butter and flour. Add all the other ingredients and mix well. The batter will thicken as it is mixed.
- Pour into the prepared pan. Bake for approximately 30 minutes, until a toothpick inserted in the middle tests cleanly.

▪ Serves 9 ▪

3/4 cup applesauce, or 1 (6-ounce) jar baby food applesauce

1/2 cup sugar, 100 grams

5 1/3 tablespoons butter, very softened

2 tablespoons milk

2 eggs

1 cup rice flour, 150 grams

1 tablespoon baking powder

1/2 teaspoon baking soda

3/4 teaspoon xanthan gum

1 teaspoon apple cider vinegar

1/2 teaspoon ground cinnamon

1/2 teaspoon salt

Banana Bread ▪ *Corn-based*

I've given you the option of using fresh bananas or baby food bananas, just in case you need a last-minute quick bread to prepare from your pantry! Either way, it's hard to resist this traditional favorite.

- Preheat the oven to 350°F. Grease a 9 x 4-inch loaf pan.
- In a large bowl, mash the bananas well. This is easier to do with a mixer. Add all the other ingredients and mix well. The batter will be thin.
- Pour into the prepared pan. Bake for 40 to 45 minutes, until a toothpick inserted in the middle tests cleanly.

▪ Serves 10 ▪

2 small bananas mashed (no more than 3/4 cup), or 1 (6-ounce) jar baby food bananas

1 teaspoon vinegar

1/2 cup sugar, 100 grams

1/4 cup oil

1 teaspoon vanilla extract

2 eggs

3/4 cup plus 2 tablespoons cornstarch, 110 grams

1 teaspoon baking soda

1/4 teaspoon xanthan gum

1/2 teaspoon salt

Banana Bread ▪ *Oat-based*

This banana bread is even better the day after it is baked. The banana permeates the bread for a mellow flavor.

- Preheat the oven to 350°F. Lightly grease an 8-inch square baking pan.
- In a large bowl, mash the bananas well. This is easier to do with a mixer. Add all the other ingredients and mix well. The batter will thicken as it is mixed.
- Pour into the prepared pan. Bake for approximately 30 minutes, until a toothpick inserted in the middle tests cleanly.

▪ Serves 9 ▪

2 small bananas mashed (no more than 3/4 cup), or 1 (6-ounce) jar baby food bananas

1/2 cup sugar, 100 grams

1/4 cup oil

1 teaspoon vanilla extract

2 eggs

1 1/4 cups oat flour, 155 grams

1 1/2 tablespoons baking powder

1/2 teaspoon xanthan gum

1/2 teaspoon salt

Banana Bread ▪ *Potato-based*

This moist, springy loaf is perfect with morning coffee or as something nice to nibble later in the day. Not too heavy, not too light.

- Preheat the oven to 350°F. Grease a 9 x 4-inch loaf pan.
- In a medium-size bowl, mash the bananas well. Add all the other ingredients and mix well. The batter will thicken as it is mixed.
- Pour into the prepared pan. Bake for 40 to 50 minutes, until a toothpick inserted in the middle tests cleanly. This loaf shrinks just a little as it cools.
- As with many gluten-free breads, this one will dry out a bit the longer it remains at room temperature. I recommend slicing and freezing individual servings.

▪ Serves 10 ▪

2 small bananas mashed (no more than 3/4 cup), or 1 (6-ounce) jar baby food bananas

1 teaspoon vinegar

1/2 cup sugar, 100 grams

1/4 cup oil

1 egg

1/4 cup milk

1 teaspoon vanilla extract

1 cup potato starch, 155 grams

1 teaspoon baking soda

1/4 teaspoon xanthan gum

1/2 teaspoon salt

NOTE: Each ounce of bananas by weight happens to measure one fluid ounce as well.

Banana Bread ▪ *Rice-based*

When I first made this recipe, I used $1/4$ cup of oil instead of the butter. While the texture, moisture, and consistency were just right, the flavor was not. Somehow, I needed to get dairy into the recipe. When using just rice, dairy provides that last little oomph to mimic traditional wheat-based flavor. Accordingly, I switched to butter and added a few tablespoons of milk. With butter being 80 percent fat (as compared to oil at 100 percent fat), I also needed to increase the amount of butter to reach the right fat content. The final result is this moist bread with mild banana flavor.

- Preheat the oven to 350°F. Lightly grease an 8-inch square baking pan.

- In a small bowl, mash the bananas well. Set aside. In a large bowl, mix the butter and flour. Add all the other ingredients, including the mashed bananas, and mix well. The batter will thicken as it is mixed.

- Pour into the prepared pan. Bake for approximately 30 minutes, until a toothpick inserted in the middle tests cleanly.

▪ Serves 9 ▪

2 small bananas mashed (no more than $3/4$ cup), or 1 (6-ounce) jar baby food bananas

$5\,1/3$ tablespoons butter, very softened

1 cup rice flour, 150 grams

$1/2$ cup sugar, 100 grams

2 tablespoons milk

1 teaspoon vanilla extract

2 eggs

1 tablespoon baking powder

$1/2$ teaspoon baking soda

$3/4$ teaspoon xanthan gum

$1/2$ teaspoon salt

Chocolate Chip Muffins ▪ *Corn-based*

This recipe makes twelve muffins. Even though it seems that the batter would fit in fewer cups, twelve is the right number. Otherwise, the batter overflows the edges of the cups during baking. This muffin is just plain yummy.

- Preheat the oven to 350°F. Line or grease a twelve-section muffin tin.

- In a large bowl, combine all the ingredients except the chips. Mix well. Continue beating for a few minutes to help the batter to thicken. Fold in the chips.

- Divide among the twelve sections of the muffin tin. Bake for 20 to 25 minutes, until a toothpick inserted in the middle tests cleanly.

▪ Makes 12 ▪

2/3 cup plain yogurt

1 teaspoon vinegar

1/2 cup sugar, 100 grams

1/4 cup oil

1 teaspoon vanilla extract

2 eggs

1 cup cornstarch, 125 grams

1 teaspoon baking soda

1/2 teaspoon xanthan gum

1/2 teaspoon salt

1/2 cup mini chocolate chips, or regular chips chopped small

Chocolate Chip Muffins ▪ *Oat-based*

These muffins are best eaten cooled, as opposed to hot from the oven. They are light, not overly sweet, and have just enough chocolate to satisfy a chocolate craving.

- Preheat the oven to 350°F. Line or grease a twelve-section muffin tin.

- In a large bowl, combine all the ingredients except chips. Mix well. The batter will thicken as it is mixed.

- Divide among the twelve sections of the muffin tin. Bake for 15 to 20 minutes, until a toothpick inserted in the middle tests cleanly.

▪ Makes 12 ▪

2/3 cup plain yogurt

1/2 cup sugar, 100 grams

1/4 cup oil

1 1/2 teaspoons vanilla extract

2 eggs

1 1/4 cups oat flour, 155 grams

1 teaspoon baking soda

1 teaspoon vinegar

1/2 teaspoon xanthan gum

1/2 teaspoon salt

1/2 cup mini chocolate chips, or regular chips chopped small

Chocolate Chip Muffins ■ *Potato-based*

- Preheat the oven to 350°F. Line or grease a twelve-section muffin tin.

- In a medium-size bowl combine the ingredients except the chips, and mix well. Add the chips to the batter and mix lightly.

- Divide among the twelve sections of the muffin tin. Bake for 17 to 23 minutes, until a toothpick inserted in the middle tests cleanly.

- These muffins shrink just a little as they cool.

■ Makes 12 ■

3/4 cup plain yogurt

1 teaspoon vinegar

1/2 cup brown sugar,
100 grams

1/4 cup oil

2 eggs

1 teaspoon vanilla extract

1 cup potato starch,
155 grams

1 teaspoon baking soda

1/4 teaspoon xanthan gum

1/2 teaspoon salt

1/2 cup mini chocolate chips,
or regular chips
chopped small

Chocolate Chip Muffins ■ *Rice-based*

Not too big, these muffins are great snack size. They taste like a fluffy, moist chocolate chip cookie.

■ Preheat the oven to 350°F. Line nine sections of a muffin tin.

■ In a medium-size bowl, mix the oil with the sugar. Add the eggs. Mix until light yellow and a little thicker. This will take a minute or two with your mixer. Add the other ingredients except the chips. Beat well. The batter will thicken a little. Stir in the chips.

■ Divide among the nine sections of the muffin tin. Bake for 20 to 25 minutes, until a toothpick inserted in the middle tests cleanly.

■ Makes 9 ■

2 tablespoons oil

1/3 cup brown sugar, 75 grams

2 eggs

1/3 cup plain yogurt

1/2 cup rice flour, 75 grams

2 teaspoons baking powder

1 teaspoon baking soda

1/2 teaspoon salt

1 teaspoon vanilla extract

1/2 teaspoon xanthan gum

1 teaspoon apple cider vinegar

1/2 cup mini chocolate chips, or regular chips chopped small

NOTE: Rice-based muffins will have a prettier domed top if one egg is replaced with two egg whites. This is not necessary for overall taste and texture.

Chocolate–Chocolate Chip Muffins ▪ *Corn-based*

Great anytime, these are pretty muffins with a nice shape, tender and chocolaty. If you're looking for a "can't believe it's gluten-free" choice, your search is over.

- Preheat the oven to 350°F. Line or grease a twelve-section muffin tin.
- In a large bowl, combine all the ingredients except the chips. Mix well. Fold in the chips.
- Divide among the twelve sections of the muffin tin. Bake for 20 to 25 minutes, until a toothpick inserted in the middle tests cleanly.

▪ Makes 12 ▪

3/4 cup plain yogurt

1/2 cup sugar, 100 grams

1/4 cup oil

1 teaspoon vanilla extract

2 eggs

1 cup cornstarch, 125 grams

1/4 cup unsweetened cocoa powder, 20 grams

1 teaspoon baking soda

1/2 teaspoon xanthan gum

1/2 teaspoon salt

1/2 cup mini chocolate chips, or regular chips chopped small

Chocolate–Chocolate Chip Muffins ■ *Oat-based*

Okay. I admit it. I love those "famous" chocolate–chocolate chip muffins. There's even a national-brand mix for these dangerous things. My kids will actually make these for themselves! I'm willing to be a big person and admit that I occasionally indulge my unrestricted dietary self in them, too.

- Preheat the oven to 350°F. Line or grease a twelve-section muffin tin.
- In a large bowl, combine all the ingredients except the chips. Mix well. The batter will thicken as it is mixed.
- Divide among the twelve sections of the muffin tin. Bake for 15 to 20 minutes, until a toothpick inserted in the middle tests cleanly.

■ Makes 12 ■

^{2}/$_3$ cup plain yogurt

^{1}/$_2$ cup sugar, 100 grams

^{1}/$_4$ cup oil

1 ^{1}/$_2$ teaspoons vanilla extract

2 eggs

1 cup oat flour, 125 grams

^{1}/$_3$ cup unsweetened cocoa powder, 30 grams

1 teaspoon baking soda

^{1}/$_2$ teaspoon xanthan gum

^{1}/$_2$ teaspoon salt

^{1}/$_2$ cup mini chocolate chips, or regular chips chopped small

Chocolate–Chocolate Chip Muffins ▪ *Potato-based*

- Preheat the oven to 350°F. Line or grease a twelve-section muffin tin.
- In a medium-size bowl, combine the ingredients except the chips, and mix well. Add the chips to batter and mix lightly.
- Divide among the twelve sections (you may fill only eleven) of the muffin tin. Bake for 17 to 23 minutes, until a toothpick inserted in the middle tests cleanly.
- These muffins shrink just a little as they cool.

▪ Makes 11 or 12 ▪

$2/3$ cup plain yogurt

$1/2$ cup sugar, 100 grams

$1/4$ cup oil

2 eggs

1 teaspoon vanilla extract

$3/4$ cup potato starch, 115 grams

$1/3$ cup unsweetened cocoa powder, 30 grams

1 teaspoon baking soda

$1/4$ teaspoon xanthan gum

$1/2$ teaspoon salt

$1/2$ cup mini chocolate chips, or regular chips chopped small

Chocolate–Chocolate Chip Muffins ▪ *Rice-based*

These muffins are reminiscent of a fluffy brownie. They are chocolaty and tasty, with a slightly domed top.

- Preheat the oven to 350°F. Line or grease nine sections of a muffin tin.
- In a medium-size bowl, mix the oil with the sugar. Add the eggs. Mix until light yellow and a little thicker. This will take a minute or two with your mixer. Add the other ingredients except the chips. Beat well. The batter will thicken a little. Stir in the chips. Divide among the nine sections of the muffin tin. Bake for 20 to 25 minutes, until a toothpick inserted in the middle tests cleanly.

▪ Makes 9 ▪

2 tablespoons oil

$1/2$ cup sugar, 100 grams

2 eggs

$1/3$ cup plain yogurt

$1/3$ cup unsweetened cocoa powder, 30 grams

$1/3$ cup rice flour, 50 grams

2 teaspoons baking powder

1 teaspoon baking soda

$1/2$ teaspoon salt

1 teaspoon vanilla extract

$1/2$ teaspoon xanthan gum

$1/2$ cup chocolate chips

Fruit Muffins ▪ *Potato-based*

The difficulty in making fruit muffins with potato (or corn, for that matter) is that the batter can be a little thin and cannot support heavy additions. If you chop your fruit small, this should not be a problem. These muffins are light, tender, and a bit sweet.

- Preheat the oven to 350°F. Line or grease a twelve-section muffin tin.

- In a medium-size bowl, combine all the ingredients except the fruit, and mix well. Chop the fruit into very small pieces. Add to the batter and mix lightly.

- Divide among the twelve sections of the muffin tin. Sprinkle the tops with sugar, if desired. Bake for 17 to 23 minutes, until a toothpick inserted in the middle tests cleanly.

- These muffins shrink just a little as they cool.

▪ Makes 12 ▪

$3/4$ cup plain yogurt

1 teaspoon vinegar

$2/3$ cup sugar, 135 grams

$1/4$ cup oil

2 eggs

1 teaspoon vanilla extract

1 cup potato starch, 155 grams

1 teaspoon baking soda

$1/4$ teaspoon xanthan gum

$1/2$ teaspoon salt

$1/2$ cup fresh or frozen blueberries, cranberries, apples, or other orchard fruit

Topping:

1 teaspoon sugar (optional)

NOTE: Vanilla is a great flavor to combine with any fruit. However, you can change the extract flavor, add $1/2$ teaspoon of cinnamon or 1 teaspoon of orange zest, or experiment with other flavor boosters.

Fruit Muffins ▪ *Rice-based*

For diversity, I have made this muffin recipe dairy-free. Add a little vanilla extract or cinnamon to accent your chosen fruit, if desired. The muffin is very light in taste and texture.

- Preheat the oven to 350°F. Line or grease nine sections of a muffin tin.
- In a medium-size bowl, combine the oil and sugar. Mix well. Add the egg and egg white. Beat until light in color. Add the remaining ingredients except the fruit, and mix well. Chop the fruit into very small pieces so that it does not fall to the bottom of the soft batter. Add to the batter and mix lightly.
- Divide among the nine sections of the muffin tin. Sprinkle the tops of the muffins with sugar. Bake for 20 to 25 minutes, until a toothpick inserted in the middle tests cleanly.

▪ Makes 9 ▪

2 tablespoons oil

$^1/_3$ cup sugar, 75 grams

1 egg

1 egg white

$^1/_2$ cup apple juice

$^1/_2$ cup plus 1 tablespoon rice flour, 85 grams

2 teaspoons baking powder

1 teaspoon baking soda

$^1/_2$ teaspoon salt

1 teaspoon vanilla extract

$^1/_2$ teaspoon xanthan gum

1 tablespoon apple cider vinegar

$^1/_2$ cup fresh or frozen blueberries, cranberries, apples, or other orchard fruit

Topping:

1 teaspoon sugar (optional)

Pumpkin Quick Bread ■ *Corn-based*

Moist, dense, and not too spicy.

- Preheat the oven to 350°F. Grease a 9 x 4-inch loaf pan.
- In a large bowl, combine all the ingredients. Mix well.
- Pour into the prepared pan. Bake for 40 to 45 minutes, until a toothpick inserted in the middle tests cleanly.

■ Serves 10 ■

3/4 cup canned pumpkin (not pumpkin pie filling)

1 teaspoon vinegar

1/2 cup sugar, 100 grams

1/4 cup oil

1 teaspoon ground cinnamon

1/2 teaspoon grated nutmeg

2 eggs

3/4 cup plus 2 tablespoons cornstarch, 110 grams

1 teaspoon baking soda

1/4 teaspoon xanthan gum

1/2 teaspoon salt

Pumpkin Quick Bread ■ *Oat-based*

Like most oat recipes, more spice is required to give that hearty pumpkin pie–like taste. While this bread uses a bit more sugar than some of the other quick breads, it is by no means too sweet.

- Preheat the oven to 350°F. Lightly grease an 8-inch square baking pan.
- In a large bowl, combine all the ingredients. Mix well. Pour immediately into the prepared pan, otherwise, the batter will not remain smooth. This affects the final appearance, but not the taste. (If the batter is not smooth in the pan, lightly smooth with moistened fingertips.)
- Bake for approximately 30 minutes, until a toothpick inserted in the middle tests cleanly.

■ Serves 9 ■

3/4 cup canned pumpkin (not pumpkin pie filling)

3/4 cup sugar, 150 grams

1/4 cup oil

1 1/2 teaspoons ground cinnamon

1/2 teaspoon grated nutmeg

1 egg

1/4 cup plain yogurt

1 1/4 cups oat flour, 155 grams

1 1/2 tablespoons baking powder

1/2 teaspoon xanthan gum

3/4 teaspoon salt

Pumpkin Quick Bread ▪ *Potato-based*

A very pretty, tasty loaf.

- Preheat the oven to 350°F. Grease a 9 x 4-inch loaf pan.
- In a medium-size bowl, combine all the ingredients and mix well. The batter will thicken as it is mixed.
- Pour into the prepared pan. Bake for 40 to 50 minutes, until a toothpick inserted in the middle tests cleanly.

▪ Serves 10 ▪

3/4 cup canned pumpkin (not pumpkin pie filling)

1 teaspoon vinegar

1/2 cup sugar, 100 grams

1/4 cup oil

2 eggs

1 teaspoon ground cinnamon

1/2 teaspoon grated nutmeg

1 cup potato starch, 155 grams

1 teaspoon baking soda

1/4 teaspoon xanthan gum

1/2 teaspoon salt

Pumpkin Quick Bread ▪ *Rice-based*

This is a very moist bread with nice pumpkin and spice flavor. It was a big hit with the people who wandered through the kitchen the day I was creating it.

- Preheat the oven to 350°F. Lightly grease an 8-inch square baking pan.
- In a large bowl, mix the oil and flour. Add all the other ingredients and mix well. The batter will thicken as it is mixed.
- Pour into the prepared pan. Bake for approximately 35 minutes, until a toothpick inserted in the middle tests cleanly.

▪ Serves 9 ▪

1/4 cup oil

1 cup rice flour, 150 grams

3/4 cup canned pumpkin (not pumpkin pie filling)

3/4 cup brown sugar, 150 grams

1 teaspoon ground cinnamon

1/2 teaspoon grated nutmeg

1 egg

1/4 cup plain yogurt

1 tablespoon baking powder

1/2 teaspoon baking soda

3/4 teaspoon xanthan gum

1/2 teaspoon salt

Sweet Muffins ▪ *Corn-based*

These muffins are best enjoyed at room temperature, as they will seem too moist when hot from the oven.

- Preheat the oven to 350°F. Line or grease a twelve-section muffin tin.
- Mix the oil with the sugar. Add the eggs. Mix until light yellow and a little thicker. This will take a minute or two with your mixer. Add the other ingredients. Beat well. The batter will thicken a little. Divide among the twelve sections of the muffin tin.
- In a bowl, combine the butter, sugar, and cinnamon for the topping. Lightly sprinkle the tops of the muffins with the mixture.
- Bake for 20 to 25 minutes, until a toothpick inserted in the middle tests cleanly.

▪ Makes 12 ▪

¼ cup oil

½ cup sugar, 100 grams

2 eggs

½ cup plain yogurt

1 ¼ cups cornstarch, 155 grams

2 teaspoons baking powder

¼ teaspoon baking soda

¼ teaspoon salt

1 teaspoon vanilla extract

1 ¼ teaspoons xanthan gum

½ teaspoon ground cinnamon

Topping:

1 tablespoon butter, softened

2 teaspoons brown sugar

Pinch of ground cinnamon

Sweet Muffins ■ *Oat-based*

This is nice for breakfast. It is the gluten-free equivalent of a cereal bar, but better.

- Preheat the oven to 350°F. Line or grease a twelve-section muffin tin.
- In a large bowl, combine all the ingredients. Mix well. The batter will thicken as it is mixed. Divide among the twelve sections of the muffin tin.
- In a bowl, combine the butter, sugar, and cinnamon for the topping. Lightly sprinkle the tops of the muffins with the mixture.
- Bake for 15 to 20 minutes, until a toothpick inserted in the middle tests cleanly.

■ Makes 12 ■

$2/3$ cup plain yogurt

$1/2$ cup sugar, 100 grams

$1/4$ cup oil

$1 1/2$ teaspoons vanilla extract

2 eggs

$1 1/4$ cups oat flour, 155 grams

1 teaspoon baking soda

1 teaspoon vinegar

$1/2$ teaspoon xanthan gum

$1/2$ teaspoon salt

$1/2$ teaspoon ground cinnamon

Topping:

1 tablespoon butter, softened

2 tablespoons brown sugar

$1/4$ teaspoon ground cinnamon

Sweet Muffins ▪ *Potato-based*

Here's your chance for an easy morning pick-me-up! The buttery topping may make you think breakfast, but enjoy them anytime.

- Preheat the oven to 350°F. Line or grease a twelve-section muffin tin.
- Mix the oil with the sugar. Add the eggs. Mix until light yellow and a little thicker. This will take a minute or two with your mixer. Add the other ingredients. Beat well. The batter will thicken a little. Divide among the twelve sections of the muffin tin.
- In a bowl, combine the butter, sugar, and cinnamon for the topping. Lightly sprinkle the tops of the muffins with the mixture.
- Bake for 25 minutes, until a toothpick inserted in the middle tests cleanly.

▪ Makes 12 ▪

¼ cup oil

½ cup sugar, 100 grams

2 eggs

½ cup plain yogurt

1 cup potato starch, 155 grams

2 teaspoons baking powder

¼ teaspoon baking soda

¼ teaspoon salt

1 ¼ teaspoons vanilla extract

1 teaspoon xanthan gum

½ teaspoon ground cinnamon

Topping:

1 tablespoon butter, softened

2 teaspoons brown sugar

Pinch of ground cinnamon

NOTE: Foil muffin tin liners are great, as the muffins do not stick to them nearly as much as with the paper liners. If you come across them, give them a try!

Sweet Muffins ▪ *Rice-based*

This is a light, tender muffin! Yes, it is really made with rice flour. You just need to trust me on this one, including the seemingly small amount of flour used.

- Preheat the oven to 350°F. Line or grease nine sections of a muffin tin.
- Mix the oil with the sugar. Add the eggs. Mix until light yellow and a little thicker. This will take a minute or two with your mixer. Add the other ingredients. Beat well. The batter will thicken a little. Divide among the nine sections of the muffin tin.
- In a bowl, combine the butter, sugar, and cinnamon for the topping. Lightly sprinkle the tops of the muffins with the mixture.
- Bake for 20 to 25 minutes, until a toothpick inserted in the middle tests cleanly.

▪ Makes 9 ▪

2 tablespoons oil

1/3 cup plus 1 tablespoon sugar, 75 grams

2 eggs

1/3 cup plain yogurt

1/2 cup rice flour, 75 grams

2 teaspoons baking powder

1 teaspoon baking soda

1/2 teaspoon salt

1 teaspoon vanilla extract

1/2 teaspoon xanthan gum

1/4 teaspoon ground cinnamon

1 tablespoon apple cider vinegar

Topping:

1 tablespoon butter, softened

1 tablespoon brown sugar

Pinch of ground cinnamon

9

...SOUPS AND STEWS

Nothing beats great soup. For me, it feels like health and love in a bowl. Some of my very favorite soups are created from odds and ends from my garden, my freezer, and the meat special at my local market. I hope this chapter inspires you to be adventurous.

The base, or underlying structure, of soups in this chapter fall into two main categories—cream soups and broth soups. By utilizing evaporated milk, you will be able to achieve a richness in your cream soups belying the ingredients. By using tender cuts of meats and a little help from bouillon cubes, you will forgo long simmering. And by using canned beans instead of dried beans, you will cut preparation time. Many soups take less than twenty minutes to prepare.

Several soups require a real broth to be good. Egg Drop Soup and Clear Pork Soup are two such recipes. Easy Crock Pot Broth recipes are included for this purpose.

While all of these soups are quite tasty, some are truly remarkable. Black Bean Soup, Fish Chowder, and Crab Soup, Maryland-Style are among my favorites. I've also included recipes for Condensed Cream of Mushroom Soup and Condensed Cream of Chicken Soup for use in your favorite casseroles.

Bean Soup

One of my most-loved soups is the wonderful, time-consuming, homey bean soup. To get you out of the kitchen fast, I've cut corners (but not flavor).

- Remove the bone and excess fat from the ham steak. Cut into very small dice and place in a medium-size saucepan. Peel and chop the onion into small dice and add to saucepan.
- Add the remaining ingredients. Bring to a boil. Cover and simmer for 30 minutes.
- If desired, remove approximately $1/2$ cup of beans and smash into a paste; then return to the soup to thicken the broth.
- Serve hot.

■ Serves 3 ■

4 ounces country ham steak

$1/2$ small onion

2 (15.5-ounce) cans small white or navy beans

1 cup water

1 teaspoon dried parsley

Beef Noodle Soup

This is a homey soup—just plain good beef noodle soup. The noodles continue to expand (but remain tasty) while standing for a long period or in the fridge as leftovers. If you are not using all the soup right away, use at least 30 percent fewer noodles or be ready to add quite a bit of broth when you reheat.

- Heat the broth, water, bouillon cube, and salt in a saucepan to boiling.
- Peel and slice the onion into thin slivers. Add to the pot, along with the rice noodles, beef, and parsley. Cover and cook until the rice noodles are tender, between 10 and 20 minutes, depending upon the brand.
- Serve hot.

■ Serves 2 ■

2 cups beef-flavored Crock Pot Broth (page 162)

$1/2$ cup water

1 beef bouillon cube

$1/4$ teaspoon salt

$1/2$ small onion

3 ounces spaghetti-style rice noodles (Tinkyada or other gluten-free brand, not clear Asian noodles)

2 ounces shredded beef

Pinch of dried parsley

Beef Vegetable Soup

Vegetable soup is a great opportunity to use up odds and ends in the freezer, even those veggies that are no longer ideal for serving as a side dish. I find broccoli, squash, and cabbage make nice additions to this soup. Once you've made soup a time or two, you'll develop a feel for what works and what doesn't. You may never want canned soup again.

- Trim the beef of any extra fat. Cut into small dice and place in a medium-size saucepan. Wash and dice the potatoes, and add to the pot. Peel and finely dice the onion, and add to the pot.
- Add the remaining ingredients. Bring to boil, then cover and simmer for at least 15 minutes.
- Serve hot.

■ Serves 5 ■

8 ounces boneless sirloin steak or chuck roast

2 small red potatoes (4 to 5 ounces)

1/2 small onion

8 ounces frozen mixed vegetables

1 (14.5-ounce) can diced tomatoes

2 tablespoons tomato paste

2 cups water

2 beef bouillon cubes

1/4 teaspoon black pepper

1/2 teaspoon salt

> **NOTE:** It is especially important to trim meat of fat and sinew because the cooking time is short.

Beef Stew

This recipe looks like it requires a lot of steps, but it is really quite easy.

- Trim the beef of any extra fat. Cut into bite-size pieces and place in a Crock Pot. Sprinkle 1 tablespoon of the cornstarch over the beef and toss lightly to coat.
- Wash the potatoes and chop into large chunks (I cut into four pieces per potato). Peel the onion and chop into similarly sized chunks. Add to the pot.
- Wash the carrots and chop off the tops. Cut into large chunks and add to the pot.
- Add the bouillon cube, 1 cup of the water, and the salt and pepper to the pot.
- Cook on high for 4 to 6 hours, or on low for 8 to 12 hours. Stir before serving, to blend. To thicken the juices, stir together the remaining 2 tablespoons of cornstarch and the 2 tablespoons of water in a cup, and add to the pot. Stir well. The existing heat should almost immediately thicken the sauce.
- Serve hot.

■ Serves 4 ■

16 ounces boneless sirloin steak or chuck roast

3 tablespoons cornstarch or potato starch

6 small white or red potatoes (approximately 12 ounces)

1 medium-size onion

2 carrots (approximately 6 ounces)

1 beef bouillon cube

1 cup plus 2 tablespoons cool water

1/2 teaspoon salt

1/4 teaspoon black pepper

Beef Stew, Crock Pot

For the record, given more time, I prefer the beef stew recipe preceding this one. However, when I need to toss everything in the Crock Pot and still come home to a nice meal, this works well. Many of the prepackaged Crock Pot meals contain ingredients that are not gluten-free.

- Place the vegetables and beef in a Crock Pot. In a small bowl, stir together the remaining ingredients. Do not worry if the bouillon cubes do not dissolve. Pour into the pot.
- Cook on high for 4 to 5 hours or low for 8 to 10 hours. Stir well but gently before serving.

■ Serves 6 ■

1 pound beef chuck stew meat or sirloin steak

2 (16-ounce) packages frozen stew vegetables

1 1/2 cups water

2 beef bouillon cubes

1 1/2 tablespoons cornstarch or potato starch

1/4 teaspoon black pepper

1/2 teaspoon salt

NOTE: In this case, frozen vegetables fare better with the shorter cooking time; the potatoes tend to fall apart. If you can, turn off the Crock Pot at 4 hours (high) or 8 hours (low). Also, because of the slightly shorter cooking time, using the better cut of meat (sirloin) will give you more tender beef.

Black Bean Soup

Eating beans never tasted better. The cilantro tempers the heat of the cayenne. Serve with a nice salad or sandwich, for a great meal. And, finally, for real indulgence, top with a little grated cheese or a dollop of sour cream.

4 ounces country ham steak

1/2 small onion

2 (15.5-ounce) cans black beans

1 cup water

1/8 teaspoon cayenne

1/4 teaspoon ground cumin seed

1 tablespoon fresh cilantro, or 1 teaspoon dried

- Remove the bone and excess fat from the ham steak. Cut into very small dice and place in a medium-size saucepan. Peel and chop the onion into small dice, and add to pot.

- Add the remaining ingredients. Bring to a boil, then cover and simmer for 15 minutes. Remove approximately 1/2 cup of beans from the pot. On a plate, smash with a fork into a paste, then return to the pot and stir.

- Serve hot.

■ Serves 3 ■

Broccoli-Cheese Soup

This rich soup is my daughter's second-most favorite soup. (Chicken Noodle places first.)

8 ounces frozen broccoli

1 (12-ounce) can evaporated milk

3/4 cup milk

1 tablespoon butter

1 chicken bouillon cube

1 teaspoon cornstarch, potato starch, or rice flour

1/4 teaspoon salt

1 cup shredded Colby cheese (approximately 3 ounces)

- Chop the broccoli into small dice and place in a medium-size saucepan. Add the remaining ingredients except the cheese, and heat over medium heat to almost boiling. Stir often to prevent settling of the thickener and avoid scorching.

- Cook until the broccoli is very tender. Add the cheese, stirring often, and cook until it has fully melted and the soup thickens.

- Serve hot.

■ Serves 3 ■

Brunswick Stew

Brunswick stew is one of my favorite meals. And it's good for you, too. It has a tiny bite from the cayenne, which may be omitted if you don't care for it. Like most homemade soups, it is even better on the second day.

- Cut the chicken into small bite-size pieces. Place in a medium-size saucepan with the oil, over medium-high heat. Peel and dice the onion, and add to the pot. Continue cooking until the chicken is cooked through, approximately 10 minutes. Wash and finely dice the potatoes (peel only if their skin is thick), and add to the pot.

- Add the remaining ingredients and bring to a boil. Simmer, uncovered, until the potatoes are very tender, about 10 minutes. Stir occasionally to keep the stew from sticking to the bottom of the pot. Simmer longer for softer vegetables.

- Serve hot.

■ Serves 5 ■

1 boneless, skinless chicken breast (approximately 6 ounces)

2 tablespoons oil

4 small new potatoes (approximately 9 ounces)

1/2 small onion

1 (14.5-ounce) can chopped tomatoes

2 tablespoons tomato paste

1 3/4 cups water

10 ounces succotash (frozen is fine)

2 chicken bouillon cubes

1/4 teaspoon black pepper

1/2 teaspoon salt

Pinch of cayenne

Chicken Corn Chowder

When my celiac friend Sheri visited my home, she thought she couldn't eat anything and was living on salads and plain rice. After trying this soup, she calls me her food angel.

- Cut the chicken into small bite-size pieces. Place in a medium-size saucepan with the butter, over medium-high heat. Peel and dice the onion, and add to the pot. Continue cooking until the chicken is cooked through, approximately 10 minutes. Wash and finely dice the potatoes (peel only if their skin is thick), and add to the pot.

- Add the remaining ingredients and bring to a boil. Simmer, uncovered, until the potatoes are very tender, about 10 minutes. Stir occasionally to keep the chowder from sticking to the bottom of the pot. Simmer longer for softer vegetables.

- Serve hot.

■ Serves 5 ■

1 boneless, skinless chicken breast (approximately 6 ounces)

4 small new potatoes (approximately 9 ounces)

2 tablespoons butter

1/2 small onion

1 (12-ounce) can evaporated milk

1 cup milk

3 chicken bouillon cubes

1/4 teaspoon black pepper

1/2 teaspoon salt

1 tablespoon cornstarch or potato starch

8 ounces fresh or frozen corn (about 2 ears)

Chicken Rice Soup, Quick

Here's a simple version of my Chicken Rice Soup. If you prefer Chicken Noodle Soup, just substitute your favorite gluten-free noodles for the rice. I use dark-meat chicken pieces because they add more flavor to the broth.

- Place the chicken in a medium-size or large saucepan. Add the onion halves, and add water to cover.

- Take three or four of the green onions and remove the roots and any ugly part of the stalk. Add to the pot. Cover with lid and bring to a boil. Cook until the chicken is done, approximately 30 minutes. Remove the chicken and onion from the pot. Allow the chicken to cool so that you can remove the bones and skin. Cut the chicken into bite-size pieces. Discard the onion.

- While the chicken is cooking, discard the roots and tops from the remaining three or four green onions; slice in half lengthwise and then into very small pieces. Set aside.

- Once the cooked chicken has been removed from the saucepan, add the chopped green onion, bouillon cubes, pepper, and rice to the broth. Stir occasionally. Add the parsley for color. Cover and cook until the rice is tender, approximately 15 minutes.

■ Serves 8 to 10 ■

2 pounds chicken thighs

7 cups water

1 small onion, unpeeled and cut in half

6–8 green onions

2 chicken bouillon cubes

$1/2$ cup uncooked long-grain rice

$1/4$ teaspoon salt

Pinch of black pepper

$1/2$ teaspoon dried parsley (optional)

Clear Chicken Soup

This soup is a lovely and impressive first course. It is light yet quite flavorful.

- Heat the broth, bouillon cube, and salt in a saucepan to boiling.
- Add the carrots and rice noodles. Cook until the rice noodles are tender, between 2 and 3 minutes. Add the broccoli and chicken. Heat through and serve.

■ Serves 2 ■

2 cups chicken-flavored Crock Pot Broth (page 162)

1 chicken bouillon cube

$1/8$ teaspoon salt

$1/2$ ounce finely sliced baby carrots

1 ounce clear rice noodles (rice sticks)

$1/2$ ounce tiny broccoli florets

$1^{1}/2$ ounces shredded chicken

Clear Pork Soup

Like its chicken counterpart, this soup is light yet quite flavorful. I wish I could think of a better name for this fine soup—one that would do it justice.

- Heat the broth and salt in a saucepan to boiling.
- Add the rice noodles and mushrooms. Cook until the rice noodles are tender, between 2 and 3 minutes.
- Serve hot.

■ Serves 2 ■

2 cups pork-flavored Crock Pot Broth (page 162)

$1/2$ teaspoon salt

1 ounce rice noodles (rice sticks)

1 ounce mushrooms, sliced very thinly

$1^{1}/2$ ounces shredded pork

Condensed Cream of Chicken Soup

For substitution in any recipe calling for one (10³/4-ounce) can of cream of chicken soup.

- Wash and finely chop the chicken. Place in a small saucepan with the butter. Cook over medium heat until the chicken is quite tender, approximately 5 minutes. Combine the remaining ingredients in a cup and stir to dissolve the starch. (You may need to use the tines of a fork to smash the bouillon cube). Add to the pot. While stirring, bring to a boil to allow the mixture to thicken.

- Use as called for in any recipe.

2 ounces boneless chicken of any kind

3 tablespoons butter

1 cup milk

2 tablespoons plus 1 teaspoon cornstarch or potato starch

1 chicken bouillon cube

Condensed Cream of Mushroom Soup

This casserole helper isn't what you think it is. Cream in the title would lead you to believe dairy is a main ingredient, but it isn't. In fact, it barely registers—that famous brand has less than 2 percent dairy. This recipe is not for eating as is—if you want to enjoy a bowl of great cream of mushroom soup, please try the other recipe on page 161. However, if you need a good substitute for a non-gluten-free commercial brand to use in a casserole, this one will do the job nicely. This recipe replaces one (10³/4-ounce) can of cream of mushroom soup.

- Wash and finely chop the mushrooms. Place in a small saucepan with the butter. Cook over medium heat until the mushrooms are very fragrant and tender, approximately 5 minutes. A little browning of the mushrooms will add to the flavor. Combine the remaining ingredients in a cup and stir to dissolve the starch. Add to the pot. Stirring, bring to a boil to allow the mixture to thicken.

- Use as called for in any recipe.

4 ounces fresh mushrooms, chopped finely

3 tablespoons butter

1 cup water

2 tablespoons plus 1 teaspoon cornstarch or potato starch

1/4 teaspoon salt

Crab Soup, Rich Cream-Style

Although the chicken bouillon cube may not seem right here, it really is. It provides softness to the background flavor and that, in turn, actually enhances the flavor of the crabmeat in this rather decadent soup. Try not to hurry the simmering time. It makes a big difference in the flavor of the soup. Our tasters preferred a small serving because the soup is truly rich.

- Finely dice the onion. Place in a medium-size saucepan with the butter, over medium-high heat. Cook until the onion is wilted. Be careful not to burn the butter.
- Add the remaining ingredients and bring to almost a boil. Simmer, uncovered, for about 10 minutes. Stir often to keep the soup from sticking to the bottom of the pot.
- Puree the soup in a blender, if desired.
- Serve hot.

1/2 small onion

2 tablespoons butter

16 ounces crabmeat

1 (12-ounce) can evaporated milk

1 cup milk

1 chicken bouillon cube

2 teaspoons Old Bay Seasoning

1/4 teaspoon black pepper

1/4 teaspoon salt

1 teaspoon dried parsley

1 tablespoon cornstarch or potato starch

■ Makes 4 1/2 cups; serves 6 to 8 ■

Crab Soup, Light Cream-Style

Here is a delicious cream soup that takes just a few minutes to prepare. It is very good, but not as rich as the other version. Garnish with a little parsley if desired.

- Wash the potatoes and pierce with a fork. Microwave on high for 1 minute. Peel the potatoes and cut into small dice. Place in a medium-size saucepan. Peel and dice the onion, and add to the pot. Add the remaining ingredients. Over medium heat, bring to almost a boil and simmer until the potatoes are tender and the flavors blend, approximately 10 minutes. Stir often to avoid scorching and prevent the thickener's settling to the bottom of the pot.
- Serve hot.

4 small new or red potatoes (about 9 ounces)

1/2 small onion

2 tablespoons butter

1 (12-ounce) can evaporated milk

1/2 cup milk

8 ounces pasteurized claw crabmeat

2 teaspoons cornstarch, potato starch, or rice flour

2 teaspoons Old Bay Seasoning

1/2 teaspoon salt

■ Serves 3 ■

Crab Soup, Maryland-Style

One of my favorites.

- Wash and dice the potatoes. Peel and finely dice the onion. Place the potatoes and onion in a medium-size saucepan. Add the remaining ingredients. Bring to a boil. Cover and simmer for about 15 minutes.
- Serve hot.

■ Serves 5 ■

2 small red potatoes (4 to 5 ounces)

1/2 small onion

8 ounces fresh pasteurized crab meat

8 ounces frozen mixed vegetables

1 (14.5-ounce) can diced tomatoes

1 tablespoon tomato paste

2 cups water

1 1/2 teaspoons Old Bay Seasoning

1/4 teaspoon black pepper

1/2 teaspoon salt

Cream of Broccoli Soup

Love broccoli soup? How about a nice, light, flavorful version? Here it is. Surprisingly, frozen broccoli makes for a better soup than does fresh.

- Combine all the ingredients, except the broccoli, in a medium-size saucepan over medium heat. Add the broccoli and cook until the broccoli is very tender. Transfer the hot soup mixture to a blender and blend, or blend with a stick blender. Serve hot.

■ Serves 3 ■

1 (12-ounce) can evaporated milk

1/2 cup milk

1 tablespoon butter

1 tablespoon cornstarch, potato starch, or rice flour

1 chicken bouillon cube

1/4 teaspoon black pepper

1/2 teaspoon salt

8 ounces frozen broccoli

Cream of Mushroom Soup

Rich, creamy, and ready in only five to ten minutes! Choose darker mushrooms for more flavor, lighter ones for a lighter taste. Enjoy!

- Wash, drain, and finely chop the mushrooms. Cook in a small saucepan with the butter, over medium heat. Add 1 tablespoon of water to the pot if the mushrooms seem too dry. Add the remaining ingredients and cook until the soup is thick and the flavors have blended.

■ Serves 2 ■

6 ounces fresh mushrooms

2 teaspoons butter

1 tablespoon water

1 (12-ounce) can evaporated milk

$1/2$ cup milk

1 tablespoon cornstarch, potato starch, or rice flour

$1/4$ teaspoon black pepper

$3/4$ teaspoon salt

Crock Pot Broth—Chicken, Pork, or Beef

Homemade broth will make any soup better but is essential for a few recipes in this book. Egg Drop Soup uses chicken broth, Wonton Soup uses pork broth, and you'll see beef broth as an option for my clear noodle soup.

You may be familiar with other recipes that call for herbs or other vegetables to turn a broth into a stock. This broth is simple and true. Final seasoning is added when the soup is prepared.

■ Wash the meat. Place in a Crock Pot. Cut the onion in quarters and add to the pot. Add the bay leaf and water. Cover with a lid and cook on high for 5 hours, or low for 8 to 10 hours.

■ Remove the meat, onion, and bay leaf from the Crock Pot. Remove the bones and excess fat from the meat. Save the meat for another meal or as an addition to a soup recipe.

■ Skim any fat from the top of the broth and discard. For the clearest broth, drain through cheesecloth.

■ Let cool.

■ Makes approximately 6 cups of chicken broth ■ or approximately 5$^1/4$ cups of pork or beef broth

1 small frying chicken, 1$^1/2$ to 1$^3/4$ pounds, or 1 boneless pork sirloin roast (approximately 2 pounds), or one beef sirloin roast (approximately 2 pounds)

1 medium onion, unpeeled

1 bay leaf (optional)

5 cups water

> NOTE: Broth may be prepared in a large pot by simmering for several hours over medium heat.

Egg Drop Soup

The secret to a good egg drop soup is the Crock Pot Broth on page 162.

- Heat the broth, bouillon cube, and salt to boiling in a small pot. Place the egg in a small cup and beat with a fork. Pour in a slow stream into the broth, stirring the broth as you pour in the egg. Remove from the heat.
- Wash and finely slice the green onion. Add for garnish.

■ Serves 2 ■

2 cups chicken-flavored Crock Pot Broth (page 162)
1 chicken bouillon cube
1/8 teaspoon salt
1 egg
1 green onion

Fish Chowder

This is a mild fish chowder in a light creamy base. Choose any light-colored skinless fish for a mild flavor. Tilapia is always good. If you want a more robust fish flavor, choose a darker fish. The spinach is optional but really enhances the dish.

- Wash the potatoes, pierce several times with a fork, and microwave until tender, about 3 minutes. Once cooked, do not peel but chop into small dice. Place in a medium-size saucepan.
- Cut the fish into small bite-size pieces. Add to the pot. Chop the onion into fine dice and add to the pot. Add the remaining ingredients, except the spinach, to the pot. Over medium heat, bring to almost a boil and simmer for approximately 10 minutes. The fish will no longer be opaque in color and the flavors will have blended.
- While the soup is cooking, wash the spinach and cut into narrow strips. Add at the last minute, just to wilt.
- Serve hot.

■ Serves 5 ■

4 small new or red potatoes (about 9 ounces)
2 small fish fillets (about 12 ounces)
1 small onion
2 tablespoons butter
1 (12-ounce) can evaporated milk
3/4 cup milk
1 teaspoon dried parsley
1/2 teaspoon salt
1 cup fresh or frozen corn
1 small handful baby spinach leaves (approximately 1/2 ounce, optional)

Leek and Potato Soup

Here is a mild soup that my husband prefers served warm. The sour cream added at the end smoothes the "green" edge of the leek, and the pepper adds just a hint of bite.

- Remove and discard the heavy green leaves and roots from the leeks. Slice the leeks lengthwise and then cut into small slices. Wash very well to remove all dirt! Place the leeks in a large pot. Cover with 6 cups of water. Set aside.

- Peel the potatoes and cut into small dice. Add to the pot. Cover with a lid. Over medium-high heat, cook until both the potatoes and leeks are tender, approximately 15 minutes after the liquid begins to boil. Add the bouillon cubes and salt. Puree in a blender until smooth. Add the black pepper and sour cream just before serving.

- Serve hot or cold.

16–18 ounces leeks

6 cups water

2 pounds red or white potatoes

2 chicken bouillon cubes

1 teaspoon salt

$1/2$ teaspoon black pepper, or to taste (optional)

$1/2$ cup sour cream

■ Makes 7 to 8 cups of soup; serves 7 to 8 ■

New England Clam Chowder

This clam chowder has a very subtle flavor.

- Wash the potatoes and pierce several times with a fork. Microwave on high for 1 minute. Peel the potatoes and cut into small dice. Place in a medium-size saucepan. Peel and dice the onion, and add to the pot. Add the remaining ingredients. Over medium heat, bring to almost a boil and simmer until the potatoes are tender and the flavors blend, approximately 10 minutes. Stir often to avoid scorching and prevent the thickener's settling to the bottom of the pot.

- Serve hot.

6 small new or red potatoes (about 12 ounces)

$1/2$ small onion

2 tablespoons butter

1 (12-ounce) can evaporated milk

1 (10-ounce) can whole baby clams

2 tablespoons clam juice

$1 1/2$ tablespoons cornstarch, potato starch, or rice flour

$1/4$ teaspoon black pepper

$1/2$ teaspoon salt

■ Serves 3 ■

One-Pot Pork and Vegetables, Crock Pot

Here is another one-pot dinner ready when you arrive home after a busy day. It takes just a few minutes to toss in the Crock Pot in the morning. Cook all day on low, or on high for 4 to 5 hours.

- Trim the pork of any excess fat. Cut across the grain into thin strips and add to a Crock Pot. Wash and roughly chop the potatoes, and peel and finely chop the onion. Add to the Crock Pot, along with the frozen vegetables.

- In a small bowl, stir together the remaining ingredients. Pour into the pot.

- Cook on high for 4 to 5 hours or low for 8 to 10 hours. Stir well but gently before serving.

■ Serves 6 ■

1 pound boneless pork

12 ounces white potatoes (about 3 medium-size)

1 small onion

1 (16-ounce) package frozen green beans or other frozen vegetables

2 cups water

2 tablespoons cornstarch or potato starch

1/4 teaspoon black pepper

1 beef bouillon cube

3/4 teaspoon dried rosemary

1 teaspoon salt

Ramen-Style Noodle Soup

This recipe was inspired by my son's teacher who makes ramen noodle soup nearly every day at school. It seems only natural that an easy, inexpensive rice version should be available, too. I know more than one college student considers this dish a study-time necessity.

- Place the noodles, bouillon cubes, and water in a small pot. Bring to a boil. Add the vegetables, if desired. Cook for approximately 3 minutes, until the noodles are tender. If desired, add cayenne to spice up your soup, and/or break the egg into the soup and stir quickly to mix. Cook for just a minute or so, until the egg is cooked.

■ Makes 2 servings ■

2 ounces thin, clear rice noodles

2 chicken or beef bouillon cubes

2 1/4 cups water

1/2 cup fresh or frozen vegetables (optional)

Large pinch of dried parsley (optional)

Pinch of cayenne (optional)

1 egg (optional)

NOTE: You can turn this simple recipe into a meal by adding a little leftover chicken, beef, or a handful of shrimp. If you do not care for clear rice noodles, clear mung bean, buckwheat, and translucent corn noodles should all be available at the nearest Asian market.

Seafood Chowder

This is my son's favorite chowder—I once made this quick-to-prepare soup for his music teacher in exchange for an earlier music lesson he'd received. It was a win-win situation for his teacher and for our schedule!

- Wash the potatoes, pierce several times with a fork, and microwave until tender, about 3 minutes. Once cooked, do not peel but chop into small dice. Place in a medium-size saucepan.

- Cut the fish into small bite-size pieces and add to the pot. Chop the onion into fine dice and add to the pot. Add all the remaining ingredients except the shrimp, clams, and scallops. Over medium heat, bring to almost a boil and simmer for approximately 10 minutes. The fish will no longer be opaque in color and the flavors will have blended. Peel the shrimp and wash the clams. Add the shrimp, clams, and scallops to the pot. Simmer for 5 minutes or so, until the clams open. Garnish with basil.

- Serve hot.

■ Serves 5 to 6 ■

4 small new or red potatoes (about 9 ounces)

1 small fish fillet (about 6 ounces)

1 small onion

2 tablespoons butter

1 (12-ounce) can evaporated milk

3/4 cup milk

1 teaspoon dried parsley

1/2 teaspoon salt

2 teaspoons Creole seasoning

1 tablespoon cornstarch or potato starch

1 cup fresh or frozen corn

6–8 large shrimp

6–8 small clams (tightly closed with no breaks in shell)

1/4 pound bay scallops

Fresh basil (for garnish)

Wonton Soup

Wontons made with rice wrappers are difficult to master at home. However, the elements of wonton soup are combined in this recipe to produce a delicious soup that will meet your flavor expectations.

2 cups pork-flavored Crock Pot Broth (page 162)

$1/2$ teaspoon salt

1 ounce rice noodles (rice sticks)

10 uncooked Asian Meatballs (page 20)

1 green onion, sliced thinly

- Heat the broth and salt to a boil in a saucepan. Add the noodles and meatballs. Cook until the noodles are tender and the meatballs are cooked through, between 3 and 5 minutes. Garnish with green onion.

- Serve hot.

■ Serves 2 ■

10

CHICKEN AND TURKEY

In this chapter you will find more than twenty diverse poultry recipes. That is three weeks with a different dish each day! And you thought you'd be stuck eating grilled chicken breast for the rest of your life!

It is very difficult for me to suggest just a few recipes from this chapter. Baked Chicken Pieces is a good start if you're tentative about your cooking skills. Cornish Hens are just right for a special meal. Orange Chicken will rival the offering of any Chinese restaurant. Turkey dishes will get you happily through the holiday season. And Sesame Chicken Stir-Fry with Bok Choy is one of my favorites.

I do hope you will try most of these recipes—all of them are easy.

Baked Chicken Pieces

This recipe was shown to me over twenty years ago by a handsome man who made it for our dinner.

4 chicken breasts, bone in, skin on
1/4 teaspoon salt
1/4 teaspoon paprika
1/4 teaspoon black pepper

- Preheat the oven to 400°F.
- Place the chicken in a small baking dish; the pieces may touch but don't overlap them. Sprinkle with the salt, paprika, and pepper. Bake for 1 hour until the skin is crisp and the juices are clear. The internal temperature of the chicken should be 185°F.

■ Serves 4 ■

Blackened Chicken

This recipe was inspired by a friend's mom as we sat upon bleachers enjoying our kids' soccer matches and sharing our love of food. She serves blackened chicken sliced over a green salad. Delicious.

1 tablespoon oil
1 tablespoon butter
1–1 1/2 tablespoons Blackened Seasoning Blend (page 440)
4 boneless chicken breasts

- Place the oil and butter in a large skillet, over medium heat. Spread the seasoning on a plate. Press one side of each chicken breast into the spices, then place the chicken, spice-side down, into the hot skillet. Cook, uncovered, for 5 minutes. Turn over the chicken and lower the heat to medium-low. Cover and cook for an additional 10 to 15 minutes, until the chicken is cooked through and no pink remains.
- To serve with salad, cut into strips and layer over greens. Otherwise, serve, seasoned side up, with sides of your choosing.

■ Serves 4 ■

Chicken and Dumplings

Here, chicken is in a tasty gravy with fluffy biscuits on top. This old-fashioned favorite takes a while to make but is surely worth the effort. This chicken gravy makes great hot chicken sandwiches, too.

- Remove the giblet packet and rinse the chicken. Rinse and save the neck, heart, and gizzard, discarding any other items in the packet, such as the liver. Place the chicken and giblets in a large pot. Add the onion and 5 cups of water. Cover with a lid. Bring to a boil, then simmer for approximately 60 minutes, until the chicken is very tender.

- Remove the chicken, giblets, and onion from the pot. Allow to cool. Remove the meat from the chicken and tear into bite-size pieces. Discard the giblets.

- To the broth in the pot, add the bouillon cubes, finely chopped onion, parsley, salt, and pepper. In a cup, mix the cornstarch with the $1/2$ cup of water and add to the broth. Stir well. Bring to a boil, and cook until thickened into a gravy. Add the chicken pieces to pot.

- Drop the biscuit batter by large spoonfuls on top of the gravy. Lower the heat to a simmer. Place a lid on the pot and cook until the biscuits are done, about 10 minutes.

- Place the biscuits in a bowl and top with the gravy.

■ Serves 8 ■

1 fryer chicken, approximately 3 $1/2$ pounds

1 medium-size onion, unpeeled and cut in half

5 cups water

Gravy:

2 chicken bouillon cubes

1 small onion, peeled and chopped finely

1 teaspoon dried parsley

1 teaspoon salt

$1/4$ teaspoon pepper

2 tablespoons cornstarch or potato starch

$1/2$ cup water

Dumplings:

1 recipe biscuits (pages 94–96), unbaked

Chicken Cacciatore

This "hunter's stew" is often made with bone-in chicken pieces, which can be awkward to eat. In this recipe, larger pieces of boneless chicken are used to retain the rugged feel of this dish. The sauce is bright and lively, with a flavor that stands up easily to gluten-free pasta, and serves a crowd!

- Wash the chicken and cut into large pieces. Set aside. Peel and slice the onion; slice the mushrooms. Set aside.

- Place the olive oil in a large skillet. Mince the garlic and add to the oil. Cook over high heat until the garlic is fragrant. Add the chicken pieces, onion, and mushrooms.

- Continue cooking over medium-high heat until the chicken is no longer pink on the outside, 7 to 10 minutes.

- Add the remaining ingredients and bring to a boil. Cover and simmer until the chicken is fully cooked and the flavors well blended, approximately 15 minutes.

■ Serves 8 ■

2 pounds boneless chicken breasts
1 large onion
8 ounces mushrooms
2 tablespoons olive oil
1 clove garlic
1 (14.5-ounce) can diced tomatoes
1 (6-ounce) can tomato paste
2 cups water
1 1/2 teaspoons dried oregano
1 1/2 teaspoons dried basil
1/2 teaspoon dried red pepper (optional)
1 1/2 teaspoons salt

NOTE: This great dish welcomes the addition of garden-fresh zucchini or tomatoes. Just add them shortly before serving, to retain some of their shape.

Chicken and Broccoli

So, you want to safely eat a little Americanized Chinese food? Chicken and Broccoli couldn't be easier. For those of us who need a little "heat" in our food, include a sprinkling of crushed red pepper flakes at the time the broccoli is added.

- Slice the chicken into thin strips. Fry in a large skillet with the oil over high heat until the chicken is cooked through, about 5 minutes.
- While the chicken is cooking, wash the broccoli and cut into smaller pieces for quicker cooking. I like to cut long, narrow trees, to thin the stems.
- As soon as the chicken is cooked, add the broccoli, garlic salt, and soy sauce. Cook until the broccoli is tender-crisp.
- If you like a thicker sauce, mix the water and cornstarch together in a cup. Pour into the sauce and stir quickly.
- Serve right away.

■ Serves 2 to 3 ■

2 small chicken breasts
   (12 ounces)
2 tablespoons oil
2 large bunches of broccoli
   crowns (12 ounces)
1/2 teaspoon garlic salt
2 tablespoons soy sauce
1/4 cup water (optional)
1/2 teaspoon cornstarch,
   potato starch, or rice flour
   (optional)

NOTE: If you do choose to venture into a Chinese restaurant, you'll want to bring your own soy sauce (such as La Choy brand) for cooking as well as condiment use, and ask that a freshly washed pan be used to prepare your dish.

Chicken Nuggets ▪ *Corn-based*

This chicken nuggets recipe is delicious. When fried, the batter stays more in shape with the chicken. It is just a tad lighter than the potato version.

- Cut the chicken into "nuggets"; set aside.
- Heat the oil, in a saucepan or dedicated fryer, to 370°F.
- In a small bowl, combine the batter ingredients. The batter will thicken if it is allowed to sit for a minute or two. Add the chicken.
- Remove the chicken pieces from the batter and place in the hot oil. Fry for 5 to 7 minutes, until the chicken is cooked through and no pink remains. The nuggets will be golden in color.

▪ Serves 4 ▪

2 boneless chicken breasts

Peanut or canola oil, for frying

Batter:

3/4 cup cornstarch, 95 grams

1/2 teaspoon salt

1/4 teaspoon pepper

1/4 teaspoon paprika

1/4 teaspoon baking powder

1/8 teaspoon baking soda

1/4 teaspoon xanthan gum

1/2 cup milk

Chicken Nuggets ▪ *Potato-based*

This potato version of chicken nuggets looks nearly identical to those famous ones your children might be missing. This recipe will serve a crowd of little ones.

- Cut the chicken into "nuggets"; set aside.
- Heat the oil, in a saucepan or dedicated fryer, to 370°F.
- In a small bowl, combine the batter ingredients. The batter will thicken if it is allowed to sit for a minute or two. Add the chicken.
- Remove the chicken pieces from the batter and place in the hot oil. Fry for 5 to 7 minutes, until the chicken is cooked through and no pink remains. The nuggets will be golden in color.

▪ Serves 4 ▪

2 boneless chicken breasts

Peanut or canola oil, for frying

Batter:

2/3 cup potato starch, 100 grams

1/2 teaspoon salt

1/4 teaspoon pepper

1/4 teaspoon paprika

1/4 teaspoon baking powder

1/8 teaspoon baking soda

1/8 teaspoon xanthan gum

1/2 cup milk

Chicken Salad

Chicken salad. It sounds like a healthy choice, doesn't it? Well, if you want sufficient dressing to truly moisten the chicken, it probably contains quite a bit of mayonnaise. This recipe is no exception. So, skip the chips and enjoy some fruit with this tasty offering. Or, substitute plain yogurt for up to half of the mayonnaise.

- Cut the chicken into small dice and place in a large bowl. Wash and finely dice the bell pepper and celery, and add to the bowl. Add the remaining ingredients and mix very well. Refrigerate to allow the flavors to blend.

■ Makes 4 cups ■

1 pound cooked boneless chicken

1/2 yellow or red bell pepper, seeded

2 celery stalks

2/3 cup mayonnaise

1 teaspoon curry powder and 1/2 teaspoon salt,

OR 1 1/2 teaspoons Creole seasoning

1 tablespoon lemon juice (brightens flavor, optional)

NOTE: No leftover cooked chicken? To quickly poach two small boneless chicken breasts, place the chicken in a small saucepan. Just barely cover with water, bring to a boil, and simmer for about 15 minutes.

Chicken Tikka

This is a terrific, simple main dish. Even if you've never tried Indian food, you're likely to enjoy it. I like to serve this dish with the Cucumber Salad (page 261). The creamy dressing cuts the heat of the spices. If you don't have all the spices listed, just use the ones you have. If you use bone-in chicken pieces, it is called Tandoori Chicken.

- Cut the chicken breasts into four or five pieces each. Combine the rest of the tikka ingredients in a large glass bowl or large resealable plastic bag. Mix well. Add the chicken pieces and allow to marinate in the refrigerator for at least 4 hours, or up to 24 hours.

- Preheat the oven to 450°F. Place the chicken pieces in a greased, shallow baking dish (do not allow the pieces to touch). Bake for 30 to 35 minutes, until nicely browned.

- Even better is to cook this dish outside on a very hot grill.

- To make the marinated onions, peel and slice the onion into a medium-size bowl. Cover with the vinegar, paprika, and salt. Mix well. The onions should be served crisp, so do not marinate for more than several hours. Serve alongside the chicken tikka.

■ Serves 4 ■

Chicken Tikka:
1 1/4–1 1/2 pounds boneless chicken breasts*
1 cup plain yogurt
1/4 cup lemon juice (juice from 1 lemon)
1 teaspoon salt
1 1/2 teaspoons paprika
1/2 teaspoon ground cardamom
1/4 teaspoon ground ginger
1/4 teaspoon crushed red pepper
1 teaspoon garlic powder
1/4 teaspoon pepper

Marinated onions (optional):
1 large onion
1/2 cup vinegar
1 teaspoon paprika
1 teaspoon salt

*Try to find chicken without added solutions for this recipe. We don't want juices to run over the pan or grill.

NOTE: This chicken dish is traditionally cooked in a tandoori oven. Unfortunately for the wheat-free diet, so is the wonderful Indian bread called naan. Do not consider this dish gluten-free if it is prepared in a tandoori oven, unless protected from cross-contamination.

Cornish Hens

Cornish hens are always appropriate for a special meal, yet I'm inclined to eat my serving with my fingers. For a no-fuss meal, make Oven-Roasted Potatoes (page 251) and one of the many salads in this book to go with them.

- Preheat the oven to 450°F. Wash the hens and pat dry with paper towels. Cut in half, straight down the center of the breast and through the back. Place on a baking sheet.

- Combine the salt, rosemary, thyme, and pepper in a small bowl. Crushing (bruising) the dry herbs will help bring out their flavor. Squeeze the lemon over both sides of the hens. Press the herb mixture onto both sides of the hens.

- Bake, breast side up, for 30 to 35 minutes, until the juices run clear and the skin is very crisp.

■ Serves 4 ■

2 Cornish hens
(approximately 3 1/2
pounds total)
1/2 teaspoon salt
1/2 teaspoon dried rosemary
1/2 teaspoon dried thyme
1/2 teaspoon pepper
Juice from 1 lemon

Curried Chicken

As with many recipes in this book, this entree is simple and tasty. The boneless chicken is stir-fried with onion with a light curry sauce prepared in the same pan.

- Cut the chicken breasts into bite-size pieces; set aside. Peel the onion and cut into bite-size pieces; set aside. Heat the oil and butter in a large skillet until quite hot. Add the chicken and cook until nearly done, approximately 10 minutes. Add the onion, peas, curry powder, and salt. Cook for just a moment, until the onion barely softens. Mix the cornstarch with the 1/2 cup of water in a cup, and pour into the pan. Stir gently but well until the sauce thickens.

■ Serves 4 ■

2 boneless chicken breasts
1 large onion
1 tablespoon oil
1 tablespoon butter
1/4 cup peas
1 tablespoon curry powder
1/2 teaspoon salt
1 tablespoon cornstarch,
potato starch, or rice flour
1/2 cup water

Fried Chicken ▪ *Corn-based*

Here are my test results for four Fried Chicken versions, with the major difference being the wash: Using a water dip before flouring doesn't do much for the chicken. No tester preferred the plain water version. Using buttermilk gives a deep mahogany color with an extra-crispy crust, but the flavor of the buttermilk version came in third. Using plain egg wash gives a mild, homey flavor with nice crust. And egg wash with extra salt and cayenne is like a mild Popeye's chicken. Among the testers, the flavor of the two egg washes tied for first. Yet, except for the water-only dredging liquid, all of these variations were really quite nice.

- Cut the chicken into desired pieces. Rinse and set aside.

- In a shallow bowl, combine the ingredients for the flour mixture. Mix well. Set aside. Choose the dredging liquid and place its ingredients in another shallow bowl. Mix very well.

- Heat the oil, in a skillet or dedicated deep fryer, to 370° to 375°F.

- Place a piece of chicken in the dredging liquid, then in the flour mixture.

- Place the coated chicken in the skillet or deep fryer. Repeat for the remaining pieces of chicken. Fry on each side in the skillet for approximately 15 minutes, or deep-fry for approximately 20 minutes.

- Drain on paper towels.

▪ Makes 8 pieces of chicken; serves 4 ▪

1 frying chicken
(2 1/2–3 pounds)

2 cups oil for a large skillet, or sufficient oil to fill a deep fryer

Flour mixture:

1 cup cornstarch, 125 grams

1 teaspoon salt

1/2–1 teaspoon pepper

1/2 teaspoon xanthan gum

1/2 teaspoon baking soda

Dredging liquid:

1 cup buttermilk

OR 2 eggs beaten with 1/2 cup water

OR 2 eggs beaten with 1/2 cup water, 1/2 teaspoon salt, and 1 teaspoon cayenne

■ ■ ■ ABOUT FRYING CHICKEN ■ ■ ■

After testing many, many versions of fried chicken, a few certainties emerged.

1. Dipping the chicken in a liquid before coating it with flour improves the flavor dramatically. However, water is not good for this purpose and, surprisingly often, buttermilk is not the first choice for flavor and texture. Egg wash is always good, and egg wash with spice is often best.
2. Xanthan gum should be included in the flour mixture.
3. The chicken loses its crispness if refrigerated overnight. Obviously, chicken must be refrigerated if there are leftovers, but fried chicken is much better eaten fresh. If necessary, reheat in a hot oven for 15 minutes, uncovered, to recrisp.

My opinion about soaking the chicken in buttermilk or a brine solution may differ from yours. Marinating originally served three purposes:

1. To tenderize the chicken. Nowadays, chicken is raised at a very fast pace, so old, tough birds are few and far between. Moreover, most chickens no longer wander about, toughening muscles, but are raised in tight pens offering little moving space. My conclusion is that most commercially raised battery chickens purchased today are young and tender.
2. To add moisture. Before coming to market, most poultry in the neighborhood grocery store will already have an "added solution," often of substantial percentage. Moisture is no longer an issue.
3. To add flavor. Think about it—Kentucky Fried Chicken and Popeye's are proof that flavored chicken is popular. My Roadside Chicken recipe is my personal proof that adding flavor makes a difference! (If you have time, marinating your chicken in the Roadside Chicken marinade before frying would be incredible!)

Based upon my analysis, flavor is the only reason to consider marinating chicken before frying. So, if you have the time and the inclination, chicken may be marinated in a mildly acidic solution full of spices for an hour or so before frying. Alternatively, additional spices may simply be added to the flour mixture or dipping liquid before frying.

Fried Chicken ▪ *Cornmeal-based*

When coating chicken with cornmeal, quite a bit adheres to the chicken. That is why the amount of cornmeal required seems so much greater than in the other fried chicken recipes. All versions of this cornmeal recipe had beautiful golden color, although the buttermilk version was a bit darker. As with all versions of the chicken, the water-only dredging liquid placed last. It wasn't bad, the others were just better. The buttermilk version was narrowly the favorite. It had the most predominant cornmeal crust. The egg-wash version was a little less imposing and placed third, with the egg wash with extra salt and cayenne placing second.

- Cut the chicken into desired pieces. Rinse and set aside.
- In a shallow bowl, combine the ingredients for the flour mixture. Mix well. Set aside. Choose a dredging liquid and place its ingredients in another shallow bowl. Mix very well.
- Heat the oil, in a skillet or dedicated deep fryer, to 370° to 375°F.
- Place a piece of chicken in the dredging liquid, then in the flour mixture.
- Place the coated chicken into the skillet or deep fryer. Repeat for the remaining pieces of chicken. Fry on each side in the skillet for approximately 15 minutes, or deep-fry for approximately 20 minutes.
- Drain on paper towels.

▪ Makes 8 pieces of chicken; serves 4 ▪

1 frying chicken
(2¹/2–3 pounds)

2 cups oil for a large skillet, or sufficient oil to fill a deep fryer

Flour mixture:

1¹/2 cups cornmeal, 140 grams

1¹/2 teaspoons salt

1 teaspoon pepper

³/4 teaspoon xanthan gum

³/4 teaspoon baking soda

Dredging liquid:

1 cup buttermilk

OR 2 eggs beaten with ¹/2 cup water

OR 2 eggs beaten with ¹/2 cup water, ¹/2 teaspoon salt, and 1 teaspoon cayenne

Fried Chicken ▪ *Potato-based*

Surprisingly, the results for the potato version of fried chicken were different from those of the corn version, although testers again thought using water as the dredging liquid was just okay. The buttermilk version gives a deep mahogany color with an almost-hard crust; however, the taste verges on oily. The plain egg wash version came in second. The egg wash with extra salt and cayenne was a clear first-place winner.

I feared that the potato starch might become gummy, as is sometimes the case when used alone. It was not at all. I would happily put either of the egg wash versions up against any traditional fried chicken.

- Cut the chicken into desired pieces. Rinse and set aside.
- In a shallow bowl, combine the ingredients for the flour mixture. Mix well. Set aside. Choose a dredging liquid and place its ingredients in another shallow bowl. Mix very well.
- Heat the oil, in a skillet or dedicated deep fryer, to 370° to 375°F.
- Place a piece of chicken in the dredging liquid, then in the flour mixture.
- Place the coated chicken in the skillet or deep fryer. Repeat for the remaining pieces of chicken. Fry on each side in the skillet for approximately 15 minutes, or deep-fry for approximately 20 minutes.
- Drain on paper towels.

▪ Makes 8 pieces of chicken; serves 4 ▪

1 frying chicken (2 1/2–3 pounds)

2 cups oil for a large skillet, or sufficient oil to fill a deep fryer

Flour mixture:

1 cup potato starch, 155 grams

1 1/2 teaspoons salt

1/2–1 teaspoon pepper

1/2 teaspoon xanthan gum

1/2 teaspoon baking soda

Dredging liquid:

1 cup buttermilk

OR 2 eggs beaten with 1/2 cup water

OR 2 eggs beaten with 1/2 cup water, 1/2 teaspoon salt, and 1 teaspoon cayenne

Fried Chicken ▪ *Rice-based*

When you coat the chicken with rice flour, it will seem like very little rice flour actually adheres to the chicken. But you actually end up with a nice coating.

For this recipe, testers thought using water was acceptable. The buttermilk version gives a deep mahogany color with a very nice, crispy crust. By a narrow margin, it ranked third. The plain egg wash version came in second by a narrow margin. The wash with extra salt and cayenne was again the favorite.

- Cut the chicken into desired pieces. Rinse and set aside.
- In a shallow bowl, combine the ingredients for the flour mixture. Mix well. Set aside. Choose a dredging liquid and place its ingredients in another shallow bowl. Mix very well.
- Heat the oil, in a skillet or dedicated deep fryer, to 370° to 375°F.
- Place a piece of chicken in the dredging liquid, then in the flour mixture.
- Place the coated chicken in the skillet or deep fryer. Repeat for the remaining pieces of chicken. Fry on each side in the skillet for approximately 15 minutes, or deep-fry for about 20 minutes.
- Drain on paper towels.

▪ Makes 8 pieces of chicken; serves 4 ▪

1 frying chicken
(2 1/2–3 pounds)

2 cups oil for a large skillet, or sufficient oil to fill a deep fryer

Flour mixture:

1 cup rice flour, 150 grams

1 teaspoon salt

1/2–1 teaspoon pepper

1/2 teaspoon xanthan gum

1/2 teaspoon baking soda

Dredging liquid:

1 cup buttermilk

OR 2 eggs beaten with 1/2 cup water

OR 2 eggs beaten with 1/2 cup water, 1/2 teaspoon salt, and 1 teaspoon cayenne

Orange Chicken ▪ *Corn-based*

To obtain that "Chinese-restaurant" quality for Orange Chicken, it is necessary to dip the chicken pieces in a light batter, then deep-fry them. If you want to avoid frying, you can enjoy a baked or broiled chicken with just the orange glaze. It is simple and good.

- Cut the chicken breasts into bite-size pieces. Set aside. In a small bowl, combine the batter ingredients. Stir well. Place the chicken pieces in the batter.

- Over medium heat, in a saucepan or dedicated fryer, heat the oil to 360°F. Remove the chicken from the batter and carefully place in the hot oil. Do not crowd the chicken pieces. (Multiple batches are to be expected.)

- Cook until the chicken is cooked through and no pink remains. This will take approximately 5 minutes, depending upon the size of pieces. The chicken will be golden in color. Place the cooked chicken on paper towels to soak up any excess oil.

- While the chicken is cooking, peel the onion and chop into bite-size pieces. Chop the bell pepper into bite-size pieces as well. Peel and finely chop the garlic. Set aside.

- Heat the olive oil in a large skillet. Add the garlic, onion, and bell pepper. Cook until the vegetables are tender-crisp.

- Prepare the glaze by combining the marmalade, water, and pepper flakes in a small saucepan. Heat to warm, stirring often. Coat the chicken well with glaze.

- Serve with plain rice, Fried Rice (page 245), or Asian Noodles (page 240).

▪ Serves 4 ▪

2 boneless chicken breasts

Peanut or canola oil, for frying

1 small onion

1/2 bell pepper, any color, seeded

1 clove garlic

1 tablespoon olive oil

Batter:

3/4 cup cornstarch, 95 grams

1/2 teaspoon salt

1/4 teaspoon baking powder

1/8 teaspoon baking soda

1/4 teaspoon xanthan gum

1/2 cup milk

Glaze:

1 1/2 cups orange marmalade

1 1/2 tablespoons water

1/4–1/2 teaspoon red pepper flakes

Orange Chicken ▪ *Potato-based*

The batter for this chicken is light, crispy, and oh so good. The glaze is so good our taste testers kept coming by looking for more (and they had just eaten lunch!).

- Cut the chicken breasts into bite-size pieces. Set aside. In a small bowl, combine the batter ingredients. Stir well. This batter will thicken a little if it sits for a minute or two. Place the chicken pieces in the batter.

- Over medium heat, in a saucepan or dedicated fryer, heat the oil to 360°F. Remove the chicken from the batter and carefully place in the hot oil. Do not crowd the chicken pieces. (Multiple batches are to be expected.)

- Cook until the chicken is cooked through and no pink remains. This will take approximately 5 minutes, depending upon size of pieces. The chicken will be golden in color. Place the cooked chicken on paper towels to soak up any excess oil.

- While the chicken is cooking, peel the onion and chop into bite-size pieces. Chop the bell pepper into bite-size pieces as well. Peel and finely chop the garlic. Set aside.

- Place the olive oil in a large skillet, Add the garlic, onion, and bell pepper. Cook until the vegetables are tender-crisp.

- Prepare the glaze by combining the marmalade, water, and pepper flakes in small saucepan. Heat to warm, stirring often. Coat the chicken well with the glaze.

- Serve with plain rice, Fried Rice (page 245), or Asian Noodles (page 240).

▪ Serves 4 ▪

2 boneless chicken breasts

Peanut or canola oil, for frying

1 small onion

1/2 bell pepper, any color, seeded

1 clove garlic

1 tablespoon olive oil

Batter:

2/3 cup potato starch, 100 grams

1/2 teaspoon salt

1/4 teaspoon baking powder

1/8 teaspoon baking soda

1/8 teaspoon xanthan gum

1/2 cup milk

Glaze:

1 1/2 cups orange marmalade

1 1/2 tablespoons water

1/4–1/2 teaspoon red pepper flakes

Poached Chicken

Are you hesitant about purchasing lunch meats? Or do you just want some moist, tender chicken for sandwiches or inclusion in a casserole? Either way, this poached chicken is a breeze.

2 boneless chicken breasts

- Place the chicken in a medium-size saucepan and add water to cover. Cover the pan and bring to a boil. Lower the heat and simmer for approximately 15 minutes, until the chicken is cooked through.

■ Serves 2 to 4 ■

NOTE: Absolutely nothing additional is needed! But if you don't want to leave well enough alone, you may wish to include a little acid (such as vinegar) and a few dried herbs to the water. Or, how about using white wine (and perhaps rosemary) in place of the water? Any change in the liquid will subtly flavor the chicken.

Poached Chicken on Greens with Orange Vinaigrette

I imagine you're feeling a little bored by the thought of poached chicken. In fact, it is actually a great way to have moist, tender chicken. This dish is ready in under thirty minutes and is perfect for when you don't want to spend much time in the kitchen.

- In a medium-size saucepan, place the chicken, onion slices, and orange juice. Cover and bring to boil. Lower the heat and simmer for approximately 15 minutes, until the chicken is cooked through. Discard the liquid.

- While the chicken cooks, wash and drain the greens. Using a potato peeler or zester, remove a small amount of zest from the oranges. Cut into long, thin strips. Add to the greens. Peel and section the oranges by peeling away entire top layer with a knife, exposing the orange flesh, without the protective membrane. Then use the knife to cut between the sections, again avoiding membranes as much as possible. Remove the seeds, if any, as well. Add the orange segments to the greens. Peel and thinly slice the onion, and add to the greens.

- In a small cup or jar, combine the orange juice, sugar, apple cider vinegar, oil, salt, and pepper. Set aside.

- Just before serving, slice the chicken, season with just a little salt, and place over the greens. Add the dressing.

■ Serves 3 ■

2 boneless chicken breasts
$1/2$ small onion, sliced thinly
2 cups orange juice

Salad:
5 ounces mixed baby greens or spinach
2 teaspoons orange zest
2 oranges
$1/2$ small onion
$1/4$ cup orange juice
2 teaspoons sugar
1 teaspoon apple cider vinegar
3 tablespoons oil (not olive oil)
$1/4$ teaspoon salt
$1/4$ teaspoon black pepper

Quesadillas

Now that you can make good Flour Tortillas (pages 103–105) anytime, how about making quesadillas, too?

- Prepare the Flour Tortillas and set aside. Poach the chicken breast (see page 185). Shred the chicken breast and cheese. Set aside.

- Prepare the sauce by combining the mayonnaise and hot sauce in a small bowl. Mix well. Set aside.

- Heat a large skillet over medium-high heat. Remove the heated skillet from the heat and spray with nonstick cooking spray. Return to the heat. Place one flour tortilla in the pan. Layer the shredded chicken, cheese, and jalapeño peppers on top of the tortilla. Spread a small amount of sauce on one side of a second tortilla. Place, sauce side down, on top of the first tortilla.

- Once the first tortilla is lightly browned, carefully flip to the other side. Continue cooking until the cheese has melted and the second tortilla is lightly browned.

- Remove from the pan. Repeat with the remaining ingredients.

■ Makes 3 ■

1 recipe Flour Tortillas (to yield ½ dozen)

1 chicken breast (approximately 8 ounces)

4 ounces cheddar or Monterey Jack cheese

Sliced jalapeño peppers, from a jar (optional)

Sauce:

2 tablespoons mayonnaise

1 teaspoon hot sauce

Really Good Turkey Burgers

Cooks often find themselves wishing their ground turkey dishes turn out as good as their ground beef dishes. That's kind of like making an apple pie with oranges and hoping it turns out. Instead, we need to embrace the differences and enjoy turkey for its own sake, not for substitution's sake.

- In a medium-size bowl, combine all the ingredients. Mix very well (hands are ideal for this job). Pat into four burgers; a 3-inch diameter is nice. Cook in a lightly greased pan or over a grill for 5 to 6 minutes on each side, until no pink remains and the center is fully cooked.

- Top with tomato or Swiss cheese, for a nice flavor combination.

■ Makes 4 large burgers ■

1 pound ground turkey

1/4 cup plain yogurt (sour cream does well, too)

1 teaspoon dried dill

1/4 teaspoon salt

1/2 small onion, peeled and chopped very finely

> **NOTE:** As with all poultry, ground turkey or chicken must be cooked to 185°F to safely destroy any potential salmonella lurking in the raw meat. Also, if using a charcoal grill, be sure the charcoal is gluten-free or your burgers are cooked in tightly sealed foil.

Roasted Chicken

A simple roasted chicken can sure be tasty. Combine a little lemon, a little rosemary, and the company of a special person, and you'll have a fine meal.

- Preheat the oven to 375°F.
- Rinse the chicken. Remove the giblets from the cavity and discard, or use for soup. Place the chicken in a small baking dish.
- Cut the lemon in half. Squeeze the juice over the chicken. Place the rosemary and squeezed lemon halves into the bird's cavity. Sprinkle the chicken with salt.
- Bake, uncovered, for 90 minutes, or until the skin is crisp and the juices are clear. The internal temperature should be 185°F.
- Pour 1 cup of the pan juices and salt into a small saucepan. Combine $1/4$ cup of water and the starch in a cup and stir well. Add to the juices and bring to a boil, then serve as gravy.

■ Serves 4 ■

1 whole chicken
  ($4^1/2$ pounds)

1 lemon

1 teaspoon dried rosemary

$1/8$ teaspoon salt

Gravy (optional):

1 cup reserved pan juices

$1/8$ teaspoon salt

$1/4$ cup water

2 teaspoons cornstarch or potato starch

Roasted Turkey

Have you always avoided hosting Thanksgiving because it means getting up early to put the turkey in the oven? Hate the idea of basting the turkey every fifteen minutes? And now, to assure a gluten-free meal, you insist on preparing the entire Thanksgiving dinner? Here's my easy, no-fuss, moist turkey to get you started.

1 turkey (10 pounds)

1 cup water

1 teaspoon dried sage (several fresh sprigs would be nice, too)

1/4 teaspoon salt

- Preheat the oven to 375°F. Open the turkey, remove the giblets, and discard any gravy packets and bits of liver. Rinse the turkey and the giblets.

- Place the neck, heart, and gizzard in the bottom of a roasting pan. Add the water. Put in a rack (if you have one) to hold the turkey. Place the sage inside the main cavity of the turkey and add the bird to the pan. Sprinkle salt over the turkey. Cover tightly with a lid or foil.

- Bake for approximately 1 hour and 45 minutes, to an internal temperature of 175° to 180°F. Remove the lid or foil. Continue baking for an additional 20 minutes, to brown the skin nicely. Remove from the oven once the thickest part of the breast measures 185°F internally. Transfer to a serving platter. Strain and reserve the broth for gravy, if desired.

■ Makes about 12 servings ■

> NOTE: Please do not rely on pop-up timers or baking schedule when roasting a turkey. Each bird is a little different, even when the same weight. The juices should run clear when pierced near the thigh. The temperature of the breast should be 185°F internally. Do not undercook, as salmonella proliferates at lower temperatures.

Sesame Chicken Stir-Fry with Bok Choy

Here's a light, refreshing dinner choice! Be careful not to overcook the bok choy! The flavor is best when the cabbage has a bit of crispness. Be sure to use baby, not mature, bok choy.

- Slice the chicken into bite-size pieces. I like to make narrow little strips. Stir-fry in a skillet with the sesame oil until the chicken is cooked through, approximately 10 minutes.

- Add the sesame seeds, bok choy, garlic salt, and soy sauce. Continue to stir-fry until the bok choy just begins to wilt.

- Serve immediately.

■ Serves 3 to 4 ■

2 chicken breasts (12 ounces)

2 tablespoons sesame oil (no substitute)

1 1/2 tablespoons sesame seeds

2 small heads baby bok choy (9 ounces)

Scant 1/2 teaspoon garlic salt

1 tablespoon soy sauce

Spicy Roadside Chicken

I have shamelessly taken the great flavor of "roadside barbecue" handed down by my sister and kicked it up by a few degrees. I prefer to cook this chicken on the grill, but a very hot oven will do. Dried herbs work well in place of poultry seasoning. Please don't fret over the large amount of spice and salt in the recipe. Most of it stays in the bowl with the other marinade ingredients.

- Combine all the ingredients, except the chicken, in a large plastic container or plastic bag. Add the chicken and toss to coat well. Allow to marinate for at least 1 hour in the refrigerator. Several hours is even better.

- Remove the chicken from the marinade and place over a hot grill or in a 400°F oven for approximately 45 minutes. Discard the marinade. The skin should be crisp and no pink should remain.

■ Makes 8 pieces ■

$^3/_4$ cup apple cider vinegar

$^1/_2$ cup oil

1 tablespoon poultry seasoning

OR 1 teaspoon dried oregano, 1 teaspoon dried rosemary, and 1 teaspoon dried tarragon

1 tablespoon black pepper

1 tablespoon cayenne

1 tablespoon paprika

1$^1/_2$ tablespoons salt

1 frying chicken, cut up (4–4$^1/_2$ pounds)

> **NOTE:** Distilled vinegar has been approved for the celiac diet. This is one controversy that seems to finally be history. However, be watchful for "flavored" or malt vinegars. You won't come across them often, but you must be cautious in reading the ingredient list. And, very important, discard any marinade used on raw chicken. Do not use on finished chicken, as salmonella may be present from the uncooked poultry. If you wish to use a marinade as a finishing baste or sauce, reserve some in a separate container before marinating the chicken, discard the liquid the chicken was marinated in, and use a clean brush or spoon to place the reserved liquid on the cooked chicken.

Teriyaki Chicken

This is another family favorite. The chicken cooks in just 5 to 10 minutes outside on a grill. Try not to overcook the chicken or it will be dry.

- Combine all the sauce ingredients in a small saucepan. Bring to a boil. Set aside.

- If using chicken breasts, slice in half to make thin cutlets. Salt and pepper the cutlets. Cook outside on a hot grill, basting with the sauce, for 5 to 10 minutes, until the chicken is cooked through.

- Alternatively, place the oil and cutlets in a large skillet, over high heat. Cook for approximately 5 minutes on each side, to cook the chicken through. The chicken should be lightly browned and no pink should remain in the center of the cutlets. Remove from the pan and place on a baking sheet. Pour approximately $1/2$ tablespoon of the sauce over each cutlet. Place under the broiler and cook until the sauce begins to bubble, just a minute or two.

- Serve hot.

■ Serves 4 ■

1 pound chicken cutlets or boneless breasts

$1/4$ teaspoon salt

Pinch of black pepper

2 tablespoons oil

Sauce:

$2/3$ cup pineapple juice

$1/3$ cup molasses or dark honey

1 teaspoon apple cider vinegar

$1 1/2$ teaspoons cornstarch or potato starch

Turkey Chili

This recipe has lots of straight-up chili flavor, just like the beef version, but the heat plays off the sweetness of the turkey and sweet potato.

- Peel and the onion and sweet potato and cut into medium dice. Place the onion and oil in a large pot. Set the sweet potatoes aside. Wash, seed, and dice the yellow bell pepper, and set aside.
- Add the turkey to the pot. Cook over medium heat until cooked through, about 5 minutes. Add the remaining ingredients. Bring to a boil. Simmer for 15 to 20 minutes, for flavors to blend.

■ Serves 8 ■

1 large onion

1 large sweet potato (about 9 ounces)

2 tablespoons oil

1 yellow bell pepper

20 ounces ground turkey

1 (15.5-ounce) can small red beans

1 (14.5-ounce) can diced tomatoes

3 cups water

$1/2$ cup tomato paste

1 teaspoon dried cilantro (optional)

$1 1/2$ tablespoons chili powder

$1/2$ teaspoon cumin

1 teaspoon salt

Turkey Cutlets (Slices) with Whole Cranberry Glaze

Are you stuck this holiday season? You want to eat safe, maybe even have a few friends over? This dish is incredibly easy yet truly delicious. The cranberry glaze makes it special. Garnish each serving with a sprig of a fresh herb if you have it.

1 tablespoon oil

2 pounds turkey cutlets (approximately 12 thin slices)

1–2 tablespoons water, as needed

Glaze:

1 cup whole cranberry sauce (canned is fine)

1/2 cup dry white wine

- Place the oil and turkey cutlets in a large pan, over medium heat, and fry until the turkey is browned on both sides. If the pan becomes dry, add 1 or 2 tablespoons of water. Cover with a lid and lower the heat. Continue cooking until the cutlets are cooked through. (Note, most cutlets are very thinly sliced and will take 5 to 10 minutes to cook through.) Place on a serving platter.

- In a small saucepan, stir the cranberry sauce and wine until blended. Heat until just warm. Serve over the turkey.

■ Serves 6 ■

Turkey Gravy from Reserved Broth

Nothing compares to homemade gravy. Enjoy!

- Place the pan juices, salt, and pepper in a medium-size saucepan. Combine the water and cornstarch. Add to the pan juices. Bring to a boil and cook until thickened. Serve hot.

■ Makes 4 cups ■

Pan juices reserved from Roasted Turkey (page 190), measured

1 teaspoon salt

$1/4$ teaspoon black pepper

Additional water to make 4 cups (with the pan juices)

6 tablespoons cornstarch or potato starch

NOTE: The biggest disadvantage to using cornstarch or potato starch in gravies is that they do not reheat well. Our initial tries at gravies often turned into one large glop after refrigeration. The secret to reheating our gluten-free gravies is to add a little water and blend well when reheating. I personally use a handheld blender, but a traditional blender or a whisk attached to a strong arm can also do the job.

11

BEEF, PORK, AND LAMB

This chapter offers many widely enjoyed beef and pork dishes.

You will find recipes for tender Baby Ribs, delicious steaks, and tasty Sloppy Joes. I have two favorite recipes in this chapter: Beef Kabobs, which are exceptionally good, and Bulgogi, a Korean beef dish.

As with most recipes in this book, none is difficult. In some instances I have recommended certain tender cuts of beef to ensure tender results. It is the tenderness of the cut of beef or pork that makes quick recipes a success.

■ ■ ■

Baby Ribs

There are two secrets to good ribs: time and the removal of the sinew—the tough, stringy membrane on the undercurve of the ribs. If you heed these secrets, you'll have very tasty ribs. Use baby back ribs or spareribs; both are good.

5 pounds pork spareribs

1 1/2 cups barbecue sauce

3/4 cup orange juice

- Preheat the oven to 350°F.

- Remove the sinew from the undercurve of the ribs where the bones are just visible. I carefully slide a paring knife under this tough, white membrane and slowly loosen it by cutting between it and the bone. If you're lucky, you can begin to pull it off in large pieces. If not, just slowly take it off.

- Place the ribs on a large, rimmed cookie sheet or a large baking pan. Mix the barbecue sauce with the orange juice. Spread 3/4 cup of this over the ribs. Cover the pan tightly with foil. Bake for 1 1/2 to 2 hours, until very tender. Remove the foil. Pour off and discard any pan juices.

- Raise the oven temperature to 450°F or heat a barbecue grill to high. Finish the ribs by spreading part of the remaining sauce over them and cooking for an additional 15 minutes. The ribs should crisp on the outside.

- Sauce not used for cooking (discard any sauce that has already been touched by the same utensil as used on the uncooked ribs up to this point) may be used for a condiment.

■ Serves 10 to 15 ■

> **NOTE:** This recipe says that it serves 10 to 15, but ribs are not usually served in "reasonable" portion size. You really must decide how "unreasonable" your portions will be for this dish. As cooking ribs takes some time and effort, I suggest you make extra to put in your freezer for a later time.

Barbecued Pork for Sandwiches

There's only one way to make great barbecued pork for sandwiches—time. The pork must be cooked until it nearly falls apart. Please note that pork tenderloin is too lean for this dish.

- Preheat the oven to 350°F.
- Place the pork roast and water in a baking pan and cover tightly. If you have no lid, foil will do. Roast until the pork is incredibly tender, approximately 3 hours. (You could also cook the pork in a Crock Pot for 8 to 10 hours on low or 4 to 6 hours on high.)
- Allow the pork to cool sufficiently to handle. Remove and discard the bone (if any) and noticeable fat. Using your hands or a fork, tear the pork into small strips. Add 1 1/2 cups of the barbecue sauce, 1/2 cup of the pan juices, and 1/2 teaspoon salt. Toss well to coat.
- Serve additional barbecue sauce on side, as desired.

■ Makes enough filling for 10 sandwiches ■

ALTERNATIVE: For something different, try the Spicy Roadside Chicken Marinade/Sauce on your pork. The recipe is on page 192.

1 pork roast
(about 3 pounds)
1/4 cup water
1 1/2 cups barbecue sauce
1/2 cup pan juices (reserved from roasting pork)
1/2 teaspoon salt

NOTE: I'm not going to suggest you suffer with making your own barbecue sauce, when several major manufacturers do a fine job of it and have a policy of clearly presenting any gluten ingredients on their labels. Kraft is one such manufacturer. I find their spicy honey barbecue sauce very nice.

Beef and Broccoli Stir-Fry

If you're cooking dinner for someone who is hesitant to try Chinese food, this is a good choice.

- Cut the sirloin steak at a 45-degree angle into very, very thin slices. Set aside. Over high heat, heat the oil in a skillet. Once the oil is quite hot, add the steak slices. Immediately add the soy sauce, black pepper, garlic salt, and red pepper flakes. Cook through. This should take no more than 5 minutes.
- While the beef cooks (or before starting cooking), place the broccoli in a microwave-safe bowl. Cover and cook on high for 3 minutes.
- Add the broccoli and onion to the skillet. Cook for just a minute or so. In a small cup, stir together the water and starch. Pour into the pan and toss well to thicken and make a light sauce.
- Serve with rice.

■ Serves 4 ■

1 pound sirloin steak, fat trimmed

2 tablespoons oil

2 tablespoons soy sauce

1/2 teaspoon black pepper

1 teaspoon garlic salt

Pinch of red pepper flakes (optional)

1 pound broccoli crowns, cut into large bite-size pieces, thick stems discarded

1/2 medium-size onion, sliced

1 cup water

2 tablespoons cornstarch or potato starch

Beef Kabobs

Tired of burgers on the grill? How about some pretty kabobs? Using small wooden skewers and beautiful fresh vegetables makes a nice presentation. The simple marinades highlight the flavors of the meat and vegetables. Try not to worry too much about the salt and fat; a lot of the marinade will remain in the bowls. This recipe is one of my favorites.

- Soak twelve to fifteen wooden skewers in water for about 1 hour before you are ready to grill. This will help to prevent them from burning while on the grill or under the broiler.

- Trim the steak of extra fat. Cut into large bite-size chunks. Place in a medium-size bowl. Add the meat marinade ingredients and toss well to coat. Set aside.

- Wash the vegetables and cut into bite-size chunks. Place in a large bowl. Add the vegetable marinade ingredients and toss well to coat. Set aside. Allow the meat and vegetables to marinate for 30 minutes, if time permits.

- Place the meat and vegetables on the skewers in random fashion. Do not crowd the items on the skewers, or longer cooking time will be required.

- Cook on a hot grill or under a hot broiler for approximately 5 minutes. The meat is best a little rare. Try to turn no more than once.

- Serve hot.

■ Serves 4 to 5 ■

1 loin top sirloin steak (1–1 1/4 pounds)

8 cherry tomatoes

1 sweet onion

1 sweet red pepper

1 small zucchini

8 small whole mushrooms

Meat marinade:

2 tablespoons olive oil

1/2 teaspoon black pepper

1/2 teaspoon garlic salt

Vegetable marinade:

2 tablespoons olive oil

1/2 teaspoon garlic salt

Beef Tips with Mushroom Sauce

Because this is a quick-to-prepare meal, you need to have a fairly tender cut of meat. If you can't locate a loin sirloin steak, substitute a better, not lesser cut. If you do not cook with wine, substitute water, but add a generous amount of freshly ground pepper before serving.

- Remove the excess fat from the steak. Cut into small bite-size pieces. Set aside. Wash and slice the mushrooms. Set aside.
- Place the butter and oil in a large skillet. Over medium-high heat, add the steak, mushrooms, and salt. Stir-fry until the meat is nearly done and the mushrooms are soft, approximately 5 minutes. Add the parsley.
- In a separate cup or bowl, combine the wine, water, and starch. Mix well to dissolve. Add to the pan. Continue cooking until the mixture thickens.
- Serve hot with rice or noodles.

■ Serves 2 ■

1 boneless steak
  ($1/2$–$3/4$ pound)
1 tablespoon butter
1 tablespoon oil
4 ounces mushrooms
$1/2$ teaspoon salt
Pinch of parsley
$1/2$ cup white wine
$1/4$ cup water
1 tablespoon cornstarch or potato starch

> NOTE: I have intentionally kept serving size to just two for this recipe, as gravies made with cornstarch or potato starch are difficult to reheat, especially if meat or vegetables are in the gravy. This recipe can be doubled with no adverse effects, just decrease the amount of butter and oil a little.

Beef Tips with Onion

This recipe takes just minutes to prepare and produces a very tasty dish.

- Remove the excess fat from the steak. Cut into small bite-size pieces. Set aside. Peel and slice the onion. Set aside.
- Place the butter and oil in a large skillet. Over medium-high heat, add the steak, onions, and soy sauce. Stir-fry until the meat is nearly done and the onions are soft, approximately 5 minutes.
- In a separate cup or bowl, combine the water and starch. Mix well to dissolve. Add to the pan. Continue cooking until the mixture thickens.
- Serve hot with rice or noodles.

■ Serves 2 ■

1 boneless loin, sirloin steak ($1/2$–$3/4$ pounds)

1 medium-size onion

1 tablespoon butter

1 tablespoon oil

2 tablespoons soy sauce

$1/2$ cup water

1 tablespoon cornstarch or potato starch

Bulgogi

Bulgogi is a slightly sweet Korean barbecue dish. Many people think they don't like Korean food because of that nation's famous, incredibly hot, pickled cabbage dish called kimchi—which is definitely an acquired taste. However, many Korean dishes are mild and quite appetizing. This is one of them.

- Cut the steak, across the grain, into very, very thin strips. Place in a large resealable plastic bag or large glass bowl. Add the marinade ingredients. Allow to marinate in the refrigerator for at least 4 hours, or overnight.
- Before cooking, slice the onion into narrow, wedgelike pieces. Heat a large skillet over high heat with the oil. Discard the marinade from the beef. Add the beef and onions to the pan. Stir-fry over high heat until the beef is cooked through, about 5 minutes. Garnish with spring onions.

■ Serves 4 ■

1 pound round steak

1 large onion

2 tablespoons oil

Spring onions, for garnish

Marinade:

1 small onion, sliced

$1/4$ cup soy sauce

$1/4$ cup water

1 teaspoon garlic salt

2 tablespoons oil

$1/3$ cup sugar

Chicken-Fried Steak

Every ounce of my dietary-conscious self says this recipe shouldn't be in the book. However, since you've promised (right?) to make it only on special occasions, I've included it here!

- Cut the steak into four pieces. (If the steak is especially thick, slice in half first.) Pound each piece as thinly as possible, no more than ¼-inch thickness. Place the remaining ingredients on a plate and mix well. Coat each piece of steak very well. Retain the excess flour mixture.

- Cook quickly in oil over high heat in a pan that is not nonstick. (We want a few tasty particles to stick to the pan for flavor.) Remove the meat and set aside. Drain off and discard the excess oil.

- In a cup, combine the milk and the reserved flour mixture. Mix well. Add to the hot pan. Add the salt and black pepper. Stir well to make "milk" gravy. Pour over top of the steak and serve.

■ Serves 4 ■

1 pound round steak

¼ cup oil, for frying

Flour Mixture:

1 cup cornstarch or potato starch

¾ teaspoon salt

¾ teaspoon pepper

1 teaspoon paprika

½ teaspoon xanthan gum

Gravy:

1 cup milk

2 teaspoons reserved flour mixture

½ teaspoon salt

½ teaspoon black pepper

NOTE: Your neighborhood meat market may have a meat tenderizer (the machine, not the spice). It takes less than a minute to tenderize with the machine, but quite a bit longer at home. Also note, potato starch makes the nicest coating on the steak.

Chili for Chili Dogs

My dad was an incredible guy who liked plain, good food. He, my sister, and I all shared his cravings for chili dogs. If you enjoy this all-American treat, try one with a bun shaped from the roll recipe in this book.

- In a small saucepan over medium heat, brown the ground beef and onion. Once cooked through (no pink remaining), add all the other ingredients and stir well. Bring to a boil, then simmer for about 10 minutes. This gives time for the flavors to soften and the sauce to thicken.

1/2 pound ground beef

1/2 small onion, peeled and chopped finely

3 tablespoons tomato paste

3/4 cup water

2 teaspoons chili powder

1/4 teaspoon black pepper

3/4 teaspoon salt

■ Tops 6 to 8 hot dogs ■

NOTE: If you want to try a hot dog my way, add a little sauerkraut, this chili topping, spicy mustard, and a little chopped onion. Yum.

Especially Good Hamburgers

Are your burgers dried-out hockey pucks? We can learn tricks from the poultry industry. They add a "solution" to their chickens and turkeys to help make them tender and juicy. It's also a low-cost way to increase profits per pound, but these minor additions do dramatically increase the juiciness and flavor of any burger, even if cooked well done.

1 pound lean ground beef

1/2 teaspoon salt

1/4 cup apple juice or water

- Combine all the ingredients in a bowl and allow to sit for 15 minutes. Pat the meat into four 3 1/2-inch-diameter patties. Cook over medium heat for up to 3 1/2 minutes per side (for well done). Ignore the urge to press down on the burgers when you flip them.

■ Serves 4 ■

NOTE: Burgers can become really special food if you're willing to experiment: 1/4 cup of red or white wine makes your burger taste like a marinated steak on a bun. Topped with a slice of Swiss or creamy Camembert is just delicious.

Fajitas

Fajitas are a quick, easy meal. Served with a little chopped avocado and salsa, they are delicious.

- Slice the steak into very, very, thin strips. Sprinkle the garlic salt over the strips and set aside. Heat the oil in a skillet over high heat. Add the steak and cook until no pink remains, 3 to 5 minutes.

- While the steak is cooking, peel and slice the peppers and onion into long strips. Cut the tomatoes into narrow wedges. Once the steak is cooked, remove the meat from the pan and discard any juices that remain in the pan.

- Add the peppers and onion to the pan. Cook over high heat until crisp-tender, 2 to 3 minutes. Return the steak to the pan. Add the tomato wedges and heat through.

- Serve right away.

■ Serves 6 ■

1 ½ pounds sirloin steak
1 teaspoon garlic salt
2 tablespoons oil
2 bell peppers (yellow, red, or orange preferred), seeded
1 medium-size onion
2 large tomatoes

Fillet Steak

This is our family's all-time favorite steak. Fillet can be expensive, but it is boneless and there is very little waste. Serving size is a little smaller than other steaks as well, thereby making this a still-affordable special meal.

- Place all the ingredients in a medium-size bowl. Mix well.

- Heat a broiler or grill to high heat. Cook the steaks from 3 to 5 minutes on each side to desired doneness. These steaks are especially good cooked rare.

■ Serves 4 ■

4 (4-ounce) fillet steaks
1 tablespoon soy sauce
½ teaspoon freshly ground black pepper
½ teaspoon garlic salt

Goulash

This hearty recipe makes quick work of this slow-cooked favorite. The flavors will be a little brighter than its long-cooked counterpart.

- Remove and discard any excess fat from the steak. Cut into large bite-size pieces. Set aside. Peel the onion and cut into large dice. Remove the stem and seeds from the bell pepper. Cut into large dice. Set aside.

- Place the oil, steak, onion, and bell pepper in a large skillet, over medium-high heat. Stir-fry until the meat is nearly browned on all sides and the onion begins to wilt.

- Add the remaining ingredients. Bring to a boil. Lower the heat to a slow boil for an additional 15 to 20 minutes, until the sauce is nicely thickened.

- Serve hot with noodles or rice.

■ Serves 8 ■

1 loin top sirloin steak
  (1 1/4–1 1/2 pounds)

1 large sweet onion

1 large red or yellow bell
  pepper

2 tablespoons olive oil

2 (14.5-ounce) cans diced
  tomatoes

1 1/2 cups water

1/4 cup tomato paste

2 tablespoons paprika

1/2 teaspoon black pepper

2 beef bouillon cubes

2 teaspoons dried parsley

1 teaspoon salt

1/4 teaspoon crushed red
  pepper (optional)

Gyros

A good gyro is a real treat. Tender leg of lamb, cooked rare, is a nice substitute for the traditional spit of pressed ground lamb or beef. The cumin is especially nice when added to the yogurt sauce. Chicken breast is a good substitute if your grocer doesn't carry a boneless leg of lamb. You may also substitute a combination of ground lamb and ground beef (mixed together) and shaped into small patties for the leg of lamb.

- Prepare the yogurt sauce first by combining all its ingredients. Set aside for the flavors to blend.

- Wash and thinly slice the lettuce; set aside. Wash and dice the tomatoes; set aside. Peel and slice the onions; set aside. Very thinly slice the lamb; set aside. Peel and mince the garlic; set aside.

- Place the olive oil in a large skillet over high heat. Add the garlic and begin cooking until fragrant. Add the lamb, salt, pepper, and cumin. Cook until the lamb has nicely browned but is still a little pink in the middle, approximately 3 minutes. Overcooking makes for tough lamb. Remove from the pan and set aside.

- Add an additional $1/2$ tablespoon of olive oil to the pan. Add the onion and fry until heated through but still crisp. Remove from the pan.

- Assemble the gyros by placing the lettuce, tomato, fried onion, and lamb on top of the flatbread. Top with crumbled feta cheese and yogurt sauce, as desired. Fold the sandwich in half and enjoy.

■ Makes 4 large sandwiches ■

Yogurt sauce:
1 cup plain yogurt

Juice from 1 lemon

$1/4$ teaspoon ground cumin (optional)

$1/2$ cucumber, seeded and diced

$1/4$ teaspoon salt

Gyro:
$1/2$ small head lettuce

2 medium-size tomatoes

1 onion

1 pound boneless lamb

1 clove garlic

1 tablespoon olive oil

$1/4$ teaspoon salt

$1/4$ teaspoon black pepper

$1/4$ teaspoon ground cumin (optional)

Gluten-free flatbread

3 ounces feta cheese, crumbled

Leg of Lamb

This simple roasted leg of lamb should be prepared rare. Even with a moist-roasting technique, it becomes less desirable when more thoroughly cooked. Wrapped in foil, it can be put in the oven and forgotten until it's time to serve. The use of rosemary is very traditional, but I prefer using the ground cumin. The juices using the cumin are especially good.

1 boneless leg of lamb (approximately 2 pounds)

1 teaspoon garlic salt

1 teaspoon dried rosemary or ground cumin

- Preheat the oven to 350°F.
- Place the lamb on large sheet of aluminum foil. Sprinkle liberally with the garlic salt and rosemary. Wrap the foil around the lamb and fold the edges to seal all the openings.
- Roast for approximately 1 hour to an internal temperature of 140°F. The lamb will be rare. Remove from the foil. Place the pan juices in a small saucepan and cook over high heat to reduce by about half.
- Slice the lamb and pour the pan juices over it just before serving.

■ Serves 6 to 8 ■

Mini Meat Loaves

There must be a million versions of meat loaf. The great thing about making mini meat loaves is the leftovers. Stored in your freezer, these meat loaves will rescue you when you go out to a restaurant with your friends and realize there is nothing safe on the menu (except for the house salad, which the preparer forgot to leave the croutons off!). So, enjoy the company of your friends while sipping something gluten-free, then come home, pull these minis out of the freezer, and microwave them.

- Preheat the oven to 375°F.

- Place the ground chuck in large bowl. Peel and dice the onion, and add to the bowl. Remove the top and seeds from the green bell pepper; cut it into small dice and add to the bowl. Add the remaining ingredients. Mix well; hands are exceptional for this job.

- Divide into four small loaves. Place in a small baking pan. Bake for 40 to 45 minutes. The meat loaf should be cooked through, with no pink remaining.

■ Serves 4 ■

1 pound ground chuck

1 small onion

1/2 small green bell pepper

1 egg

1/2 cup ketchup

1/2 teaspoon salt

1/4 teaspoon pepper

1 1/2 teaspoons cornstarch or potato starch

New York Strip Steak

I'm told by inside sources (okay, my sister begged it from an insider at a great steakhouse) that the best steaks are made with McCormick Grill Mates Montreal Steak Seasoning. You can substitute 1/4 teaspoon of salt and 1/4 teaspoon of pepper for the seasoning, if necessary. This steak would be great prepared on the grill, as well.

2 New York strip steaks (approximately 1 pound total)

3/4 teaspoon McCormick Montreal Steak Seasoning or 1/4 teaspoon salt and 1/4 teaspoon pepper

1 tablespoon oil

- Season the steaks on both sides with seasoning. Press the spices into the meat. Set aside.

- Place a medium-size skillet (do not use a nonstick pan) over medium heat. Once very hot, add the oil and tilt the pan to coat. Quickly add the steaks and cook for approximately 3 minutes on the first side. Turn the steaks and cook for another 3 minutes. This cooking time is for medium-rare.

■ Serves 2 ■

> **NOTE:** For those of us who can't leave well enough alone, top the steaks with the Caramelized Onions on page 441.

Orange Beef

Summer interns frequented our home in the early 1990s. One special intern, now an administrative law judge, prepared this dish for our young family. A nonstick skillet really saves cleanup time for this dish.

- Trim the sirloin steak of any excess fat. Cut the steak into very, very thin slices. Set aside. Peel and finely dice the garlic; set aside. Peel and slice the onion; set aside.

- Place the oil and garlic in a large skillet, over high heat. Add the beef and cook until almost all the pink is gone, 3 to 4 minutes. Add the remaining ingredients except the cornstarch and water. Stir for 1 more minute.

- Keep the pan over high heat. Combine the starch and water in a cup, and add to the pan. Stir until the sauce thickens.

- Serve hot.

■ Serves 4 ■

1 pound sirloin steak

1 clove garlic

1 small onion

1 tablespoon oil

1/2 cup orange marmalade

Pinch of red pepper flakes (optional)

1/4 teaspoon salt

1 tablespoon cornstarch or potato starch

2 tablespoons water

NOTE: Using a potato peeler to make a nice ribbon of orange zest creates a pretty garnish.

"Philly" Cheesesteak

Are you a cheesesteak purist? I was until I had a cheesesteak at the Old Pike Inn in our hometown. Unfortunately, that restaurant has closed. But their cheesesteak and chicken wings are vivid in my memory and have found their way to these pages. This recipe makes filling for four hearty sandwiches.

- Cut the sirloin steak at 45-degree angle into very, very thin slices. Set aside. Heat the oil in the pan over high heat. Once the pan is very hot, add the steak slices. Immediately add the soy sauce and black pepper. Cook through. Remove from the pan.

- Add the onion, bell pepper, mushrooms, and garlic salt to the pan. Lower the heat to medium. Sauté until all the vegetables are wilted and tender. Layer the cheese over the vegetables and allow it to melt. Turn off the heat.

- Divide the meat among the four rolls and top with the vegetables and melted cheese. Add mayo and/or hot hoagie spread to the rolls as desired.

■ Serves 4 ■

1 pound sirloin steak, fat trimmed

1 tablespoon oil

1 tablespoon soy sauce

1/2 teaspoon black pepper

1 medium-size onion, sliced

1 red or yellow bell pepper, seeded and sliced

4–5 ounces white mushrooms, sliced

1/4 teaspoon garlic salt

8 thin slices provolone cheese

4 gluten-free sub rolls

Mayonnaise

Hot hoagie spread

Pork Chops Smothered with Apples and Onion

Cameo and Gala apples are bright and sweet tasting and hold their shape when cooked. If you cannot find Cameo or Gala apples, look for another with similar characteristics. I do not recommend apples that fall apart during cooking, such as Golden Delicious or Fuji.

- Place the oil in a large skillet. Over medium-high heat, pan-fry the chops until browned on both sides, approximately 1 minute per side.

- Peel and slice the onion and apples. Remove the chops from the pan. Add the onion, apples, and salt. Cook until the onions begin to soften and are fragrant. Add 1 tablespoon of the brown sugar. Stir to dissolve.

- Lower the heat to medium-low and place the chops back in the pan. Cover and continue cooking until the chops are done, approximately 5 minutes. Place the chops on a serving plate.

- Raise the heat back to high. Add to the pan the remaining 1 tablespoon of brown sugar and the butter. Cook until dissolved. The sauce will thicken slightly.

- Place the apple mixture over the chops and sprinkle generously with fresh pepper.

- Serve hot.

■ Serves 4 ■

2 tablespoons oil

4 thinly sliced pork chops
(1 1/4–1 1/2 pounds)

1 large onion

2 Cameo or Gala apples

1/4 teaspoon salt

2 tablespoons brown sugar

1 tablespoon butter

Freshly ground black pepper

Pork Roast with Gravy

Believe it or not, it is important to use a pork roast that is not a tenderloin or center-cut pork roast. Otherwise, the flavor is just not there. This recipe showcases the essence of a good pork roast. It couldn't be simpler or better tasting.

- Preheat the oven to 350°F.
- Season the outside of the pork with the salt.
- Place the water and then the pork roast in an oven-safe casserole and cover with a lid or foil. Roast, covered, for 2 hours, then remove the covering and continue to roast until the meat reaches an internal temperature of 170°F, approximately 1 hour.
- Place the pan juices into large measuring cup and add water to make $1\frac{1}{2}$ cups. In a separate cup, combine the water and cornstarch. Add the salt and the cornstarch mixture to the pan juices. Microwave on high for 2 to 3 minutes, until nicely thickened. Add freshly ground pepper to taste.
- Serve the gravy alongside the roast, over noodles or rice.

■ Serves 8 ■

1 bone-in pork shoulder or butt roast (4–5 pounds)
$\frac{1}{4}$ teaspoon salt
$\frac{1}{4}$ cup water

Gravy:

Reserved pan juices, plus water to make $1\frac{1}{4}$ cups
$\frac{1}{4}$ teaspoon salt
$1\frac{1}{2}$ tablespoons cornstarch or potato starch
Freshly ground pepper

NOTE: The pork roast may also be prepared in a Crock Pot by cooking it on high for 5 hours or on low for 8 to 10 hours. There is no need to add water to the Crock Pot when preparing it this way.

Sausage with Peppers and Onions (Sandwiches)

If you've never cooked rope sausage on a grill, you have to try this recipe! It proves that the simple foods are sometimes the best. I prefer to use spicy sausage, but traditional is good as well. Be sure to check the ingredient list for possible gluten. Wheat should be clearly listed. Rye, barley, oats, malt, and caramel coloring are all unlikely, but read carefully.

4 gluten-free hoagie-style rolls
1 pound rope sausage
1 green bell pepper
1 red or yellow bell pepper
1 onion
1 tablespoon olive oil
1/4 teaspoon salt

- Preheat a grill until very hot. Open the rolls and lightly toast on the grill, if desired. Set aside.
- Cut the rope sausage into four pieces. Place on the grill and cook for approximately 5 minutes on each side, until cooked through. (Closing the grill speeds the cooking time.)
- While the sausages cook, clean the seeds and stems from the peppers. Slice into strips. Peel and slice the onion as well. Set aside.
- In a skillet over high heat (or on top of the grill, in a pan), place the olive oil, peppers, and onion. Add the salt. Sauté until well cooked but a little crispness remains, 2 to 3 minutes.
- Top the rolls with the sausages, then the pepper mixture. Serve with mustard, if desired.

■ Serves 4 ■

Sloppy Joes

My recipe for Sloppy Joes is fashioned lightly after Manwich brand Original Sloppy Joe Sauce. Because some of you are avoiding corn (specifically, high-fructose corn syrup), I wanted to include my corn-free recipe here. These homemade Sloppy Joes are ready in about 20 minutes.

- In a large saucepan over medium heat, brown the ground beef, onion, and bell pepper. Once the meat is cooked through (no pink remains), add the tomato paste and 1 can of the water. Mix the starch with the remaining can of water. Stir well and add to the pan. Add the remaining ingredients and stir well. Bring to a boil.

- Simmer over low heat for 10 to 15 minutes, to allow the flavors to blend and the sauce to thicken.

■ Serves 6 ■

1 pound ground beef

1 medium-size onion, peeled and chopped finely

1 small green bell pepper, seeds removed, chopped finely

1 (6-ounce) can tomato paste

2 (6-ounce) cans water

1 tablespoon cornstarch or potato starch

1 1/2 teaspoons chili powder

1 teaspoon salt

1/2 teaspoon black pepper

1/4 teaspoon cayenne (optional)

1 teaspoon sugar

Sour Beef

Seen as Sauerbraten on German menus, this roasted beef is often marinated and then roasted in vinegar and spices. I've shied away from the expected cloves and ginger, for a more understated interpretation.

- Place all ingredients except the starch and the 1½ tablespoons of water in a Crock Pot. Position the roast so that it is substantially covered by the liquid. Cook until the meat is very tender, 5 to 6 hours on high or 10 to 12 hours on low.

- Remove the meat from the Crock Pot. Set aside. Test the pan juices for flavor. Add up to ¼ additional teaspoon of salt, as needed.

- Place 1½ cups of the pan juices into a microwave-safe cup or bowl. In a separate bowl, combine the starch and the 1½ tablespoons of water. Stir well and add to the pan juices. Microwave on high for 1 to 2 minutes, to thicken.

- Slice the beef and top with the thickened juices.

■ Serves 7 to 8 ■

1 sirloin or chuck roast (2½–3 pounds)
1 cup apple cider vinegar
1 teaspoon dried rosemary
½ cup plus 1½ tablespoons water
½ teaspoon salt
1½ teaspoons cornstarch or potato starch

Bagels, corn- and rice-based (page 52); Waffles, corn-based (page 68);
Coffee Cake, rice-based (page 57); Pancakes, oat-based (page 65)

Lemonade Pie (page 396) using Pie Crust, rice-based (page 403)

Dinner Rolls, potato- and sorghum-based (page 90);
coleslaw; and Spicy Roadside Chicken (page 192)

Hamburger Rolls, corn- and cornmeal-based (page 86); Dinner Rolls, potato- and sorghum-based (page 90); Hot Dog Rolls, corn-based (page 85)

Fish and Chips, corn-based (page 228)

Cheese Crackers, potato-based (page 30)

Especially Good Hamburger (page 205)
on a Roll, corn- and cornmeal-based (page 86)

Yellow Wedding Cake (page 348) with Traditional Icing (page 326)

Brownies, potato-based (page 354)

Crab Soup,
Maryland Style (page 160)

Shrimp with Fresh Vegetables (page 237)

Fortune Cookies, corn-based (page 363),
rice-based (page 366), and potato-based (page 369)

Spaghetti Sauce

Manufacturers spend who knows how much money perfecting those cans and jars of spaghetti sauce. However, the moment I begin a sauce from scratch, my family wanders into the kitchen with, "Mmm. . . that smells really good." This sauce stands up boldly to the pasta. Use less red pepper flakes if your palate prefers a milder taste.

- In a large saucepan, heat the oil. Add the garlic and onion. Cook over medium heat until fragrant and the onion softens. Add the ground meat and cook until no pink remains. Stir and break up any large pieces during this cooking time.

- Add the remaining ingredients. Stir very well. Bring to a boil, then lower the heat to a simmer. Simmer, covered, for 15 minutes, to allow the flavors to blend. Stir occasionally. If you like the sauce to be thicker, simmer, uncovered, for an additional 5 minutes.

■ Makes 4 cups of sauce; serves 6 ■

2 tablespoons olive oil

1 large clove garlic, peeled and chopped finely

1 medium-size onion, peeled and chopped

1 pound lean ground beef

1 (14.5-ounce) can diced tomatoes

1 (14.5-ounce) can water

1 (6-ounce) can tomato paste

1 teaspoon dried oregano

3/4 teaspoon red pepper flakes

1/2 teaspoon dried basil

1/2 teaspoon black pepper

1/2 teaspoon dried thyme

1 1/2 teaspoons salt

Stove-top Hamburger Casserole

Like most families, we enjoy a quick, easy-to-prepare pasta dish made on the stove. You can make it, too. Here is an easy, mild version to get you started. Alter the spices to meet your taste, just watch the liquid-to-pasta ratio.

- Place the ground beef in a large skillet. Peel and dice the onion, and add to the pan. Cook over medium-high heat until the beef is cooked through, about 5 minutes. Drain off excess fat, if any. Add the remaining ingredients, except the cornstarch and 2 tablespoons of the water, in the order given. Stir well to blend. Bring to a boil.

- Cover and simmer until the noodles are very tender, approximately 20 minutes. Once the noodles are tender, stir the starch and 2 tablespoons of water in a cup. Add to the pan and stir gently to thicken the remaining liquid.

■ Serves 4 ■

1 pound ground beef

1 medium-size onion

1 teaspoon dried parsley

1 1/2 tablespoons chili powder

1 teaspoon salt

1/4 teaspoon black pepper

6 ounces uncooked gluten-free pasta (2 cups)

3 1/2 cups plus 2 tablespoons water

1/4 teaspoon crushed red pepper (optional)

2 teaspoons cornstarch or potato starch

2 tablespoons water

NOTE: For a complete meal in one pan, add 1 1/2 cups of your favorite frozen vegetables.

Sweet-and-Sour Pork ■ *Corn-based*

Here is another popular Americanized Chinese dish.

- Cut the pork into bite-size pieces. Set aside. In a small bowl, combine the batter ingredients. Stir well. Place the pork in the batter.

- Over medium heat, in a saucepan or a dedicated fryer, heat the oil to 370°F. Remove the pork from the batter and carefully place in the hot oil. Do not crowd the pork. (Multiple batches are to be expected.)

- For the sauce, drain, but reserve the juice from the pineapple. Peel onion and seed bell pepper. Cut into bite-sized pieces.

- In a small saucepan, combine the drained pineapple chunks, 1/4 cup of reserved juice, chili sauce, and sugar. Cook over medium heat until the flavors blend and the sugar is completely dissolved. Add onion and bell pepper. Heat through.

- Place over the pork just before serving.

■ Serves 2 ■

1/2 pound lean boneless pork

1 small onion

1/2 bell pepper, any color

1 tablespoon oil

Peanut or canola oil, for frying

Batter:

3/4 cup cornstarch, 95 grams

1/2 teaspoon salt

1/4 teaspoon baking powder

1/8 teaspoon baking soda

1/4 teaspoon xanthan gum

1/2 cup milk

Sweet-and-sour sauce:

1 (8-ounce) can pineapple chunks in own juice

1 (7.5-ounce) jar sweet chili sauce

4 teaspoons sugar

Sweet-and-Sour Pork ▪ *Potato-based*

- Cut the pork into bite-size pieces. Set aside. In a small bowl, combine the batter ingredients. Stir well. Place the pork in the batter.

- Over medium heat, in a saucepan or a dedicated fryer, heat the oil to 360°F. Remove the pork from the batter and carefully place in the hot oil. Do not crowd the pork. (Multiple batches are to be expected.)

- For the sauce, drain, but reserve the juice from the pineapple. Peel onion and seed bell pepper. Cut into bite-sized pieces.

- In a small saucepan, combine the drained pineapple chunks, 1/4 cup of the reserved juice, chili sauce, and sugar. Cook over medium heat until the flavors blend and the sugar is completely dissolved. Add onion and bell pepper. Heat through.

- Place over the pork just before serving.

▪ Serves 2 ▪

1/2 pound lean boneless pork

1 small onion

1/2 bell pepper, any color

1 tablespoon oil

Peanut or canola oil, for frying

Batter:

2/3 cup potato starch, 100 grams

1/2 teaspoon salt

1/4 teaspoon baking powder

1/8 teaspoon baking soda

1/8 teaspoon xanthan gum

1/2 cup milk

Sweet and sour sauce:

1 (8-ounce) can pineapple chunks in own juice

1 (7.5-ounce) jar sweet chili sauce

4 teaspoons sugar

12

FISH AND SEAFOOD

I am really pleased to bring you the recipes in this chapter. I once preferred eating seafood at restaurants because my attempts at home came up short. Fortunately, times have changed!

Blackened Fish is one of my favorite recipes in this chapter. Steamed Salmon is so very easy—and, it is amazing with Lemon Butter Sauce! And to those of you who miss fish and chips, you will love the Fish and Chips in this chapter. My favorite shrimp recipe may be Shrimp with Fresh Vegetables, but the Cajun Shrimp comes in a close second.

The recipes that have a batter coating, such as Fish and Chips and Fried Oysters, should be served quickly after making. As with their traditional wheat counterparts, steam from the fish or seafood on the inside will soften the exterior.

When you're stuck and don't know what to cook, seafood is a very quick, tasty option. These recipes are nearly foolproof.

Bay Scallops with Lemon and Rosemary

Looking for a fast, tasty entrée? Serve over your favorite gluten-free pasta.

- Heat a small skillet over high heat. Add the butter and let melt. Add the scallops, lemon juice, rosemary, and salt. Simmer for approximately 2 minutes, until the scallops are fully cooked.

■ Serves 2 ■

1 tablespoon butter
$3/4$ pound bay scallops
Juice of $1/2$ lemon
1 teaspoon dried rosemary
$1/4$ teaspoon salt

Blackened Fish

I prefer to use tilapia fish fillets for this recipe. However, any firm skinless fillet should be fine.

- Place the oil and butter in large skillet over medium heat. Spread the seasoning on a plate. Press one side of each fillet into the spices and place the fillets, spice side down, in the hot skillet. Cook until the fish loses all opaque appearance, 5 to 8 minutes. If the fillets are especially thick, turn over to finish cooking the upper side.
- Serve immediately, seasoned side up.

■ Serves 4 ■

1 tablespoon oil (not olive)
1 tablespoon butter
$1–1\frac{1}{4}$ tablespoons Blackened Seasoning Blend (page 440)
4 tilapia fillets (about $1\frac{1}{4}$ to $1\frac{1}{2}$ pounds)

NOTE: Oil is added to raise the flash point of the butter, which is critical for the flavor. Both fats will burn, but the oil will get hotter before it burns. Despite the best of intentions, you are likely to have a little browning of the fat. This is not a bad thing.

Cajun Shrimp

A fine gentleman from New Orleans was displaced from the restaurant he loved by Hurricane Katrina. He worked on a construction project near our home and treated us to some of his cooking. This simple dish is remarkably good. I make it with olive oil for the health benefits, but true decadence calls for butter in its place.

1 pound raw shrimp
  (medium to larger size)

1 tablespoon Cajun seasoning

2 tablespoons olive oil

1 medium-size onion

■ Peel and devein the shrimp. Toss with half of the Cajun seasoning. Set aside. In a large skillet, heat the olive oil. Peel the onion and slice into $\frac{1}{4}$-inch strips. Add to the oil, along with the remaining Cajun seasoning. Cook over medium-high heat until the onion is soft. Add the shrimp and cook until done. The shrimp will turn from translucent to pink.

■ Serves 2 ■

Crab Cakes

Living on the East Coast not too far from the Chesapeake Bay, I can't help but be a fan of Old Bay Seasoning. These crab cakes take only a few minutes to make and taste great. Please make the effort to find shallots in your local market. The food testers didn't know what was different about these crab cakes (it was the shallots), but they all spoke about how good they were!

- Place the crabmeat in a small bowl. Sort through the crabmeat for pieces of shell and discard any you find. (You are unlikely to find any, but check anyway.) If you use claw crabmeat, you may wish to break up the larger pieces of crabmeat. Lightly beat the egg in a separate bowl or small cup. Add half of the egg to the crabmeat; discard the rest. Add the remaining ingredients and mix gently but well.

- Heat a large skillet over medium heat. Spray with nonstick spray (away from the heat) or add a little butter to the pan. Butter has a low smoking point, so keep an eye on the pan if you use butter!

- Divide the mixture into three large balls. Place each into the pan and press down with a spatula to approximately $1/2$-inch thickness. The crab cakes will become less fragile while they cook.

- Cook to a light golden brown, approximately 3 to 5 minutes per side, and serve.

■ Makes 3 large crab cakes ■

8 ounces pasteurized fresh crab, drained

$1/2$ egg

1 rounded teaspoon mayonnaise

1 teaspoon Old Bay Seasoning*

1 teaspoon cornstarch, potato starch, or rice flour

1 small shallot, peeled and minced (approximately 1 tablespoon)

*Old Bay Seasoning is made by one of my favorite spice companies—McCormick & Co. They are sensitive to the needs of the gluten-free community and will clearly list gluten or wheat in their ingredient label. They also make a nice Creole seasoning for those of you with a Cajun preference.

ABOUT FRESH CRABMEAT

Unless you want to pick the crabs yourself, choose pasteurized fresh crabmeat. It is far better than the fresh-picked crabmeat available at most markets. It is often found in small plastic tubs with metal lids (8 ounces) or larger cans (16 ounces). It has a long refrigerator life until opened. Two varieties of pasteurized crabmeat are available, lump and claw. Lump crabmeat is from the body of the crab. It is milky white, slightly more delicate, a little prettier, and usually more expensive than claw crabmeat. Claw crabmeat is a little darker, a little heartier in texture, and every bit as tasty in this recipe.

Fish and Chips ▪ *Corn-based*

In making this dish, we tested tilapia and catfish. There is no comparison—use tilapia in this method. Save the catfish for pan-frying. I personally find this corn version closer to the real thing than the potato version.

■ Rinse and pat dry the fillets, and slice in half lengthwise. Set aside. Mix the batter ingredients in a bowl and set aside. This batter will thicken a bit as it sits.

■ Wash and dry the potatoes. Slice into narrow french fries and set aside.

■ Heat the oil to 370°F in a saucepan or dedicated fryer.

■ Place the fries in the hot oil. Cook for approximately 4 minutes. Remove from the oil. Drain on paper towels. The fries will be pale in color and not yet ready to eat.

■ At this point, the batter should be the consistency of a nice gravy. If it is thinner than that, add up to ¼ teaspoon additional xanthan gum and mix well to thicken. Dip the fillets in the batter and place in the hot oil. Cook until golden brown, approximately 4 minutes. (If the fillets stick to the bottom of the fryer, do not try to remove until they have spent several minutes in the oil. Otherwise, the coating will pull away from the fish and the results will be disappointing.) Remove from the oil. Drain on paper towels. Sprinkle with salt if desired.

■ Return the fries to the oil. Cook until golden brown, approximately 2 more minutes.

■ Serves 4 ■

---

4 small fish fillets (approximately 1 pound)

Peanut or canola oil (sufficient amount to deep-fry)

Batter:

¾ cup cornstarch, 95 grams

1½ teaspoons Old Bay Seasoning or Creole seasoning (I prefer Creole in this case)

¼ teaspoon baking powder

⅛ teaspoon baking soda

¼ teaspoon xanthan gum

¾ cup milk

Chips:

2 large russet baking potatoes

Salt

Fish and Chips ▪ *Oat-based*

Oat creates a light, flavorful coating on the fish. It is not quite as crisp as the other versions, but it is very pleasant.

- Rinse and pat dry the fillets, and slice in half lengthwise. Set aside. Mix the batter ingredients in a bowl and set aside. This batter will thicken a bit as it sits.

- Wash and dry the potatoes. Slice into narrow french fries and set aside.

- Heat the oil to 370°F in a saucepan or dedicated fryer.

- Place the fries in the hot oil. Cook for approximately 4 minutes. Remove from the oil. Drain on paper towels. The fries will be pale in color and not yet ready to eat.

- At this point, the batter should be the consistency of a nice gravy. If it is thinner than that, add up to 1/4 teaspoon additional xanthan gum and mix well to thicken. Dip the fillets in the batter and place in the hot oil. Cook until golden brown, approximately 4 minutes. (If the fillets stick to the bottom of the fryer, do not try to remove until they have spent several minutes in the oil. Otherwise, the coating will pull away from the fish and the results will be disappointing.) Remove from the oil. Drain on paper towels. Sprinkle with salt if desired.

- Return the fries to the oil. Cook until golden brown, approximately 2 more minutes.

▪ Serves 4 ▪

4 small fish fillets (approximately 1 pound)

Peanut or canola oil (sufficient amount to deep-fry)

Batter:

3/4 cup oat flour, 90 grams

1 1/2 teaspoons Old Bay Seasoning or Creole seasoning (I prefer Creole in this case)

1/4 teaspoon baking powder

1/8 teaspoon baking soda

1/2 teaspoon xanthan gum

1 egg

3/4 cup milk

Salt

Chips:

2 large russet baking potatoes

Salt

Fish and Chips ▪ *Potato-based*

As in the corn version, use tilapia for this dish. Tilapia is farm-raised, usually available fresh instead of frozen, and ideally suited to the dish. Oh, and the fries taste a lot like Boardwalk fries—and that's a good thing.

■ Rinse and pat dry the fillets, and slice in half lengthwise. Set aside. Mix the batter ingredients in a bowl and set aside. This batter will thicken a bit as it sits.

■ Wash and dry the potatoes. Slice into narrow french fries and set aside.

■ Heat the oil to 370°F in a saucepan or dedicated fryer.

■ Place the fries in the hot oil. Cook for approximately 4 minutes. Remove from the oil. Drain on paper towels. The fries will be pale in color and not yet ready to eat.

■ At this point, the batter should be the consistency of a nice gravy. If it is thinner than that, add up to ¼ teaspoon additional xanthan gum and mix well to thicken. Dip the fillets in the batter and place in the hot oil. Cook until golden brown, approximately 4 minutes. (If the fillets stick to the bottom of the fryer, do not try to remove until they have spent several minutes in the oil. Otherwise, the coating will pull away from the fish and the results will be disappointing.) Remove from the oil. Drain on paper towels. Sprinkle with salt if desired.

■ Return the fries to the oil. Cook until golden brown, approximately 2 more minutes.

▪ Serves 4 ▪

4 small fish fillets (approximately 1 pound)

Peanut or canola oil (sufficient amount to deep-fry)

Batter:

⅔ cup potato starch, 100 grams

1½ teaspoons Old Bay Seasoning or Creole seasoning

¼ teaspoon baking powder

⅛ teaspoon baking soda

⅛ teaspoon xanthan gum

½ cup milk

Chips:

2 large russet baking potatoes

Salt

Fish and Chips ▪ *Rice-based*

Rice provides a light, crispy, yet soft coating for the fish in this recipe. Please note that it really needs a sprinkle of salt after it is fried, for the best flavor.

▪ Rinse and pat dry the fillets, and slice in half lengthwise. Set aside. Mix the batter ingredients in a bowl and set aside. This batter will thicken a bit as it sits.

▪ Wash and dry the potatoes. Slice into narrow french fries and set aside.

▪ Heat the oil to 370°F a saucepan or dedicated fryer.

▪ Place the fries to the hot oil. Cook for approximately 4 minutes. Remove from the oil. Drain on paper towels. The fries will be pale in color and not yet ready to eat.

▪ At this point, the batter should be the consistency of a nice gravy. If it is thinner than that, add up to ¼ teaspoon additional xanthan gum and mix well to thicken. Dip the fillets in the batter and place in the hot oil. Cook until golden brown, approximately 4 minutes. (If the fillets stick to the bottom of the fryer, do not try to remove until they have spent several minutes in the oil. Otherwise, the coating will pull away from the fish and the results will be disappointing.) Remove from the oil. Drain on paper towels. Sprinkle with salt if desired.

▪ Return the fries to the oil. Cook until golden brown, approximately 2 more minutes.

▪ Serves 4 ▪

4 small fish fillets (approximately 1 pound)

Peanut or canola oil (sufficient amount to deep-fry)

Batter:

¾ cup rice flour, 115 grams

1 ½ teaspoons Old Bay Seasoning or Creole seasoning (I prefer Creole in this case)

¼ teaspoon baking powder

⅛ teaspoon baking soda

½ teaspoon xanthan gum

1 egg

1 cup milk

Salt

Chips:

2 large russet baking potatoes

Salt

Fried Catfish

Here is catfish in its simplest, and perhaps best, presentation. This is the only way I make catfish.

- Combine your choice of flour, salt, and pepper on a plate. Mix well. Set aside.
- Combine the eggs and water in a shallow bowl. Mix very well. Set aside.
- Heat the oil in large skillet over medium-high heat. Dip the fish first in the egg mixture, then in the flour mixture. Coat well.
- Place the fillets, curved side down, into the hot oil. Cook until nicely browned. Turn (a spatula works well) and continue cooking until the fish is browned on the other side and no longer opaque in the middle. The entire process should take 5 to 6 minutes.
- Sprinkle with additional salt to taste. Serve hot.

■ Serves 4 ■

$^1/_2$ cup cornmeal, millet flour, or rice flour

$^1/_2$ teaspoon salt

$^1/_2$ teaspoon pepper

2 eggs

$^1/_4$ cup water

4 small catfish fillets, approximately 1 $^3/_4$ pounds

$^1/_4$ cup oil

> **NOTE:** Our taste testers preferred cornmeal as their first choice. The rice flour had similar texture but was just a little lighter in coating the fish. Finally, the millet provided a seemingly thicker coating on the fish. The flavor of all three was pleasant.

Fried Oysters ▪ *Corn-based*

We tested several flours for the adventure of creating a gluten-free fried oyster, and the results were clear: corn tasted the best and produced the closest eating experience. Like traditional fried oysters, the outside is slightly crisp with a tender inside next to the oyster. But, appearances are very different. Unfortunately, this approach makes for fewer servings, but they are good.

▪ Heat the oil to 370°F in a saucepan or dedicated fryer.

▪ Drain the oysters. Set aside. In a bowl, mix the ingredients for the batter, except for 1/4 cup of cornmeal, which should be placed in a dish.

▪ One by one, coat the oysters lightly with the cornmeal, then dip into the batter. Place in the hot oil and fry until golden, just a minute or so.

▪ Serve hot.

▪ Serves 4 ▪

1 (8-ounce) container fresh oysters

Peanut or canola oil (sufficient amount to deep-fry)

Batter:

1/2 cup cornmeal, 70 grams

1/2 cup cornstarch, 65 grams

1 teaspoon salt

1/2 teaspoon xanthan gum

1/8 teaspoon baking soda

1 egg

3/4 cup milk

Mahimahi

Mahimahi is a firm, meaty fish but is certainly not fishy. A simple pan preparation of this fish works well. A little lime juice and salt enhance the flavor. Either of these salsas would be very traditional with this fish. However, I've included sautéed mushrooms as a surprisingly good alternative, preferred as the first-choice accompaniment by some taste testers.

- Place the olive oil in a medium-size nonstick pan and heat over medium heat. Add the fillets, pretty side down. Lower the heat just a little, to medium-low. Cook the fillets for approximately 10 minutes on each side. Cover with a lid for faster cooking. The fillets should be cooked through and not opaque in the middle. Sprinkle with salt and a squeeze of lime juice.

- For either salsa, combine all the ingredients in a small bowl. Allow the mixture to sit for a few minutes for the flavors to combine.

- For sautéed mushrooms, place the mushrooms and butter in a saucepan. Cook over medium-low heat until the mushrooms are very soft, approximately 5 minutes.

■ Makes 2 large servings ■

1 tablespoon olive oil (or 2, if not using nonstick pan)

2 mahimahi fillets, about 1 inch thick (1–1 1/4 pounds)

Salt

Squeeze of lime juice

Pineapple salsa:

1 (8-ounce) can pineapple chunks in own juice

1/2 small onion, peeled and diced finely

Zest from 1 lime, chopped very finely

Juice of 1 lime

Mango salsa:

1/2 mango

1/2 small onion, peeled and diced finely

Zest from 1/2 lime, chopped very finely

Juice of 1 lime

1 teaspoon sugar (if mango is not fully ripe)

Sautéed mushrooms:

8 button mushrooms, sliced

2 tablespoons butter

Hint of salt

Perch with Lemon-Caper Butter

Perch is a mild white fish that takes only minutes to prepare. This dish is prepared on top of the stove. Simplicity serves perch well.

1 tablespoon oil
1 pound perch fillets
1 tablespoon capers
Juice of 1 lemon
¼ cup butter

- Place the oil in a large skillet and heat over medium heat. Place the fillets in the skillet, skin side down, and cover with lid. Cook for approximately 5 minutes, until the fish separates easily and no opaqueness remains. Transfer the fish to a serving plate.
- Add the capers, lemon juice, and butter to the pan. As soon as the butter melts, stir and pour over the fillets.

■ Serves 4 ■

Red Snapper with Tomato and Capers

Isn't it fun to order fish at restaurants? Somehow, the chef knows how to make it special. This is one of those dishes. This recipe is full of flavor yet leaves room for dessert. You may substitute tilapia fillets if you are unable to obtain red snapper.

2 tablespoons olive oil
2 cloves garlic, chopped
1 (14.5-ounce) can diced tomatoes
2 teaspoons Cajun seasoning
3 tablespoons capers
4 fresh red snapper fillets (approximately 4 ounces each)

- Preheat the broiler to a high setting.
- Place the olive oil and garlic in a large skillet over medium heat. Sauté until fragrant, approximately 1 minute. Do not brown the garlic. Add the tomatoes and Cajun seasoning. Stir and simmer for 3 to 5 minutes so that the flavors meld. Add the capers and stir.
- Spray a shallow nonglass baking dish with nonstick cooking spray. Place the fillets in bottom of the baking dish in a single layer. Pour the tomato mixture evenly over the fillets.
- Place under the broiler for approximately 5 minutes. The fish is ready when the flesh, separated with a fork, is no longer opaque.

■ Makes 4 servings ■

Shrimp Scampi

This is simple and tasty—a great last-minute dish when unexpected guests arrive. If you do not care for wine, omit it and add a large squeeze of lemon juice just before serving.

- Place olive oil and butter in a large skillet over medium heat; add the garlic and cook until fragrant.
- Add the remaining ingredients. Cook until the shrimp is cooked through, 3 to 4 minutes.
- Serve with pasta or rice.

1 tablespoon olive oil

2 tablespoons butter

1 clove garlic, minced

1 pound raw shrimp (medium to large), peeled

1/3 cup dry white wine

1/4 teaspoon salt

■ Serves 3 ■

Shrimp with Fresh Vegetables

This dish a celebration of fresh flavors. Very easy, but so yummy.

- Peel the shrimp. Rinse all the vegetables. Cut the broccolini into very small pieces or the broccoli into florets or tiny "trees." Remove the strings from the sugar snap peas. Slice the squash in half lengthwise, then into small slices. Set all aside.
- Place the olive oil and butter in a large skillet over medium heat. Add the remaining ingredients and stir-fry until the shrimp is cooked through, 3 to 5 minutes, and the vegetables are tender-crisp.
- Serve soon after making, to avoid overcooking with residual heat.

1 pound raw shrimp (medium to large)

5 ounces broccolini or broccoli florets

4 ounces sugar snap peas

1 small yellow squash (about 6 ounces)

1 small zucchini squash (about 6 ounces)

1 tablespoon olive oil

1 tablespoon butter

1/2 teaspoon salt

■ Serves 4 ■

Steamed Salmon

This may be the easiest recipe in this cookbook. I use it for dinner parties. I use it to make fish for Salade Niçoise. I also use it for special, more private occasions. This recipe serves five to six, but you could substitute individual-size fillets (3 to 4 ounces) for fewer servings. Clean-up couldn't be easier. For over-the-top salmon, serve with Lemon Butter Sauce (page 238).

1 salmon fillet (between 1 3/4 and 2 pounds)

4 lemons

Pinch of salt

- Preheat the oven to 400°F.
- Rinse and pat dry the salmon fillet. Set aside.
- Cut a piece of aluminum foil a little over two times the length of the salmon. Place on a baking sheet. Spray foil with nonstick cooking spray.
- Place the fish, skin side down, in the center of the foil.
- Slice 1 lemon into thin slices. Layer over the salmon in a pretty design. Fold the foil loosely over the salmon and fold the edges over twice, to form a sealed packet.
- Place in the preheated oven. Bake for 20 to 25 minutes, until the fish flakes and is no longer translucent in the middle.
- Cut another lemon in half. Squeeze the juice over the cooked salmon and sprinkle with salt. Cut the remaining lemons into wedges to serve alongside the salmon. Serve hot or cold.

■ Serves 5 to 6 ■

NOTE: This recipe is great on the grill. Heavy-duty foil is a little easier to handle for this purpose, as the foil packet should be placed directly on the cooking rack. The fish will take approximately 15 minutes to cook in a hot, closed grill.

Lemon Butter Sauce

This sauce tastes great because it is made from great ingredients. Just a tablespoon or two of sauce over the fish, drifting into freshly steamed vegetables, is just delicious.

- In a small saucepan, melt the butter. Add the lemon juice and stir well. Add the heavy cream and cook over low heat until the sauce thickens slightly.

■ Makes almost $^1/_2$ cup sauce ■

4 tablespoons ($^1/_4$ cup) butter

Juice of 1 large lemon

$^1/_4$ cup heavy cream

Pinch of salt

13

PASTA, RICE, AND POTATOES

If you're a pasta junkie like me, you may be wondering if you're ever going to enjoy a plate of spaghetti again. I can honestly tell you that, yes, you will.

Tinkyada is among the most enjoyed gluten-free pastas available today. Where available? You may even find this brand in your local grocery store. I have tested it and find it very good. These noodles are slightly heavier in taste than traditional noodles. Gluten-free noodles come in many shapes and sizes. A small serving of gluten-free pasta may be as satiating as a larger serving of traditional pasta.

Like many prepared gluten-free foods, gluten-free noodles are a little expensive. However, compared to ordering out, the cost is very modest. So, enjoy!

Another good choice is Asian noodles. On a quick trip to my local Asian market, I found buckwheat noodles, rice sticks, mung bean noodles, and cornstarch sticks. Each has its own flavor and slightly different cooking instructions. Just 30 seconds to a minute can make a huge difference in your results. With the exception of the buckwheat noodles, you will see that most of the Asian noodles are translucent in color. They are also very affordable.

Should you be unable to locate gluten-free pastas, some very good rice and potato dishes are included in this chapter. Au Gratin Potatoes, Fried Rice, and Yams are all delicious alternatives to pasta.

■ ■ ■

Asian Noodles

At our favorite Chinese restaurant, you can order noodles in place of rice. One evening at home, I decided to surprise my daughter with these noodles—so simple. By the way, adding salt does not enhance this dish.

- Prepare the noodles according to the package directions. Rinse with very hot water if the noodles have cooled. Drain well. Place in a large serving bowl.

- In a small saucepan, combine the soy sauce and sugar. Heat on the stove-top until the sugar dissolves completely. Alternatively, combine in a microwave-safe bowl and microwave until the sugar dissolves. Pour over the noodles and toss well to coat.

- Garnish with slices of green onion.

■ Serves 2 ■

4 ounces gluten-free spaghetti noodles (not clear rice noodles)

1 tablespoon soy sauce

2 teaspoons sugar

Sliced green onion, for garnish (optional)

Au Gratin Potatoes

If you are a person who makes ham on the holidays, try making these potatoes to go with it. The potatoes and onion are smothered in a creamy cheese sauce. If you do not care for onion, substitute one more potato in its place. These potatoes take a while to bake, but are truly worth the effort.

2 cups milk

8 ounces shredded cheddar cheese

2 tablespoons cornstarch or potato starch

1 teaspoon salt

$1/2$ teaspoon pepper

1 medium-size onion

$1 1/2$ pounds white or red potatoes (about 4 medium)

- Preheat the oven to 350°F. Lightly grease a 9-inch square (or similarly sized) casserole dish.

- In a microwave-safe bowl, combine the milk, 4 ounces of the cheese, the starch, the salt, and the pepper. Microwave on high for approximately $4^1/2$ minutes, stirring occasionally, until the sauce has thickened. Set aside.

- Peel and very thinly slice the onion. Set aside. Wash the potatoes and slice into thin slices.

- In the prepared casserole dish, repeatedly layer the potatoes, onions, sauce, and cheese in that order until used. I usually have three layers of each.

- Place in the oven, cover, and bake for 40 minutes. Uncover and bake for approximately 30 minutes, until the potatoes are tender and the top is nicely browned.

■ Serves 9 ■

Baked Ziti

This is one of my family's favorite dinners. And it is a whole lot easier to prepare than lasagne. I like Jimmy Dean's spicy sausage because it bring great flavor to the dish without the need for a long list of dried spices. This ziti is surprisingly mild, with a light sauce.

- Preheat the oven to 350°F. Lightly grease a casserole dish.
- Cook the pasta al dente (a little firm) in a large pot. Drain well. Set the noodles aside to cool.
- In the same large pot, cook the sausage until no pink remains. Break into little bits while cooking. Drain away the excess grease, if any. Turn off the heat.
- Add the tomatoes, tomato paste, water, oregano, and salt to the sausage in the pot. Mix well. Add the noodles, cottage cheese, and nearly all of the mozzarella cheese. Stir well.
- Pour into the prepared casserole dish. Top with the remaining mozzarella cheese.
- Bake, covered with foil, for 30 minutes, then uncover and bake for an additional 15 minutes to allow the cheese on top to brown.
- Serve hot.

■ Serves 9 ■

8 ounces gluten-free pasta

8 ounces sausage

1 (14.5-ounce) can diced tomatoes

3 tablespoons tomato paste

1/4 cup water

1 teaspoon dried oregano

1/2 teaspoon salt

1 cup small-curd cottage cheese

12 ounces mozzarella cheese, shredded

Broccoli and Rice au Gratin

This recipe was inspired by one of those rice mixes that are so great for making a dinner side dish. Unfortunately, a lot of those mixes contain wheat. Fortunately, our version is much tastier than the product that inspired us.

- In a medium-size saucepan, combine all the ingredients except the broccoli. Stir frequently and bring to a boil. Be careful not to scorch the mixture. As soon as the mixture boils, lower the heat to low, cover, and simmer for 10 minutes. Stir occasionally to prevent sticking to the bottom of the pan. Add the broccoli. Cover and continue to cook over low heat until the rice and broccoli are tender, 5 to 10 minutes. If the sauce is thin, continue cooking, uncovered, for a few minutes.

■ Serves 4 ■

1 cup rice
1 1/4 cups water
1 3/4 cups milk
1 teaspoon cornstarch or potato starch
1/2 teaspoon salt
1/4 teaspoon black pepper
2 ounces cheddar cheese, grated (approximately 1/2 cup)
2 tablespoons grated Parmesan cheese
1 1/2 cups broccoli florets

Cajun Rice

Some of those seasoned rice mixes are quite good but are not gluten-free. Luckily, making your own great Cajun rice is easy.

- Peel and dice the onion. Seed and dice the bell pepper. Place the onion, bell pepper, and sausage in a medium-size saucepan. Break up the sausage into crumbles. If the sausage renders a lot of fat, drain and discard the fat. Add the butter, Creole seasoning, black pepper, and rice. Stir gently for a minute or so. Add the spring onion and heat through.
- Serve hot.

■ Serves 2 as a main dish, 4 as a side dish ■

1/2 medium-size onion
1/2 small red bell pepper
1/4 pound sausage
2 tablespoons butter
2 teaspoons Creole seasoning
1/4 teaspoon freshly ground black pepper
2 cups cooked rice
1 spring onion, chopped finely

Fried Potatoes

Ever want to have some nice fried potatoes when you order your breakfast out at a restaurant? They're one of my favorites. Unfortunately, they are often cooked on the same griddle as traditional pancakes and French toast. So, unless you can talk the cook into making a fresh batch in a fresh pan, you might like to try this at home.

2–3 large white potatoes (russet or Yukon Gold will tend to fall apart) (approximately 1 pound)
1 medium-size onion
2–3 tablespoons oil
1/4 teaspoon salt
1/4 teaspoon black pepper

- Wash the potatoes. Pierce each potato several times with a fork or knife. Microwave the potatoes for approximately 7 minutes.
- While the potatoes cook, peel and slice the onion into thin slices. Set aside.
- Slice the potatoes into thin slices. Set aside.
- Over medium-high heat, place 2 tablespoons of the oil and the onions in a large skillet. Cook for 30 seconds or so to start cooking of the onion. Add the potato slices, salt, and pepper.
- Mix gently and continue cooking over medium-high heat. Turn occasionally to nicely brown the potatoes. Add the extra 1 tablespoon of oil if needed. The actual frying time will be approximately 5 minutes.

■ Serves 4 ■

Fried Rice

When we eat at Chinese restaurants, I'm as interested in the rice as I am in the other entrées. Whether you like rice with ham, pork, chicken, or shrimp, all are tasty, and the choice is yours.

- ■ In a large skillet over high heat, cook the onion in the oil. Set aside. Scramble and cook the egg. Set aside. Cook the meat through. Add everything to the pan in the order listed. Sauté together for a few minutes for the flavors to blend.

■ Serves 2 ■

1 small onion, chopped
2 tablespoons oil
1 egg
6 ounces boneless pork chop, ham, boneless chicken, or shrimp
2 cups cooked rice
2 tablespoons soy sauce
1/4 teaspoon black pepper
1/2 cup frozen peas

Hash Browns

To have really crisp hash browns, you need to grate a potato or two. They cook surprisingly fast, but must be watched closely, as quite browned is good and burnt is unpleasant. I like to add a little onion to the potatoes.

- ■ Wash the potatoes. Grate into a bowl, add the salt, and toss well to distribute the salt.
- ■ Place 2 tablespoons of the oil in a large skillet over medium-high heat. Place approximately 1/2 cup of the potatoes in the hot oil. Press to 1/4-inch thickness with a spatula. Continue with the remaining potatoes.
- ■ Cook for approximately 2 minutes, until dark golden brown on bottom. Turn and cook for an additional 2 minutes, until again nicely browned. Serve right away for best texture.
- ■ Sprinkle with additional salt as desired.

■ Serves 6 ■

2–3 large white potatoes (approximately 1 pound)
2–3 tablespoons oil
1/4 teaspoon salt

Lemon Rice

This easy rice dish is perfect with steamed salmon. Pair it with fresh green beans for a beautiful meal.

- Cook the rice according to the package directions. Set aside.

- Slice the onions and zest into small pieces. Place the onion, lemon, and butter in a medium-size skillet. Sauté over medium-high heat until the butter melts and the onion is slightly cooked, 3 to 4 minutes. Add the rice, salt, and pepper. Toss well and serve.

■ Serves 4 ■

2 cups long-grain rice

4 spring onions, or $1/4$ cup finely chopped onion

Zest of 1 lemon

4 tablespoons ($1/4$ cup) butter

$1/4$ teaspoon salt

$1/8$ teaspoon pepper

NOTE: My favorite way to cook long-grain rice for this recipe is to place 4 cups of water and 2 cups of rice into a saucepan with both heavy sides and bottom. Bring to a boil over high heat. Stir briefly. Turn off the heat and immediately cover with a lid. Ignore for about 15 minutes, and you'll have perfect rice.

Macaroni and Cheese, Baked

Several taste testers and I butted heads on this dish. I liked using pepper Jack cheese to have "heat" accompanying the creamy, yet slightly sharp taste of the cheddar. They preferred plain Monterey Jack cheese. Take your choice.

- Preheat the oven to 350°F.
- Cook the pasta according to the package directions. Rinse and drain well. Set aside.
- Shred the 8 ounces of cheddar cheese and set aside. Separately, shred the 2 ounces of cheese for the topping as well.
- In a microwave-safe bowl, combine the sauce ingredients. Microwave and stir in 20-second intervals until the cheese has melted and the sauce thickens slightly. The frequent stirring is necessary to avoid a scrambled-egg effect.
- Combine the pasta, sauce, and 8 ounces of shredded cheese. Mix well.
- Place in an oven-safe casserole. Cover and bake for 30 minutes. Uncover and sprinkle with the remaining cheese. Bake for 15 to 25 more minutes, until the top just begins to brown.
- Serve hot.

■ Serves 9 ■

8 ounces gluten-free elbow noodles or penne pasta (Tinkyada is nice)

8 ounces cheddar cheese

Sauce:

3/4 cup milk

2 eggs

1 tablespoon cornstarch or potato starch

3/4 teaspoon salt

4 ounces Monterey Jack or pepper Jack cheese

Topping:

2 ounces cheddar cheese

Macaroni and Cheese, Stove-top

This recipe tastes a lot like that famous blue-box brand.

- Cook the pasta according to the package directions. Rinse and drain well. Set aside.
- In a large glass bowl, combine the sauce ingredients. Stir well. Microwave on high for 2 to 3 minutes, stirring at least once with a whisk.
- Pour the sauce over the cooked noodles and stir well. Serve hot.

■ Serves 6 ■

6 ounces gluten-free elbow noodles or penne pasta (Tinkyada is nice)

Sauce:

1 cup milk

1 tablespoon cornstarch, potato starch, or rice flour

4 ounces shredded cheddar cheese

1/4 teaspoon salt

Macaroni Salad

This recipe tastes very much like the Amish macaroni salad at many delis. To avoid using an extra pan, cook the egg in the same pot (and at the same time) as the pasta.

- Prepare the pasta according to the package directions. Rinse with cold water and drain very well. Allow to dry well, or pat away most of the water with a fresh towel.
- In a medium-size bowl, combine the ingredients for the sauce. Add the egg, carrots, bell pepper, onion, and pasta. Mix well.
- Refrigerate for at least 30 minutes to allow the flavors to blend.

■ Serves 4 ■

4 ounces gluten-free rice pasta (not clear rice noodles) (1 1/2 cups uncooked)

1 hard-boiled egg, chopped finely

2 tablespoons finely chopped baby carrots

2 tablespoons finely chopped green bell pepper

1 tablespoon finely chopped onion

Sauce:

1/2 cup mayonnaise

2 tablespoons sugar

1 teaspoon prepared mustard

2 teaspoons vinegar

Mashed Potatoes

Because some of you may be grudgingly accepting the need to cook, I've include some real basics. This is one of them. There are two important things about making mashed potatoes. The first is to use russet potatoes. Yukon Gold potatoes will also do the job, but using white potatoes or red potatoes can cause lumps. (If you like the hominess of lumps, use any potato.) The second is to use hot milk.

4 large russet potatoes
(approximately 2 pounds)

Scant 1 cup milk

1/4 teaspoon salt

2 tablespoons butter
(optional)

- Place approximately 6 cups of water in a medium-size saucepan. Wash the potatoes, peel, and cut into small chunks. Place in the saucepan. (The potatoes are added to water right away to prevent discoloration.). Cook over medium-high heat until the potatoes are tender. This will take approximately 15 minutes from the time the water boils. The tines of a fork should move easily through a potato. However, the potatoes should not be falling apart, either.
- When the potatoes are almost done, heat the milk in the microwave for about 1 minute. Set aside.
- Remove the potatoes from the heat and drain well. Return the potatoes to the saucepan. Add the salt and butter (if desired). Add 1/2 to 3/4 cup of the milk and beat with a mixer or potato masher. The potatoes should take on a creamy, smooth texture. Add more milk as needed to reach the correct texture.
- Serve hot.

■ Serves 4 ■

> NOTE: My favorite potato peeler is made by Oxo Good Grips.

Oven-Roasted Potatoes

These spicy potatoes may help you forget french fries (and the cross-contamination worries of restaurants). I use $1/4$ teaspoon of cayenne when I make these potatoes but I didn't want to scare you, so the recipe halves that.

- Preheat the oven to 400°F.
- Wash the potatoes and cut into large bite-size pieces. Do not peel. Shake off the excess water and place the potatoes on a baking sheet. Cover with the remaining ingredients. Toss well to coat.
- Bake for 40 to 45 minutes, until the potatoes are tender on the inside and crisp on the outside. Toss the potatoes once during the baking process, if you remember to.

■ Serves 4 to 6 ■

2 pounds white potatoes
2 tablespoons olive oil
$1/4$ teaspoon salt
$1/8$ teaspoon cayenne
1 teaspoon dried rosemary
$1/4$ teaspoon black pepper

Oven-Roasted Sweet Potato Hash

There is a great little bar/restaurant in Decatur, Georgia, called Feast. They have a wonderful stone pizza oven that they make magic in. A 700°F oven does amazing things to fish and Cornish hens. I can't duplicate their hens, but this is my version of their sweet potato hash.

- Preheat the oven to 400°F.
- In a medium-size to large baking dish, combine all the ingredients. Toss well to coat. Bake for 45 minutes, until the potatoes are tender on the inside, crisp on the outside.

■ Serves 3 to 4 ■

1 pound sweet potatoes, diced small
2 tablespoons olive oil
1 tablespoon lemon juice
Pinch of salt

Parsleyed Potatoes

These potatoes are quick and easy, not to mention tasty. I like to serve them at dinner as a side dish. They go equally well with fish, chicken, or beef.

- Wash the potatoes and cut in half. Place, unpeeled, in a medium-size saucepan and add water to cover. Bring to a boil. Continue cooking until the potatoes are tender, about 10 minutes from the time the water boils. A fork should pierce the potatoes easily. Turn off the heat. Drain the potatoes and return to the hot pan. Add the butter, parsley, and salt. Stir well to evenly coat the potatoes.

■ Serves 4 ■

12–14 small new potatoes (between 1 1/4 and 1 1/2 pounds)
2 tablespoons butter
1 tablespoon dried parsley
Scant 1/4 teaspoon salt

Parmesan-Garlic Noodles

This dish is served often at our home. Don't be tempted to do a "real cooking" version of this recipe. Sautéing garlic and using fresh Parmesan do nothing to enhance the results. The more difficult method of preparing this dish lost 4 to 0 in our taste test.

- Cook the noodles and drain. Place in a serving dish and add the remaining ingredients and mix well.
- Serve hot.

■ Serves 4 ■

8 ounces of your favorite pasta, cooked and rinsed
1/4 cup butter
3/4 teaspoon garlic salt
1/2 teaspoon black pepper
1 1/2 tablespoons grated Parmesan cheese

Sweet Potato Soufflé

Our Cajun chef/painter introduced us to this recipe. His name was John, and I'll bet he can be found in one of the finer restaurants in Louisiana today. This is just a yummy accompaniment to a nice dinner.

1 1/2 pounds sweet potatoes
2 tablespoons honey
Pinch of salt
1 tablespoon butter

- Peel and chop the sweet potatoes into large pieces. Place in a large microwave-safe bowl. Rinse and drain. Cover loosely with plastic wrap and microwave until tender, approximately 8 minutes. Drain off and discard any liquid. Alternatively, you may cook the sweet potatoes (covered with water) in a saucepan, until tender.
- Add the honey, butter, and salt. Beat with a mixer or potato masher until creamy.

■ Serves 4 ■

NOTE: To make this holiday fare, consider placing potatoes in shallow baking dish, adding chopped candied nuts and/or marshmallows, and browning under the broiler for a minute or two.

Candied Nuts for Sweet Potato Soufflé (optional)

- Lightly grease a baking sheet.
- Place the pecans in a small skillet. Add the orange marmalade. Cook over medium-low heat until the pan is nearly dry, approximately 5 minutes. You will notice that a bit of the marmalade will begin to caramelize on the sides of the pan.
- Place the nuts on the prepared baking sheet and spread out. Sprinkle lightly with salt. Allow to cool.

1 cup pecan halves
1/3 cup orange marmalade
Pinch of salt

■ Makes 1 cup ■

Twice-Baked Potatoes

These potatoes should be on the list of things you don't make very often. But, hey, you need great munchies for a big-game party, right? They are definitely hearty in taste.

- Wash the potatoes and pierce several times with a fork. Microwave on high for 10 to 12 minutes, when the potatoes should be cooked through. Cook the sausage, breaking it into bits, and set aside.

- Cut the potato in half lengthwise. Scoop out center of each potato and place in a bowl, remembering to leave a margin of the potato flesh inside its skin. Retain the exterior "bowls" of potato. You should be able to remove almost 2 cups of cooked potato (approximately 12 ounces) from the skins.

- Add the sour cream, 3/4 of the cheese, the salt, and the sausage. Mix well with a fork. Place the filling back into the potato skins. Top with the remaining cheese.

- Bake on a baking sheet at 375°F until hot, approximately 25 minutes. They will take longer if you have prepared these ahead of time. Top with slices of green onion as a garnish, as desired.

■ Serves 8 ■

4 russet potatoes
(about 1 3/4 pounds)

1/2 pound sausage meat

3/4 cup low-fat sour cream
or plain yogurt

4 ounces Colby cheese,
shredded

1/4 teaspoon salt

2 green onions (optional)

Veggie Packets

These little packets are great when you're going to a friend's house for a barbecue or when you want a fun, no-fuss side dish. Although this dish is a simple blend of potatoes and onion, you can easily modify the recipe to your personal taste.

- Preheat the oven to 400°F.
- Wash and thinly slice the potatoes. Peel and thinly slice the onions. Set both aside.
- Cut four squares of foil. Lightly spray the foil with nonstick spray.
- Divide the potatoes and onions among the foil squares. Sprinkle the olive oil, thyme, salt, and pepper on top of the vegetables. Fold each square of foil into a packet and seal tightly.
- Bake for 30 minutes, until the potatoes and onions are very tender. Serve hot.

■ Serves 4 ■

4 medium-size white potatoes, approximately 1 1/2 pounds

1 medium-size onion

Nonstick cooking spray

3 tablespoons olive oil

1 teaspoon dried thyme

1/8 teaspoon salt

1/8 teaspoon pepper

Yams

This is my nephew's favorite dish at Thanksgiving.

- Preheat the oven to 375°F. Lightly grease a medium-size casserole dish.
- Peel the sweet potatoes. Cut into large chunks; I cut them to approximately 1 x ½ x 2 inches. Place in the prepared casserole. Sprinkle the remaining ingredients over the sweet potatoes.
- Bake, covered, for 1 hour. Spoon the sauce over the sweet potatoes when serving.

■ Serves 6 ■

3 medium-size sweet potatoes (about 1 ½ pounds)
1 ounce raisins (1 snack-size box)
¼ cup chopped pecans
½ cup brown sugar

14

▪▪▪ SALADS

This chapter contains a variety of salads to accompany any meal.

Many store-bought salads may be gluten-free in their own right, although you must check the ingredient listings to be sure. Of additional concern, however, is cross-contamination. It can occur at the deli counter, the salad bar, and even from shared serving spoons.

Even at home, sharing a jar of mayo with a "traditional" sandwich maker can be a source of cross-contamination.

These are my very favorite salads, some from my family, others from my favorite restaurants. Potato Salad, Traditional, is fashioned after my grandmother's and Potato Salad, German, is styled after my mother's.

Caesar Salad

Caesar salad is one of my very favorite salads. We'll make our own speedy croutons in a toaster. And for safety, we'll exclude the traditional partially cooked egg and use a yolk in our quickly cooked dressing. Although not conventional, the addition of thin strips of ham makes this a delicious main-course salad.

- To make the salad, wash the lettuce and drain well. Tear it into bite-size pieces and place in a large serving bowl. Peel the onion, slice into small slivers, and sprinkle over the top of the greens. Peel and slice the eggs and add to the bowl. If using a wedge of cheese, use a potato peeler to slice little ribbons of Parmesan to add to the bowl. (If using packaged grated cheese, just sprinkle over the salad.) Set aside.

- To make the croutons, toast the bread as you would for breakfast. Allow to cool. Toast for a second time (and third if needed), but watch closely to avoid burning. You want the bread to dry out but not burn. While still hot, spray both sides of the toast with the nonstick spray. Sprinkle both sides with garlic salt. Cut into small cubes. Set aside.

- Combine all the dressing ingredients in a small bowl. Mix well. If time permits, allow to sit for a few minutes for the flavors to mingle.

- Just before serving, add the croutons and your desired amount of dressing to the bowl of salad. Toss to coat.

■ Serves 6 ■

10 ounces romaine lettuce

1/2 small red onion (optional)

2 ounces fresh Parmesan cheese, 55 grams

2 hard-boiled eggs

Croutons:

2 slices gluten-free bread (thinly sliced is better)

Nonstick cooking spray

1/4 teaspoon garlic salt

Dressing:

2 tablespoons oil

1/4 cup mayonnaise

2 tablespoons apple cider vinegar

1/4 teaspoon garlic salt

Pinch of black pepper

1 teaspoon sugar

1 tablespoon grated Parmesan cheese (canned is fine)

Coleslaw

I used to consider coleslaw an annoyance put on a plate by restaurants solely to fill an empty spot. Perhaps it was the ultimate marketing effort by cabbage growers? Then, I tasted the coleslaw made by my mother-in-law, Lucile. Wonderful! She was unable to give me exact measurements, but careful tasting and her general guidelines proved successful. Please measure your ingredients carefully the first time you make this dish. You may substitute evaporated milk for the cream if you want a lower-fat recipe.

1 small head of cabbage
(about 1 pound)
$^1/_3$ cup sugar
$^1/_2$ teaspoon salt
$^1/_2$ cup cream
2 tablespoons cider vinegar

■ Finely shred the cabbage, or purchase the bagged kind. Place in a large, nonreactive bowl. Sprinkle with the sugar and salt. Stir well. Add the other ingredients. Stir well. The sugar crystals will dissolve if the slaw is allowed to sit for a few minutes before serving. The slaw is also nice chilled overnight.

■ Makes eight $^1/_2$-cup servings ■

Cranberry Salad

I make Cranberry Salad just once or twice a year. It is a favorite of everyone gathered at the table. If you have a food processor, this recipe takes about five minutes to put together. I usually chop or slice everything in my recipes by hand, which is a bit of a task for this dish. If you do not have a food processor, I suggest a sharp knife and good company to help chop.

- Combine the fruit, nuts, and celery in very large, nonreactive bowl. Set aside. In a separate bowl, combine sugar, gelatin, and boiling water. Stir until the sugars are totally dissolved. Add 3/4 cup of the retained juices and stir.

- Pour the liquid over the fruit mixture. Mix very well. Ladle into individual serving cups or a larger serving bowl. Cover and chill in the refrigerator for at least 6 hours; overnight is even better.

■ Makes 8 1/2 cups; serves 12 to 16 ■

12 ounces fresh cranberries, chopped finely

1 (15.5-ounce) can sliced pears, chopped (retain juice)

1 (8-ounce) can crushed pineapple (retain juice)

1 large cluster seedless grapes (12–16 ounces), cut in half

4 ounces pecans, chopped finely

3 stalks celery, sliced as thinly as possible

3/4 cup sugar

3 (3-ounce) boxes powdered gelatin dessert, strawberry or raspberry preferred

1 1/2 cups boiling water

NOTE: This recipe makes a lot. I like to save some in the refrigerator to use on turkey sandwiches later—very tasty.

Cucumber Salad

This salad is a great accompaniment to a fiery dish, because the dairy seems to cool the palate. The browned fennel seed adds something extra but, even without it, this simple salad is delicious.

- Wash and peel the cucumber. Cut in half and slice thinly. Place in a serving bowl. Add the other ingredients and mix well. If desired, brown the fennel seed in the butter and add to the salad. Allow the flavors blend for at least 10 minutes prior to serving.

■ Serves 3 ■

1 medium-size cucumber (12–15 ounces)

1/2 cup low-fat plain yogurt

Scant 1/4 teaspoon salt

Juice of 1/2 lemon

1/2 teaspoon fennel seed (optional)

1 teaspoon butter (optional)

Fruit and Green Salad

I often serve this salad at dinner parties. It is special but not difficult to prepare. The secret is in the freshness of the ingredients, rather than which ones you choose. Substitute any fresh fruit for the plums and pears. You can also substitute a soft lettuce, such as Boston, for the baby greens.

5–6 ounces baby greens

1 small red onion

2 plums

2 pears

1/2 lemon

Celery Seed Dressing (page 442), or another sweet-and-sour dressing of your choice

- Wash the lettuce and shake off excess water. Tear into bite-size pieces and place in a large serving bowl. Peel the onion and cut in half. Slice each half into small slivers. Sprinkle over the top of the greens. Set aside.

- Wash, peel, pit, and slice the plums and pears into a small bowl. Squeeze the lemon over the fruit, to prevent browning. Toss the fruit to distribute the lemon juice all over. Place the fruit on top of the salad.

- Toss with your preferred dressing.

■ Serves 8 ■

> NOTE: You would think while eating out that a salad or trip to the salad bar would be a great safety net. Maybe, maybe not. Unfortunately, those pretty little croutons may not stay snug in their own little compartment. The hands of the food preparers may have just picked up some wayward croutons and then rearranged the tomatoes. To be safe, make your own salads.

Fruit Salad

Besides using fresh, delicious fruit, the secret of a good fruit salad is adding a hint of dressing to accentuate the flavors.

- Wash, peel, and dice the cantaloupe, watermelon, and honeydew. Place in a large bowl. Wash, hull, and slice the strawberries, and add to the bowl. Peel the kiwi and dice very small, and add to the bowl.

- In a separate cup, mix the orange juice, lemon juice, and sugar if needed. Stir well. Pour over the fruit and toss to coat. Refrigerate for several hours for the flavors to blend.

■ Serves 10 to 12 ■

1/2 cantaloupe
1/2 seedless baby watermelon
1/2 honeydew melon
1 pint fresh strawberries
1 kiwi
1/2 cup orange juice
Juice of 1/2 lemon
2 tablespoons sugar
(if fruit is not very sweet)

Japanese Salad of Cabbage, Carrots, and Rice Noodles with Sesame Dressing

Inspired by our favorite Japanese restaurant, this salad is a delicious first course. Do not let the simplicity of the recipe deter you from giving it a try.

- Cook the rice noodles according to package directions. Drain, rinse well with cold water, then dry on a paper towel. Set aside.

- Cut the cabbage and carrots into very fine julienne strips.

- Arrange the noodles and vegetables in three small clusters on four small serving plates.

- Combine all the ingredients for the dressing in a small bowl or jar. Stir or shake well to mix. Pour approximately 2 tablespoons of the dressing over top of the salad clusters just before serving.

■ Serves 4 ■

1 ounce thin, clear rice noodles
3 ounces cabbage
2 carrots (approximately 2 ounces)

Dressing:
1/4 cup sesame oil (no substitute)
1/4 cup mayonnaise
1 tablespoon plus 1 teaspoon soy sauce
1/4 teaspoon salt

Kimchi, Fresh

For those of you who like Korean food, this is a quick version of the cuisine's famous pickled cabbage. Traditional kimchi is made with mi-won (monosodium glutamate) but not everyone has it in their kitchen. Accordingly, I've opted to omit it. The longer the kimchi marinates, the better it is. To further veer from tradition, I like to add a little extra sugar just before serving. This makes for a hot-and-sweet pickled cabbage. Other cabbages, radishes, cucumbers, and turnips can be substituted for the bok choy.

8 ounces baby bok choy

1 spring onion

$1/2$ teaspoon ground red pepper

$1/2$ teaspoon sugar plus $1 1/2$ teaspoons sugar (optional)

$1 1/2$ teaspoons apple cider vinegar

- Wash, core, and chop the bok choy. Wash and roughly chop the spring onion, discarding the roots.

- Place all the ingredients except the optional $1 1/2$ teaspoons of sugar in a small resealable plastic bag. Allow to marinate at room temperature for at least 1 hour. Refrigerate for at least 12 additional hours for the raw edge of the red pepper to mellow. Add the additional sugar just before serving, if desired.

■ Serves 2 ■

Potato Salad, German

My mom is German. She taught us how to make this dish when we were young. If you prefer the sweeter style of German potato salad, just add a little sugar to the dressing and a few crumbled slices of bacon to the dish. But I must remain a purist. This is how my mom does it.

2 pounds red potatoes
$^1/_3$ cup red wine vinegar
$^1/_3$ cup water
2 tablespoons oil
$^1/_2$ teaspoon salt
1 small onion

- Wash the potatoes. Place, uncut and unpeeled, into a medium-size saucepan and add water to cover. Bring to a boil and cook until tender, about 15 minutes.

- While the potatoes are cooking, mix remaining ingredients, except the onion, in a large measuring cup. Peel and finely chop the onion. Add to the cup and allow the flavors to blend.

- Once tender, drain the potatoes and allow to cool until you can just handle them. Peel the potatoes and slice thinly into a large bowl. Pour the dressing over the potatoes and allow the flavors to blend. Serve warm or cold.

■ Serves 8 ■

Potato Salad, Traditional

Here is the old-fashioned potato salad with a cooked salad dressing that few people still make. The dressing takes just a few minutes in the microwave and everyone will be impressed when you serve it at a family gathering.

- Wash the potatoes. Place, uncut and unpeeled, in a medium-size saucepan and add water to cover. Bring to a boil and cook until tender, about 15 minutes. Once the water boils, you can add the eggs to the water to hard-cook them at the same time.

- While the potatoes cook, prepare the dressing. Place all the ingredients in a large glass bowl or other microwave-safe container. Stir well to combine. Microwave on high for 2 to 4 minutes to cook the dressing, stirring periodically. (It is important that the egg become fully cooked to avoid food poisoning.) Set aside to cool.

- Drain the potatoes and allow to cool. Wash and chop the onion, hard-boiled eggs, and celery. Place in a large serving bowl and set aside. Peel the potatoes and cut into small cubes. Add to the serving bowl.

- Add the dressing and mix gently but well. Refrigerate until serving.

■ Serves 8 ■

2 pounds red or white potatoes

1 small onion

3 hard-boiled eggs

2 stalks celery

Dressing:

1/2 cup sugar

1 egg

1 teaspoon cornstarch, potato starch, or rice flour

2 tablespoons apple cider vinegar

1/2 teaspoon prepared mustard

1 cup mayonnaise

1 teaspoon salt

1/2 teaspoon pepper

1/2 teaspoon celery seed (optional)

Salade Niçoise

When it's just me and my husband, we'll sometimes enjoy this salad for lunch or dinner. I hope this recipe inspires you to use whatever you have on hand in a new way. I think of this salad as the French version of our American chef salad.

- If using fresh fish, place on a microwave-safe plate and cover with plastic wrap. Microwave on high for approximately 2 minutes, until the fish is cooked through and the thickest part is no longer opaque. Alternatively, place the fish in a steamer and cook for several minutes.

- Place the eggs and potatoes in a small saucepan. Cover with water and cook until the potatoes are tender, approximately 15 minutes. Add the green beans and cook for approximately 5 minutes, until tender-crisp. Drain and allow to cool.

- Arrange greens on serving plates. Top with remaining ingredients and your favorite vinaigrette.

■ Serves 2 ■

4 ounces steamed fish (salmon, tuna, or even canned albacore tuna)

4 small red or white potatoes

2 eggs

1/2 cup fresh green beans

3 cups baby salad greens

1 tablespoon capers

1 tablespoon minced onion

Spinach Threads with Sesame Oil

This dish is popular at a nearby Chinese restaurant. Serving sizes are small, as the flavor is quite distinct. It's a nice start or side to a meal, though be aware—this is a love-it-or-hate-it recipe.

- Roll the spinach into a tight bundle and slice thread thin. Add the remaining ingredients except the sesame seeds, and toss well to coat. Refrigerate for at least 1 hour for the spinach to almost wilt. Sprinkle with the sesame seeds.

■ Serves 2 ■

2 ounces baby spinach

1 tablespoon sesame oil (no substitute)

1 1/2 teaspoons rice wine vinegar (no substitute)

Pinch of salt

1/2 teaspoon toasted sesame seeds

NOTE: Sesame seeds are available in toasted form in most grocery stores. If you cannot locate them, use plain sesame seeds instead.

Tomato and Onion Salad

Here's a simple salad that shows off the fresh flavor of tomatoes.

- Wash the tomatoes. Cut in half and then into bite-size wedges (they're pretty this way). Place in a serving bowl. Set aside. Peel half of the onion and cut into very thin wedges (again, a pretty cresent shape). Add to the serving bowl. Wash and chop the cilantro. Add to the serving bowl.

- In a small bowl, combine the dressing ingredients. Mix well. Pour over the salad. Mix gently but well. Allow the flavors to blend for at least 10 minutes prior to serving.

■ Serves 4 ■

2 fresh tomatoes
(10–12 ounces)

$1/2$ sweet onion
(3–4 ounces)

1 small handful fresh cilantro
(optional)

Dressing:

$1/4$ cup red wine vinegar

$1/4$ cup water

1 tablespoon olive oil

$1/2$ teaspoon salt

Freshly ground black pepper

Zucchini, Tomato, and Feta Salad with Balsamic Dressing

Sometimes I think I'm trying to convince you to eat your vegetables! If you're a little adventurous with me, you'll be enjoying things you never knew tasted good—like raw zucchini!

- Wash the zucchini and cut into very small cubes. Place in a medium-size serving bowl. Wash the tomatoes and cut in half. Place in the serving bowl. Crumble the feta cheese into the serving bowl. Wash and chop the basil, discarding any larger stems. Add to the serving bowl.

- Combine all the dressing ingredients in a small bowl or jar. Mix well. Toss the dressing with the salad and allow flavors to blend for at least 10 minutes before serving.

■ Makes 1/2 cup dressing ■

2 baby zucchini squash (about 8 ounces)

1 pint cherry or grape tomatoes

4 ounces feta cheese

Handful of fresh basil

Dressing:

1/2 cup olive oil

2 tablespoons balsamic vinegar

1/2 teaspoon salt

1 tablespoon sugar

1 teaspoon dried basil (if fresh not used in the salad)

15

VEGETABLES

Vegetables are a very important part of a gluten-free diet. If you're like many newly diagnosed individuals, your body has been having difficulty absorbing sufficient nutrients. You may even be taking vitamins or other supplements.

I hope the recipes in this chapter will inspire you to eat more fresh vegetables. They are readily available and will help your body get back on track.

If your favorite vegetables are not in season, consider frozen ones. Be careful to read ingredient listings for sauces, as they may contain unacceptable flours. Frozen vegetables, without sauces, are often free of sodium and packaged at peak flavor.

Use canned vegetables if you need to, but remember that their sodium content is usually quite high.

Most of the vegetable recipes in these pages are very easy. Fresh flavor simply enhanced is a good combination. For example, when I serve Broccoli with Brown Butter, our guests regularly ask for the recipe.

Don't forget to try the Cheese Sauce recipe (page 442) over freshly steamed broccoli or cauliflower.

Asparagus

Are you tempted to skip this vegetable because you've only "enjoyed" the mushy or tough kind? If so, you'll be missing out. Asparagus should look bright in color, have firm (but not woody) stalks, a tightly closed top, and snap when broken in two. If it is wiggly in the store, don't bring it home.

1 pound fresh asparagus

1 lemon

Pinch of salt

- Wash the asparagus and snap off the ends. (If you hold the stalk in your hand bend at the very end of the stalk with your other hand, the stalk will snap at the desired point. This removes the tough or woody end.) Cut half of the lemon into slices. Set aside.

- Place the asparagus in a shallow pan that can accommodate its length and add water to cover. Cover the pan with a lid. Bring to a boil and cook until barely approaching tender. For stalks thinner than a pencil, this will take about 2 minutes after the water boils. For thicker stalks, this will take up to 5 minutes after the water boils. (The asparagus will continue to cook from the retained heat.)

- Remove from the heat and drain. Place on a serving dish. Squeeze the uncut half of the lemon lightly over the asparagus and sprinkle with a hint of salt. Garnish with the lemon slices. Serve hot.

■ Serves 6 ■

Asparagus in Vinaigrette

Cold asparagus can be delicious served alone or in a salad. Two secrets to this easy preparation: do not overcook the asparagus and use a flavorful (but not overpowering) vinaigrette.

1 pound fresh asparagus

$1/3$ cup favorite vinaigrette (bottled is fine—check out Kraft)

- Prepare the asparagus as indicated in the prior recipe, to point of drainage. Immediately run cold water over the asparagus to stop the cooking.

- Place the asparagus in a serving dish or resealable plastic bag. Pour in the vinaigrette. Chill for a minimum of 20 minutes, or overnight.

■ Serves 6 ■

Baked Beans

Isn't it just amazing where you'll find suspect ingredients? Canned baked beans often aren't gluten-free. Well, good baked beans are always a doctored-up version of the canned ones, anyway. I won't ask you to use dried beans, but you do have to work a little to prepare this recipe. I hope you enjoy these beans!

2 slices bacon, diced

1 small onion, diced finely

2 (15.5-ounce) cans small white beans, undrained

$1/2$ cup molasses

1 teaspoon prepared yellow mustard

3 tablespoons tomato paste

$1/4$ teaspoon salt

- In a medium-size saucepan, fry the bacon until crisp. Add the onion once the fat begins to be released from the bacon. When the bacon is crisp, drain the excess fat and discard. Add all the other ingredients. Stir well. Bring to a boil. Lower the heat to low and simmer, uncovered, for at least 15 minutes, or until the sauce thickens. Stir occasionally to prevent sticking.

■ Serves 7 ■

Black Beans

My family enjoys almost every cuisine. I hope you'll venture to try new foods. This Cuban staple takes just a few minutes to make.

- In a small saucepan over high heat, combine the olive oil, garlic, and onion. Sauté together until fragrant. Carefully (the oil will spatter), add the black beans. Add the cayenne. Stir, cover, lower the heat, and simmer for at least 10 minutes.
- Serve with rice.

■ Serves 3 ■

1 tablespoon olive oil

1 clove garlic, chopped finely

1/2 small onion, chopped finely

1 (15.5-ounce) can black beans, undrained

Pinch of cayenne

Pinch of ground cumin (optional, but nice)

1 small bay leaf

Broccoli with Brown Butter

This recipe produces beautiful, bright green broccoli with a subtle flavor that you'll like but won't quite be able to describe. Time after time, I'm asked "How'd you make the broccoli?"

- Wash the broccoli and cut into individual "trees." Cut any thick stems to facilitate quick cooking. Melt the butter in a large skillet over high heat. Allow the butter to brown but not burn. Add the broccoli and salt. Cover with a lid for the first minute or so to help cook the broccoli. Add 1 tablespoon of water if the pan becomes dry. Continue cooking, covered, until the broccoli is tender yet crisp, about 3 minutes.

■ Serves 4 ■

1–1 1/4 pounds fresh broccoli crowns

2 tablespoons butter

Pinch of salt

"Clam Bake" Potatoes and Corn

This is one of my favorites to make when having steaks or steamed crabs. It is a crowd-pleaser. Don't let the simple preparation fool you; the end results are just delicious!

2 pounds white potatoes (not russet)

4 ears corn

$1/2$ to $3/4$ teaspoon Old Bay Seasoning

■ Shuck and wash the corn. Break in half. Set aside. Wash the potatoes and cut (do not peel) into very large pieces. Small potatoes should be left whole. Place the potatoes in a large pot and cover with water. Bring to a boil and cook until just tender, 10 to 15 minutes. Add the corn; bring the water back to a boil and cook for 35 minutes. Drain and place on a serving platter. Sprinkle liberally with Old Bay Seasoning. Serve hot!

■ Serves 6 to 8 ■

NOTE: Fresh green beans (whole) are a nice addition to this dish. Just add them to the pot at the same time you add the corn.

Corn and Tomato Sauté

Vegetables can taste so good with so little effort. This recipe is especially tasty with fresh corn, but frozen white corn will do. If you're a garlic lover like me, your taste buds may tell you to add garlic to this dish, but I suggest you try it as written. It really is better.

2 ears corn, or 1 1/2 cups frozen white corn

1/2 pint (1 cup) cherry or grape tomatoes

2 tablespoons olive oil

1 tablespoon grated Parmesan cheese

Pinch of salt

Pinch of freshly ground pepper

■ Wash the corn and tomatoes. Slice the corn kernels off cob. Cut the tomatoes in half. Heat the oil over medium heat in a medium-size skillet. Add the corn and cook until nearly tender. Add the tomatoes and cook just long enough to warm. Add the Parmesan, salt, and pepper. Toss gently but well, to mix. Serve immediately.

■ Makes 4 large servings ■

Fresh Green Beans with Heat

I like to have fresh green beans often when they are in season. Their flavor is bright. Their texture is crisp. And they require only a minute or two in boiling water and a pinch of salt after. However, if you want something a little more interesting, give this a try. Most of the oil stays behind in the pan. And you'll have delicious beans that are a bit out of the ordinary.

1 1/2 tablespoons oil

1/2 teaspoon crushed red pepper

8 ounces fresh green beans

1/2 teaspoon salt

■ In a small bowl, combine the oil and red pepper. Set aside. (If you have time, allow the oil and red pepper to sit for 5 to 10 minutes.)

■ Wash the green beans and snip off the ends. Drain very well.

■ Place the oil mixture and salt in a large skillet over high heat. Once quite hot, add the beans. Stir-fry for approximately 2 minutes, until the beans are tender-crisp. Remove from the oil and place on serving dish.

■ Serves 4 ■

Grape Tomatoes with Parmesan and Garlic

This is my favorite tomato dish. What more can I say?

- In a large saucepan, melt the butter. Add the tomatoes and top with the pepper, garlic salt, and Parmesan. Cook over high heat until heated through. You want the tomatoes to hold their shape, not soften too much.

■ Serves 4 ■

2 tablespoons butter

1 pint grape tomatoes

$1/3$ teaspoon black pepper

$1/2$ teaspoon garlic salt

1 tablespoon Parmesan cheese

Green Bean Casserole

This recipe is adapted from the famous Green Bean Casserole recipe published on Campbell's soup cans and French's Original French Fried Onions. Credit for this holiday favorite belongs to them. To make it gluten-free is a labor of love, but it may make you a rock star to the celiac in the room.

- Preheat the oven to 350°F.
- Combine the milk, pepper, mushroom soup, green beans, and all but $1/2$ cup of the onion rings in a medium-size casserole dish.
- Bake for 30 minutes, until hot throughout. Top with the remaining onion rings. Bake for 5 additional minutes, or until the onions have crisped.

■ Serves 8 to 10 ■

$3/4$ cup milk

$1/8$ teaspoon black pepper

1 recipe Condensed Cream of Mushroom Soup, page 158

2 (14.5-ounce) cans cut green beans, drained

$1 1/3$ cups Onion Rings (prepared extra thin), pages 41–43

> NOTE: It is difficult to locate gluten-free condensed cream of mushroom soup commercially. Several are available in ready-to-serve form. You may substitute them in place of our condensed version if you reduce the amount of milk. If you choose a prepared soup, read the label carefully.

Green Beans with Ham

This slow-cooked favorite was served at nearly every holiday gathering when I was growing up. You can toss these into a Crock Pot or cook them on the stove top.

3 (14.5-ounce) cans cut green beans

1 small ham hock

- In medium-size saucepan, place the green beans and ham hock. Cover with a lid and bring to a boil. Lower the heat and simmer for at least 60 minutes. Turn off the heat. Remove the ham hock and allow it to cool until you can handle it (or just work carefully). Remove the lean pieces of meat from the ham hock and return it to the beans.

■ Serves 7 ■

NOTE: If using a Crock Pot, cook on high for 4 to 5 hours, or low for 8 to 10 hours.

Indian-Style Vegetables

Many Indian dishes are simmered for a long period of time, first with ghee (clarified butter) and then combined with yogurt and spices, for a wonderful sauce. In preparing these vegetables, I use butter for flavor but combine it with a little oil to raise the "burning" point of the butter.

- Peel the potatoes and cut into large bite-size pieces. Cook, covered with water, in a small saucepan until just tender.

- While the potatoes are cooking, wash and quarter the mushrooms. Set aside.

- Wash the cauliflower, discard the leaves and stem, and cut into large bite-size pieces. Add the cauliflower to the potatoes during the last 5 minutes of cooking. Drain.

- In a large pot over high heat, combine the butter and oil. Add the cooked vegetables, garam masala, salt, and water. Stir frequently and cook until all the vegetables are tender and the flavors have blended.

■ Serves 6 ■

4–6 medium-size potatoes (approximately 12 ounces)

9–10 large button mushrooms (approximately 6 ounces)

1 small head of cauliflower (approximately 24 ounces) or approximately 16 ounces after leaves and stem are removed

2 tablespoons butter

1 tablespoon oil

1 tablespoon garam masala

1 teaspoon salt

1/4 cup water

NOTE: Use a white all-purpose or red potato for this dish. The potato should hold its shape, not fall entirely to pieces. A russet potato would fall apart and not look very nice. Garam masala is an Indian spice found in the local grocery store. If you do not have any, substitute half paprika and half cardamom (also used in chicken tikka).

Marinara Sauce

This light tomato sauce is bright with flavor. It doesn't overpower Asian rice sticks or even spaghetti squash. I hope you enjoy it.

- Place the tomatoes in a small bowl and chop into smaller pieces.
- In a medium-size saucepan over medium heat, sauté the garlic in olive oil until fragrant. Add the tomatoes and any juice, salt, and pepper to the pan. Lower the heat to low.
- Once the tomato sauce is almost to a boil, add the basil and stir well. Simmer for just a moment or two.

■ Serves 2 ■

1 (14.5-ounce can) diced tomatoes

1 clove garlic, minced

1 tablespoon olive oil

Pinch of salt

Small pinch of cayenne or black pepper

$1/4$–$1/2$ ounce fresh basil, stemmed and chopped finely

Root Vegetable Chips

The vegetables in this dish may be baked quite crisp and taste like a trendy healthy snack food. Alternatively, they may be deep-fried until crispy. That probably rules out any health benefits, but they are yummy.

1 medium-size potato (5–6 ounces)

1 small sweet potato (5–6 ounces)

1 large or 2 medium-size carrots (5 ounces)

2 tablespoons oil

1/4 teaspoon salt

- Preheat the oven to 400°F.

- Wash the potatoes. Remove any green or damaged areas. Set aside. Wash and peel the carrots. Remove and discard the tops.

- Place the oil in a medium-size bowl. Using a potato peeler or mandoline, make long slices or chips from the vegetables and add to the bowl. When the vegetable becomes too small to safely slice, discard the remainder.

- Add the salt to the bowl and toss well to coat.

- Spread the slices on a large cooling rack so that air may reach all the surfaces. Place in the oven for approximately 10 minutes. Remove the crisp slices. Continue baking the remaining slices for 5 to 10 minutes, as needed. Sprinkle with additional salt, if desired.

■ Serves 4 ■

Spaghetti Squash

Want to try something different and delicious? If you were to make this easy-to-prepare squash and top it with the Marinara Sauce on page 280, you would have a remarkably good meal. And, it would take you less than 15 minutes from start to finish.

1 spaghetti squash, approximately 2 pounds

- Wash the squash and cut in half lengthwise. This will be hard, so please be careful. Cut the squash into multiple pieces if it makes it easier for you to handle it. Remove and discard the seeds from the center of the squash.

- Place the squash in a microwave-safe bowl. Cover loosely with plastic wrap. Microwave on high for 10 minutes, until the squash is quite tender when pierced with a fork. Run the tines of a fork lengthwise along the inside of the squash. Almost magically, it will have the spaghetti appearance this squash is famous for. Although the squash is very tender, the spaghetti strands are almost crunchy in texture.

- Place in a serving bowl and top as desired.

■ Serves 2 ■

NOTE: Our testers felt that the squash at room temperature is more noodlelike. Very hot, the squash is more vegetable-like.

Squash, Sautéed

This is my daughter's favorite vegetable. It's quick and easy! You can use only zucchini squash or both zucchini and yellow squash.

- Wash the squash, remove and discard the ends, and cut in half lengthwise. Cut into ¼- to ½-inch sticks. Heat the oil in a medium-size skillet. Add the squash and sprinkle with garlic salt. Cook to your desired level of tenderness, just a minute or two. (We keep the squash a little crisp.)
- Serve hot.

■ Serves 6 ■

4 young squash, about
  1 ½ pounds
1 ½ tablespoons olive oil
½ teaspoon garlic salt

Sugar Snap Peas

Sugar snap peas are so very yummy. Don't mistake them for flat snow peas (although they are delicious, too). It takes a few minutes to remove any tough strings on the pods, but is well worth the effort.

- Wash the peas. Remove the strings from the sides of the pods. This is easiest to accomplish by snapping off a tiny bit at each end and pulling along the outside edge of the pod.
- Over medium heat, place the butter, then the peas, and finally the salt in a skillet. Cook, stirring frequently, for approximately 3 minutes.

■ Serves 6 ■

1 ¼ pounds sugar snap peas
1 tablespoon butter
Pinch of salt

Summer Vegetables

I like to serve this dish as a side to a plate of spaghetti. It is especially nice if you want something a little more substantial to go with rice noodles.

- Wash and dice the eggplant, zucchini, and yellow squash. Do not peel.
- In a large skillet over medium-high heat, place the oil, then all the remaining ingredients. Cover and cook for approximately 5 minutes. Stir occasionally. The vegetables will be tender but not mushy.

■ Serves 6 ■

1 small eggplant (8 ounces)

1 small–medium zucchini squash (10 ounces)

1 small–medium yellow squash (10 ounces)

2 tablespoons olive oil

1 teaspoon dried oregano

$1/2$ teaspoon salt

16 ∎ ▪ ▫ ▫

▪▪▪ CAKES

Gluten-free cakes can be wonderful but, like most baked items, are only as good as the recipes.

There is a science to making a cake. To ensure success, follow these easy rules:

1. Measure carefully. Weight measurement is best.
2. Use Rumford baking powder if baking powder is called for in the recipe.
3. Use Hershey's cocoa if cocoa powder is an ingredient in the recipe. I believe its flavor is better than some others when paired with gluten-free flours.
4. When using a loan, its intf paernal measurements should be approximately 4½ x 9 x 2½ inches (or one that has a capacity of 65 cubic inches).

If you'd like to understand more about gluten-free cakes, read on.

Just as wheat flour has certain characteristics, each gluten-free flour has its own unique characteristics. Cornstarch needs less sugar to achieve the correct sweetness level. Potato starch makes for a tighter crumb in some recipes and needs less binder. Rice uses far less flour by weight and requires more eggs.

Gluten-free cake batters take on a wider range of appearance than do traditional cake batters. This is not a bad thing, just surprising the first time you mix up certain recipes.

In traditional baking, gluten is the natural binder in white flour. (If you're not familiar with gluten, think of the stretchy insides of a good loaf of bread.) Bread flour is milled from wheat that produces more gluten, and cake flour utilizes wheat that produces less gluten. All-purpose flour provides the "middle ground" of gluten. If you don't mix all-purpose flour too much, gluten formation is limited. If you mix it a lot, more gluten is formed. Plain, ordinary white flour is truly a marvel.

The gluten-free substitute for gluten is xanthan gum. Xanthan helps us to duplicate gluten's binding effect. When baking without wheat, we must use different ratios of xanthan gum to achieve different results. Add to that, the rules for each gluten-free flour are a little different. Generally speaking, potato starch requires less xanthan gum, corn and rice require a little more, and oats require the least of all. And, just when you have it figured out, a recipe will shock you by not following the rules at all.

Xanthan gum performs its binding activity in two places. First, in the mixing bowl, you will notice that your batter gets thicker the longer you beat it. (If you look at the ingredient list for a traditional cake or muffin mix, you may see xanthan gum. Traditional cake mix batters will often start thin, then thicken as you beat them.) In the recipes that use larger amounts of xanthan gum, overbeating can cause a very thick batter, verging on a dough. If this happens, your cake will bake up with a funny-looking top.

There are two major raising agents used in these pages—baking soda and baking powder. Baking soda interacts with an acid (such as vinegar, brown sugar, or cocoa powder) to create little bubbles of air. Baking powder has an acid included in its formulation. In theory, $1/4$ teaspoon of baking soda used in the presence of an acid should have the same raising effect as 1 teaspoon of baking powder. This is true, but only up to a point. In fact, with gluten-free baking, structural stability is at risk. (To those of you who have never baked gluten-free, you're thinking I've spent one too many hours in the kitchen, which may be true. But those of you who have experienced the heartache of a sunken cake, you're nodding your head up and down, wanting to know more.)

It is for structural stability (or should I say pursuit of springy texture) that sometimes I use just baking soda. Other times, I use both baking soda and baking powder, and still other times I use just baking powder. Without baking soda, your cake may fall. Without baking powder, the texture of a cake may be too tight. And using more baking soda in a pound cake helps to produce a tight crumb.

When mixing a recipe, it is important not to have your baking soda and an added acid—such as vinegar—come into contact prematurely. The reason it is so important to keep these ingredients far away from each other when first adding them to the mixing bowl, is to prevent a volcano-like school experiment from happening in your batter.

Also, not all baking powders are created equal! Two major brands that I've tested extensively are made by the Clabbergirl Company—Rumford baking powder and Clabbergirl baking powder. Also of note, Rumford is aluminum-free.

Rumford performs most of its chemical activity in the mixing bowl, and the rest in the oven. Clabbergirl does most of its chemical activity in the oven, and a smaller amount in the bowl. All recipes in this book have been successfully made using Rumford baking powder. Spot-testing with Clabbergirl makes for different results: that batter can actually overflow the baking pan! If you use another brand, use one that acts like Rumford (or reduce baking powder by one-third and keep your fingers crossed).

I have manipulated every common baking ingredient to its limits so that we can produce truly delicious foods. Think about it. Making a light, springy cake with rice flour may seem like making whipped cream with sand. It is possible, but we must measure carefully and push ingredients to their limits of performance.

Finally, I humbly acknowledge that someone out there may well figure out how to make a single-grain angel food cake that is just right. If they do, mazel tov! Until then, enjoy the angel food and sponge cakes in my first book, *The Gluten-Free Kitchen*.

■ ■ ■

Carrot Cake ▪ *Corn-based*

This carrot cake is moist and flavorful. For those who are avoiding dairy, this would be a good choice.

- Preheat the oven to 350°F. Lightly grease a 9-inch round or square baking pan.

- In a medium-size bowl, mix the oil with the sugar. Add the eggs. Mix until lighter and thicker. This will take a minute or two with your mixer. Add the other ingredients. Beat well. The batter will become quite thick. Pour into the prepared baking pan. Bake for 30 to 40 minutes, until a toothpick inserted in the middle tests cleanly.

▪ Serves 9 ▪

1/3 cup oil

3/4 cup brown sugar, 150 grams

2 eggs

1/4 cup apple juice

1 1/4 cups cornstarch, 155 grams

2 teaspoons baking powder

1/4 teaspoon baking soda

1/4 teaspoon salt

1 teaspoon ground cinnamon

Scant 3/4 teaspoon xanthan gum

1/3 cup chopped nuts (optional)

1 cup grated carrots, packed, 100 grams

Carrot Cake ▪ *Oat-based*

This carrot cake is slightly crumbly. If you plan to layer the cake, increase the xanthan gum by approximately $1/8$ teaspoon.

- ▪ Preheat the oven to 350°F. Lightly grease a 9-inch round or square baking pan.
- ▪ In a medium-size bowl, mix the oil with the sugar. Add the eggs and egg white. Mix until light and thick. This will take a minute or two with your mixer. Add the other ingredients. Beat well. The batter will thicken a bit. Pour into the prepared baking pan. Bake for 30 to 40 minutes, until a toothpick inserted in the middle tests cleanly.

▪ Serves 9 ▪

$1/3$ cup oil

$3/4$ cup sugar, 150 grams

2 eggs

1 egg white

$1/2$ cup apple juice

$1 1/3$ cups oat flour, 160 grams

1 tablespoon baking powder

$1/4$ teaspoon baking soda

$1/4$ teaspoon salt

1 teaspoon vanilla extract

1 teaspoon ground cinnamon

$1/4$ teaspoon xanthan gum

1 cup grated carrots, packed, 100 grams

Carrot Cake ■ *Potato-based*

Like the corn version, this carrot cake is moist and flavorful. If you have the opportunity, serve this cake warm. This one gets high marks.

- Preheat the oven to 350°F. Lightly grease a 9-inch round or square baking pan.

- In a medium-size bowl, mix the oil with the sugar. Add the eggs. Mix until lighter and thicker. This will take a minute or two with your mixer. Add the other ingredients. Beat well. The batter will thicken a little. Pour into the prepared baking pan. Bake for 30 to 40 minutes, until a toothpick inserted in the middle tests cleanly.

■ Serves 9 ■

1/3 cup oil

3/4 cup brown sugar, 150 grams

2 eggs

1/4 cup apple juice

1 cup potato starch, 155 grams

2 teaspoons baking powder

1/4 teaspoon baking soda

1/4 teaspoon salt

3/4 teaspoon ground cinnamon

1/2 teaspoon xanthan gum

1/3 cup chopped nuts (optional)

1 cup grated carrots, packed, 100 grams

NOTE: If you choose to add nuts to this version of the carrot cake, chop them very small so that they do not sink to the bottom of the batter.

Carrot Cake ▪ *Rice-based*

This carrot cake is perhaps the most delicate in flavor and texture of all my carrot cakes. My son called this cake "yummy." It also keeps well.

- Preheat the oven to 350°F. Lightly grease a 9-inch round or square baking pan.
- In a medium-size bowl, mix the oil with the sugar. Add the eggs and egg white. Mix until light and thick. This will take a minute or two with your mixer. Add the other ingredients. Beat well. The batter will thicken a bit. Pour into the prepared baking pan. Bake for 30 to 40 minutes, until a toothpick inserted in the middle tests cleanly.

▪ Serves 9 ▪

1/2 cup oil

3/4 cup sugar, 150 grams

2 eggs

1 egg white

1/3 cup apple juice

1 cup rice flour, 150 grams

1 tablespoon baking powder

1/4 teaspoon baking soda

1/4 teaspoon salt

1/2 teaspoon vanilla extract

1/2 teaspoon ground cinnamon

1/2 teaspoon xanthan gum

1 cup grated carrots, packed, 100 grams

Homemade Chocolate Cake ▪ *Corn-based*

This cake is medium-textured and its chocolate flavor is just right.

- Preheat the oven to 350°F. Lightly grease a 9-inch round or square baking pan.
- In a medium-size bowl, mix the oil with the sugar. Add the eggs. Mix until lighter and thicker. This will take a minute or two with your mixer. Add the other ingredients. Beat well. The batter will become quite thick. Pour into the prepared baking pan. Bake for 30 to 40 minutes, until a toothpick inserted in the middle tests cleanly.

▪ Serves 9 ▪

1/3 cup oil

3/4 cup sugar, 150 grams

2 eggs

1/2 cup plain yogurt

1 1/2 teaspoons vanilla extract

3/4 cup plus 2 tablespoons cornstarch, 110 grams

1/4 cup unsweetened cocoa powder, 20 grams

2 teaspoons baking powder

1/2 teaspoon baking soda

1/2 teaspoon salt

1/2 teaspoon xanthan gum

Homemade Chocolate Cake ▪ *Oat-based*

Chocolaty and moist—an all-around nice cake.

- Preheat the oven to 350°F. Grease a 9-inch round or square pan.

- In a small bowl, combine the cocoa powder and water. Stir well. Allow to cool for several minutes. While the cocoa mixture cools, combine all the dry ingredients in a medium-size bowl and stir well. (This will distribute the xanthan gum throughout the flour, for better absorption.)

- Add the remaining ingredients, including the cocoa mixture, to the bowl. Mix well, scraping the sides of the bowl at least once. The batter will remain quite thin.

- Pour the batter into the prepared pan. Bake for 30 minutes, until a toothpick inserted in the middle tests cleanly. Let cool.

- Frost as desired.

▪ Serves 9 ▪

$1/2$ cup unsweetened cocoa powder, 40 grams
$3/4$ cup boiling water
1 cup oat flour, 125 grams
$3/4$ cup sugar, 150 grams
1 teaspoon baking soda
2 teaspoons baking powder
$1/4$ teaspoon xanthan gum
$1/2$ teaspoon salt
$1/4$ cup oil
2 eggs
1 egg white
1 teaspoon vanilla extract

NOTE: For those of you interested in why this recipe was formulated in this fashion, I'll pass on what I think is very interesting information. First, a hot liquid helps to release flavor from the cocoa. Water carries a more straightforward chocolate flavor than milk, so water is used. The extra egg white is added to develop more little pockets of air for the raising agent to work within. Little xanthan gum is required, as the oat flour has a little binding property by itself. And, finally, the vanilla softens the flavor of the cocoa, which is naturally bitter.

Homemade Chocolate Cake ■ *Potato-based*

This is a soft, squishy, moist chocolate cake. It will retain its moist texture for several days.

- Preheat the oven to 350°F. Lightly grease a 9-inch square baking pan.
- In a medium-size bowl, mix the melted butter with the sugar. Add the eggs. Mix until light and thick. Add the other ingredients. Beat until thick and creamy. Pour into the prepared baking pan. Bake for 40 to 50 minutes, until a toothpick inserted in the middle tests cleanly.

■ Serves 9 ■

1/4 pound butter (1/2 cup), melted

1 cup sugar, 100 grams

2 eggs

1/2 cup milk

3/4 cup potato starch, 115 grams

1/4 cup unsweetened cocoa powder, 20 grams

3/4 teaspoon baking soda

1/4 teaspoon salt

1 teaspoon vanilla extract

1 1/4 teaspoons xanthan gum

Homemade Chocolate Cake ■ *Rice-based*

This is an excellent chocolate cake. As you can see in this recipe, working with rice sometimes involves more fat, eggs, and sugar, but it is worth it in this case. Refrigerate or freeze after baking to maintain the best texture.

- Preheat the oven to 350°F. Lightly grease a 9 x 13-inch baking pan.
- In a medium-size bowl, cream the butter and sugar. Add the eggs and egg whites. Mix until light yellow and a little thicker. This will take a minute or two with your mixer. Add the other ingredients. Mix well.
- Pour into the prepared baking pan. Bake for 30 to 40 minutes, until a a toothpick inserted in the middle tests cleanly. The cake will spring back lightly when touched and will begin to pull away from the sides of the pan ever so slightly when done.

■ Serves 15 ■

12 tablespoons (3/4 cup) butter

1 1/3 cups sugar

3 eggs

3 egg whites

3/4 cup milk

3/4 cup unsweetened cocoa powder, 60 grams

1 cup rice flour, 150 grams

1 tablespoon plus 1 teaspoon baking powder

2 teaspoons baking soda

3/4 teaspoon salt

1 1/2 teaspoons vanilla extract

1 1/4 teaspoons xanthan gum

Homemade Yellow Cake ▪ *Corn-based*

This is a medium-bodied yellow cake. Although it contains no butter, it tastes buttery.

- ▪ Preheat the oven to 350°F. Lightly grease a 9-inch round or square baking pan.
- ▪ In a medium-size bowl, mix the oil with the sugar. Add the eggs. Mix until light and thick. This will take a minute or two with your mixer. Add the other ingredients. Beat well. The batter will thicken a little. Pour into the prepared baking pan. Bake for 30 to 40 minutes, until a toothpick inserted in the middle tests cleanly.

▪ Serves 9 ▪

$^1/_3$ cup oil

$^3/_4$ cup sugar, 150 grams

2 eggs

$^1/_4$ cup milk

1 $^1/_4$ cups cornstarch, 155 grams

2 teaspoons baking powder

$^1/_4$ teaspoon baking soda

$^1/_4$ teaspoon salt

1 teaspoon vanilla extract

1 $^3/_4$ teaspoons xanthan gum

Homemade Yellow Cake ▪ *Potato-based*

This medium-bodied yellow cake is reminiscent of homemade traditional yellow cake.

- ▪ Preheat the oven to 350°F. Lightly grease a 9-inch round or square baking pan.
- ▪ In a medium-size bowl, mix the oil with the sugar. Add the eggs. Mix until light and thick. This will take a minute or two with your mixer. Add the other ingredients. Beat well. The batter will thicken a little. Pour into the prepared baking pan. Bake for 30 to 40 minutes, until a toothpick inserted in the middle tests cleanly.

▪ Serves 9 ▪

$^1/_3$ cup oil

1 cup sugar, 200 grams

2 eggs

$^1/_3$ cup milk

1 cup potato starch, 155 grams

2 teaspoons baking powder

$^1/_4$ teaspoon baking soda

$^1/_4$ teaspoon salt

1 teaspoon vanilla extract

1 $^1/_2$ teaspoons xanthan gum

ABOUT NUT CAKES

Much to my surprise, nut cakes were difficult to formulate. The ground nuts are drying and must also be calculated as a flour. The moisture ratio and the required rise were difficult to perfect. Use of a 9-inch round baking pan provided best results.

Please know, however, that should your cake not look perfect, it will still taste great. We tested scores of recipes to be sure that you wouldn't end up with a pretty but dry cake. Instead, we've pushed the envelope, giving you a moist one that is also attractive.

I suggest serving these cakes with a simple chocolate glaze to accentuate the flavor of the nut. They are also nice without icing. I've used ground pecans (my favorite) in most of the recipes, but ground walnuts or other nuts can certainly be substituted.

Nut Cake ■ *Corn-based*

This cake has a slightly depressed surface, but the flavor and texture are perfect.

- Preheat the oven to 350°F. Lightly grease a 9-inch round or square baking pan.
- In a medium-size bowl, mix the oil with the sugar. Add the eggs. Mix until lighter and thicker. This will take a minute or two with your mixer. Add the other ingredients. Beat well. The batter will become quite thick. Pour into the prepared baking pan. Bake for 30 to 40 minutes, until a toothpick inserted in the middle tests cleanly.

■ Serves 9 ■

1/3 cup oil

3/4 cup sugar, 150 grams

2 eggs

1/3 cup plain yogurt

1 cup cornstarch, 125 grams

1/4 cup ground nuts, 25 grams

2 teaspoons baking powder

1/2 teaspoon baking soda

1/2 teaspoon salt

1 teaspoon vanilla extract

1 teaspoon vinegar

1/2 teaspoon xanthan gum

Nut Cake ■ *Oat-based*

This cake would be good with or without icing. The texture is between that of a fluffy cake and a nut bread, not too sweet with a slight hit of oat flavor.

■ Preheat the oven to 350°F. Lightly grease a 9-inch round or square baking pan.

■ In a medium-size bowl, mix the oil with the sugar. Add the eggs and egg white. Mix until light and thick. This will take a minute or two with your mixer. Add the other ingredients. Beat well. The batter will thicken a bit. Pour into the prepared baking pan. Bake for 30 or 40 minutes, until a toothpick inserted in the middle tests cleanly.

■ Serves 9 ■

1/3 cup oil
3/4 cup sugar, 150 grams
2 eggs
1 egg white
1/2 cup milk
1 1/3 cups oat flour, 160 grams
1/4 cup ground pecans, 25 grams
1 tablespoon baking powder
1/4 teaspoon baking soda
1/4 teaspoon salt
1 1/2 teaspoons vanilla extract
1 teaspoon vinegar
1/2 teaspoon xanthan gum

Nut Cake ■ *Potato-based*

This cake has a soft nut undertone. The texture is light.

■ Preheat the oven to 350°F. Lightly grease a 9-inch round or square baking pan.

■ In a medium-size bowl, mix the oil with the sugar. Add the eggs. Mix until lighter and thicker. This will take a minute or two with your mixer. Add the other ingredients. Beat well. The batter will thicken a little. Pour into the prepared baking pan. Bake for 30 to 40 minutes, until a toothpick inserted in the middle tests cleanly.

■ Serves 9 ■

1/3 cup oil
3/4 cup sugar, 150 grams
2 eggs
1/3 cup plain yogurt
1 cup potato starch, 155 grams
1/4 cup ground nuts, 25 grams
1 tablespoon baking powder
1/2 teaspoon baking soda
1/4 teaspoon salt
1 teaspoon vanilla extract
1/2 teaspoon vinegar
1/2 teaspoon xanthan gum

Nut Cake ▪ *Rice-based*

This version is probably the mildest in flavor. Use a stronger-tasting nut, such as walnut, for more flavor. A simple chocolate glaze would complement this cake.

- Preheat the oven to 350°F. Lightly grease a 9-inch round or square baking pan.

- In a medium-size bowl, mix the oil with the sugar. Add the eggs and egg white. Mix until light and thick. This will take a minute or two with your mixer. Add the other ingredients. Beat well. The batter will thicken a bit. Pour into the prepared baking pan. Bake for 30 to 40 minutes, until a toothpick inserted in the middle tests cleanly.

▪ Serves 9 ▪

$^1/_2$ cup oil

$^3/_4$ cup sugar, 150 grams

2 eggs

1 egg white

$^1/_3$ cup plain yogurt

1 cup rice flour, 150 grams

$^1/_4$ cup ground pecans, 25 grams

1 tablespoon baking powder

$^1/_4$ teaspoon baking soda

$^1/_4$ teaspoon salt

1 $^1/_2$ teaspoons vanilla extract

$^1/_2$ teaspoon xanthan gum

ABOUT POUND CAKES

Pound cakes are similar to nut cakes in their tendency to sink a little in the middle, especially the corn versions. After scores of tests, I've tweaked it about as far as my single flours will let me go. Some rules for baking gluten-free pound cakes with single flours may seem strange, but are worth sharing:

1. Use baking soda, with the accompanying acid, for a more stable rise. Theoretically, baking soda combined with an acid should act the same as baking powder, which already has an acid in its formulation. But this is just not the case. The subtle differences make for different textures as well as affect structural stability.
2. Use less cornstarch by weight than potato starch by weight.
3. Use higher xanthan gum–to–flour ratio when using cornstarch than when using potato starch. This is counterintuitive, given potato starch has a lower xanthan gum ratio than does cornstarch when making breads.
4. Using more flour does not fix the minor sinking. Neither does using less raising agent or using less liquid. In fact, more flour makes for a high-rising mess when using cornstarch.
5. Increasing xanthan gum, which often adds stability, can backfire, making for pulled in sides and a loaf that can be gummy.

Pound Cake, Chocolate ▪ *Corn-based*

This cake is not overly sweet, has a tight crumb, and is pretty irresistible.

- Preheat the oven to 350°F. Grease a large loaf pan.
- In a large bowl, cream together the sugar and butter. Add the eggs. Mix until light, thick, and fluffy. Add the remaining ingredients. Beat until thick and creamy. (I like to use a whisk blade on my mixer, thereby incorporating as much air as possible.) Scrape down the edges once during the mixing process.
- Pour the batter into the prepared pan. Bake for 45 to 50 minutes, until a toothpick inserted in the middle tests cleanly.

▪ Makes 1 large loaf; serves 10 ▪

3/4 cup sugar, 150 grams

1/4 pound butter (1/2 cup), very softened

3 eggs

3/4 cup plus 2 tablespoons cornstarch, 110 grams

1 teaspoon xanthan gum

1/3 cup unsweetened cocoa powder, 30 grams

1/4 teaspoon salt

1/2 cup milk

2 teaspoons baking powder

1 teaspoon baking soda

1 teaspoon vanilla extract

Pound Cake, Chocolate ∎ *Oat-based*

This is a not-too-heavy but very chocolaty pound cake. It is also not overly sweet. The top of the cake is level, instead of domed. The crumb is very traditional. I had the urge to put strawberries and whipped cream on top of this chocolate cake! However, it is moist and can certainly be eaten alone.

■ Preheat the oven to 350°F. Grease a medium-size loaf pan.

■ In a small bowl, combine the cocoa powder and water. Stir well. Allow to cool for several minutes. While the cocoa mixture cools, combine all the dry ingredients in a medium-size bowl and stir well. (This will distribute the xanthan gum throughout the flour, for better absorption.)

■ Add the remaining ingredients, including the cocoa mixture. Mix well, scraping the sides of the bowl at least once. The batter will not be too thick.

■ Pour the batter into the prepared pan. Bake for 45 to 50 minutes, until a toothpick inserted in the middle tests cleanly. Let cool.

■ Serves 10 ■

1/2 cup unsweetened cocoa powder, 40 grams

3/4 cup boiling water

1 cup oat flour, 125 grams

3/4 cup sugar, 150 grams

1 teaspoon baking soda

1 teaspoon baking powder

1/4 teaspoon xanthan gum

1/2 teaspoon salt

1/4 cup oil

3 eggs

1 teaspoon vanilla extract

Pound Cake, Chocolate ■ *Potato-based*

This cake has a nice chocolate flavor and is quite soft. This is my favorite of the chocolate pound cakes.

- Preheat the oven to 350°F. Grease a large loaf pan.

- In a large bowl, cream together the sugar and butter. Add the eggs. Mix until light, thick, and fluffy. Add the remaining ingredients. Beat until thick and creamy. (I like to use a whisk blade on my mixer, thereby incorporating as much air as possible.) Scrape down the edges once during the mixing process.

- Pour the batter into the prepared pan. Bake for 40 to 45 minutes, until a toothpick inserted in the middle tests cleanly.

■ Makes 1 large loaf; serves 10 ■

3/4 cup sugar, 150 grams

1/4 pound butter (1/2 cup), very softened

3 eggs

3/4 cup potato starch, 115 grams

3/4 teaspoon xanthan gum

1/3 cup unsweetened cocoa powder, 30 grams

1/4 teaspoon salt

1/2 cup milk

2 teaspoons baking powder

1 teaspoon baking soda

1 teaspoon vanilla extract

Pound Cake, Chocolate ▪ *Rice-based*

Rice flour is so underrated! It makes this moist, delicious pound cake, with a tight crumb. The top is relatively flat and the texture is very consistent throughout. If you want to try making a pound cake, this would be a good place to start.

- Preheat the oven to 350°F. Grease a medium-size loaf pan.

- In a small bowl, combine the cocoa powder and water. Stir well. Allow to cool for several minutes. While the cocoa mixture cools, combine the oil and sugar in a medium-size bowl. Mix well. Add the eggs and beat until light. Add the remaining ingredients, including the cocoa mixture. Mix well, scraping the sides of the bowl at least once. The batter will thicken a bit.

- Pour the batter into the prepared pan. Bake for 45 to 55 minutes, until a toothpick inserted in the middle tests cleanly. Let cool.

▪ Serves 9 ▪

1/2 cup unsweetened cocoa powder, 40 grams

1/3 cup boiling water

1/3 cup oil

1 cup sugar, 200 grams

3 eggs

1/4 cup milk

3/4 cup rice flour, 115 grams

1 teaspoon baking soda

1 teaspoon baking powder

1 teaspoon xanthan gum

1/2 teaspoon salt

1 teaspoon vanilla extract

Pound Cake, Lemon–Poppy Seed ■ *Corn-based*

This pound cake is best at room temperature. The lemon flavor is subtle and pleasing.

- Preheat the oven to 350°F. Grease a large loaf pan.

- In a large bowl, cream together the sugar and butter. Add the eggs. Mix until light, thick, and fluffy. Add the remaining ingredients. Beat until thick and creamy. (I like to use a whisk blade on my mixer, thereby incorporating as much air as possible.) Scrape down the edges once during the mixing process.

- Pour the batter into the prepared pan. Bake for 45 to 50 minutes, until a toothpick inserted in the middle tests cleanly. Let cool in the pan to help retain the structure.

■ Makes 1 large loaf; serves 10 ■

3/4 cup sugar, 150 grams

1/4 pound butter (1/2 cup), very softened

3 eggs

3/4 cup plus 2 tablespoons cornstarch, 110 grams

1 teaspoon xanthan gum

1/2 teaspoon salt

1/4 cup plus 1 tablespoon milk

3 tablespoons lemon juice

2 teaspoons baking powder

1 teaspoon baking soda

1 teaspoon poppy seeds

Pound Cake, Lemon ■ *Potato-based*

This cake is for lemon purists. It has definite lemon flavor, but very buttery undertones. You may want a second piece.

- Preheat the oven to 350°F. Grease a large loaf pan.

- In a large bowl, cream together the sugar and butter. Add the eggs. Mix until light, thick, and fluffy. Add the remaining ingredients. Beat until thick and creamy. (I like to use a whisk blade on my mixer, thereby incorporating as much air as possible.) Scrape down the edges once during the mixing process.

- Pour the batter into the prepared pan. Bake for 45 to 50 minutes, until a toothpick inserted in the middle tests cleanly.

■ Makes 1 large loaf; serves 10 ■

3/4 cup sugar, 150 grams

1/4 pound butter (1/2 cup), very softened

3 eggs

1 cup potato starch, 155 grams

1 1/4 teaspoons xanthan gum

1/2 teaspoon salt

1/4 cup lemon juice

1/4 cup milk

2 teaspoons baking powder

1 teaspoon baking soda

1 teaspoon lemon zest

Pound Cake, Lemon ■ *Rice-based*

This pound cake has delicate lemon flavor with a springy texture. Not my favorite lemon pound cake, but if you need to use rice flour, this will do nicely.

- Preheat the oven to 350°F. Grease a medium-size loaf pan.
- In a medium-size bowl, combine the butter and sugar. Mix well. Add the eggs and beat until light. Add the remaining ingredients. Mix well, scraping the sides of the bowl at least once. Continue beating until the batter thickens.
- Pour the batter into the prepared pan. Bake for 45 to 55 minutes, until a toothpick inserted in the middle tests cleanly. Let cool.

■ Serves 10 ■

$5\frac{1}{3}$ tablespoons ($\frac{1}{3}$ cup) butter

1 cup sugar, 200 grams

3 eggs

1 cup rice flour, 150 grams

$\frac{2}{3}$ cup milk

3 tablespoons lemon juice

1 teaspoon baking powder

1 teaspoon xanthan gum

1 teaspoon baking soda

$\frac{1}{2}$ teaspoon salt

1 teaspoon lemon zest

Pound Cake, Rum ■ *Corn-based*

This cake is fashioned after the famous Bacardi rum cake. It has great flavor. For simplicity, I've baked it in a large loaf pan instead of a fluted pan.

- Preheat the oven to 350°F. Grease a large loaf pan.
- In a large bowl, cream together the sugar and butter. Add the eggs. Mix until light, thick, and fluffy. Add the remaining ingredients. Beat until thick and creamy. (I like to use a whisk blade on my mixer, thereby incorporating as much air as possible.) Scrape down the edges once during the mixing process.
- Pour the batter into the prepared pan. Bake for 45 to 50 minutes, until a toothpick inserted in the middle tests cleanly.

■ Makes 1 large loaf; serves 10 ■

$\frac{3}{4}$ cup sugar, 150 grams

$\frac{1}{4}$ pound butter ($\frac{1}{2}$ cup), very softened

3 eggs

$\frac{3}{4}$ cup plus 2 tablespoons cornstarch, 110 grams

1 teaspoon xanthan gum

$\frac{1}{2}$ teaspoon salt

5 tablespoons milk

3 tablespoons rum

2 teaspoons cider vinegar

2 teaspoons baking powder

1 teaspoon baking soda

Pound Cake, Rum ▪ *Potato-based*

Substituting Grand Marnier for rum makes this cake absolutely wonderful, but the original rum is pretty nice, too. When substituting distilled liqueurs, be watchful for suspect ingredients, such as caramel coloring.

- Preheat the oven to 350°F. Grease a large loaf pan.
- In a large bowl, cream together the sugar and butter. Add the eggs. Mix until light, thick, and fluffy. Add the remaining ingredients. Beat until thick and creamy. (I like to use a whisk blade on my mixer, thereby incorporating as much air as possible.) Scrape down the edges once during the mixing process.
- Pour the batter into the prepared pan. Bake for 45 to 50 minutes, until a toothpick inserted in the middle tests cleanly.

▪ Makes 1 large loaf; serves 10 ▪

3/4 cup sugar, 150 grams
1/4 pound butter (1/2 cup), very softened
3 eggs
1 cup potato starch, 155 grams
1 1/4 teaspoons xanthan gum
1/2 teaspoon salt
3 tablespoons rum
2 teaspoons cider vinegar
1/4 cup milk
2 teaspoons baking powder
1 teaspoon baking soda

Pound Cake, Vanilla ▪ *Corn-based*

This cake is soft with a nice, buttery flavor.

- Preheat the oven to 350°F. Grease a large loaf pan.
- In a large bowl, cream together the sugar and butter. Add the eggs. Mix until light, thick, and fluffy. Add the remaining ingredients. Beat until thick and creamy. (I like to use a whisk blade on my mixer, thereby incorporating as much air as possible.) Scrape down the edges once during the mixing process.
- Pour the batter into the prepared pan. Bake for 45 to 50 minutes, until a toothpick inserted in the middle tests cleanly.

▪ Makes 1 large loaf; serves 10 ▪

3/4 cup sugar, 150 grams
1/4 pound butter (1/2 cup), very softened
3 eggs
1 1/4 cups cornstarch, 155 grams
1 teaspoon xanthan gum
1/2 teaspoon salt
1/2 cup milk
2 teaspoons baking powder
1 teaspoon baking soda
2 teaspoons cider vinegar
2 teaspoons vanilla extract

Pound Cake, Vanilla ▪ *Potato-based*

This soft pound cake melts in your mouth and has buttery undertones. For a firmer cake, add an extra 1/8 teaspoon of xanthan gum. This cake could win a blue ribbon in any baking contest.

- Preheat the oven to 350°F. Grease a large loaf pan.
- In a large bowl, cream together the sugar and butter. Add the eggs. Mix until light, thick, and fluffy. Add the remaining ingredients. Beat until thick and creamy. (I like to use a whisk blade on my mixer, thereby incorporating as much air as possible.) Scrape down the edges once during the mixing process.
- Pour the batter into the prepared pan. Bake for 45 to 50 minutes, until a toothpick inserted in the middle tests cleanly.

▪ Makes 1 large loaf; serves 10 ▪

3/4 cup sugar, 150 grams
1/4 pound (1/2 cup) butter, very softened
3 eggs
1 cup potato starch, 155 grams
3/4 teaspoon xanthan gum
1/2 teaspoon salt
1/2 cup milk
2 teaspoons baking powder
1 teaspoon baking soda
2 teaspoons cider vinegar
2 teaspoons vanilla extract

Pound Cake, Vanilla ▪ *Rice-based*

This is an all-around nice pound cake. I prefer the potato version, but this one will do nicely if rice is your flour of choice.

- Preheat the oven to 350°F. Grease a medium-size loaf pan.
- In a medium-size bowl, cream the butter and sugar. Add the eggs and beat until light. Add the remaining ingredients. Mix well, scraping the sides of the bowl at least once. Continue beating until the batter thickens.
- Pour the batter into the prepared pan. Bake for 45 to 55 minutes, until a toothpick inserted in the middle tests cleanly. Let cool.

▪ Serves 10 ▪

5 1/3 tablespoons (1/3 cup) butter
1 cup sugar, 200 grams
3 eggs
1 cup rice flour, 150 grams
2/3 cup milk
2 teaspoons apple cider vinegar
1 teaspoon baking powder
1 teaspoon xanthan gum
1 teaspoon baking soda
1/2 teaspoon salt
1 teaspoon vanilla extract

Shortcake, Blueberry ▪ *Potato-based*

This is the slightly sweet counterpart of our traditional biscuits. Enjoy at room temperature. Otherwise, there is a gummy edge, which tends to be the nature of potato starch when used alone. This recipe uses blueberries as they are available throughout the year, even if frozen.

▪ Preheat the oven to 375°F. Grease a baking sheet.

▪ In a medium-size bowl, blend together all the ingredients for the biscuits except the milk and vinegar. Add the milk and vinegar, and mix well. The dough will be quite fragile. Pat the dough out on the prepared baking sheet to ½- to ¾-inch thickness. Cut into nine square biscuits and separate with the side of a knife.

▪ Bake for 15 to 20 minutes, until the biscuits begin to brown. Do not underbake. Remove from the baking sheet with spatula (handling by hand will cause the structure to partially collapse) and move to a cooling rack. Let cool until room temperature.

▪ If using fresh berries, wash and drain. If using frozen, thaw and drain. Sprinkle the berries with the sugar and vanilla.

▪ In individual serving dishes, top each biscuit with the fruit and then the whipped cream.

▪ Serves 9 ▪

Biscuits:

¼ pound (½ cup) butter

1 cup plus 2 tablespoons potato starch, 175 grams

1⅛ teaspoon xanthan gum

1 tablespoon baking powder

½ teaspoon baking soda

2 tablespoons sugar

½ teaspoon vanilla extract

½ teaspoon salt

¾ cup milk

1 teaspoon vinegar

Topping:

1½ pounds fresh or frozen blueberries

2 tablespoons sugar

½ teaspoon vanilla extract

1 recipe Whipped Cream (page 332), prepared

Shortcake, Peach ▪ *Oat-based*

This is a sweet version of our traditional biscuits. These biscuits are paired with spiced peaches to stand up to the whole-grain flavor of the oats.

- ▪ Preheat the oven to 375°F. Grease a baking sheet.

- ▪ In a medium-size bowl, blend together all the biscuit ingredients except the milk and vinegar. Add the milk and vinegar, and mix well. The dough will be quite fragile. Pat the dough out on the prepared baking sheet to 1/2-inch thickness. Cut into nine square biscuits and separate with the side of a knife.

- ▪ Bake for 15 to 20 minutes, until the biscuits begin to brown.

- ▪ If using fresh peaches, wash, peel, and slice. Toss with lemon juice right away to prevent browning. If using frozen, thaw and drain. Sprinkle the fruit with the sugar, vanilla, and cinnamon. Mix well.

- ▪ In individual serving dishes, top each biscuit with the fruit and then the whipped cream.

▪ Serves 9 ▪

Biscuits:
1/4 pound (1/2 cup) butter

1 1/3 cups oat flour, 165 grams

1 teaspoon xanthan gum

1 tablespoon baking powder

1/2 teaspoon baking soda

2 1/2 tablespoons sugar

1/2 teaspoon vanilla extract

1/2 teaspoon ground cinnamon or grated nutmeg

1/2 teaspoon salt

3/4 cup milk

1 teaspoon vinegar

Glaze (optional):
1 tablespoon melted butter

Topping:
1 1/2 pounds fresh or frozen peaches

1 teaspoon lemon juice

2 tablespoons sugar

1/2 teaspoon vanilla extract

1/2 teaspoon ground cinnamon or grated nutmeg

1 recipe Whipped Cream (page 332), prepared

Shortcake, Strawberry ▪ *Corn-based*

This is a slightly sweet version of our traditional biscuits, teamed with strawberries, because they are just so good.

- Preheat the oven to 375°F. Grease a baking sheet.

- In a medium-size bowl, blend all the ingredients for the biscuits except the milk and vinegar. Add milk and vinegar, and mix well. The dough will be quite fragile. Pat the dough out on the prepared baking sheet to $^1/_2$- to $^3/_4$-inch thickness. Cut into nine square biscuits and separate with the side of a knife.

- Bake for 15 to 20 minutes, until the biscuits begin to brown.

- Wash and slice the berries. Sprinkle with a little sugar if they are not sweet.

- In individual serving dishes, top each biscuit with the fruit and then the whipped cream.

▪ Serves 9 ▪

Biscuits:

$^1/_4$ pound ($^1/_2$ cup) butter

$1 ^1/_3$ cups cornstarch, 165 grams

$1 ^1/_4$ teaspoons xanthan gum

1 tablespoon baking powder

$^1/_2$ teaspoon baking soda

$1 ^1/_2$ tablespoons sugar

$^1/_2$ teaspoon salt

$^1/_2$ teaspoon vanilla extract

$^3/_4$ cup milk

1 teaspoon vinegar

Topping:

1 pound strawberries

1 tablespoon sugar (optional)

1 recipe Whipped Cream (page 332), prepared

Shortcake, Strawberry ■ *Rice-based*

Your guests will certainly enjoy this sweetened traditional biscuit base.

■ Preheat the oven to 375°F. Grease a baking sheet.

■ In a medium-size bowl, blend together all the ingredients for the biscuits, except the milk and vinegar. Add the milk and vinegar, and mix well. The dough will be quite fragile. Pat the dough out on the prepared baking sheet to $1/2$-inch thickness. Cut into nine square biscuits and separate with the side of a knife.

■ Bake for 15 to 20 minutes, until the biscuits begin to brown.

■ Wash and slice the berries. Sprinkle with a little sugar if they are not sweet.

■ In individual serving dishes, top each biscuit with the fruit and then the whipped cream.

■ Serves 9 ■

Biscuits:

$1/4$ pound ($1/2$ cup) butter

1 cup rice flour, 150 grams

1 $1/4$ teaspoons xanthan gum

1 tablespoon baking powder

$1/2$ teaspoon baking soda

2 $1/2$ tablespoons sugar

$1/2$ teaspoon vanilla extract

$1/2$ teaspoon salt

$3/4$ cup milk

1 teaspoon vinegar

Topping:

1 pound strawberries

1 tablespoon sugar (optional)

1 recipe Whipped Cream (page 332), prepared

Snacking Cake ■ *Oat-based*

This is a very moist, dense spice cake with raisins and nuts. No frosting is needed. It was developed from a recipe I received many years ago from Norm Palmer, a fine cook and special lady.

- Preheat the oven to 350°F. Grease a 9-inch square baking pan.
- Combine the rolled oats and boiling water in a small bowl; set aside. Put all the other ingredients in a large bowl. Add the oat mixture. Mix until all the flour lumps are gone. Pour into the prepared pan. Bake for 30 to 35 minutes, until the cake is golden brown and tests cleanly with a toothpick.

■ Serves 9 ■

1/2 cup quick rolled oats
3/4 cup boiling water
3/4 cup oat flour
1 cup brown sugar
1/2 cup oil
2 eggs
1 teaspoon baking soda
1/4 teaspoon salt
1/4 teaspoon grated nutmeg (optional)
1/2 teaspoon ground cinnamon
1/4 teaspoon xanthan gum
1/2 cup raisins, chopped
1/2 cup nuts, chopped

Soft Chocolate Cake ■ *Corn-based*

The batter for this cake is so thin, you might think you made a mistake. You have not. It makes for a perfectly soft and squishy cake. Be sure to ice this cake, as the top isn't the prettiest. However, the nice chocolate flavor and texture taste and look good.

- Preheat the oven to 350°F. Lightly grease a 9 x 13-inch baking pan.
- In a medium-size bowl, mix the oil with the sugar. Add the eggs. Mix until light and thick. This will take a minute or two with your mixer. Add the other ingredients. Beat well. The batter will be quite thin. Pour into the prepared baking pan. Bake for 30 to 40 minutes, until a toothpick inserted in the middle tests cleanly.

■ Serves 15 ■

3/4 cup oil
1 1/4 cups sugar, 250 grams
3 eggs
2/3 cup milk
1 1/4 cups cornstarch, 155 grams
1/4 cup unsweetened cocoa powder, 20 grams
3/4 teaspoon baking soda
3/4 teaspoon salt
1 3/4 teaspoons vanilla extract
2 1/2 teaspoons xanthan gum

Soft Chocolate Cake ▪ *Potato-based*

This cake has an understated chocolate flavor. We paired it with the Chocolate–Peanut Butter Velvet Icing (page 330). Yes!

- Preheat the oven to 350°F. Lightly grease a 9 x 13-inch baking pan.

- In a medium-size bowl, mix the oil with the sugar. Add the eggs. Mix until light and thick. This will take a minute or two with your mixer. Add the other ingredients. Beat well. The batter will be quite thin initially, but thickens a bit with additional mixing. Pour into the prepared baking pan. Bake for 30 to 40 minutes, until a toothpick inserted in the middle tests cleanly.

▪ Serves 15 ▪

3/4 cup oil

1 1/2 cups sugar, 300 grams

3 eggs

2/3 cup milk

1 cup potato starch, 155 grams

1/4 cup unsweetened cocoa powder, 20 grams

3/4 teaspoon baking soda

3/4 teaspoon salt

2 teaspoons vanilla extract

2 1/2 teaspoons xanthan gum

Soft Yellow Cake ▪ *Corn-based*

If you want that traditional boxed cake mix taste and texture, this is it.

- Preheat the oven to 350°F. Lightly grease a 9 x 13-inch baking pan.

- In a medium-size bowl, mix the oil with the sugar. Add the eggs. Mix until light and thick. This will take a minute or two with your mixer. Add the other ingredients. Beat well. The batter will thicken a bit during the mixing process. Pour into the prepared baking pan. Bake for 35 to 40 minutes, until a toothpick inserted in the middle tests cleanly.

▪ Serves 15 ▪

3/4 cup oil

1 1/4 cups sugar, 250 grams

3 eggs

2/3 cup milk

1 1/2 cups cornstarch, 190 grams

2 teaspoons baking powder

1/4 teaspoon baking soda

1/2 teaspoon salt

2 teaspoons vanilla extract

2 1/2 teaspoons xanthan gum

Soft Yellow Cake ■ *Potato-based*

This is a wonderfully soft and squishy cake, modeled after a traditional boxed-type yellow cake mix.

- Preheat the oven to 350°F. Lightly grease a 9 x 13-inch baking pan.
- In a medium-size bowl, mix the oil with the sugar. Add the eggs. Mix until light and thick. This will take a minute or two with your mixer. Add the other ingredients. Beat well. While the batter thickens a little, it will still be quite thin. Pour into the prepared baking pan. Bake for 30 to 35 minutes, until a toothpick inserted in the middle tests cleanly.

■ Serves 15 ■

$^3/_4$ cup oil

1 $^1/_2$ cups sugar, 300 grams

3 eggs

$^3/_4$ cup milk

1 $^1/_2$ cups potato starch, 235 grams

1 tablespoon baking powder

$^1/_4$ teaspoon baking soda

$^1/_2$ teaspoon salt

1 $^1/_2$ teaspoons vanilla extract

2 $^1/_4$ teaspoons xanthan gum

NOTE: Feel free to top this wonderful cake with some canned icing. Although many are fine, remember to read the label carefully. Alternatively, the icings in this book are pretty easy to make, and you'll know exactly what's in them!

Soft Yellow Cake ■ *Rice-based*

This cake has a very flat top, with the slightest upturned lip at the side. It is soft, buttery, and moist with a medium texture. Refrigerate or freeze after baking, to maintain the best texture.

- Preheat the oven to 350°F. Lightly grease a 9 x 13-inch baking pan.
- In a medium-size bowl, mix the butter and sugar. Add the eggs and egg whites. Mix until light yellow and a little thicker. This will take a minute or two with your mixer. Add the other ingredients. Mix well.
- Pour into the prepared baking pan. Bake for 35 to 40 minutes, until a toothpick inserted in the middle tests cleanly. The cake will spring back lightly when touched and will begin to pull away from the sides of the pan ever so slightly when done.

■ Serves 15 ■

10²/₃ tablespoons (²/₃ cup) butter

1¹/₃ cups sugar

3 eggs

3 egg whites

1 cup plain yogurt

1¹/₄ cups rice flour, 190 grams

1 tablespoon plus 2 teaspoons baking powder

1¹/₂ teaspoons baking soda

³/₄ teaspoon salt

2 teaspoons vanilla extract

1¹/₄ teaspoons xanthan gum

1 tablespoon apple cider vinegar

Spice Cake ■ *Corn-based*

Soft in texture, this is the spice version of the traditional boxed cake.

- Preheat the oven to 350°F. Lightly grease a 9 x 13-inch baking pan.
- In a medium-size bowl, mix the oil with the sugar. Add the eggs. Mix until light and thick. This will take a minute or two with your mixer. Add the other ingredients. Beat well. The batter will thicken a bit during the mixing process. Pour into the prepared baking pan. Bake for 30 to 40 minutes, until a toothpick inserted in the middle tests cleanly.

■ Serves 15 ■

³/₄ cup oil

1¹/₄ cups sugar, 250 grams

3 eggs

²/₃ cup milk

1¹/₂ cups cornstarch, 190 grams

2 teaspoons baking powder

¹/₄ teaspoon baking soda

¹/₂ teaspoon salt

1 teaspoon vanilla extract

2¹/₂ teaspoons xanthan gum

³/₄ teaspoon ground cinnamon

¹/₄ teaspoon grated nutmeg

Spice Cake ▪ *Oat-based*

You may have noticed the absence of a yellow cake made with oats. The flavor of the oats is too strong, and you end up with a strange (though not unpleasant) flavor. However, the addition of spices makes for a very nice cake.

- Preheat the oven to 350°F. Grease a 9-inch round or square pan.
- In a medium-size bowl, combine all the dry ingredients. Stir well. (This will distribute the xanthan gum throughout the flour, for better absorption.)
- Add the remaining ingredients. Mix well, scraping the sides of the bowl at least once during the mixing process. The batter will remain quite thin.
- Pour the batter into the prepared pan. Bake for 30 to 35 minutes, until a toothpick inserted in the middle tests cleanly. Let cool.
- Frost as desired.

▪ Serves 9 ▪

1 $1/3$ cups oat flour, 160 grams
$3/4$ cup sugar, 150 grams
1 teaspoon baking soda
2 teaspoons baking powder
$1/4$ teaspoon xanthan gum
$1/2$ teaspoon salt
$1/2$ teaspoon ground cinnamon
$1/4$ teaspoon grated nutmeg
$2/3$ cup milk
2 teaspoons cider vinegar
$1/4$ cup oil
2 eggs
1 egg white
1 teaspoon vanilla extract

Spice Cake ■ *Potato-based*

This cake is soft and squishy; again, much like one from a traditional boxed cake mix. For me, the vanilla cuts the harsh edge of the cinnamon.

- ■ Preheat the oven to 350°F. Lightly grease a 9 x 13-inch baking pan.
- ■ In a medium-size bowl, mix the oil with the sugar. Add the eggs. Mix until light and thick. This will take a minute or two with your mixer. Add the other ingredients. Beat well. While the batter thickens a little, it will still be quite thin. Pour into the prepared baking pan. Bake for 30 to 35 minutes, until a toothpick inserted in the middle tests cleanly.

■ Serves 15 ■

$3/4$ cup oil

$1 1/2$ cups sugar, 300 grams

3 eggs

$3/4$ cup milk

$1 1/2$ cups potato starch, 235 grams

1 tablespoon baking powder

$1/4$ teaspoon baking soda

$1/2$ teaspoon salt

$3/4$ teaspoon vanilla extract (optional)

$2 1/4$ teaspoons xanthan gum

$3/4$ teaspoon ground cinnamon

$1/4$ teaspoon grated nutmeg

Spice Cake ▪ *Rice-based*

This is a very flat-topped cake that is moist with a medium texture. Refrigerate or freeze after baking, to maintain the best texture.

- Preheat the oven to 350°F. Lightly grease a 9 x 13-inch baking pan.
- In a medium-size bowl, mix the butter and sugar. Add the eggs and egg whites. Mix until light yellow and a little thicker. This will take a minute or two with your mixer. Add the other ingredients. Mix well.
- Pour into the prepared baking pan. Bake for 35 to 40 minutes, until a toothpick inserted in the middle tests cleanly. The cake will spring back lightly when touched and will begin to pull away from the sides of the pan ever so slightly when done.

▪ Serves 15 ▪

10²/₃ tablespoons (²/₃ cup) butter

1¹/₃ cups sugar, 270 grams

3 eggs

3 egg whites

1 cup plain yogurt

1¹/₄ cups rice flour, 190 grams

1 tablespoon plus 2 teaspoons baking powder

1¹/₂ teaspoons baking soda

³/₄ teaspoon salt

1 teaspoon vanilla extract

1 teaspoon ground cinnamon

¹/₄ teaspoon grated nutmeg

1¹/₄ teaspoons xanthan gum

1 tablespoon apple cider vinegar

Strawberry Cake ▪ *Corn-based*

This cake is made in honor of my young friend Braden. It is soft and the gelatin creates a hot pink color.

- Preheat the oven to 350°F. Lightly grease two 8- or 9-inch round cake pans.
- In a medium-size bowl, mix the oil with the sugar and gelatin. Add the eggs. Mix until light and thick. This will take a minute or two with your mixer. Add the other ingredients. Beat well. The batter will be thin, even after beating for a few minutes. Pour into the prepared cake pans. Bake for 30 to 35 minutes, until a toothpick inserted in the middle tests cleanly.

▪ Serves 15 ▪

³/₄ cup oil

³/₄ cup sugar, 150 grams

1 (3-ounce) box powdered strawberry gelatin

3 eggs

²/₃ cup milk

1¹/₂ cups cornstarch, 190 grams

2 teaspoons baking powder

¹/₄ teaspoon baking soda

¹/₄ teaspoon salt

Scant 2¹/₄ teaspoons xanthan gum

Strawberry Cake ■ *Potato-based*

This is light and "cake-mix" squishy. A little Cool Whip and fresh strawberries would be nice with this cake. Cool Whip is gluten-free as of this writing, but always recheck labels!

- Preheat the oven to 350°F. Lightly grease two 8- or 9-inch round cake pans.
- In a medium-size bowl, mix the oil with the sugar and gelatin. Add the eggs. Mix until light and thick. This will take a minute or two with your mixer. Add the other ingredients. Beat well. The batter will thicken considerably. Pour into the prepared cake pans. Bake for 30 to 35 minutes, until a toothpick inserted in the middle tests cleanly.

■ Serves 15 ■

3/4 cup oil

3/4 cup sugar, 150 grams

1 (3-ounce) box powdered strawberry gelatin

3 eggs

3/4 cup milk

1 1/2 cups potato starch, 235 grams

1 tablespoon baking powder

1/4 teaspoon baking soda

1/4 teaspoon salt

Scant 2 teaspoons xanthan gum

"Toll House" Cake ■ *Oat-based*

Combined with a traditional chocolate icing, this cake is reminiscent of an oversized, fluffy chocolate chip cookie. The batter is too thin to support the nuggets of chocolate, so the chocolate icing is necessary to complete the job. You may be tempted to use brown sugar instead of white sugar in this recipe, but do not, as that would actually make the cake taste "oatier."

1 1/3 cups oat flour, 160 grams
3/4 cup sugar, 150 grams
1 teaspoon baking soda
2 teaspoons baking powder
1/4 teaspoon xanthan gum
1/2 teaspoon salt
2/3 cup milk
2 teaspoons apple cider vinegar
1/4 cup oil
2 eggs
1 egg white
2 teaspoons vanilla extract

- Preheat the oven to 350°F. Grease a 9-inch round or square pan.
- In a medium-size bowl, combine all the dry ingredients. Stir well. (This will distribute the xanthan gum throughout the flour, for better absorption.)
- Add the remaining ingredients. Mix well, scraping the sides of the bowl at least once. The batter will remain quite thin.
- Pour the batter into the prepared pan. Bake for 30 to 35 minutes, until a toothpick inserted in the middle tests cleanly. Let cool.
- Frost with any chocolate icing in this cookbook.

■ Serves 9 ■

White Cake ■ *Corn-based*

This cake has just the right soft and squishy texture.

- Preheat the oven to 350°F. Lightly grease a 9 x 13-inch baking pan.
- In a medium-size bowl, mix the oil with the sugar. Add the egg whites. Mix well for several minutes. Add the other ingredients. Beat well. The batter will thicken a bit during the mixing process. Pour into the prepared baking pan. Bake for 35 to 40 minutes, until a toothpick inserted in the middle tests cleanly.

■ Serves 15 ■

1 cup oil
1 1/4 cups sugar, 250 grams
5 egg whites
2/3 cup milk
1 1/2 cups cornstarch, 190 grams
2 teaspoons baking powder
1/4 teaspoon baking soda
1/2 teaspoon salt
2 teaspoons vanilla extract
2 1/2 teaspoons xanthan gum

White Cake ■ *Potato-based*

This has a soft and squishy texture and a very pleasant flavor.

- Preheat the oven to 350°F. Lightly grease a 9 x 13-inch baking pan.
- In a medium-size bowl, mix the oil with the sugar. Add the egg whites. Mix until very well blended and the frothiness disappears. Add the other ingredients. Beat well. Although the batter will thicken a little, it will still be quite thin. Pour into the prepared baking pan. Bake for 30 to 35 minutes, until a toothpick inserted in the middle tests cleanly.

■ Serves 15 ■

1 cup oil
1 1/2 cups sugar, 300 grams
5 egg whites
2/3 cup milk
1 1/2 cups potato starch, 235 grams
1 tablespoon baking powder
1/4 teaspoon baking soda
1/2 teaspoon salt
1 1/2 teaspoons vanilla extract
2 1/4 teaspoons xanthan gum

17

ICINGS

If you try a few of the recipes in this chapter, you may never purchase store-bought icing again, even though many of them are gluten-free.

Traditional icings are technically buttercreams, even though they may not contain butter. The traditional icings in this chapter are a little richer and, in my opinion, truer in flavor than store-bought icings. Butter is in part responsible for the superior flavor of these recipes. Real lemon juice, coffee, peanut butter, and freshly melted chocolate squares impart great flavor as well. If you must avoid dairy, switch to shortening or dairy-free margarine. The small amount of milk may be replaced with a dairy-free substitute such as soy milk, as well.

It is important when making the traditional icings to beat the icing until the raw sugar taste is gone.

If you were to make a traditional icing with shortening and clear flavoring, you would have the icing used on most wedding cakes. It is very sweet. It is also the preferred icing for piping decorations, especially flowers and string work.

Velvet icings have been expanded since my first book, although the publisher kindly permitted me to include those original recipes here as well. Each of these icings is a play on the original Red Velvet icing many of us know and love. The finished velvet icings are somehow more sophisticated than traditional icings. The texture is also lighter and richer than traditional icings.

These velvet frostings are ideal for special-occasion cakes, especially wedding cakes. Your guests will appreciate a wedding cake that not only looks good but tastes good, too.

For those who cannot tolerate corn and must be careful of the cornstarch in confectioners' sugar, velvet frostings are a nice option. Alternatively, consider making your own confectioners' sugar with a bit of potato starch. A Corn-Free Confectioners' Sugar recipe is here as well.

There is another kind of buttercream that contains eggs, but I have not included it in this book, as the velvet frostings are much easier to prepare and are delicious. Surprisingly, this egg-inclusive style of buttercream is not always mentioned in serious cake-making cookbooks.

You will also find one other delicious option to frost a cake—whipped cream. The whipped cream recipes in this chapter taste oh so good, but almost as important, they are very stable. You can actually frost a cake and serve it days later. You can even pipe decorative borders with these whipped creams.

I made a friend a small torte with blackberry whipped cream. She asked that I use it on her wedding cake. This delicious alternative for frosting a wedding cake is best used in an air-conditioned setting.

Confectioners' Glaze

This glaze would be typical to top cinnamon rolls or sweet breads. It would also be good to add just a little extra to a pound cake.

1 cup confectioners' sugar

2 tablespoons milk

1/2 teaspoon vanilla extract

- Combine the ingredients in a small cup until well blended. Pour over a cake or sweet yeast-style breads.

■ Makes 1 cup ■

Chocolate Glaze

This is a quick, light glaze for a cake or even to use with doughnuts. The small amount of butter adds richness. Cooking the cocoa releases more chocolate flavor.

1 tablespoon butter

2 tablespoons unsweetened cocoa powder, 10 grams

2 tablespoons milk

1/2 teaspoon vanilla extract

1 cup confectioners' sugar, 120 grams

- Combine the butter, cocoa powder, and milk in a small, microwave-safe cup. Microwave for 30 to 40 seconds, until the butter melts. Pour into a medium-size bowl. Add the vanilla and confectioners' sugar. Beat until the raw sugary texture is gone.

■ Makes approximately 3/4 cup ■

Corn-Free Confectioners' Sugar

Many commercial brands of confectioners' sugar use cornstarch as an ingredient. You can special-order or perhaps find corn-free confectioners' sugar in a health food store. Or, you can take just a minute to make some. My efforts were successful when using a traditional blender, but failed when using a hand blender or food processor.

1/3 cup sugar
1/2 teaspoon potato starch

■ Place the sugar and potato starch in a blender. Blend on the highest setting for approximately 1 minute, until the sugar is powdery. There will be a cloud of dust when you remove the lid from the blender, so you may want to allow it to rest for 10 or 15 seconds before removing the lid.

■ Makes just under 1/2 cup ■

Traditional Icing, Chocolate

Better than canned. Chocolaty good.

■ Chop the chocolate squares into small pieces. Place in a microwave-safe cup or bowl. Microwave on high for 1 to 2 minutes, until the chocolate has melted. Set aside to cool.

■ In a medium-size bowl, combine the butter, sugar, and vanilla. Mix until the butter is in tiny pieces. Add the milk, 1 tablespoon at a time. Beat on high speed until the undissolved sugar taste is gone, at least 1 minute and up to 3 minutes, depending upon your mixer. Slowly add the melted chocolate and beat well to combine.

2 (1-ounce) squares unsweetened baking chocolate
12 tablespoons (3/4 cup) butter
1 pound confectioners' sugar
1 teaspoon vanilla extract
1/4 cup milk

■ Makes enough icing for two 8- to 9-inch round ■
layers or one 9 x 13-inch rectangular cake

NOTE: Chocolate pieces will retain their shape when microwaved. It is necessary to stir them to see that they are actually melted.

Traditional Icing, Lemon

Going the extra mile to make homemade icing can make a big difference in taste. Rather than using artificial flavor, I've opted for real lemon flavor. The taste is bright and fresh.

12 tablespoons (^{3}/4 cup) butter

1 pound confectioners' sugar

5 tablespoons frozen lemonade concentrate

▦ In a medium-size bowl, combine the butter and sugar. Mix until the butter is in tiny pieces. Add the lemon concentrate, 1 tablespoon at a time. Beat at high speed until the undissolved sugar taste is gone, at least 1 minute and up to 3 minutes, depending upon your mixer.

■ Makes enough icing for two 8- to 9-inch round ■ layers or one 9 x 13-inch rectangular cake

Traditional Icing, Mocha

Not quite chocolate; not quite coffee. Understatedly good.

2 (1-ounce) squares unsweetened baking chocolate

^{1}/2 teaspoon instant coffee granules

1 tablespoon hot water

12 tablespoons (^{3}/4 cup) butter

1 pound confectioners' sugar

1 teaspoon vanilla extract

3 tablespoons milk

▦ Chop the chocolate squares into small pieces. Place in a microwave-safe cup or bowl. Microwave on high for 1 to 2 minutes, until the chocolate has melted. Set aside to cool.

▦ In another small cup, combine the coffee and hot water. Stir to dissolve. Set aside.

▦ In a medium-size bowl, combine the butter, sugar, and vanilla. Mix until the butter is in tiny pieces. Add the coffee mixture, then the milk, 1 tablespoon at a time. Beat at high speed until the undissolved sugar taste is gone, at least 1 minute and up to 3 minutes, depending upon your mixer. Slowly add the melted chocolate and beat well to combine.

■ Makes enough icing for two 8- to 9-inch round layers ■ or one 9 x 13-inch rectangular cake

Traditional Icing, Peanut Butter

Have you ever had a craving for chocolate cake with peanut butter icing, like school cafeterias used to serve? It turns out that it is just as good today as it was back then. If you have never had good peanut butter icing, it tastes a lot like peanut butter fudge.

4 tablespoons
 ($^1/_4$ cup) butter
$^1/_2$ cup peanut butter
1 pound confectioners' sugar
1 teaspoon vanilla extract
$5^1/_2$–6 tablespoons milk

■ In a medium-size bowl, combine the butter, peanut butter, sugar, and vanilla. Mix until the butter is in tiny pieces. Add the milk, 1 tablespoon at a time. Beat at high speed until the undissolved sugar taste is gone, at least 1 minute and up to 3 minutes, depending upon your mixer.

■ Makes enough icing for two 8- to 9-inch round ■
layers or one 9 x 13-inch rectangular cake

Traditional Icing, Vanilla

I have used this icing on everyday cakes as well as wedding cakes. It has more flavor than traditional wedding cake icing, which is often made with shortening.

12 tablespoons
 ($^3/_4$ cup) butter
1 pound confectioners' sugar
1 teaspoon vanilla extract
$^1/_4$ cup milk

■ In a medium-size bowl, combine the butter, sugar, and vanilla. Mix until the butter is in tiny pieces. Add the milk, 1 tablespoon at a time. Beat at high speed until the undissolved sugar taste is gone, at least 1 minute and up to 3 minutes, depending upon your mixer.

■ Makes enough icing for two 8- to 9-inch round ■
layers or one 9 x 13-inch rectangular cake

Velvet Icing, Chocolate ■ *Corn- or potato-based*

This recipe, reprinted with permission, is a modification of Chocolate Velvet Icing in my first book, *The Gluten-Free Kitchen.*

- In microwave-safe bowl, combine milk, cocoa, and cornstarch. Stir well. Microwave this mixture on high for 2 to 4 minutes, until quite thick. Stir periodically to better incorporate ingredients. These ingredients may also be cooked in a saucepan over medium heat. Stir constantly if using this method.

- Cover the thickened milk mixture with plastic wrap touching its surface, or spray surface with nonstick spray. Either approach will help prevent a skin from forming. Cool to room temperature. If a skin forms, you can discard it later.

- In a medium bowl, cream butter, sugar, and vanilla. Mix until light and fluffy. Add vanilla extract. Set aside. Add milk mixture (with the skin removed if necessary) and beat until frosting looks like whipped cream. This will take several minutes.

■ Makes enough frosting for two ■
8- or 9-inch cake layers

For full-size cake:

1 cup milk

$1/4$ cup cocoa

$2 1/2$ tablespoons cornstarch or potato starch

1 cup butter

1 cup sugar

2 teaspoons vanilla extract

*For petite cake
(8- or 9-inch cake):*

$1/2$ cup milk

2 tablespoons cocoa

1 tablespoon plus
$3/4$ teaspoon cornstarch or potato starch

$1/2$ cup butter

$1/2$ cup sugar

1 teaspoon vanilla extract

Velvet Icing, Lemon ■ *Corn- or potato-based*

I've made a few wedding cakes for family, friends, and charity raffles. One such occasion called for lemon icing. While traditional icing is good, this version is more subtle and downright delicious. Don't be surprised if your milk curdles from the lemon juice. Lemon extract alone does not do the job well.

3/4 cup milk

1/4 cup lemon juice

2 1/2 tablespoons cornstarch or potato starch

1/2 pound (1 cup) butter

1 cup sugar

1 teaspoon lemon extract

■ In a microwave-safe bowl, combine the milk, lemon juice, and starch. Stir well. Microwave this mixture on high for 2 to 4 minutes, until thick. Stir periodically to better incorporate the ingredients. These ingredients may also be cooked in a saucepan over medium heat. Stir constantly if using this method.

■ Cover the thickened mixture with plastic wrap touching its surface, or spray the surface with nonstick cooking spray. Either approach will help prevent a skin from forming. Let cool to room temperature. If a skin forms, you can discard it later.

■ In a medium-size bowl, cream the butter, sugar, and lemon extract. Mix until light and fluffy. Add the milk mixture (with the skin removed, if necessary) and beat until the frosting looks like whipped cream. This will take several minutes.

■ Makes enough frosting for two ■
8- or 9-inch cake layers

Velvet Icing, Mocha ■ *Corn- or potato-based*

Don't expect to have leftover cake if you use this frosting—your guests will take extra servings home. At first the vanilla may seem counterintuitive, given the other flavors, but is necessary to soften the bitter edge of both the coffee and the chocolate.

- In a microwave-safe bowl, combine the milk and starch. Stir well. Microwave this mixture on high for 2 to 4 minutes, until thick. Stir periodically to better incorporate the ingredients. These ingredients may also be cooked in a saucepan over medium heat. Stir constantly if using this method.

- Cover the thickened mixture with plastic wrap touching its surface, or spray the surface with nonstick cooking spray. Either approach will help prevent a skin from forming. Let cool to room temperature. If a skin forms, you can discard it later.

- In a medium-size bowl, cream the butter and sugar. Set aside.

- Melt the chocolate in a separate bowl in the microwave, approximately 1 minute on high. Let cool to room temperature. In a cup, dissolve the coffee in the hot water. Add to the butter mixture. Mix until light and fluffy. Add the milk mixture (with the skin removed, if necessary) and beat until the frosting looks like whipped cream. This will take several minutes. Slowly beat in the melted chocolate until combined.

■ Makes enough frosting for two ■
8- or 9-inch cake layers

1 cup milk

2$^1/_2$ tablespoons cornstarch or potato starch

$^1/_2$ pound (1 cup) butter

1 cup sugar

1$^1/_2$ (1-ounce) squares unsweetened baking chocolate

$^1/_2$ teaspoon instant coffee granules

1 tablespoon hot water

1 teaspoon vanilla extract

Velvet Icing,
Peanut Butter ■ *Corn- or potato-based*

This peanut butter frosting is very light in color and texture. It has a true peanut butter taste and is not overly sweet. The Chocolate–Peanut Butter variation below was actually preferred by our resident peanut butter lover.

1 cup milk

2¹⁄₂ tablespoons cornstarch or potato starch

¹⁄₄ pound (¹⁄₂ cup) butter

¹⁄₂ cup peanut butter

1 cup sugar

1 teaspoon vanilla extract

- ■ In a microwave-safe bowl, combine the milk and starch. Stir well. Microwave this mixture on high for 2 to 4 minutes, until thick. Stir periodically to better incorporate the ingredients. These ingredients may also be cooked in a saucepan over medium heat. Stir constantly if using this method.

- ■ Cover the thickened mixture with plastic wrap touching its surface, or spray the surface with nonstick cooking spray. Either approach will help prevent a skin from forming. Let cool to room temperature. If a skin forms, you can discard it later.

- ■ In a medium-size bowl, cream the butter, peanut butter, sugar, and vanilla. Mix until light and fluffy. Add the milk mixture (with the skin removed, if necessary) and beat until the frosting looks like whipped cream. This will take several minutes.

■ Makes enough frosting for two ■
8- or 9-inch cake layers

VARIATION: Velvet Frosting, Chocolate–Peanut Butter: Melt 2 (1-ounce) squares of unsweetened chocolate in a bowl in the microwave oven for approximately 1 minute. Let cool to room temperature and add to the frosting. Beat well.

Velvet Icing, Vanilla ▪ *Corn- or potato-based*

This recipe, reprinted with permission from *The Gluten-Free Kitchen,* is based on one given to me by my grandmother to top a Red Velvet Cake. My daughter says it is the best. I've used this recipe on several wedding cakes. Like me, the guests loved it. My favorite cake to use this with is a petite chocolate cake.

- In microwave-safe bowl, combine the milk and cornstarch. Stir well. Microwave this mixture on high for 2 to 4 minutes, until quite thick. Stir periodically to better incorporate ingredients. These ingredients may also be cooked in a saucepan over medium heat. Stir constantly if using this method.

- Cover thickened milk mixture with plastic wrap touching its surface, or spray surface with nonstick spray. Either approach will help prevent a skin from forming. Cool to room temperature. If a skin forms, you can discard it later.

- In a medium bowl, cream butter, sugar, and vanilla. Mix until light and fluffy. Add milk mixture (with the skin removed if necessary) and beat until frosting looks like whipped cream. This will take several minutes.

▪ Makes enough frosting for two ▪
8- or 9-inch cake layers

For full-size cake:
1 cup milk
2 1/2 tablespoons cornstarch or potato starch
1 cup butter
1 cup sugar
2 teaspoons vanilla extract

For petite cake (8- to 9-inch round cake):
1/2 cup milk
1 tablespoon plus 3/4 teaspoon cornstarch or potato starch
1/2 cup butter
1/2 cup sugar
1 teaspoon vanilla extract

Whipped Cream

This very stable whipped cream is used in the Black Forest Cake (page 336). Adapted from the whipped cream recipe in my first book, the extra stability comes from just a little bit of xanthan gum. We gluten-free cooks all have xanthan gum in our cabinets, so why not use it to make us (and our cakes and other desserts) look good, too? This whipped cream easily holds for a week in the fridge.

1 cup heavy cream

2 tablespoons confectioners' sugar

2 teaspoons vanilla liqueur, or 1/2 teaspoon vanilla extract

1/8 teaspoon xanthan gum

■ In a medium-size bowl, combine the cream, 1 tablespoon of the confectioners' sugar, and the vanilla liqueur. Beat to almost soft peaks. Mix the xanthan gum and the remaining 1 tablespoon of confectioners' sugar in a small cup. Sprinkle over the top of the cream. Beat to soft peaks.

NOTE: Use of a distilled vanilla liqueur extends the flavor, giving a longer mellow vanilla taste than just vanilla extract. A fine vanilla extract is often based in bourbon, which would also provide a better flavor.

■ Serves 8 ■

VARIATION: For an incredible option, omit the vanilla liqueur or extract and add 1 tablespoon of seedless jam. Black raspberry is very good.

Whipped Cream, Chocolate

This is the chocolate version of my very stable whipped cream. Use to frost a torte or to top an ice-cream or brownie sundae. This whipped cream tastes like a cloud of wonderful hot cocoa—but not hot, of course.

1 cup heavy cream

1 tablespoon unsweetened cocoa powder

1 teaspoon vanilla extract

2 tablespoons confectioners' sugar

1/8 teaspoon xanthan gum

■ In a medium-size bowl, combine the cream, cocoa powder, and vanilla. Beat to almost soft peaks. Mix the xanthan gum and confectioners' sugar in a small cup. Sprinkle over the top of the cream. Beat to soft peaks.

■ Serves 8 ■

18

WEDDING AND OTHER SPECIAL CAKES

This chapter has special cakes, small and large! From Black Forest Cake to wedding cake layers, you will find celebrations waiting to happen.

Isn't it ironic that beautiful wedding cakes are sometimes dry and tasteless?

To ensure success with these recipes, please note these important points:

1. Measure carefully. Weight measurement is best.
2. Use Rumford baking powder if baking powder is an ingredient in the recipe.
3. Use Hershey's cocoa if cocoa powder is an ingredient in the recipe. I believe the flavor is better than some others when paired with gluten-free flours.

4. Use high-sided baking pans (such as Wilton 2- to 3-inch) for all the cakes in this chapter, as many of the cakes near 2 inches in height.

The wedding cake layers and sheet cakes in this chapter are made from potato starch, which is well tolerated by most individuals. Two versions, yellow and chocolate, are included to tempt your taste buds. The medium textures are ideal for celebration cakes. You can even make and freeze the layers well ahead of the event! (Wrap tightly to avoid absorption of other freezer flavors.) The sheet cakes and larger wedding cake layers have large, flat tops for writing good wishes and are beautiful when decorated. They also serve a crowd!

When I started formulating wedding cake layers, ranging in 2-inch size intervals from 6 to 14 inches, this chapter suddenly began to look like a specialized cookbook in its own right. My sanity was at risk as hundreds of beautiful options came to mind. Ultimately, I opted to keep it simple. After all, taste is most important, followed by a pretty presentation. So doable!

Wedding cake layers *can* be made by the most novice bakers. Just measure very carefully. Do not be tempted to make up a big batch of batter and pour it into multiple pans. Take it one layer at a time until you're done. It's not hard; it just takes time. I have tested each and every one of these layers. Although nonstick cooking spray did a fine job in preventing the layers from sticking to the pan during testing, it is best to line the bottom of each lightly greased pan with a circle of baking parchment for extra confidence in extracting your layers.

Once you get into the very large layers, 12 or 14 inches, the structure of the cake changes a little. I have reduced the amount of xanthan gum and added a little extra baking soda and/or acid (vinegar) to help stabilize the structure of the yellow cakes. The very top edges of these largest layers will pull in just a little during cooling. This will not affect the decorated appearance or texture of the cake itself, so don't be alarmed.

Making a layer larger than 14 inches creates a very large amount of batter, more than can be held in the bowl of my standard KitchenAid stand mixer, and probably in your stand mixer as well. These pans are so big that some home ovens are a little small for the job. And, honestly, manhandling a cake that big is a little difficult, especially when stacking layers. Accordingly, if you want to make a layer larger than 14 inches in diameter, you'll need to experiment a little with the recipe. (My suggestion is to increase all ingredients incrementally from the 12- or 14-inch recipe and decrease the ratio of xanthan gum. You may also need to bake the cake at a slightly lower temperature to have the center set before the edges overbake.)

If you are using a pan size that I have not calculated, you should calculate the pan's volume and use the recipe which is closest in volume, but which *does not exceed* the volume of the new pan. Using a larger volume of batter will cause the batter to overflow during baking.

Let's walk through two examples together.

As you may recall from math class, the volume of a rectangular pan or square would be calculated as:

Volume (V) = length x width x height

For example, a 9-inch square pan that is 2 inches tall would be calculated as:

V = 9 x 9 x 2
V = 162 cubic inches

In this case, you would want to use the recipe for a 10-inch round, 2-inch high pan, which has a volume of 157 cubic inches—the closest volume without going over the 162 cubic inches of your preferred pan.

In the case of a round pan, volume would be calculated as:

Volume (V) = (π x radius^2) x height

For example, a 9-inch round pan (the diameter is 9 inches; the radius is half that, or 4.5 inches) that is 2 inches tall would be calculated as:

V = (3.14 x 4.5^2 [4.5 x 4.5]) x 2
    [Note that (π = approximately 3.14; and 4.5 x 4.5 = 20.25]
V = (3.14 x 20.25) x 2
V = 53.59 x 2
V = 107.18 cubic inches

In this case, you would want to use the recipe for 8-inch round, 2-inch high pan, which has a volume of 100 cubic inches—the closest volume without going over the 107 cubic inches of your preferred pan.

Embellish these cakes to suit your imagination. Fruit and cream between layers would be delicious. Splitting the layers and filling them jam would be very pretty and tasty. Top with the very stable Whipped Cream (page 332) for a decadent surprise (just don't leave the cake in a warm room for too long). Or, use velvet icing (see pages 327–331) for a soft presentation. Decorate with fresh flowers or simple piped decorations.

If the thought of making a wedding cake is just too much, take these recipes to your trusted baker (professional, family, or friend) who understands the seriousness of cross-contamination and wants to help. A very clean, wheat-free baking environment is essential.

I hope that these cakes bring a little extra joy to whatever special occasion you are celebrating.

■ ■ ■

Black Forest Cake

This cake is a dolled-up version of a chocolate cake. It is rich, delicious, and very attractive. This would make a great special-occasion cake. While this is made with chocolate cake, it would be beautiful for a spring bridal shower, made with a white or yellow cake.

- Bake the chocolate cake of your choosing. Let cool completely.

- In a medium-size bowl, combine the cherry pie filling and liqueur. Mix well to blend. Set aside.

- Place the first layer of cake on a serving plate. Top with most of the cherry mixture, keeping $1/2$ inch or more away from the edge of the cake. Reserve five or ten cherries for decoration.

- Place the second layer on top of the cherry mixture. Gently ice the cake with the whipped cream. Garnish with the reserved cherries.

■ Serves 12 ■

1 large chocolate cake, baked in two 9-inch round pans

1 (21-ounce) can gluten-free cherry pie filling or homemade cherry pie filling (page 390)

1 $1/2$ tablespoons vanilla liqueur or kirsch

2 recipes Whipped Cream (page 332)

Coconut Cake

A traditional version of this cake has been served for many years during family gatherings at Easter. It was only this year that I realized I use a white cake, whereas everyone else uses a yellow cake.

- Prepare the yellow or white cake of your choosing. Substitute ¼ cup of coconut milk for an equal amount of milk in the recipe if extra coconut flavor is desired. Let cool.

- Place the first layer of cake on a serving plate. Ice with the velvet icing. Sprinkle approximately ½ cup of coconut on top of the icing.

- Place the second layer on top of the first layer. Ice the top and sides of the entire cake. Sprinkle or gently press the remaining coconut on the top and sides of the cake.

■ Serves 12 ■

1 large soft yellow or white cake, baked in two 8- or 9-inch round pans

¼ cup coconut milk (optional)

1 (7-ounce) package sweetened grated coconut

1 recipe Velvet Icing, Vanilla (page 331)

NOTE: It is especially pretty to dye a small portion of the coconut green and make a nest in the center top of the cake. Then a few jelly beans can be nestled among the green grass—just like an Easter egg hunt.

Ice-Cream Cake

Any recipe that makes a single 9-inch layer is ideal for making an ice-cream cake. Among these are Carrot Cake, Homemade Chocolate Cake, Homemade Yellow Cake, Nut Cake, and Orange Cake.

■ Bake your cake of choice and let cool.

■ Slice the cake in half horizontally. Place one half-layer in a lightly greased 9-inch springform pan. Spread the softened ice cream on top of the cake. Place the remaining half-layer on top of the ice cream.

■ Place in the freezer for at least 3 or 4 hours, for the ice cream to firm. I prefer to chill this cake overnight.

■ Transfer the cake from the springform pan to a serving plate. Ice as you would a traditional cake. Return to the freezer until serving time. (If storing for more than several hours, wait for the icing to become very firm and then cover the cake with foil.)

■ Serves 9 ■

1 recipe single-layer cake, to be baked in one 9-inch round pan

6 cups ice cream or sherbet, softened

1 recipe icing of choice or 2 recipes Whipped Cream (page 332)

NOTE: For an easier-to-prepare cake, do not slice the cake in half. Simply place the entire layer into the springform pan, followed by the ice cream. If you want to be adventurous, place Fudge Sauce (page 444), chocolate chips, or jam between the layers.

Orange Cake ▪ *Potato-based*

My friend Mireille suggested an orange cake as a good special cake to have in this book. She was right. This cake is light, soft, and airy. I suggest a dusting of confectioners' sugar or a simple glaze of confectioners' sugar blended with orange juice to top the cake.

- Preheat the oven to 350°F. Lightly grease a 9-inch round, 2-inch high baking pan (An 8-inch pan is too small.)

- Mix the oil and sugar in a medium-size bowl. Add the eggs and beat until light and creamy. Add the other ingredients. Mix well. The batter will thicken just a little but remain very thin.

- Pour into the prepared baking pan. Bake for approximately 40 minutes, until a toothpick inserted in the middle tests cleanly. The cake will spring back lightly when touched and will begin to pull away from the sides of the pan ever so slightly when done.

▪ Serves 8 ▪

1/2 cup oil

1 cup sugar, 200 grams

2 eggs

1/2 cup milk

1/4 cup frozen orange juice concentrate

1 1/4 cups potato starch, 195 grams

1 teaspoon baking powder

1/2 teaspoon baking soda

1/2 teaspoon salt

1/2 teaspoon vanilla extract

1 teaspoon apple cider vinegar

3/4 teaspoon xanthan gum

1 1/2 teaspoons orange zest (optional)

NOTE: For different flavors, substitute frozen lemon or lime concentrate. But if you do, omit the vanilla and reduce the baking powder to 1/2 teaspoon.

Red Velvet Cake ■ *Potato-based*

I don't think a cookbook would be quite complete without at least one Red Velvet Cake. I've chosen to make this a single layer baked in a 9-inch round pan so there aren't too many leftovers, and so it could be used for a delicious and unexpected ice-cream cake as well. You may notice that I have streamlined the mixing directions (compared to traditional Red Velvet Cake), but the texture and flavor should be exactly as you recall.

■ Preheat the oven to 350°F. Lightly grease a 9-inch round baking pan.

■ Mix the oil and sugar in a medium-size bowl. Add the eggs and beat until light and creamy. Add the other ingredients. Mix well. The batter will thicken just a little but remain very thin.

■ Pour into the prepared baking pan. Bake for approximately 30 minutes, until a toothpick inserted in the middle tests cleanly. The cake will spring back lightly when touched and will begin to pull away from the sides of the pan ever so slightly when done.

■ Serves 8 ■

1/2 cup oil

1 cup sugar, 200 grams

2 eggs

2/3 cup milk

1 cup potato starch, 155 grams

1 tablespoon unsweetened cocoa powder

1 teaspoon red food coloring

1/2 teaspoon baking soda

1/2 teaspoon salt

1 teaspoon vanilla extract

1 teaspoon apple cider vinegar

3/4 teaspoon xanthan gum

Sheet Cake, Chocolate

(12 x 19 x 13/4) ■ *Potato-based*

If you are making a large birthday cake, this is the one for you. It makes a beautiful half-sheet cake, 12 x 19 inches, with a very flat top. Finished, the cake is approximately 1 1/2 inches tall, shy of the height used for wedding layers, but sized very much like one you'd pick up at a bakery. Use a double recipe of any icing to cover and decorate the cake.

- Preheat the oven to 350°F. Lightly grease a half-sheet pan.

- Mix the oil and sugar in a large bowl. Add the eggs and beat until light and creamy. Add the other ingredients. Mix well. The batter will thicken just a little but remain very thin.

- Pour into the prepared pan. Bake for approximately 35 minutes, until a toothpick inserted in the middle tests cleanly. The cake will spring back lightly when touched and will begin to pull away from the sides of the pan ever so slightly when done.

■ Serves 48 ■

1 1/2 cups oil

3 cups sugar, 600 grams

6 eggs

2 cups milk

3 cups potato starch, 470 grams

1 cup unsweetened cocoa powder, 90 grams

1 1/2 teaspoons baking soda

1 1/2 teaspoons salt

1 tablespoon vanilla extract

1 1/4 teaspoons xanthan gum

NOTE: If you prefer a softer, lighter cake, reduce the amount of cocoa powder to 3/4 cup (60 grams) and increase the amount of xanthan gum by 1/8 teaspoon.

Sheet Cake, Vanilla

(12 x 19 x 1³/4) ■ *Potato-based*

This 12 x 19-inch cake is lighter and more tender than the chocolate sheet cake. It rises right up to the top of the pan, and settles slightly to a 1 ¹/2-inch finished height. The top is even and smooth. This is a very typical, sweet party cake. It serves a crowd! Any icing will complement this cake.

- Preheat the oven to 350°. Lightly grease a half-sheet pan.

- Mix the oil and sugar in a large bowl. Add the eggs and beat until light and creamy. Add the other ingredients. Mix well. The batter will thicken just a little but remain very thin.

- Pour into the prepared pan. Bake for approximately 35 minutes, until a toothpick inserted in the middle tests cleanly. The cake will spring back lightly when touched and will begin to pull away from the sides of the pan ever so slightly when done.

■ Serves 48 ■

1 ¹/2 cups oil

3 cups sugar, 600 grams

6 eggs

1 ¹/2 cups milk

3 cups potato starch, 470 grams

2 tablespoons baking powder

¹/2 teaspoon baking soda

1 ¹/2 teaspoons salt

1 tablespoon vanilla extract

1 teaspoon apple cider vinegar

1 ³/4 teaspoons xanthan gum

Torte ▪ *Corn-based*

This is a short, slightly eggy sponge cake. It is perfect for layering with custard, cream, or jam. Topped with fresh fruit, it makes an impressive dessert.

- Preheat the oven to 350°F. Lightly grease an 8- or 9-inch square baking pan.

- Mix the eggs and sugar in a medium-size bowl until light, very pale, and thick. Add the other ingredients. Mix well to remove all lumps. (I like to use a whisk blade on my mixer, thereby incorporating as much air as possible.) Scrape down the sides of the bowl at least once during the mixing process. Your batter will have the consistency of mayonnaise.

- Spread the batter in the prepared baking pan and bake for 20 to 25 minutes, until a toothpick inserted in the middle tests cleanly. The cake will be very lightly browned.

- Let cool. Cut into two or three equal strips. Layer with cream, custard, softened ice cream, or fresh fruit.

▪ Serves 4 to 6 ▪

2 eggs

1/3 cup sugar, 65 grams

5 1/3 tablespoons (1/3 cup) butter, very softened

2/3 cup cornstarch, 85 grams

1/4 teaspoon xanthan gum

Pinch of salt

1/3 cup milk

2 teaspoons baking powder

1/2 teaspoon vanilla extract (optional)

> **NOTE:** I've made the flavoring optional in this recipe because the cake is quite mild and should pick up the flavors from your fillings and toppings. If you want more defined flavor in the layers, by all means add 1/2 teaspoon of your favorite flavoring.

Torte ■ *Potato-based*

This is a very thin, spongy cake. It has a tighter crumb than the corn version. The vanilla extract is an important ingredient, otherwise the taste is too bland. This cake bakes evenly, making it ideal for layering with pudding, cream, or fruit.

2 eggs

1/3 cup sugar, 65 grams

5 1/3 tablespoons (1/3 cup) butter, very softened

2/3 cup potato starch, 100 grams

1/8 teaspoon xanthan gum

Pinch of salt

1/3 cup milk

2 teaspoons baking powder

1/2 teaspoon vanilla extract (or other flavoring of choice)

■ Preheat the oven to 350°F. Lightly grease an 8- or 9-inch square baking pan.

■ Cream the eggs and sugar in a medium-size bowl until light and thick. Add the remaining ingredients. Beat until light. (I like to use a whisk blade on my mixer, thereby incorporating as much air as possible.) Scrape down the sides of the bowl at least once during the mixing process. Your batter will not be quite as thick as mayonnaise.

■ Spread the batter in the prepared baking pan and bake for 20 to 25 minutes, until a toothpick inserted in the middle tests cleanly. The cake will be very lightly browned.

■ Let cool. Cut into two or three equal strips. Layer with cream, custard, softened ice cream, or fresh fruit.

■ Serves 4 to 6 ■

Torte ■ *Rice-based*

This recipe screams, "Make me!" It is one of my very favorite rice-based cakes. I once trimmed away the very edges of the cake and layered it with Smucker's seedless black raspberry jam and iced it with whipped cream (to which I added a hint of jam). The cake is soft, moist, and eggy. If refrigerated, the cake will seem quite dense.

2 eggs

1/3 cup sugar (65 grams)

4 tablespoons butter, very softened

1/3 cup rice flour, 50 grams

1/2 teaspoon xanthan gum

Pinch of salt

1/3 cup milk

2 teaspoons baking powder

■ Preheat the oven to 350°F. Lightly grease an 8- or 9-inch square baking pan.

■ Mix the eggs and sugar in a medium-size bowl until light, very pale, and thick. Add the other ingredients. Mix well to remove all lumps. (I like to use a whisk blade on my mixer, thereby incorporating as much air as possible.) Scrape down the sides of the bowl at least once during the mixing process. Your batter will have the consistency of mayonnaise. (Do not be surprised if this takes several minutes.)

■ Spread the batter in the prepared baking pan and bake for 20 to 25 minutes, until a toothpick inserted in the middle tests cleanly. The cake will be lightly browned.

■ Let cool. Cut into two or three equal strips. Layer with cream, custard, softened ice cream, or fresh fruit.

■ Serves 4 to 6 ■

Wedding Layers, Chocolate ■ *Potato-based*

The texture of this cake is between that of a homemade cake and a pound cake. It domes during baking, making leveling likely, especially for the 6-inch and 8-inch layers. The flavor is quite chocolaty but not overpowering. Each layer is just shy of 2 inches tall.

- Preheat the oven to 350°F. Lightly grease the pan.
- Mix the oil with the sugar in a medium-size bowl. Add the eggs. Mix until light and thick. This will take a minute or two with your mixer. Add the other ingredients. Beat until the batter is well blended and begins to thicken. Pour into the prepared pan. The batter will fill approximately half the height of the pan. Bake until lightly browned and a toothpick inserted in the middle tests cleanly.

Measurements for Wedding Layers, Chocolate

Ingredient	6" x 2" round pan 57 cubic inches 934 cubic centimeters		8" x 2" round pan 100 cubic inches 1,639 cubic centimeters		10" x 2" round pan 157 cubic inches 2,573 cubic centimeters	
	Cup Measure	Metric Weight	Cup Measure	Metric Weight	Cup Measure	Metric Weight
oil	1/4 cup		1/2 cup		3/4 cup	
sugar	1/2 cup	100 grams	1 cup	200 grams	1 1/2 cups	300 grams
eggs	1		2		3	
milk	1/3 cup		2/3 cup		1 cup	
potato starch	1/2 cup	80 grams	1 cup	155 grams	1 1/2 cups	235 grams
cocoa	3 tablespoons	15 grams	1/3 cup	30 grams	1/2 cup	40 grams
baking powder	n/a		n/a		n/a	
baking soda	1/4 teaspoon		1/2 teaspoon		3/4 teaspoon	
salt	1/4 teaspoon		1/2 teaspoon		3/4 teaspoon	
vanilla	1/2 teaspoon		1 teaspoon		1 1/2 teaspoons	
xanthan gum	1/4 teaspoon		1/2 teaspoon		3/4 teaspoon	
Estimated Baking Time	30 minutes		40 minutes		40–45 minutes	
Estimated Servings per Single Layer	8		15		24	

Ingredient	12" x 2" round pan 226 cubic inches 3,703 cubic centimeters		14" x 2" round pan 308 cubic inches 5,047 cubic centimeters	
	Cup Measure	Metric Weight	Cup Measure	Metric Weight
oil	1 cup		1 1/2 cups	
sugar	2 cups	400 grams	3 cups	600 grams
eggs	4		6	
milk	1 1/3 cups		2 cups	
potato starch	2 cups	310 grams	3 cups	470 grams
cocoa	2/3 cup	60 grams	1 cup	90 grams
baking powder	n/a		n/a	
baking soda	1 teaspoon		1 1/2 teaspoons	
salt	1 teaspoon		1 1/2 teaspoons	
vanilla	2 teaspoons		1 tablespoon	
xanthan gum	1 teaspoon		1 1/4 teaspoons	
Estimated Baking Time	45 minutes		50 minutes	
Estimated Servings per Single Layer	34		46	

Wedding Layers, Yellow ▪ *Potato-based*

This cake is soft, moist, light to medium in texture. It tastes buttery despite having no butter. Although it domes during baking, it settles into an almost flat top, even when baking strips are not used. The recipes are for single layers only. Each layer is approximately 2 inches tall.

- ▪ Preheat the oven to 350°F. Lightly grease the pan.
- ▪ Mix the oil with the sugar in a medium-size bowl. Add the eggs. Mix until light and thick. This will take a minute or two with your mixer. Add the other ingredients. Beat until the batter is well blended and begins to thicken. Pour into the prepared pan. The batter will fill approximately half the height of the pan. Bake until lightly browned and a toothpick inserted in the middle tests cleanly.

Measurements for Wedding Layers, Yellow

Ingredient	6" x 2" round pan 57 cubic inches 934 cubic centimeters		8" x 2" round pan 100 cubic inches 1,639 cubic centimeters		10" x 2" round pan 157 cubic inches 2,573 cubic centimeters	
	Cup Measure	Metric Weight	Cup Measure	Metric Weight	Cup Measure	Metric Weight
oil	1/4 cup		1/2 cup		3/4 cup	
sugar	1/2 cup	100 grams	1 cup	200 grams	1 1/2 cups	300 grams
eggs	1		2		3	
milk	1/4 cup		1/2 cup		3/4 cup	
potato starch	1/2 cup	80 grams	1 cup	155 grams	1 1/2 cups	235 grams
baking powder	1 teaspoon		2 teaspoons		1 tablespoon	
baking soda	pinch		scant 1/4 teaspoon		1/4 teaspoon	
salt	1/4 teaspoon		1/2 teaspoon		3/4 teaspoon	
vanilla	1/2 teaspoon		1 teaspoon		1 1/2 teaspoons	
xanthan gum	1/2 teaspoon		1 teaspoon		1 1/2 teaspoons	
apple cider vinegar	n/a		n/a		n/a	
Estimated Baking Time	35 minutes		40 minutes		40 minutes	
Estimated Servings per Single Layer	8		15		24	

Ingredient	12" x 2" round pan 226 cubic inches 3,703 cubic centimeters		14" x 2" round pan 308 cubic inches 5,047 cubic centimeters	
	Cup Measure	Metric Weight	Cup Measure	Metric Weight
oil	1 cup		1 1/2 cups	
sugar	2 cups	400 grams	3 cups	600 grams
eggs	4		6	
milk	1 cup		1 1/2 cups	
potato starch	2 cups	310 grams	3 cups	470 grams
baking powder	1 tablespoon plus 1 teaspoon		2 tablespoons	
baking soda	1/4 teaspoon		1/2 teaspoon	
salt	1 teaspoon		1 1/2 teaspoons	
vanilla	2 teaspoons		1 tablespoon	
xanthan gum	scant 1 1/2 teaspoons		1 3/4 teaspoons	
apple cider vinegar	1/2 teaspoon		1 teaspoon	
Estimated Baking Time	40–45 minutes		50 minutes	
Estimated Servings per Single Layer	34		46	

19

··COOKIES

Is there anything better than a home-made cookie? Not for me!

Some of the gluten-free cookies available commercially are either hard, gritty, or crumble in the packaging. Admittedly, there are times when a hard cookie is just what you want, and some of the commercial cookies are down-right tasty. Unfortunately, they can also be a little expensive.

Fortunately, your taste buds and your budget can both benefit from a few minutes in the kitchen. Most of the recipes in this chapter make moist, tender and generally soft cookies. If you're looking for a crisper cookie, you simply need to bake the cookies just a little longer.

To ensure success with these recipes, please note these important points:

1. Measure carefully. Weight measurement is best.
2. Use Rumford baking powder if baking powder is an ingredient in the recipe.
3. Use Hershey's cocoa if cocoa powder is called for in the recipe. I believe its flavor is better than some others when paired with gluten-free flours.

I suggest you first try these cookies in their original formulations, then experiment! A little melted chocolate drizzled over a delicate sugar cookie is awesome. The addition of chopped nuts to the brownie recipe is also a treat. Or how about a little icing on the oatmeal cookies?

Perhaps a little silly, but I have a recurring daydream of someone making a fine dinner for their gluten-intolerant girlfriend and surprising her with a marriage proposal in a fortune cookie at the end of the meal. The oat version is my favorite fortune cookie recipe.

On a more serious note, unlike most of the recipes in this book, certain of the rice-based cookies come across as a little gritty when made with Bob's Red Mill brand of rice flour. You may wish to try one of the more finely ground rice flours or put Bob's in a blender for a few seconds, before making the rice-based cookies. That said, don't allow this bit of perceived grittiness scare you away from trying a recipe. The overall taste and texture more than offset this minor characteristic.

Brownies ▪ *Corn-based*

These are dense and chocolaty. Traditional brownies aren't this good!

- Preheat the oven to 350°F. Lightly grease a 9-inch square baking pan.
- In a medium-size bowl, combine and mix all the ingredients. Do not cream the sugar and butter first. The batter will be very thick. Press into the prepared pan. Bake for 25 to 35 minutes, until a toothpick inserted in the middle tests cleanly and the top begins to appear dry. If you sneak a brownie while hot, it will seem too moist. It needs to cool for a few minutes.

▪ Makes 16 small brownies ▪

$1/4$ pound ($1/2$ cup) butter, melted

1 cup sugar, 200 grams

1 egg

1 cup cornstarch, 125 grams

$1/4$ cup unsweetened cocoa powder, 20 grams

$1/4$ teaspoon salt

1 teaspoon vanilla extract

$3/4$ teaspoon xanthan gum

Brownies ▪ *Oat-based*

Have you ever had one of those no-bake chocolate-oatmeal cookies called Ragged Robbins? These brownies taste just like that, only in a dense, cakey, brownie way. Likely, you'll want more than one.

- Preheat the oven to 350°F. Lightly grease a 9-inch square baking pan.
- In a medium-size bowl, combine and mix all the ingredients. Do not cream the sugar and butter first. The batter will be very thick. Spread in the prepared pan. Bake for 30 to 35 minutes, until a toothpick inserted in the middle tests cleanly and the top begins to appear dry.

▪ Makes 16 small brownies ▪

$1/4$ pound ($1/2$ cup) butter, melted

1 cup sugar, 200 grams

2 eggs

1 cup oat flour, 120 grams

$1/4$ cup unsweetened cocoa powder, 20 grams

$1/4$ teaspoon salt

1 teaspoon vanilla extract

$1/4$ teaspoon xanthan gum

Brownies ■ *Potato-based*

A little chewy, a tiny bit gooey, with the classic crinkle on the top, they taste great, too. Several of these brownies were sampled by Billie Keller, the resident chocoholic at our local school. Always one to say the right thing, she opened the packet, thanked me, and commented on how cute they were. Then she took a bite, made some mmmm noises, and said, "Oh my gosh, these are delicious!"

■ Preheat the oven to 350°F. Lightly grease a 9-inch square pan.

■ In a medium-size bowl, combine and mix all the ingredients. Do not cream the sugar and butter first.

■ Pour into the prepared pan. Bake for 25 to 35 minutes, until a toothpick inserted in the middle tests cleanly. If you sneak a brownie while hot, it will seem too moist. It needs to cool for a few minutes.

■ Makes 16 small brownies ■

1/4 pound (1/2 cup) butter, melted

1 cup sugar, 200 grams

1 egg

3/4 cup potato starch, 115 grams

1/4 cup unsweetened cocoa powder, 20 grams

1/4 teaspoon salt

1 teaspoon vanilla extract

1/2 teaspoon xanthan gum

Brownies ■ *Rice-based*

These are dense, full of chocolate flavor, and a little chewy. I would store the extras in the freezer.

■ Preheat the oven to 350°F. Lightly grease a 9-inch square pan.

■ In a medium-size bowl, combine and mix all the ingredients. Do not cream the sugar and butter first. The batter will be very thick. Spread in the prepared pan. Bake for 30 to 35 minutes, until a toothpick inserted in the middle tests cleanly and the top begins to appear dry.

■ Makes 16 small brownies ■

1/4 pound (1/2 cup) butter, melted

1 cup sugar, 200 grams

2 eggs

3/4 cup rice flour, 115 grams

1/4 cup unsweetened cocoa powder, 20 grams

1/4 teaspoon salt

1 teaspoon vanilla extract

1/2 teaspoon xanthan gum

Brownies ▪ *Baby rice cereal–based*

Not quite a brownie, not quite a candy, this is a chewy, chocolaty confection that grows on you. It is reminiscent of no-bake chocolate-oatmeal fudge. And it requires no xanthan gum!

- Preheat the oven to 350°F. Lightly grease a 9-inch square baking pan.
- In a medium-size bowl, combine and mix all the ingredients. Do not cream the sugar and butter first. The batter will seem very crumbly. Press firmly into the prepared pan. Bake for 30 to 35 minutes, until a toothpick inserted in the middle tests cleanly and the top begins to appear dry.

▪ Makes 16 small brownies ▪

1/4 pound (1/2 cup) butter, melted

1 cup sugar, 200 grams

1 egg

1 1/3 cups baby rice cereal

1/4 cup unsweetened cocoa powder, 20 grams

1/4 teaspoon salt

1 teaspoon vanilla extract

Chocolate Chip Cookies ▪ *Corn-based*

- Preheat the oven to 375°F. Grease a cookie sheet.
- Cream the buttter and sugar in a medium-size bowl. Add the egg. Mix until light and thick. Add all the other ingredients except the chips. Beat until thick and creamy. Beat in the chips. Drop by rounded teaspoonfuls onto the prepared pan. Press to a 1/4-inch thickness with moistened fingertips. Bake for 8 to 9 minutes, until lightly browned. Allow to cool for just a minute or so, for easier removal from cookie sheet. (Nonstick spray on your spatula is helpful, too!) Transfer from the cookie sheet to a rack and let cool completely.

▪ Makes 36 cookies ▪

1/4 pound (1/2 cup) butter

1/2 cup dark brown sugar, packed firmly, 115 grams

1 egg

1 tablespoon milk

1 cup cornstarch, 125 grams

3/4 teaspoon baking soda

1 tablespoon baking powder

1/4 teaspoon salt

1 1/2 teaspoons vanilla extract

1 1/4 teaspoons xanthan gum

1 cup semisweet chocolate chips

Chocolate Chip Cookies ▪ *Oat-based*

This is a very nice cookie with a light cakelike texture, a crisp edge (be sure to bake long enough), and a mild flavor.

- Preheat the oven to 375°F. Grease a cookie sheet.
- Cream the butter and sugar in a medium-size bowl. Add the eggs. Mix until lighter and thicker. Add all the other ingredients except the chips. Beat until thick and creamy. Beat in the chips. Drop by rounded teaspoonfuls onto the prepared pan. Bake for 8 to 9 minutes, until lightly browned. Allow to cool for just a minute or so, for easier removal from the cookie sheet. Transfer from the cookie sheet to a rack and let cool completely.

▪ Makes 36 cookies ▪

$1/4$ pound ($1/2$ cup) butter

$1/2$ cup dark brown sugar, packed firmly, 115 grams

2 eggs

1 tablespoon plain yogurt

1 cup oat flour, 120 grams

$3/4$ teaspoon baking soda

1 tablespoon baking powder

$1/4$ teaspoon salt

$1 1/2$ teaspoons vanilla extract

$1 1/2$ teaspoons xanthan gum

1 cup semisweet chocolate chips

Chocolate Chip Cookies ▪ *Potato-based*

This cookie has all the nuances of a real chocolate chip cookie: a little crispness outside, tenderness inside, and that bite of baking soda. You will absolutely feel like you're cheating on your diet.

- Preheat the oven to 375°F. Grease a cookie sheet.
- Cream the butter and sugar in a medium-size bowl. Add the egg. Mix until light and thick. Add all the other ingredients except the chips. Beat until thick and creamy. Beat in the chips. Drop by rounded teaspoonfuls onto the prepared pan. Press to a $1/4$-inch thickness with moistened fingertips. Bake for 8 to 9 minutes, until lightly browned. Transfer from the cookie sheet to a rack and let cool completely.

▪ Makes 36 cookies ▪

$1/4$ pound ($1/2$ cup) butter

$1/2$ cup dark brown sugar, packed firmly, 115 grams

1 egg

2 tablespoons water

1 cup potato starch, 155 grams

1 teaspoon baking soda

2 teaspoons baking powder

$1/4$ teaspoon salt

$1/2$ teaspoon vanilla extract

$1 1/4$ teaspoons xanthan gum

1 cup semisweet chocolate chips

Chocolate Chip Cookies ■ *Rice-based*

This was the first rice-only cookie I made. It took quite a few tries to figure out what must be included to make a really good rice-based cookie. Flavor, texture, and taste were all very important for the formulation. If you like your cookies a bit crisp on the outside, increase baking time by a minute or two.

- Preheat the oven to 375°F. Grease a cookie sheet.
- Cream the butter and sugar in a medium-size bowl. Add the egg. Mix until light and thick. Add all the other ingredients except chips. Beat until thick and creamy. Beat in the chips. Drop by rounded teaspoonfuls onto the prepared pan. Press to a ¼-inch thickness with moistened fingertips. Bake for approximately 8 minutes, until lightly browned. Transfer from the cookie sheet to a rack and let cool completely.

■ Makes 40 cookies ■

¼ pound (½ cup) butter

½ cup dark brown sugar, packed firmly, 115 grams

1 egg

2 tablespoons plain yogurt

1¼ cups rice flour, 190 grams

¾ teaspoon baking soda

1 tablespoon baking powder

¼ teaspoon salt

1 teaspoon vanilla extract

2½ teaspoons xanthan gum

1 cup semisweet chocolate chips

Chocolate Cookies ∎ *Corn-based*

These are soft and fudgy, but not too sweet. Do not be alarmed that these cookies poof a little during baking. They settle into a traditional appearance while cooling.

- ∎ Preheat the oven to 375°F. Grease a cookie sheet.
- ∎ Cream the butter and sugar in a medium-size bowl. Add the egg. Mix until light and thick. Add all the other ingredients except the chips. Beat until thick and creamy. Beat in the chips. Drop by rounded teaspoonfuls onto the prepared pan. Flatten the tops slightly with moistened fingertips. Bake for 8 to 10 minutes, until no wet spots are visible. Transfer from the cookie sheet to a rack and let cool completely.

∎ Makes 36 cookies ∎

1/4 pound (1/2 cup) butter

1/2 cup sugar, packed firmly, 100 grams

1 egg

1 tablespoon plus 2 teaspoons milk

3/4 cup cornstarch, 95 grams

1/4 cup unsweetened cocoa powder, 20 grams

3/4 teaspoon baking soda

1 teaspoon baking powder

1/4 teaspoon salt

1 1/2 teaspoons vanilla extract

1 1/2 teaspoons xanthan gum

1 cup semisweet chocolate chips (optional)

NOTE: If you want to omit the chips, I recommend pressing the dough to a 1/4-inch thickness with moistened fingertips, sprinkling with a touch of sugar, and baking for 12 minutes. This adds just a bit of extra crispness to the outside of the cookie. This crispier cookie would be great for making an ice-cream sandwich!

Chocolate Cookies ▪ *Oat-based*

Plain and simple, these are good chocolate cookies. Add up to 1 cup of chocolate chips, if desired. Try not to overbake, otherwise the cookies will seem a little dry.

▪ Preheat the oven to 375°F. Grease a cookie sheet.

▪ Cream the butter and sugar in a medium-size bowl. Add the eggs. Mix until lighter and thicker. Add the other ingredients, and beat until thick and creamy. The dough will be very soft. Drop by rounded teaspoonfuls onto the prepared pan. Press to a ¼-inch thickness with moistened fingertips, for a flatter cookie, if desired. Bake for 8 to 9 minutes, until set and no shine remains. Allow to cool for just a minute or so, for easier removal from the cookie sheet. Transfer from the cookie sheet to a rack and let cool completely.

▪ Makes 36 cookies ▪

¼ pound (½ cup) butter

½ cup dark brown sugar, packed firmly, 115 grams

2 eggs

2 tablespoons plain yogurt

¾ cup oat flour, 90 grams

⅓ cup unsweetened cocoa powder, 30 grams

¾ teaspoon baking soda

1 tablespoon baking powder

½ teaspoon salt

1½ teaspoons vanilla extract

1½ teaspoons xanthan gum

Chocolate Cookies ▪ *Potato-based*

These cookies are soft and chocolaty, but not too sweet.

- Preheat the oven to 375°F. Grease a cookie sheet
- Cream the butter and sugar in a medium-size bowl. Add the egg. Mix until light and thick. Add all the other ingredients except the chips. Beat until thick and creamy. Beat in the chips. Drop by rounded teaspoonfuls onto the prepared pan. Flatten the tops slightly with moistened fingertips. Bake for 8 to 10 minutes, until lightly browned. Transfer from the cookie sheet to a rack and let cool completely.

▪ Makes 36 cookies ▪

$1/4$ pound ($1/2$ cup) butter

$1/2$ cup sugar, packed firmly, 100 grams

1 egg

2 tablespoons water

$3/4$ cup potato starch, 115 grams

$1/4$ cup unsweetened cocoa powder, 20 grams

1 teaspoon baking soda

2 teaspoons baking powder

$1/4$ teaspoon salt

1 teaspoon vanilla extract

$1 1/4$ teaspoons xanthan gum

1 cup semisweet chocolate chips (optional)

NOTE: If you want to omit the chips, I recommend pressing the dough to a $1/4$-inch thickness with moistened fingertips, sprinkling with a touch of sugar, and baking for 12 minutes. This adds just a bit of extra crispness to the outside of the cookie. Like its corn counterpart, this crispier cookie would be great for making an ice-cream sandwich!

Chocolate Cookies ▪ *Rice-based*

These chocolate cookies are very versatile. If you do not flatten them before baking, they become pretty little domed cookies. Pressed to a $\frac{1}{4}$-inch thickness (as in the directions), they are a traditional soft chocolate cookie. And finally, pressed to a $\frac{1}{8}$-inch thickness (and baked for about ten minutes), they become a crisp cookie. The flavor of these cookies is quite chocolaty, but there is room for up to 1 cup of chocolate chips, if desired.

- Preheat the oven to 375°F. Grease a cookie sheet.
- Cream the butter and sugar in a medium-size bowl. Add the egg. Mix until light and thick. Add the other ingredients. Beat until thick and creamy. Drop by rounded teaspoonfuls onto the prepared pan. Press to a $\frac{1}{4}$-inch thickness with moistened fingertips. Bake for approximately 8 minutes, until lightly browned. Transfer from the cookie sheet to a rack and let cool completely.

▪ Makes 36 cookies ▪

$\frac{1}{4}$ pound ($\frac{1}{2}$ cup) butter

$\frac{1}{2}$ cup dark brown sugar, packed firmly, 115 grams

1 egg

2 tablespoons plain yogurt, 30 grams

1 cup rice flour, 150 grams

$\frac{1}{3}$ cup unsweetened cocoa powder, 30 grams

$\frac{3}{4}$ teaspoon baking soda

1 tablespoon baking powder

$\frac{1}{2}$ teaspoon salt

1 teaspoon vanilla extract

2$\frac{1}{4}$ teaspoons xanthan gum

ABOUT FORTUNE COOKIES

When you first make fortune cookies, I suggest you bake them one at a time, until you have the hang of it. You will be folding a hot cookie rather quickly. Here's the detailed process:

1. Prepare fortunes on very small slips of paper, approximately $1/4$ x 2 inches. Have them ready ahead of time.
2. When baking, it is very important to bake for the right length of time. Too little, and you have a chewy center; too long, you have a burnt cookie. Look for the cookie to be browned for at least $1/4$ inch from the edges.
3. Remove the hot cookies from the oven. As soon as you can handle them, quickly remove the cookies one at a time from the cookie sheet and place a fortune in the center of each.
4. Working quickly, fold each fortune-topped cookie in half, leaving a soft bend at the fold rather than pressing down into a flat semicircle. Then, place one finger in the center of the fold (so the cookie will bend there), and bring the two ends of folded seam together. You should have the ideal cookie shape. Any odd-shaped bit of cookie may be trimmed with scissors.
5. Placing the cookies in a muffin tin or small cups, tips down, helps to hold their shape until they cool.

Fortune Cookies ▪ *Corn-based*

A classic, this cookie tastes almost identical to those served in a Chinese restaurant after dinner. I strongly suggest you make one test cookie before plunging in and putting the whole batch into the oven. It is important that the batter be thin, but not too thin. If the batter is too thick (due to slight differences in measuring ingredients), you will have a cookie that is a little pliable, instead of crisp, in the center.

2 egg whites
1/2 cup sugar, 100 grams
Pinch of salt
1/2 teaspoon vanilla extract
2/3 cup cornstarch, 80 grams
1 tablespoon oil
2 tablespoons milk
1/2 teaspoon xanthan gum
Pinch of baking soda

▪ Preheat the oven to 375°F. Grease a cookie sheet.

▪ Mix all the ingredients in a medium-size bowl, until well blended. I like to use a mixer with a whisk attachment. Be sure no lumps remain.

▪ Drop 1 tablespoonful of batter onto the prepared pan. The batter will spread during the baking. On the off-chance that your batter seems thick, spread the batter into a 3-inch circle. Place up to four rounds of batter on the baking sheet. (It is difficult to shape more than four baked cookies at a time before they become unbendable.)

▪ Bake for 8 to 10 minutes, until the edges of the cookies are browned substantially. The bottoms of the cookies should be browned. Do not underbake.

▪ Remove each cookie from the cookie sheet and place a fortune in the center; fold the cookie in half (see About Fortune Cookies, page 362). Bring the ends of the fold together to complete the cookie shape. Let cool completely.

▪ Makes 10 cookies ▪

Fortune Cookies ▪ *Oat-based*

When spreading these cookies, take extra care to be sure the center of the dough is spread very thin, otherwise the cookie will be soft in the middle after baking. Despite using whole-grain oat flour, these cookies have very good "fortune cookie" flavor and crunch.

2 egg whites
1/2 cup sugar, 100 grams
Pinch of salt
1/2 teaspoon vanilla extract
1/2 cup oat flour, 60 grams
1 tablespoon oil
2 tablespoons milk
1/4 teaspoon xanthan gum
Pinch of baking soda

▪ Preheat the oven to 375°F. Grease a cookie sheet.

▪ Mix all the ingredients in a medium-size bowl until well blended. I like to use a mixer with the whisk attachment. Be sure no lumps remain.

▪ Drop 1 scant tablespoonful of batter onto the prepared pan. Spread into a 3 1/2- to 4-inch circle. Moistened fingertips work well for this. Place up to four rounds of batter on the cookie sheet. (It is difficult to shape more than four baked cookies at a time before they become unbendable.)

▪ Bake for approximately 9 minutes, until the edges of the cookies are browned substantially. The bottoms of the cookies will be browned. Loosen the cookies from the sheet right away, but allow to cool for a minute so that they begin to firm.

▪ Remove a cookie from the pan and place a fortune in the center; fold the cookie in half (see About Fortune Cookies, page 362). Bring the ends of the fold together to complete the cookie shape. Let cool.

▪ Makes 12 cookies ▪

Fortune Cookies ▪ *Potato-based*

These fortune cookies are sweet and crunchy when they turn out just right. If underbaked, they will have a chewy center when cool. The center crisps after baking (which makes judging the whole process a little difficult). It is, however, so worth the effort. Just do not underbake!

- Preheat the oven to 375°F. Grease a cookie sheet.

- Mix all the ingredients in a medium-size bowl, until well blended. I like to use a mixer with the whisk attachment. Be sure no lumps remain.

- Drop 1 tablespoonful of batter onto the prepared pan. The batter will be thin. If the batter thickens upon sitting (it will), spread out into a 3-inch circle. Place up to four rounds of batter on the cookie sheet. (It is difficult to shape more than four baked cookies at a time before they become unbendable.)

- Bake for 10 to 12 minutes, until the edges of the cookies are browned substantially. The bottoms of the cookies will be browned.

- Remove a cookie from the pan and place a fortune in the center; fold the cookie in half (see About Fortune Cookies, page 362). Bring the ends of the fold together to complete the cookie shape. Let cool.

▪ Makes 10 cookies ▪

2 egg whites
1/2 cup sugar, 100 grams
Pinch of salt
1/2 teaspoon vanilla extract
1/2 cup plus 2 tablespoons potato starch, 95 grams
1 tablespoon oil
2 tablespoons milk
1/2 teaspoon xanthan gum
Pinch of baking soda

Fortune Cookies ▪ *Rice-based*

The batter for this cookie is a little thicker and easier to spread in a circle prior to baking. The taste is not quite as dead-on as the potato and corn versions, but is perhaps even more pleasing. There is a definite grit to the texture of this cookie.

2 egg whites
1/2 cup sugar, 100 grams
Pinch of salt
1/2 teaspoon vanilla extract
1/2 cup rice flour, 75 grams
1 tablespoon oil
2 tablespoons milk
1/2 teaspoon xanthan gum
Pinch of baking soda

- Preheat the oven to 375°F. Grease a cookie sheet.

- Mix all the ingredients in a medium-size bowl until well blended. I like to use a mixer with the whisk attachment. Be sure no lumps remain.

- Drop 1 scant tablespoonful of batter onto the prepared pan. Spread into a 3 1/2- to 4-inch circle. Moistened fingertips work well for this. Place up to four rounds of batter on the baking sheet. (It is difficult to shape more than four cookies at a time before they become unbendable.)

- Bake for approximately 10 minutes, until the edges of the cookies are browned substantially. The bottoms of the cookies will be browned. Let cool for a minute or so, to allow the cookies to firm a little.

- Remove a cookie from the pan and place a fortune in the center; fold the cookie in half (See About Fortune Cookies, page 362). Bring the ends of the fold together to complete the cookie shape. Let cool.

▪ Makes 12 cookies ▪

Lebkuchen ■ *Corn-based*

Lebkuchen is a German Christmas cookie that has a thin, almost-transparent glazed top. With one bite, you will think they are a flavorful, chewy treat. After several, they may be your favorite.

- Preheat the oven to 350°F. Grease a 9-inch square or round baking pan.

- In a medium-size bowl, combine all the ingredients, including the raisins and nuts. Beat until well mixed. The batter will be very sticky and very thick. With wet fingertips, press the dough into the prepared baking pan. Bake for 30 to 35 minutes, until a toothpick inserted in the middle tests cleanly and the top is nicely browned. Let cool.

- In a small cup, stir together the confectioners' sugar and enough of the water to make a thin glaze. Pour on top of the cooled cake. Cut into small squares or wedges.

■ Makes 16 small servings ■

1/4 cup honey

2 teaspoons oil

2 tablespoons milk

1/2 cup sugar, 100 grams

1 1/4 cups cornstarch, 155 grams

1/4 teaspoon salt

1/2 teaspoon grated lemon zest

1/2 teaspoon ground cinnamon

1/2 teaspoon ground allspice

3/4 teaspoon xanthan gum

1/3 cup raisins

1/3 cup chopped nuts

Glaze:

1/2 cup confectioners' sugar

2 teaspoons water (approximately)

Lebkuchen ■ *Oat-based*

This German bar cookie has just a bit of chewiness and is full of flavor. It is the driest of the Lebkuchen versions, but by no means too dry.

■ Preheat the oven to 350°F. Grease a 9-inch square or round baking pan.

■ In a medium-size bowl, combine all the ingredients, including the raisins and nuts. Beat until well mixed. The batter will be very sticky and very thick. With wet fingertips, press the dough into the prepared baking pan. Bake for approximately 35 minutes, until a toothpick inserted in the middle tests cleanly and the top is nicely browned. Let cool.

■ In a small cup, stir together the confectioners' sugar and enough of the water to make a thin glaze. Pour on top of the cooled cake. Cut into small squares or wedges.

■ Makes 16 small servings ■

¼ cup honey

2 teaspoons oil

2 tablespoons milk

½ cup sugar, 100 grams

1 cup oat flour, 120 grams

¼ teaspoon salt

½ teaspoon grated lemon zest

½ teaspoon ground cinnamon

½ teaspoon ground allspice

¼ teaspoon xanthan gum

⅓ cup raisins

⅓ cup chopped nuts

Glaze:

½ cup confectioners' sugar

2 teaspoons water (approximately)

Lebkuchen ∎ *Potato-based*

This spicy, thin bar cookie is very flavorful. It is slightly chewy.

- Preheat the oven to 350°F. Grease a 9-inch square or round baking pan.
- In a medium-size bowl, combine all the ingredients, including the raisins and nuts. Beat until well mixed. The batter will be very sticky and very thick. With wet fingertips, press the dough into the prepared baking pan. Bake for 35 to 40 minutes, until a toothpick inserted in the middle tests cleanly and the top is nicely browned. Let cool.
- In a small cup, stir together the confectioners' sugar and enough of the water to make a thin glaze. Pour on top of the cooled cake. Cut into small squares or wedges.

∎ Makes 16 small servings ∎

1/4 cup honey

2 teaspoons oil

2 tablespoons milk

1/2 cup sugar, 100 grams

1 cup potato starch, 155 grams

1/4 teaspoon salt

1/2 teaspoon grated lemon peel

1/2 teaspoon ground cinnamon

1/2 teaspoon ground allspice

1/2 teaspoon xanthan gum

1/3 cup raisins

1/3 cup chopped nuts

Glaze:

1/2 cup confectioners' sugar

2 teaspoons water (approximately

Lebkuchen ■ *Rice-based*

Rice flour surprises me again and again. Used in Lebkuchen, it makes a moist, slightly chewy bar cookie. No one will be able to tell it is not a traditional recipe.

- Preheat the oven to 350°F. Grease a 9-inch square or round baking pan.

- In a medium-size bowl, combine all the ingredients, including the raisins and nuts. Beat until well mixed. The batter will be very sticky and very thick. With wet fingertips, press the dough into the prepared baking pan. Bake for approximately 35 minutes, until a toothpick inserted in the middle tests cleanly and the top is nicely browned. Let cool.

- In a small cup, stir together the confectioners' sugar and enough of the water to make a thin glaze. Pour on top of the cooled cake. Cut into small squares or wedges.

■ Makes 16 small servings ■

1/4 cup honey

2 teaspoons oil

2 tablespoons milk

1/2 cup sugar, 100 grams

3/4 cup rice flour, 115 grams

1/4 teaspoon salt

1/2 teaspoon grated lemon peel

1/2 teaspoon ground cinnamon

1/2 teaspoon ground allspice

1/2 teaspoon xanthan gum

1/3 cup raisins

1/3 cup chopped nuts

Glaze:

1/2 cup confectioners' sugar

2 teaspoons water (approximately)

Oatmeal Cookies ■ *Corn- and oat-based*

This is a good recipe to try if you want to slowly incorporate oats into your gluten-free diet. Please choose an oat that is certified to be gluten-free. Many mills process oats as well as wheat through a series of screens that separate (for the most part) the different grains.

- Preheat the oven to 375°F. Grease a cookie sheet.
- Cream the butter and sugar in a medium-size bowl. Add the egg. Mix until light and thick. Add the other ingredients. Beat until thick and creamy. Drop by rounded teaspoonfuls onto the prepared pan. Press to a ¼-inch thickness with moistened fingertips. Bake for 9 to 10 minutes, until lightly browned. Transfer from the cookie sheet to a rack and let cool completely.

■ Makes 36 cookies ■

¼ pound (½ cup) butter
½ cup dark brown sugar, packed firmly, 115 grams
1 egg
1 tablespoon milk
1 cup cornstarch, 125 grams
¾ teaspoon baking soda
1 tablespoon baking powder
¼ teaspoon salt
1 teaspoon vanilla extract
1 ¼ teaspoons xanthan gum
1 cup rolled oats

Oatmeal Cookies ■ *Potato- and oat-based*

Oatmeal cookies are one of my favorites, although I do add chocolate chips to the batter. If you want to incorporate chips as well, I suggest 1 cup of semisweet chocolate morsels.

- Preheat the oven to 375°F. Grease a cookie sheet.
- Cream the butter and sugar in a medium-size bowl. Add the egg. Mix until light and thick. Add the other ingredients. Beat until thick and creamy. Drop by rounded teaspoonfuls onto the prepared pan. Press to a ¼-inch thickness with moistened fingertips. Bake for 9 to 10 minutes, until lightly browned. Transfer from the cookie sheet to a rack and let cool completely.

■ Makes 36 cookies ■

¼ pound (½ cup) butter
½ cup dark brown sugar, packed firmly, 115 grams
1 egg
1 tablespoon milk
1 cup potato starch, 155 grams
1 teaspoon baking soda
2 teaspoons baking powder
¼ teaspoon salt
½ teaspoon vanilla extract
1 teaspoon xanthan gum
1 cup rolled oats

Oatmeal-Raisin Cookies ▪ *Oat-based*

I've included vanilla in the flavoring of this cookie to soften the whole-oat taste. This may be my favorite oatmeal cookie.

- Preheat the oven to 375°F. Grease a cookie sheet.
- Cream the butter and sugar in a medium-size bowl. Add the eggs. Mix until lighter and thicker. Add all the other ingredients except the raisins. Beat until thick and creamy. Beat in the raisins. The dough will be very soft. Drop by rounded teaspoonfuls onto the prepared pan. Bake for 8 to 9 minutes, until lightly browned. Allow to cool for just a minute or so, for easier removal from the cookie sheet. Transfer from the cookie sheet to a rack and let cool completely.

▪ Makes 40 cookies ▪

$1/4$ pound ($1/2$ cup) butter

$1/2$ cup dark brown sugar, packed firmly, 115 grams

2 eggs

1 tablespoon plain yogurt

1 cup oat flour, 120 grams

$3/4$ teaspoon baking soda

1 tablespoon baking powder

$1/4$ teaspoon salt

1 teaspoon vanilla extract

$1/2$ teaspoon ground cinnamon

$1/4$ teaspoon grated nutmeg

$1 1/2$ teaspoons xanthan gum

$2/3$ cup rolled oats, 60 grams

$1/2$ cup raisins, loosely packed, 60 grams

Oatmeal-Raisin Cookies ▪ *Rice-based*

These cookies have a little spice, poha flakes (flattened rice), and raisins. They feel healthy and tasty all at once. Poha flakes can be found at some health food stores and Asian or Indian markets. I find the poha flakes a bit hard, but you can let the batter sit for a while to soften them a little. Certified-gluten-free oats may be substituted for the poha flakes.

- Preheat the oven to 375°F. Grease a cookie sheet.
- Cream the butter and sugar in a medium-size bowl. Add the eggs. Mix until light and thick. Add all the other ingredients except the raisins. Beat until thick and creamy. Beat in the raisins. Drop by rounded teaspoonfuls onto the prepared pan. Press to a ¼-inch thickness with moistened fingertips. Bake for approximately 8 minutes, until lightly browned. Transfer from the cookie sheet to a rack and let cool completely.

▪ Makes 40 cookies ▪

¼ pound (½ cup) butter

½ cup dark brown sugar, packed firmly, 115 grams

2 eggs

2 tablespoons plain yogurt, 30 grams

1¼ cups rice flour, 190 grams

¾ teaspoon baking soda

1 tablespoon baking powder

¼ teaspoon salt

½ teaspoon ground cinnamon

¼ teaspoon grated nutmeg

2½ teaspoons xanthan gum

½ cup poha flakes, 40 grams

½ cup raisins, loosely packed, 60 grams

> **NOTE:** If you prefer no spice or raisins in your oatmeal cookies, substitute 1 teaspoon of vanilla extract in place of the cinnamon and nutmeg and omit the raisins. Also, add up to 1 cup of chocolate chips, if you like.

Peanut Butter Cookies ■ *Corn-based*

These cookies are everything you'd want in a peanut butter cookie, tender with understated peanut butter taste.

■ Preheat the oven to 375°F. grease a cookie sheet.

■ Cream the butter, peanut butter, and sugar in a medium-size bowl. Add the eggs. Mix until lighter and thicker. Add all the other ingredients except the chips. Beat until thick and creamy. Add the chips, if desired; then drop by rounded teaspoonfuls onto the prepared pan. If not using chips, dip a fork into cornstarch and press the tops of the cookies with the bottom of the fork; press a second time crosswise to make a crisscross pattern. Bake for 8 to 9 minutes, until lightly browned. Allow to cool for just a minute or so, for easier removal from the cookie sheet. Transfer from the cookie sheet to a rack and let cool completely.

■ Makes 36 cookies ■

4 tablespoons (¼ cup) butter

½ cup peanut butter

½ cup dark brown sugar, packed firmly, 115 grams

2 eggs

2 tablespoons plain yogurt

1 ¼ cups cornstarch, 155 grams

¾ teaspoon baking soda

1 tablespoon baking powder

½ teaspoon salt

1 teaspoon vanilla extract

2 teaspoons xanthan gum

1 cup chocolate chips (optional)

Peanut Butter Cookies ▪ *Oat-based*

The dough for these cookies is very soft. Unless you want to refrigerate the dough for several hours after mixing, you need to make a choice: embrace the plain, ordinary cookie top; put up to 1 cup of chocolate chips in the dough; or top each with a Hershey kiss. These cookies have a mild peanut butter flavor; they're one of my favorite oat-version cookies.

- Preheat the oven to 375°F. Grease a cookie sheet.
- Cream the butter, peanut butter, and sugar, in a medium-size bowl. Add the eggs. Mix until lighter and thicker. Add all the other ingredients. Beat until thick and creamy. Drop by rounded teaspoonfuls onto the prepared pan. Bake for 8 to 9 minutes, until lightly browned. Allow to cool for just a minute or so, for easier removal from the cookie sheet. Transfer from the cookie sheet to a rack and let cool completely.

▪ Makes 36 cookies ▪

4 tablespoons ($^1/_4$ cup) butter

$^1/_2$ cup peanut butter

$^1/_2$ cup dark brown sugar, packed firmly, 115 grams

2 eggs

2 tablespoons plain yogurt

1 cup oat flour, 120 grams

$^3/_4$ teaspoon baking soda

1 tablespoon baking powder

$^1/_4$ teaspoon salt

1 teaspoon vanilla extract

$1^1/_2$ teaspoons xanthan gum

Peanut Butter Cookies ▪ *Potato-based*

This has the taste of a traditional peanut butter cookie, but is just a little bit moister—and still tender.

- Preheat the oven to 375°F. Grease a cookie sheet.
- Cream the butter, peanut butter, and sugar, in a medium-size bowl. Add the eggs. Mix until lighter and thicker. Add all the other ingredients except the chips. Beat until thick and creamy. Add the chips, if desired; then drop by rounded teaspoonfuls onto the prepared pan. If not using chips, dip the fork into potato starch and press the tops of the cookies with the bottom of the fork; press a second time crosswise to make a crisscross pattern. Bake for 8 to 9 minutes, until lightly browned. Allow to cool for just a minute or so, for easier removal from the cookie sheet. Transfer from the cookie sheet to a rack and let cool completely.

▪ Makes 36 cookies ▪

4 tablespoons (1/4 cup) butter

1/2 cup peanut butter

1/2 cup dark brown sugar, packed firmly, 115 grams

2 eggs

2 tablespoons plain yogurt

1 cup potato starch, 155 grams

3/4 teaspoon baking soda

1 tablespoon baking powder

1/2 teaspoon salt

1 teaspoon vanilla extract

1 3/4 teaspoons xanthan gum

1 cup chocolate chips (optional)

NOTES ON FORMULATING A
RICE-BASED PEANUT BUTTER COOKIE

Some recipes come together quickly, whereas others prove more difficult. Underlying food theory for alternative flours must be developed, with rice being among the most difficult.

When calculating the formulation for the rice version of a peanut butter cookie, it is natural to first look at the addition of peanut butter to a plain cookie recipe. But remember, making cookies is a lot like algebra. The equation must always be balanced; otherwise, the results are not good. (i.e., the addition of a liquid requires the reduction in another liquid).

Knowing that peanut butter is roughly 50 percent fat (not all of the fat is "bad" fat) means that we need to use twice as much peanut butter for the amount of fat removed. So, we remove ¼ cup of butter and add ½ cup peanut butter. (The fact that butter is approximately 80 percent fat is not a material issue in this analysis.)

Then, we think about what the other 50 percent of peanut butter (the nonfat part) is like. We presume it to be a near liquid. So, we reduce the liquid in the recipe by several tablespoons. And . . . the resulting cookie is dry in the bowl and dry in taste. We were so wrong about the 50 percent nonfat part of peanut butter being a near liquid! (And, suddenly my testing on nut cakes comes to mind—the testing that showed ground nuts must be treated as a flour—I should have known better than to think of peanut butter, which is essentially simply well-ground peanuts, as a liquid!)

Seeing the dryness of the dough and the finished cookie, we know we have gone in the absolute wrong direction. That 50 percent nonfat element of peanuts is actually drying to a cookie batter—it absorbs liquid. This means we need *more* moisture, not less. So, we add back the 2 tablespoons of liquid (in this case, plain yogurt) and add 2 more tablespoons of liquid. The resulting cookie is, again, not quite right. After baking, the cookie has lost its pretty little fork indentations and the flavor is too light.

Finally, we know what we must do. We must go in between the two options. First, we need to use 3 tablespoons of liquid (instead of the 4 last used). Second, we must increase the salt to enhance the flavor. And, finally, we have to add some vanilla to boost the flavor, as well.

We have success. The resulting tasty cookie is the rice-based recipe that follows.

Peanut Butter Cookies ■ *Rice-based*

At long last, a perfect rice-based peanut butter cookie.

- Preheat the oven to 375°F. Grease a cookie sheet.
- Cream the butter, peanut butter, and sugar, in a medium-size bowl. Add the egg. Mix until light and thick. Add the other ingredients. Beat until thick and creamy. Drop by rounded teaspoonfuls onto the prepared pan.
- Dip a fork into the rice flour and press the tops of the cookies with the bottom of the fork; press a second time crosswise to make a crisscross pattern, while pressing to a 1/4-inch thickness.
- Bake for 8 to 10 minutes, until lightly browned at the edges. Transfer from the cookie sheet to a rack and let cool completely.

■ Makes 36 cookies ■

4 tablespoons (1/4 cup) butter

1/2 cup peanut butter

1/2 cup sugar, 100 grams

1 egg

3 tablespoons yogurt

1 teaspoon apple cider vinegar

1 1/4 cups rice flour, 190 grams

3/4 teaspoon baking soda

1 tablespoon baking powder

1/4 teaspoon salt

1 teaspoon vanilla extract

2 1/2 teaspoons xanthan gum

Pecan Cookies ▪ *Corn-based*

This is a tender, melt-in-your-mouth cookie with delicate nut flavor.

- Preheat the oven to 375°F. Grease a cookie sheet.
- Cream the butter and sugar in a medium-size bowl. Add the egg. Mix until light and thick. Add the other ingredients. Beat until thick and creamy. Drop by rounded teaspoonfuls onto the prepared pan. Bake for approximately 9 minutes, until lightly browned on the top and edges, and golden on the bottom. Allow to cool for just a minute or so, for easier removal from the cookie sheet. Transfer from the cookie sheet to a rack and let cool completely.

▪ Makes 32 cookies ▪

1/4 pound (1/2 cup) butter
1/2 cup sugar, 100 grams
1 egg
1 cup cornstarch, 125 grams
3/4 teaspoon baking soda
1 tablespoon baking powder
1/2 teaspoon salt
1 1/2 teaspoons vanilla extract
1 1/4 teaspoons xanthan gum
1 tablespoon apple cider vinegar
1/4 cup ground pecans

Pecan Cookies ▪ *Oat-based*

These cookies aren't the prettiest gluten-free cookies in this book, but they do taste good! It's almost like the flavor of the nut is first to be noticed, then the oats, but then you can't quite be sure.

- Preheat the oven to 375°F. Grease a cookie sheet.
- Cream the butter and sugar in a medium-size bowl. Add the eggs. Mix until lighter and thicker. Add the other ingredients and beat well. Drop by rounded teaspoonfuls onto the prepared pan. Bake for approximately 11 minutes, until lightly browned on top and golden on the bottom. Transfer from the cookie sheet to a rack and let cool completely.

▪ Makes 36 cookies ▪

1/4 pound (1/2 cup) butter
1/2 cup sugar, 100 grams
2 eggs
1 cup oat flour, 120 grams
3/4 teaspoon baking soda
1 tablespoon baking powder
1/2 teaspoon salt
1 1/2 teaspoons vanilla extract
1 tablespoon apple cider vinegar
1 1/2 teaspoons xanthan gum
1/4 cup ground pecans

Pecan Cookies ▪ *Potato-based*

This was the pecan cookie most favored by our taste testers. They couldn't explain why: "They are just better." I would describe the cookie as tender and flavorful.

- Preheat the oven to 375°F. Grease a cookie sheet.
- Cream the butter and sugar in a medium-size bowl. Add the egg. Mix until light and thick. Add the other ingredients and mix well. Drop by rounded teaspoonfuls onto the prepared pan. Bake for 9 to 11 minutes, until the top and edges are lightly browned and the bottom is golden. Transfer from the cookie sheet to a rack and let cool completely.

▪ Makes 36 cookies ▪

1/4 pound (1/2 cup) butter
1/2 cup sugar, 100 grams
1 egg
1 tablespoon water
1 cup potato starch, 155 grams
1 teaspoon baking soda
2 teaspoons baking powder
1/2 teaspoon salt
1/2 teaspoon vanilla extract
1 tablespoon apple cider vinegar
1 1/4 teaspoons xanthan gum
1/4 cup ground pecans

Pecan Cookies ▪ *Rice-based*

These pecan cookies are most like a pecan sandy. The dough looks like ordinary cookie dough and holds its shape.

- Preheat the oven to 375°F. Grease a cookie sheet.
- Cream the butter and sugar in a medium-size bowl. Add the egg. Mix until light and thick. Add the other ingredients and beat well. Drop by rounded teaspoonfuls onto the prepared pan. Press the dough to a 1/4-inch thickness with moistened fingertips. Bake for 9 to 11 minutes, until lightly browned on the top and edges and golden on the bottom. Transfer from the cookie sheet to a rack and let cool completely.

▪ Makes 36 cookies ▪

1/4 pound (1/2 cup) butter
1/2 cup sugar, 100 grams
1 egg
1 tablespoon plain yogurt
1 1/4 cups rice flour, 190 grams
3/4 teaspoon baking soda
1 tablespoon baking powder
1/2 teaspoon salt
1 teaspoon vanilla extract
1 tablespoon apple cider vinegar
2 1/2 teaspoons xanthan gum
1/4 cup ground pecans

Sugar Cookies ■ *Corn-based*

Here is a very traditional sugar cookie, a little crisp, but still tender.

- Preheat the oven to 375°F.
- Cream the butter and sugar in a medium-size bowl. Add the egg. Mix until light and thick. Add the other ingredients. Beat until thick and creamy. Drop by rounded teaspoonfuls onto the prepared pan. Press to a ¼-inch thickness with moistened fingertips. Top with sugar or sprinkles, if desired. Bake for 8 to 10 minutes, until lightly browned. Do not underbake! These cookies will seem flexible when transferring them from the pan to a rack. They will crisp while cooling.

■ Makes 36 cookies ■

¼ pound (½ cup) butter

½ cup sugar, 110 grams

1 egg

1½ tablespoons milk

1 cup cornstarch, 125 grams

½ teaspoon baking soda

1 tablespoon plus 1 teaspoon baking powder

¼ teaspoon salt

2 teaspoons vanilla extract

1¼ teaspoons xanthan gum

Topping:

1 tablespoon sugar or sprinkles

Sugar Cookies ▪ *Potato-based*

These cookies are light and delicate in flavor. Go easy if you top them with sprinkles—too many will easily overpower these cookies.

- Preheat the oven to 375°F. Grease a cookie sheet.
- Cream the butter and sugar in a medium-size bowl. Add the eggs. Mix until light and thick. Add the other ingredients. Beat until thick and creamy. Drop by rounded teaspoonfuls onto the prepared pan. Press to a ¼-inch thickness with moistened fingertips. Top with sprinkles, if desired. Bake for 8 to 9 minutes, until lightly browned. Transfer from the cookie sheet to a rack and let cool completely.

▪ Makes 36 cookies ▪

¼ pound (½ cup) butter

½ cup sugar, 100 grams

2 eggs

1 cup potato starch, 155 grams

2 teaspoons baking powder

¼ teaspoon baking soda

Pinch of salt

½ teaspoon vanilla extract

1 ¼ teaspoons xanthan gum

Sprinkles (optional)

> **NOTE:** This mixing process is very important, especially for potato starch. First, it coats the flour and prevents the cookies from drying out too quickly. Second, it prevents the cookies from becoming too gummy.

Sugar Cookies ▪ *Rice-based*

These cookies are flattened with the bottom of a glass dipped first in water, then in sugar, just as our family did when we were little. If you prefer, sprinkles work well on top, too. These cookies are light in flavor and texture.

- ▪ Preheat the oven to 375°F. Grease a cookie sheet.

- ▪ Cream the butter and sugar. Add the egg. Mix until light and thick. Add the other dough ingredients. Beat until thick and creamy. Drop by rounded teaspoonfuls onto the prepared pan.

- ▪ Place the sugar for the topping in a small dish. Dip the bottom of a glass into water, then into the sugar. Press the cookies to a ¼-inch thickness with the bottom of the glass. (Or press to a ¼-inch thickness with moistened fingertips and top with sprinkles.)

- ▪ Bake for approximately 8 minutes, until lightly browned. Transfer from the cookie sheet to a rack and let cool completely.

▪ Makes 36 cookies ▪

¼ pound (½ cup) butter

½ cup sugar, 100 grams

1 egg

2 tablespoons plain yogurt

1 teaspoon apple cider vinegar

1 ¼ cups rice flour, 190 grams

¾ teaspoon baking soda

1 tablespoon baking powder

¼ teaspoon salt

1 teaspoon vanilla extract

2½ teaspoons xanthan gum

Topping:

2 tablespoons sugar

Water

OR sprinkles

Toffee Bars ▪ *Corn-based*

A tender, rich base layer. Melted morsels and chopped pecans on top. Decadent, wonderful for young and old alike.

- Preheat the oven to 350°F. Lightly grease a 9-inch round or square baking pan.

- Combine all the ingredients, except the milk, in a medium-size bowl. Mix until the dough resembles a fine crumb. Add the milk and beat well.

- Press into the bottom of the prepared pan. Prick the top with a fork. Bake until golden brown, approximately 25 minutes.

- In a small pan, cook the brown sugar and butter until both are melted and begin to boil. Immediately set a timer for 7 minutes and continue cooking, stirring the whole time. The butter and brown sugar will slowly blend together. This mixture is exceedingly hot and should not be touched by hand. Pour the mixture over the top of the base layer.

- Place the chopped pecans and then the chocolate chips over the top of the sugar mixture. Cover the pan so that the heat from the sugar mixture will melt the chips. Alternatively, the entire pan may also be placed in a hot oven for a minute or two, to melt the chips.

- Once the chips melt, remove the cover, spread the melted chocolate lightly with knife, and let cool. Cut into small pieces.

▪ Makes 16 pieces ▪

Base:

4 ounces cream cheese

4 tablespoons (1/4 cup) butter

3/4 cup cornstarch, 95 grams

1/3 cup sugar, 65 grams

1/4 teaspoon xanthan gum

1/4 teaspoon baking soda

1 tablespoon milk

Topping:

1/2 cup brown sugar

5 1/3 tablespoons (1/3 cup) butter

3/4 cup chopped pecans

1 cup semisweet chocolate chips

NOTE: It is customary to melt the butter and sugar without stirring, to prevent any sugar crystals from dropping into the mixture and causing the caramel to become gritty. I have had good success with stirring constantly. A teaspoon or so of corn syrup added to the mixture (at the beginning) will also deter formation of sugar crystals.

20

PIES AND TARTS

So, what does this cookbook bring to pies that hasn't been done before? Actually, a lot.

First, better pie crusts. I talk about this more later, but they are the best gluten-free pie crusts I have ever made.

Second, fillings that are cooked on the stove or in the microwave oven. Cooking fillings on the stove and placing them in a prebaked pie crust help prevent moisture from being absorbed into the pie crust. Soggy pie crusts are low on my list of good things to eat. Even when a pie is baked in the oven, gluten-free pie crusts perform better if they are at least partially prebaked.

The fillings fall into two major categories—custard and fruit. Custard fillings are creamy and delicious. Fruit fillings celebrate the fresh flavor of fruits. The process of making custard fillings is consistent: partial cooking of the base, then tempering eggs and completion of cooking. It seems odd the first time you make it, but it sure is faster than waiting by a hot oven.

Working with fruit has one major variable—the cooking time of the fruit. When working with berries, which cook quickly, the entire filling can be mixed and cooked quickly. When working with fruit that requires longer cooking (such as peaches or rhubarb—yes, rhubarb is really a vegetable, but it is a fruit for our purposes), the fruit will be partially cooked, then a thickener (dissolved in liquid) is added with just a little final cooking.

There are a few choices for topping pies. If you are very agile with handling pie crusts, you can certainly put the uncooked fruit filling into the crust, place a top crust or genuine lattice over it, and bake it. Alternatively, you can pre-bake strips of crust for a mock-lattice top, or bake streusel and sprinkle it on top of the cooked fruit filling.

And, finally, if you need more tempting options, you can top any baked fruit pie with meringue (and bake briefly for color) or top with whipped cream.

If you're looking for a dessert that comes together quicker than a pie, I suggest taking any one of the pie fillings and layering it with whipped cream into a beautiful parfait.

Apricot Tart ▪ *Rice-based*

If you've never baked with apricots, you're in for a surprise! Unlike most fruit, apricots take on a tartness during baking. The sweet vanilla glaze is a nice offset. You will either love the tartness of the apricots (as I do) or you will probably not like it even a little bit. The crust is barely sweet and breadlike in texture.

- ▪ Preheat the oven to 375°F. Lightly grease a baking sheet.

- ▪ To make the crust, place the egg whites in a medium-size bowl. Beat until very frothy, with big and little bubbles. Add the remaining crust ingredients. Mix well until thickened. It should seem soft and thick, like softly whipped cream.

- ▪ On the prepared baking sheet, press the dough to just under ¼-inch thickness. (Moistened fingertips help with the process.) You may free-form the shape into a circle or rectangle, whatever you like. If shaping into a circle, the size will be approximately 11 inches in diameter.

- ▪ Peel and cut the apricots into small wedges. Press the wedges into the dough in a pretty, overlapping pattern.

- ▪ Bake for approximately 20 minutes, until the dough is lightly browned and the apricots are tender.

- ▪ Combine the topping ingredients in a small cup. Mix well to dissolve the starch. Microwave for approximately 30 seconds, to thicken. Brush over the top of the tart.

▪ Serves 12 ▪

Crust:

3 egg whites

1 tablespoon oil

½ cup milk

½ cup rice flour, 75 grams

2 teaspoons baking powder

¼ teaspoon baking soda

2 tablespoons sugar

¼ teaspoon salt

1¾ teaspoons xanthan gum

1 tablespoon apple cider vinegar

1 teaspoon vanilla extract

Filling:

8–9 fresh apricots, just under 1½ pounds

Topping:

2 tablespoons sugar

½ teaspoon vanilla extract

2 tablespoons water

½ teaspoon cornstarch or potato starch

Banana Cream Pie

If you're craving traditional banana pudding (with vanilla wafers), this pie is a fast alternative. The light custard/pudding is studded with many thin slices of banana.

- In a large, microwave-safe bowl, combine all the ingredients for the filling except the eggs and bananas. Microwave on high for 4 to 5 minutes, stirring occasionally, until the mixture is quite thick.

- Place the eggs in a small bowl. Slowly add approximately 1 cup of the filling to the eggs while beating quickly, to temper the eggs (to avoid scrambling them). Add the egg mixture to the bowl of filling. Microwave for 1 minute or so to bring the mixture to a boil. Do not skip this step.

- When the filling is almost ready, slice the bananas into thin slices. Place approximately half of the bananas into the bottom of the pie crust. Pour half of the filling over the bananas. Arrange the remaining bananas on top of the filling. Cover with the remaining filling. A light spray of nonstick cooking spray will help prevent a skin from forming over the top of the filling. Refrigerate for several hours before serving.

- Top with whipped cream or meringue, if desired.

■ Makes one 9-inch pie ■

Crust:
Prebaked gluten-free pie crust or cookie crumb crust

Filling:
1/2 cup sugar, 100 grams

3 tablespoons cornstarch or potato starch

1 1/2 teaspoons vanilla extract

2 1/2 cups milk

2 bananas

2 eggs

Topping (optional):
Whipped cream or meringue

Blueberry Pie

This blueberry pie is very pretty and very strong in flavor, although not too sweet. If you prefer a sweeter pie, increase the sugar by several tablespoons. If you wish to tone down the blueberry flavor, consider topping with streusel or whipped cream. Or just make your slices a little smaller than usual.

- Rinse the blueberries. Place the blueberries and the remaining ingredients in a large, microwave-safe bowl. Stir well but gently. Microwave on high for approximately 7 minutes, stirring gently every 2 minutes or so. The juices should be clear, thickened, and boiling.

- Pour into the prebaked crust. If you wish to top the filling with streusel, place on top of the pie before cooling. If you wish to top the filling with whipped cream, place on top of the pie after cooling.

- Refrigerate.

■ Makes one 9-inch pie ■

Crust:

1 prebaked gluten-free pie crust

Filling:

2 pints blueberries (approximately 1 3/4 pounds)

1/3 cup sugar

1/4 cup water

2 tablespoons cornstarch or potato starch

1/2 teaspoon vanilla extract

Topping (optional):

Prebaked streusel or whipped cream

Cherry Streusel Pie

Sour cherries are among my favorite fruits. This pie takes such a short amount of time once the crust is ready. It is also very good without streusel.

- Wash and pit the cherries. Place in a large, microwave-safe bowl (I like to pit the cherries over the bowl, to catch the few tablespoons of the juice in the process). Add the sugar and starch. Stir well but gently. Microwave on high for approximately 8 minutes, stirring occasionally, until the cherries are tender and the juices clear, thickened, and boiling.

- Pour into the prebaked crust. Smooth the top of the filling, for a better presentation. Allow the pie to cool for approximately 10 minutes, then sprinkle the top with the streusel.

- Refrigerate before serving to allow the filling to set.

■ Serves 8 ■

Crust:
1 prebaked gluten-free pie crust

Filling:
1 quart sour cherries (approximately 1 3/4 pounds)
1/2 cup sugar
3 tablespoons cornstarch or potato starch

Topping:
Prebaked streusel

Custard Pie, No-Bake

This pie has a very smooth custard. It is very good plain, but a dollop of whipped cream and a sprinkling of nutmeg makes it extra nice. Two tablespoons of Grand Marnier substituted for the vanilla would be a good flavor option.

- Have the pie crust ready and cooled. Set aside.

- In a large saucepan, combine all the ingredients for custard except the egg yolks, and stir well. Over medium heat, and stirring often, bring the mixture to almost a boil. The custard should be thickening. Remove from the heat.

- Place the egg yolks in a small bowl. Slowly add approximately 1 cup of the filling to the egg yolks while beating quickly, to temper the eggs (to avoid scrambling them). Add the yolk mixture to the saucepan. Return to the heat and bring to boil. Do not skip this step.

- Pour the custard into the pie shell. A light spray of nonstick cooking spray will help prevent a skin from forming over the top of the custard. Refrigerate until quite cold, preferably overnight. Top with whipped cream and a sprinkle of nutmeg, if desired.

■ Serves 8 ■

Crust:

1 prebaked gluten-free pie crust

Custard:

1/2 cup sugar

1 teaspoon vanilla extract

2 (12-ounce) cans evaporated milk

3 1/2 tablespoons cornstarch or potato starch

6 egg yolks

Topping:

1 recipe Whipped Cream (page 332, if desired)

1/4 teaspoon nutmeg (if desired)

Custard Pie, Chocolate No-Bake

More sophisticated than a chocolate pie and not too sweet—it's richer, smoother, and denser.

- Have a pie crust ready and cooled. Set aside.

- In a large saucepan, combine all the ingredients for the custard except the egg yolks, and stir well. Over medium heat, and stirring often, bring the mixture to almost a boil. The custard should be thickening. Remove from the heat.

- Place the egg yolks in a small bowl. Slowly add approximately 1 cup of the filling to the egg yolks while beating quickly, to temper the eggs (to avoid scrambling them). Add the yolk mixture to the saucepan. Return to the heat and bring to boil. Do not skip this step.

- Pour the custard into the pie shell. A light spray of nonstick cooking spray will help prevent a skin from forming over top of the custard. Refrigerate until quite cold, preferably overnight. Top with whipped cream, if desired.

■ Serves 8 ■

Crust:

1 prebaked gluten-free pie crust

Custard:

1/2 cup sugar

1 teaspoon vanilla extract

2 (12-ounce) cans evaporated milk

3 1/2 tablespoons cornstarch or potato starch

2 (1-ounce) squares unsweetened chocolate, chopped roughly

6 egg yolks

Topping:

1 recipe Whipped Cream (page 332, if desired)

Easy Miniature Pies

This recipe would be great on a buffet. I've recommended two fillings, but let your imagination take over this simple recipe.

- Use foil cupcake liners to line twelve sections of a muffin tin. Place one cookie in the bottom of each liner.

- Divide the pie filling among the twelve liners.

- Crush the remaining six cookies and sprinkle over the filling. Refrigerate until ready to serve. Remove the foil liners from each pie just before placing on serving plate.

■ Serves 12 ■

18 gluten-free cookies

1 recipe of Lemonade Pie filling (page 396) or Pudding, Instant Chocolate (page 427)

▪▪▪ A NOTE ABOUT GARNISHES AND FLAVORS ▪▪▪

A dollop of whipped cream with a curl of chocolate makes a pie beautiful! (Warm the edge of a plain Hershey bar and peel off a curl with a potato peeler.) An extra strawberry sliced to its top and fanned out is also very pretty. A sprinkle of cinnamon or nutmeg is surprisingly attractive. Add a drizzle of chocolate syrup or strawberry sauce on a plate and you're a gourmet! Really, you've gone to a lot of trouble to make your homemade gluten-free food. You deserve to have it be a treat to the eye as well.

As for flavorings, I'm a big fan of plain old vanilla and chocolate, but the difference between a very good dessert and an extraordinary dessert is sometimes as simple as a change in flavors. Vanilla can be omitted and a tablespoon or so of Grand Marnier or rum (or another gluten-free alcohol) substituted in its place. Compared to imitation flavorings, the alcohol gives a longer, smoother finish on the palate.

Kuchen, Peach ▪ *Corn-based*

This German treat has a sweet dough crust and a light, nutty topping. Use the freshest fruit you can find in season, for the best results. I've used peaches in this recipe.

- Preheat the oven to 375°F. Lightly grease a 9 x 13-inch baking pan.
- To make the dough, combine the butter and sugar in a medium-size bowl. Add the egg whites and beat until very frothy. Add the remaining dough ingredients. Mix well. The dough will be rather thin. Place the dough in the middle of the prepared baking pan. With wet fingertips, press the dough to evenly cover the bottom of the pan.
- Peel and pit the peaches and cut into thin wedges. Arrange in a pretty pattern on top of the dough. Combine the sugar, pecans, butter, cornstarch, and preferred spice in a small bowl. Sprinkle over the top of the peaches.
- Bake for 35 to 40 minutes, until golden brown.

▪ Serves 12 ▪

Dough:
2 tablespoons butter
3 tablespoons sugar
3 egg whites
1/2 cup plain yogurt
1 1/4 cups cornstarch, 155 grams
1 teaspoon baking powder
1/2 teaspoon baking soda
1 teaspoon vanilla extract
1 teaspoon xanthan gum
1 tablespoon apple cider vinegar
1/4 teaspoon salt

Topping:
2 pounds peaches
2 tablespoons sugar
1/2 cup finely chopped pecans
2 tablespoons butter
1 teaspoon cornstarch
1/8 teaspoon grated nutmeg or ground cinnamon

NOTE: Juicy fruits such as peaches pair better with this sweet, breadlike crust. If you use apples, choose a variety such as Yellow Delicious, which softens during baking.

Kuchen, Plum ▪ *Corn-based*

My mom used to make plum kuchen when we were kids. A bit of the dough mixture is retained to make a sweet crumb topping. Fresh fruit may be substituted for the canned plums, but these are quite tasty.

- Preheat the oven to 350°F. Lightly grease a springform pan or 9-inch pie plate.

- Combine all the dough ingredients, except the milk and egg white, in a medium-size bowl. Mix until the mixture resembles a fine crumb. Remove and reserve ¼ cup of the crumbs. Beat the egg white in a separate cup until frothy. Add the egg white and milk to the main portion of the crumb mixture. Beat well.

- Press the dough into bottom of the prepared pan. (Moistened fingertips help with this task.)

- Drain the plums, cut in half and remove the pits, and drain again. Arrange in a pretty pattern over the base layer. In a small bowl, combine remaining topping ingredients to make a nice crumbly mixture. Sprinkle over the fruit.

- Bake for 25 to 30 minutes, until the topping is golden brown and the base layer tests cleanly with a toothpick.

▪ Serves 9 ▪

Dough:

4 ounces cream cheese

4 tablespoons (¼ cup) butter

¾ cup cornstarch, 95 grams

¼ cup sugar, 50 grams

¼ teaspoon salt

2 teaspoons baking powder

½ teaspoon xanthan gum

¼ teaspoon baking soda

¼ cup milk

1 egg white

Topping:

1 (30-ounce) can purple plums in heavy syrup

¼ cup reserved crumbs

2 teaspoons sugar

¼–½ teaspoon milk

Drop or two of vanilla extract

Lemonade Pie ▪ *Corn- or rice-based*

The filling for this pie is bright, tart, and delicious. If you prefer the taste of lime, substitute frozen limeade concentrate. By using concentrate, you get the taste of freshly picked fruit and the ease of quick preparation.

- In a medium-size saucepan, combine all the filling ingredients. Mix well with a whisk until the starch is completely dissolved.

- Heat over medium heat until the mixture thickens and just begins to boil. Remove from the heat. Pour into the prepared pie crust.

- Top with meringue, if desired. Refrigerate for at least several hours.

▪ Serves 6 ▪

Crust:

1 prebaked gluten-free pie crust

Filling:

1 (12-ounce) can frozen lemonade concentrate

1 cup water

2 eggs

1/4 cup cornstarch or potato starch

Topping (optional):

Meringue

Peach Tart ▪ *Rice-based*

This tart has a bread-textured, sweet crust and is spiced with a heavy hand. Your peaches should be just ready to eat, not hard, but not super-soft. In this recipe, err on the side of too much fruit.

▪ Preheat the oven to 375°F. Lightly grease a baking sheet.

▪ To make the crust, place the egg whites in a medium-size bowl. Beat until very frothy, with big and little bubbles. Add the remaining crust ingredients. Mix well until thickened. It should seem soft and thick, like softly whipped cream.

▪ On the prepared baking sheet, press the dough to just under ¼-inch thickness. (Moistened fingertips help with the process.) You may free-form the shape into a circle or rectangle, whatever you like. If shaping into a circle, the size will be approximately 11 inches in diameter.

▪ Peel and pit the peaches and cut into wedges. Press the peaches into the dough in a pretty, overlapping pattern.

▪ Combine the topping ingredients in a small cup. Mix well. Sprinkle over the peaches.

▪ Bake for approximately 30 minutes, until the dough is lightly browned and the peaches are tender.

▪ Serves 12 ▪

Crust:

3 egg whites

1 tablespoon oil

½ cup milk

½ cup rice flour, 75 grams

2 teaspoons baking powder

¼ teaspoon baking soda

2 tablespoons sugar

¼ teaspoon salt

1¾ teaspoons xanthan gum

1 tablespoon apple cider vinegar

1 teaspoon vanilla extract

Filling:

4–5 medium-size peaches (approximately 1⅓ pounds)

Topping:

1 tablespoon sugar

¼ teaspoon grated nutmeg

¼ teaspoon ground cinnamon

Prebaked streusel

Peach Melba Pie

This pie is made up of my two favorite fruits. A thick layer of lightly sweetened peach filling is served with raspberry sauce on the side. The raspberry sauce can also be "plated" under the pie or simply passed around at time of serving. Note that the alcohol in the sauce breaks down the structure of the peach filling if left on the pie for an extended period of time, turning the filling into a puddle (yes, I learned from personal experience). This pie is very good with ice cream.

- Prepare the raspberry sauce and set aside to cool. If possible, make the sauce several hours ahead.
- Rinse and peel the peaches, pit, and slice into a large, microwave-safe bowl. Add the lemon juice as soon as possible to keep the peaches from browning. Add the sugar and stir well but gently. Microwave on high for approximately 5 minutes, stirring occasionally, until the peaches are very tender. (If your fruit is very firm, it will take a little longer.) Once the peaches are cooked through, test for sweetness. If your peaches are not sweet enough, add a tablespoon or two of sugar and stir well.
- In a small bowl, combine the starch and water. Add to the peach mixture and stir quickly but gently. Continue microwaving for approximately 2 minutes, until the juices are clear, thickened, and boiling.
- Pour into the prebaked crust. Smooth the top of the filling for a better presentation. Refrigerate for 15 to 30 minutes prior to adding the sauce.
- Garnish with freshly washed berries and sauce as the servings are plated.

■ Makes one 9-inch pie ■

Crust:
1 prebaked gluten-free pie crust

Filling:
4–5 medium-size peaches (approximately 1 3/4 pounds)
Juice of 1/2 lemon
1/3 cup sugar
2 tablespoons cornstarch or potato starch
2 tablespoons water

Topping:
1 recipe Raspberry Sauce (page 447)
1/2 cup fresh raspberries
Ice cream or whipped cream (optional)

■ ■ ■ ABOUT PIE CRUSTS ■ ■ ■

I began this section with two approaches to pie crust in mind: the first, to use cream cheese as the fat, the second, to use oil.

The first approach was incredibly successful, and those recipes follow. They are the best gluten-free pie crusts I have ever made.

The oil approach was not successful. The crusts were pretty and relatively easy to roll, but unpleasant to eat—this, despite duplicating the fat, protein, and liquid ratios of the cream cheese. In using cream cheese, there is something about dairy that goes beyond food science calculations. Similarly, margarine just can't measure up to butter.

You may also note that I have limited the amount of xanthan gum to bind the crust. This is to keep the crust tender. Because the dough is a little fragile, I roll out the pie crust using baking parchment. It is available in wider widths than waxed paper (although two overlapping pieces of standard-width paper will do the job). The extra width makes rolling out the crust just a little bit easier.

These pie crusts are easier to roll out when the dough is cool. Do not bring your cream cheese or butter to room temperature before mixing. If the dough warms, it can become rather sticky. If needed, place the dough in the fridge for 10 or 15 minutes before rolling out, to make it easier to handle.

When the crust is placed into the pie plate, be sure to anchor the edges of the crust to the edge of the pie plate by pressing a decorative pinch between your fingers. Otherwise, your crust may slide down the sides of the pie plate, which is only funny much after the fact.

And, finally, do not be deterred by needing a patch or two in your pie crust. Just press in a little extra dough wherever needed. It doesn't hurt the final results one bit.

Pie Crust ▪ *Corn-based*

This pie crust is tender, with a flaky texture.

- Preheat the oven to 400°F.
- Combine all the ingredients in a medium-size bowl. The mixture will first become a fine crumb, then finally a ball (clump) of dough.
- Place the dough on a sheet of baking parchment (or two sheets of waxed paper). Cover with another sheet of paper and roll out into a large circle, 12 to 13 inches in diameter.
- Remove the top sheet and turn the dough upside down into a 9-inch pie plate. Carefully remove the remaining sheet of paper. Trim, tuck, and pinch the dough at the edge of the pie plate. Pinching the dough between your fingers will help adhere it to the pie plate and reduce the chance of the crust's slipping into the plate during baking.
- Prick the crust all over with a fork to deter air bubbles and slippage.
- Bake for approximately 15 minutes, until quite golden in color. Let cool. Fill as desired.

▪ Makes one 9-inch pie crust ▪

4 ounces cream cheese

2 tablespoons butter

3/4 cup cornstarch, 95 grams

Pinch of salt

1 teaspoon sugar

1/4 teaspoon xanthan gum

1/4 teaspoon baking soda

Pie Crust ▪ *Oat-based*

Of all the pie crusts, this dough is perhaps the most difficult to ease away from the baking parchment. But a little extra effort produces a very nice pie crust with whole-grain flavor.

- Preheat the oven to 400°F.

- Combine all the ingredients in a medium-size bowl. The mixture will first become a fine crumb, then finally a ball (clump) of dough.

- Place the dough on a sheet of baking parchment (or two sheets of waxed paper). Cover with another sheet of paper and roll out into a large circle, 12 to 13 inches in diameter.

- Remove the top sheet and turn the dough upside down into 9-inch pie plate. Carefully remove the remaining sheet of paper. Trim, tuck, and pinch the dough at the edge of the pie plate. Pinching the dough between your fingers will help adhere it to the pie plate and reduce the chance of the crust's slipping into the plate during baking.

- Prick the crust all over with a fork to deter air bubbles and slippage.

- Bake for approximately 15 minutes, until quite golden in color. Let cool. Fill as desired.

▪ Makes one 9-inch pie crust ▪

4 ounces cream cheese
2 tablespoons butter
3/4 cup oat flour, 90 grams
1 1/2 teaspoons sugar
Pinch of salt
1/2 teaspoon xanthan gum
1/4 teaspoon baking soda

Pie Crust ▪ *Potato-based*

This crust is quite flaky. It is better at room temperature as warm, it can have a slight gummy edge. (Our taster was pretty darn picky that day!)

- Preheat the oven to 400°F.

- Combine all the ingredients in a medium-size bowl. The mixture will first become a fine crumb, then finally a ball (clump) of dough.

- Place the dough on a sheet of baking parchment (or two sheets of waxed paper). Cover with another sheet of paper and roll out into a large circle, 12 to 13 inches in diameter.

- Remove the top sheet and turn the dough upside down into 9-inch pie plate. Carefully remove the remaining sheet of paper. Trim, tuck, and pinch the dough at the edge of the pie plate. Pinching the dough between your fingers will help adhere it to the pie plate and reduce the chance of the crust's slipping into the plate during baking.

- Prick the crust all over with fork to deter air bubbles and slippage.

- Bake for approximately 15 minutes, until quite golden in color. Do not underbake. Let cool. Fill as desired.

▪ Makes one 9-inch pie crust ▪

4 ounces cream cheese

2 tablespoons butter

$^2/_3$ cup potato starch, 100 grams

Pinch of salt

1 teaspoon sugar

Scant $^1/_4$ teaspoon xanthan gum

$^1/_4$ teaspoon baking soda

Pie Crust ▪ *Rice-based*

Much to my surprise, this was the best of the pie crusts. I never imagined rice could perform so well in this application.

- Preheat the oven to 400°F.
- Combine all the ingredients in a medium-size bowl. The mixture will first become a fine crumb, then finally a ball (clump) of dough.
- Place the dough on a sheet of baking parchment (or two sheets of waxed paper). Cover with another sheet of paper and roll out into large circle, 12 to 13 inches in diameter.
- Remove the top sheet and turn the dough upside down into a 9-inch pie plate. Carefully remove the remaining sheet of paper. Trim, tuck, and pinch the dough at the edge of the pie plate. Pinching the dough between your fingers will help adhere it to the pie plate and reduce the chance of the crust's slipping into the plate during baking.
- Prick the crust all over with a fork to deter air bubbles and slippage.
- Bake for 15 to 20 minutes, until quite golden in color. Let cool. Fill as desired.

▪ Makes one 9-inch pie crust ▪

4 ounces cream cheese

2 tablespoons butter

2/3 cup rice flour, 100 grams

Pinch of salt

1 teaspoon sugar

1/2 teaspoon xanthan gum

1/4 teaspoon baking soda

Potato Pie

Perhaps it was one too many days in the kitchen, but I got to thinking about pies made with potatoes. Sweet potato pie is good, right? Well, why not make a super-fast spiced pie by using mashed potatoes? Your guests will have a hard time distinguishing the flavor, but they will enjoy the subtle flavors in a pumpkin pie–like texture.

- Place the water and potato flakes in a large saucepan and stir. Add the milk. Stir well to remove any lumps. Add the remaining ingredients and stir well. Cook, stirring often, over medium-low heat, until the mixture thickens and just begins to boil.
- Pour into the prebaked crust and chill well; overnight is best.

■ Serves 8 ■

1 cup boiling water

1 cup instant mashed potato flakes

1 (12-ounce) can evaporated milk

3/4 cup brown sugar

1/2 cup apple butter

1/2 teaspoon salt

1/2 teaspoon ground cinnamon

1/4 teaspoon grated nutmeg

3 eggs

1 tablespoon cornstarch or potato starch

2 teaspoons vanilla extract

Pumpkin Pie

This is a traditional pumpkin pie made easy, cooked for just a few minutes on top of the stove and poured into a prepared crust. Serve with a little whipped cream if you like.

- Place all the ingredients in a large saucepan. Stir well. Cook, stirring often, over medium-low heat, until the mixture thickens and just begins to boil. Pour into the prebaked pie crust and chill well; overnight is best.

■ Serves 8 ■

Crust:

1 prebaked gluten-free pie crust

Filling:

1 1/2 cups milk

1 (15–16 ounce) can pumpkin (not pumpkin pie filling)

3/4 cup sugar

1/4 teaspoon salt

1/2 teaspoon ground cinnamon

1/4 teaspoon grated nutmeg

3 eggs

1 tablespoon cornstarch or potato starch

1 teaspoon vanilla extract

Raspberry Pie

A handful of raspberries tastes great. A pie made with raspberries, accentuated by a hint of vanilla, is wonderful. Use $1/4$ cup sugar if your berries are sweet, $1/2$ cup if they are tart.

- Rinse the raspberries. Place the damp berries and remaining ingredients in a large, microwave-safe bowl. Stir well but gently. Microwave on high for 5 to 6 minutes, stirring gently every 2 minutes or so. The juices should be clear, thickened, and boiling.

- Pour into the prebaked crust. Spray the top of pie with nonstick cooking spray to keep the surface area soft. Let cool. Prepare the whipped cream or meringue and top as desired.

- Refrigerate.

■ Makes one 9-inch pie ■

Crust:

1 prebaked gluten-free pie crust

Filling:

2 pints raspberries (just over 1 pound)

$1/4$ cup sugar

3 tablespoons water

2 tablespoons cornstarch or potato starch

$1/2$ teaspoon vanilla extract

Topping (optional):

Whipped cream or meringue

Rhubarb Pie

My good friend George Schamel guided me in the making of this pie. He said it shouldn't be too sweet and should be a little tart. Okay, he was vague. The filling is made on top of the stove, so you can modify the sugar to your own taste. Also, young rhubarb stalks are not as tart as more mature rhubarb stalks. The leaves of this plant should be discarded, as they are poisonous.

1 prebaked gluten-free pie crust
4 cups thinly sliced rhubarb stems (1–1 $^1/_4$ pounds)
$^3/_4$ cup sugar
$^1/_2$ cup water
2 tablespoons cornstarch or potato starch

- In a medium-size saucepan, combine the rhubarb, sugar, and $^1/_4$ cup of the water. Cook over low to medium heat until the rhubarb becomes very soft and the sauce is boiling. Combine the starch and remaining $^1/_4$ cup of water in a cup. Stir well.

- Add the starch mixture to the filling and stir well. The sauce should begin to thicken almost immediately.

- Pour into the prebaked pie crust. Refrigerate.

■ Makes one 9-inch pie ■

VARIATION: Substitute 2 cups of thinly sliced strawberries for 2 cups of the rhubarb.

Rustic Apple and Pear Pie

This is an open-faced pie for which the dough is rolled out, then folded up around the filling. I opted for sweet Yellow Delicious apples and barely ripe pears. The dried cherries add a pop of flavor and color.

- Preheat the oven to 400°F. Lightly grease a baking sheet.

- Roll the pie crust dough between two pieces of baking parchment into a circle approximately 15 inches in diameter. Remove the top sheet of parchment. Turn the dough over onto the baking sheet. Carefully remove the remaining sheet of parchment. Set aside.

- In a large bowl, combine the ingredients for the filling. Place in center of the crust. Spread to fill the center 12 inches of the crust. Carefully fold the edges of the crust over the filling toward the center of the pie.

- Bake for 10 minutes at 400°F. Lower the oven temperature to 350°F and continue baking until the fruits are very tender, approximately 40 minutes. The juices will be clear and bubbly.

■ Makes one 12-inch pie ■

Crust:

1 recipe traditional gluten-free pie crust dough, unbaked

Filling:

3 cups peeled, cored, sliced apples

1 cup peeled, cored, sliced pears

1/2 cup dried cherries or cranberries

1/2 cup sugar

2 tablespoons cornstarch or potato starch

Streusel ■ *Corn-based*

- Preheat the oven to 375°F.
- Combine all the ingredients except the milk, and mix until powdery. Add the milk and mix until crumbly.
- Sprinkle over the top of pies or tarts before baking. Alternatively, bake for approximately 15 minutes, until golden brown and cooked through, and then sprinkle over desserts.

■ Serves 4 ■

4 tablespoons ($^1/_4$ cup) butter

1 cup cornstarch, 125 grams

$^1/_3$ cup sugar

$^1/_4$ teaspoon baking soda

$^1/_2$ teaspoon vanilla extract

$^1/_4$ teaspoon xanthan gum

2 tablespoons milk

Streusel ■ *Oat-based*

- Preheat the oven to 375°F.
- Combine all the ingredients except the milk, and mix until powdery. Add the milk and mix until crumbly.
- Sprinkle over the top of pies or tarts before baking. Alternatively, bake for approximately 15 minutes, until golden brown and cooked through, and then sprinkle over desserts.

■ Serves 4 ■

4 tablespoons ($^1/_4$ cup) butter

$^1/_4$ cup oat flour

$^1/_3$ cup oatmeal

$^1/_4$ cup packed brown sugar

1 teaspoon vanilla extract

Pinch of xanthan gum

Streusel ▪ *Potato-based*

- Preheat the oven to 375°F.
- Combine all the ingredients except the milk, and mix until powdery. Add the milk and mix until crumbly.
- Sprinkle over the top of pies or tarts before baking. Alternatively, bake for approximately 15 minutes, until golden brown and cooked through, and then sprinkle over desserts.

▪ Serves 4 ▪

4 tablespoons ($1/4$ cup) butter

$3/4$ cup potato starch, 115 grams

$1/3$ cup sugar

$1/4$ teaspoon baking soda

$1/2$ teaspoon vanilla extract

$1/4$ teaspoon xanthan gum

1 teaspoon milk

Streusel ▪ *Rice-based*

- Preheat the oven to 375°F.
- Combine all the ingredients except the milk, and mix until powdery. Add the milk and mix until crumbly.
- Sprinkle over the top of pies or tarts before baking. Alternatively, bake for approximately 15 minutes, until golden brown and cooked through, and then sprinkle over desserts.

▪ Serves 4 ▪

4 tablespoons ($1/4$ cup) butter

$1/2$ cup rice flour, 75 grams

$1/2$ teaspoon baking powder

$1/4$ cup packed brown sugar

1 teaspoon vanilla extract

$1/4$ teaspoon xanthan gum

"Toll House" Pie

This pie is designed after a chocolate chip cookie. Place the filling in a cookie crumb crust or a traditional crust. I prefer this pie very cold.

- In a large, microwave-safe bowl, combine all the ingredients for the filling, except the eggs and chips. Microwave on high for 4 to 5 minutes, stirring occasionally, until the mixture is quite thick.

- Place the eggs in a small bowl. Slowly add approximately 1 cup of the filling to the eggs while beating quickly, to temper the eggs (to avoid scrambling them). Add the egg mixture to the bowl of filling. Microwave for a minute or so, to bring the mixture to a boil. Do not skip this step.

- Press a sheet of plastic wrap on top of the pudding, to prevent a skin from forming. Refrigerate for about 1 hour, to reduce the temperature of the pudding. Remove the plastic wrap and fold in the chocolate chips. Pour into the prebaked pie crust.

- Spray the top with nonstick spray to prevent a crust from forming. Refrigerate until very cold; overnight is best.

■ Makes one 9-inch pie ■

Crust:
1 prebaked gluten-free pie crust

Filling:
1/2 cup dark brown sugar, 115 grams

3 tablespoons cornstarch or potato starch

1 teaspoon vanilla extract

2 1/2 cups milk

2 eggs

1 cup chocolate chips

NOTE: Chocolate curls are also a nice garnish for a pie. The easiest way to make them is to take a Hershey's chocolate bar, warm it for a minute between your hands, and peel "curls" off the edges of the bar with a potato peeler.

21

OTHER DESSERTS

This chapter is an eclectic mix of additional desserts.

To complement a sophisticated meal, Cran-Apple Poached Pears, Zabaglione with Liqueur, or Fresh Berries with Custard Sauce are all very nice.

To accompany a more casual meal, try the Bread Pudding, one of the crisps, or one of the cobblers. If you want something light, try Scalloped Apples or a pudding. And, if you want decadence, try one of the trifles.

My personal favorite recipes in this chapter are the Vanilla Crème with Strawberry Sauce and the chocolate Soufflé.

Applesauce

Homemade applesauce is delicious. Although you can buy gluten-free applesauce in your local market, homemade is worth the effort. A combination of apples makes for a nice balance of flavor. Avoid Red Delicious apples, as their flavor is a little bland. I suggest two Yellow Delicious apples (for sweetness) with two others of any variety. No sugar is needed, but a little can be added at the end if you like your applesauce quite sweet.

2 cups water

1 tablespoon lemon juice or lime juice

4 large apples, about 1 1/2 pounds

Pinch of ground cinnamon (optional)

2 tablespoons sugar (only if needed)

■ In a medium-size bowl, place the water and lemon juice. This liquid is to prevent the apples from turning brown. Peel, core, and slice the apples into the liquid.

■ Remove the apples from the liquid and place in a large, microwave-safe bowl. Discard the liquid. Microwave the apples on high for up to 10 minutes, until all are soft and easily pierced with a fork (Stayman or other tart apples take longer to cook than Yellow Delicious).

■ Pour the cooked apples into a blender. Blend until smooth. Taste for sweetness. Add the cinnamon and sugar, if desired.

■ Makes 2 cups, serves 4 ■

NOTE: The best applesauce of all time is made from Lotte apples. It is the first apple of the season here in Maryland. It is very tart and added sugar is necessary. In addition to her potato salad, my grandmother was famous for her Lotte applesauce.

Bread Pudding

This bread pudding may be even better than its traditional counterpart. Baked in a glass pie pan, it is surprisingly pretty for such a simple dish. Although apples or raisins can be added before baking, this pudding stands well alone. To go above and beyond, you could serve some scalloped apples on the side or use the traditional caramel sauce on the following page. I used the Single-Grain Loaf (corn and cornmeal version) in this recipe, which was absolutely perfect.

6 slices gluten-free bread, 300 grams

1 cup milk

3 eggs

1/3 cup sugar

1 teaspoon vanilla extract

1/8 teaspoon ground cinnamon

- Preheat the oven to 350°F. Lightly grease a pie tin.

- Cut the bread into small cubes. Place in a large bowl. Set aside.

- In a small bowl, combine the milk, eggs, sugar, and vanilla. Stir well to dissolve the sugar and blend in the eggs. Pour over the bread cubes, being sure all the pieces are moistened.

- Gently place the mixture into the prepared pie tin. Sprinkle cinnamon over the top. Bake for 40 to 50 minutes, until the top is golden and the liquid is set throughout.

- Serve hot or cold.

■ Serves 6 ■

Caramel Sauce

This is the easiest sauce to make. However, if you touch the melted sugar with your finger in the process of making it, you will be badly burned—please be careful. Should your sugar become a little more brown than you desire, the addition of vanilla helps cut the harsh edge.

1 cup sugar
1 cup heavy cream
$1/4$ teaspoon vanilla extract (optional)

- In a large skillet (do not use nonstick), place $1/2$ cup of the sugar. Cook over high heat until melted and golden brown in color. The darker the color, the stronger the flavor. Do not use plastic utensils. If you feel you must stir the sugar, use a metal whisk.

- Remove from the heat and slowly add the cream. (The entire pan of sauce will bubble wildly when the cream is added.) Return to the heat. Add the remaining $1/2$ cup of sugar and the vanilla. Slowly bring back to a boil. Once at a full boil, remove from the heat and cool. The sauce thickens as it cools.

■ Makes approximately 1 cup ■

Chocolate Dessert Waffles ■ *Corn-based*

This recipe makes the world's quickest dessert for chocolate-lovers. In just a few minutes, you'll be ready to serve this waffle under a scoop of ice cream covered with hot fudge sauce!

1 egg
$1/2$ cup cornstarch, 60 grams
$1/4$ cup unsweetened cocoa powder, 20 grams
$1 1/2$ teaspoons baking powder
3 tablespoons oil
$1/4$ teaspoon salt
$1/2$ cup sugar
$1/2$ cup milk
$1/4$ teaspoon xanthan gum
$1/2$ teaspoon vanilla extract

- Preheat your waffle iron.
- Place all the ingredients in a medium-size bowl. Mix very well. The batter will seem thin but will thicken considerably if allowed to sit for a minute or two. It will better fill the waffle iron when the batter is thicker. Pour approximately half of the batter into the waffle iron. Cook to your desired level of browning, about $1 1/2$ minutes.

■ Makes two 8-inch waffles; serves 4 ■

Cobbler, Blueberry ▪ *Rice-based*

The topping for this cobbler is quite sweet and the fruit layer is less sweet. Use of rice flour in the fruit layer makes for a richer, heavier presentation for the fruit. Use of cornstarch or potato starch makes for a clear, brighter presentation. I prefer using cornstarch or potato starch in the fruit layer, but want to also offer the rice-only option. The batter bakes almost crisp on the outside and quite tender on the inside. I've used frozen blueberries, which are available year-round.

- Preheat the oven to 350°F. Lightly grease a pie plate or casserole.

- In a medium-size bowl, combine the ingredients for the fruit layer. Mix well and place in the bottom of the prepared baking dish.

- In a bowl, cream together the butter and sugar. Add the egg and egg white. Beat until quite light in color and thickened. Stir in the remaining ingredients to form a soft batter.

- Pour over the fruit. It does not matter if all the pieces of fruit are not fully covered.

- Bake for 55 to 65 minutes, until a toothpick inserted in the crust tests cleanly. The top will be a dark golden color and will feel firm to the touch. Any visible juices will be opaque and bubbly.

▪ Serves 6 ▪

Fruit layer:

1 (16-ounce) package frozen blueberries

1/3 cup sugar

1 1/2 tablespoons rice flour, or 1 tablespoon cornstarch or potato starch

1/2 teaspoon vanilla extract

1/4 cup water

Batter:

3 tablespoons butter

1/2 cup sugar

1 egg

1 egg white

1/3 cup milk

1/3 cup rice flour, 75 grams

1 teaspoon baking powder

3/4 teaspoon baking soda

1/4 teaspoon salt

1/2 teaspoons vanilla extract

Scant 1/2 teaspoon xanthan gum

1 teaspoon apple cider vinegar

NOTE: If you prefer a clear, more traditional-tasting fruit layer, substitute 1 tablespoon of cornstarch or potato starch for the 1 1/2 tablespoons of rice flour.

Cobbler, Peach ▪ *Corn-based*

Here in Maryland where I live, we are lucky to have a fabulous assortment of peaches in the summer. The season doesn't last all year, of course, but frozen peaches have great flavor and are used in this recipe.

- ▪ Preheat the oven to 350°F. Lightly grease a pie plate or casserole.

- ▪ In a medium-size bowl, combine the ingredients for the fruit layer. Mix well and place in bottom of the prepared baking dish.

- ▪ In a bowl, cream together the butter and sugar. Add the cornstarch and mix well. Stir in the remaining ingredients to form a soft batter.

- ▪ Pour over the fruit. It does not matter if all the pieces of fruit are not fully covered.

- ▪ Bake for 50 to 60 minutes, until a toothpick inserted in the crust tests cleanly. The top will be lightly browned and any visible juices will be clear.

▪ Serves 6 ▪

Fruit layer:

1 (16-ounce) package frozen peaches

2 tablespoons sugar

1 tablespoon cornstarch

Batter:

4 tablespoons ($1/4$ cup) butter

$1/4$ cup sugar

$1/2$ cup cornstarch, 60 grams

$1/4$ teaspoon salt

$1/2$ cup milk

1 egg

2 teaspoons baking powder

$1/2$ teaspoon xanthan gum

$1/4$ teaspoon baking soda

$1/2$ teaspoon vanilla extract

NOTE: Instead of frozen, $2^1/2$ cups of freshly sliced peaches may be substituted. Adjust the baking time to approximately 30 minutes. If you have accidentally underbaked your cobbler, place individual servings in a dish and microwave for a minute or so.

Cobbler, Peach ▪ *Potato-based*

Like its corn counterpart, this cobbler reminds me of the Bisquick version from my childhood. It is a little homely in appearance but long on taste. Like other potato-based dishes, it has better texture and appeal if allowed to cool for a few minutes after baking.

▪ Preheat the oven to 350°F. Lightly grease a pie plate or casserole.

▪ In a medium-size bowl, combine the ingredients for the fruit layer. Mix well and place in the bottom of the prepared baking dish.

▪ In a bowl, cream together the butter and sugar. Add the cornstarch and mix well. Stir in the remaining ingredients to form a soft batter.

▪ Pour over the fruit. It does not matter if all the pieces of fruit are not fully covered.

▪ Bake for 50 to 60 minutes, until a toothpick inserted in the crust tests cleanly. The top will be lightly browned and any visible juices will be clear.

▪ Serves 6 ▪

Fruit layer:

1 (16-ounce) package frozen peaches

2 tablespoons sugar

1 tablespoon potato starch

Batter:

4 tablespoons ($1/4$ cup) butter

$1/3$ cup sugar

$1/2$ cup potato starch, 80 grams

$1/4$ teaspoon salt

$1/2$ cup milk

1 egg

2 teaspoons baking powder

Scant $1/2$ teaspoon xanthan gum

$1/4$ teaspoon baking soda

$1/2$ teaspoon vanilla extract

Cran-Apple Poached Pears

Pears can be poached with virtually any liquid. These pears are made festive for the holidays by using the popular holiday cranberry. If you don't care for the taste of cranberry, substitute apple cider for the cran-apple juice and a cinnamon stick for the cranberry garnish.

1 1/2 cups cranberry-apple juice

1/4 cup sugar

4 not-quite-ripe pears

12–15 fresh cranberries

- Place the cranberry-apple juice and sugar in a medium-size saucepan. Heat over medium heat to dissolve the sugar.

- Peel the pears and cut in half from the bottom to the stem, but not quite all the way up; leave the stem intact. Remove the seeds with a melon baller or the tip of a small spoon. Cut a bit from the base of the pear to provide a flat surface for it to sit upright. Place the pears upright in the pan and cover.

- Cook at a slow boil until the pears are very tender, 15 to 20 minutes. Transfer the pears to serving plate(s).

- Raise the heat to high and cook the liquid, uncovered, until the juices begin to thicken. Approximately 1/3 cup of syrup will remain. Add the cranberries and heat them through. Spoon over the pears just before serving. Serve warm or cold.

■ Serves 4 ■

Crisp, Apple ▪ *Potato-based*

I used widely available Fuji apples for this recipe. They are naturally sweet, so very little sugar is needed in the recipe. I precooked the apple mixture briefly to ensure a pleasant filling.

- Preheat the oven to 375°F.

- Peel, core, and dice apples, tossing with lemon juice in a large bowl to prevent browning. Add the other filling ingredients and mix well. Divide among six individual ovenproof casserole dishes. Set aside.

- Combine all the topping ingredients, except the milk, in a bowl and mix to a fine crumb. Add the milk and mix well. Sprinkle over the filling. Bake for 30 to 40 minutes, until the topping is lightly browned and cooked through. The filling will be bubbly.

▪ Serves 4 ▪

Filling:

4 Fuji apples, 1 3/4 pounds

Juice of 1/2 lemon

2 tablespoons sugar

1 tablespoon potato starch

1/2 teaspoon ground cinnamon

2/3 cup water

Topping:

4 tablespoons (1/4 cup) butter

3/4 cup potato starch, 115 grams

1/3 cup sugar

1/4 teaspoon baking soda

1/2 teaspoon vanilla extract

1/4 teaspoon xanthan gum

1 teaspoon milk

Crisp, Blueberry ▪ *Corn-based*

Make this recipe any time of year with frozen blueberries. This is great served with ice cream. The topping is quite sweet.

- Preheat the oven to 375°F.
- In a medium-size bowl, combine all the filling ingredients. Gently mix well. Place in a small ovenproof casserole dish. Set aside.
- In a bowl, combine all the topping ingredients except the milk, and mix until powdery. Add the milk and mix until crumbly. Sprinkle over the filling. Do not overlap the crumbles too much or they will take longer to bake. Bake for 35 to 45 minutes, until the topping is golden brown and cooked through. The filling will be bubbly. Check the deepest part of crispy coating to be sure it is done.

▪ Serves 4 ▪

Filling:

1 1/2 pints fresh or frozen blueberries (3 cups)

1/3 cup sugar

1 1/2 tablespoons cornstarch

1/2 teaspoon vanilla extract

Topping:

4 tablespoons (1/4 cup) butter

1 cup cornstarch, 125 grams

1/3 cup sugar

1/4 teaspoon baking soda

1/2 teaspoon vanilla extract

1/4 teaspoon xanthan gum

2 tablespoons milk

Crisp, Cherry ▪ *Oat-based*

Cherry pie filling makes this dish super-fast to prepare, but I think the make-it-yourself version is a little better. It is a little less sweet, a little more tart in taste—a nicer pairing with the sweet, crispy topping.

- Preheat the oven to 375°F.
- If using canned pie filling, divide among four individual ovenproof dishes. Set aside.
- If using canned cherries, combine the cherries, the liquid from the can, and the sugar, cornstarch, and water in microwave-safe bowl. Microwave on high for 5 to 7 minutes, stirring occasionally, until nicely thickened. Once thickened, divide among four individual ovenproof dishes. Set aside.
- Combine the topping ingredients in a bowl and mix until crumbly. Sprinkle over the filling. Bake for 25 minutes, until the topping is golden brown and the filling is bubbly.

▪ Serves 4 ▪

Filling:

1 (21-ounce can) premium cherry pie filling (see note)

OR

1 (14.5-ounce) can pitted red tart pie cherries

1/2 cup sugar

2 tablespoon cornstarch or potato starch

1/2 cup water

Topping:

4 tablespoons (1/4 cup) butter

1/4 cup oat flour

1/3 cup oatmeal

1/4 cup packed brown sugar

1 teaspoon vanilla extract

Pinch of xanthan gum

> **NOTE:** If you are avoiding corn, please note that ready-made cherry pie filling often has corn syrup and/or cornstarch as an ingredient.

Crisp, Cherry ▪ *Rice-based*

The rice topping is very sweet. Consider serving this dish over a scoop or two of vanilla ice cream.

- ▪ Preheat the oven to 375°F.
- ▪ If using canned pie filling, divide among four individual ovenproof dishes. Set aside.
- ▪ If using canned cherries, combine the cherries, the liquid from the can, and the sugar, cornstarch, and water in a microwave-safe bowl. Microwave on high for 5 to 7 minutes, stirring occasionally, until nicely thickened. Once thickened, divide among four individual ovenproof dishes. Set aside.
- ▪ Combine the topping ingredients in a bowl and mix until crumbly. Sprinkle over the filling. Bake for 25 minutes, until the topping is golden brown and the filling is bubbly.

▪ Serves 4 ▪

Filling:

1 (21-ounce) can premium cherry pie filling (see note, page 421)

OR

1 (14.5-ounce) can pitted red tart pie cherries

1/2 cup sugar

2 tablespoon cornstarch or potato starch

1/2 cup water

Topping:

4 tablespoons (1/4 cup) butter

1/2 cup rice flour, 75 grams

1/2 teaspoon baking powder

1/4 cup packed brown sugar

1 teaspoon vanilla extract

1/4 teaspoon xanthan gum

Flan

Flan is a silky custard inverted and baked on top of burnt sugar syrup. We will simplify the traditional recipe by making it all on top of the stove. Be very careful when handling the sugar syrup; it is dangerously hot.

- Place the sugar in a small skillet (not nonstick). Without stirring, over medium-low heat, melt the sugar until it is fully dissolved and lightly browned. Immediately—and very carefully—pour equal amounts of the syrup into six small ramekins. Set aside.

- In a large saucepan, combine all the ingredients for the custard except the egg yolks, and stir well. Over medium heat, and stirring often, bring the mixture to almost a boil. The custard should be thickening. Remove from the heat.

- Place the egg yolks in a small bowl. Slowly add approximately 1 cup of the custard mixture to the egg yolks while beating quickly to temper the eggs (to avoid scrambling them). Add the yolk mixture to the saucepan. Return to the heat and bring to boil (do not skip this step).

- Pour the custard into the ramekins over the sugar syrup. Refrigerate until very cold, ideally overnight. To prevent a film from forming on top of the custard, spray the top of custard sauce with nonstick spray or press piece of plastic wrap to top, before chilling.

Syrup:
3/4 cup sugar

Custard:
1/2 cup sugar

1/2 teaspoon vanilla extract

2 (12-ounce) cans evaporated milk

3 tablespoons cornstarch or potato starch

6 egg yolks

■ Serves 6 ■

> **NOTE:** If you accidentally make sweet scrambled eggs, use your blender to smooth out the custard. It will be fine.

Fresh Berries with Custard Sauce

This is one of my all-time-favorite dinner party desserts. It looks and tastes great and can be made ahead of time. I've even made the sauce in the microwave! If you are avoiding dairy, please try the Zabaglione recipe (page 437).

- Place the berries, sugar, and vanilla in a medium-size bowl. Stir well. Refrigerate until serving time.

- In a microwave-safe bowl, combine all the custard ingredients except the egg yolks. Microwave on high for approximately 3 minutes, stirring occasionally, until the mixture boils. It will still be quite thin. Remove the bowl from the oven.

- In a separate bowl, place the egg yolks. Add about $1/2$ cup of the cooked mixture, stirring quickly to temper the eggs. Add the egg mixture to the cooked custard and return the bowl to the microwave. Microwave for an additional 30 seconds, or until the mixture boils (do not skip this step). Stir well.

- Place in the refrigerator until serving time. To prevent a film from forming on top of the custard, spray the top of custard sauce with nonstick spray or press piece of plastic wrap to top, before chilling. Let cool to at least room temperature.

- Just before serving, place the berries in pretty serving dishes. Stir the custard sauce well and pour over the top of the berries.

■ Serves 4 to 6 ■

Fruit:

1 pound strawberries or blueberries, sliced

1 $1/2$ tablespoons sugar

$1/4$ teaspoon vanilla extract (optional)

Custard sauce:

1 $1/2$ cups milk, preferably whole

1 tablespoon cornstarch or potato starch

1 teaspoon vanilla extract

3 tablespoons sugar

3 egg yolks

NOTE: Let your imagination go wild with this recipe: try fresh peaches with a small splash of brandy, banana slices with a little brown sugar and rum, raspberries with a hint of vanilla, and so on.

Ice-Cream Cones ▪ *Corn-based*

Homemade ice-cream cones or beautiful, edible desert cups are a real treat—and easy and fast to make.

> 2 egg whites
> 1/2 cup sugar, 100 grams
> Pinch of salt
> 1/2 teaspoon vanilla extract
> 2/3 cup cornstarch, 80 grams
> 2 tablespoons oil
> 1 teaspoon water

▪ Mix all the ingredients until well blended. I like to use a mixer with whisk attachment. Be sure no lumps remain.

▪ Grease and heat a small skillet to medium-high.

▪ Pour approximately 2 tablespoons of batter into the hot pan. Swirl to coat the pan. Work fast, but be careful! Cook until the batter is golden brown on the bottom and the top no longer looks moist. Flip and cook until the other side is golden brown.

▪ Remove from the pan and shape immediately into a ice-cream cone, or use to line a section of a muffin tin, or drape over an upside-down cup or glass. Let cool.

▪ Makes 8 cones ▪

Ice-Cream Cones ▪ *Potato-based*

Fill these cones with berries and whipped cream or custard sauce, for a special treat.

> 2 egg whites
> 1/2 cup sugar, 100 grams
> Pinch of salt
> 1/4 teaspoon vanilla extract
> 1/2 cup potato starch, 80 grams
> 2 tablespoons oil

▪ Mix all the ingredients until well blended. I like to use a mixer with whisk attachment. Be sure no lumps remain.

▪ Grease and heat a small skillet to medium-high.

▪ Pour approximately 2 tablespoons of batter into the hot pan. Swirl to coat the pan. Work fast, but be careful! Cook until the batter is golden brown on the bottom and the top no longer looks moist. Flip and cook until the other side is golden brown.

▪ Remove from the pan and shape immediately into a ice-cream cone, or use to line a section of a muffin tin, or drape over an upside-down cup or glass. Let cool.

▪ Makes 8 cones ▪

Ice-Cream Cones ▪ *Rice-based*

This is the most challenging of the ice-cream cones to make. They are difficult to turn over, but if you use a large nonstick skillet, they can be turned with a large spatula. They are perhaps the most tasty of the bunch.

2 egg whites
1/2 cup sugar, 100 grams
Pinch of salt
1/2 teaspoon vanilla extract
1/2 cup rice flour, 75 grams
2 tablespoons oil
1 teaspoon water

▪ Mix all the ingredients until well blended. I like to use a mixer with whisk attachment. Be sure no lumps remain.

▪ Grease and heat a small skillet to medium-high.

▪ Pour approximately 2 tablespoons of batter into the hot pan. Swirl to coat the pan. Work fast, but be careful! Cook until the batter is golden brown on the bottom and the top no longer looks moist. Flip and cook until the other side is golden brown.

▪ Remove from the pan and shape immediately into a ice-cream cone, or use to line a section of a muffin tin, or drape over an upside-down cup or glass. Let cool.

▪ Makes 8 cones ▪

Pudding, Instant Chocolate

Because instant puddings have corn in them, and some need to avoid corn, I wanted to include this recipe. By using low-speed mixing, a traditional texture is achieved. Using a whisk attachment at high speed produces a very light, fluffy pudding.

- In a medium-size bowl, place the sugar, xanthan gum, and cocoa. Mix well to combine (this prevents the xanthan gum from clumping). Add the vanilla and milk. Mix until quite thick. Divide between two individual serving dishes. Serve right away or refrigerate for a slightly thicker set.

■ Serves 2 ■

1/4 cup confectioners' sugar, 30 grams (see note)

1 teaspoon xanthan gum

1 tablespoon unsweetened cocoa powder

1/2 teaspoon vanilla extract

1 cup whole milk or 1/2 cup milk plus 1/2 cup cream

Pudding, Instant Vanilla

Like the chocolate version of instant pudding, this recipe becomes light and fluffy if mixed with a whisk. It makes a great accent over fresh fruit if whipped quite light. Because no coloring is added, the pudding is white in color. Add a drop or two of yellow food coloring if you want a more traditional appearance.

- In a medium-size bowl, place the sugar and xanthan gum. Mix well to combine (this prevents the xanthan gum from clumping). Add the vanilla and milk. Mix until quite thick. Divide between two individual serving dishes. Serve right away or refrigerate for a slightly thicker set.

■ Serves 2 ■

1/4 cup confectioners' sugar, 30 grams

1 teaspoon xanthan gum

1/2 teaspoon vanilla extract

1 cup whole milk, or 1/2 cup milk plus 1/2 cup cream

Pudding, Microwave
Chocolate ▪ *Cornstarch or potato starch–based*

Chocolate cornstarch pudding was often served at my family gatherings. Grandpap was able to eat his way through three generations of guests at the holiday table. And, if it was there, he always had room for cornstarch pudding.

- In a microwave-safe bowl, combine the sugar, cornstarch, and cocoa. Mix well (this prevents lumps). Add the remaining ingredients and mix well. Microwave on high for 2 to 3 minutes, stirring occasionally, until the mixture is quite thick. Divide between 2 individual serving dishes.

▪ Serves 2 ▪

2 tablespoons sugar, 25 grams

1 tablespoon cornstarch or potato starch

1 tablespoon unsweetened cocoa powder

1/2 teaspoon vanilla extract

2 teaspoons dried egg whites

1 cup whole milk

Pudding, Microwave
Vanilla ▪ *Cornstarch or potato starch–based*

Using eggs technically makes this a custard, but most people who taste it would just call it a good pudding. This recipe takes less than five minutes to make. Enjoy.

- In a microwave-safe bowl, combine the sugar and cornstarch. Mix well (this prevents lumps). Add the remaining ingredients and mix well to combine. Microwave on high for 2 to 3 minutes, stirring occasionally, until the mixture is quite thick.
- Divide between two individual serving dishes.

▪ Serves 2 ▪

2 tablespoons sugar, 25 grams

1 tablespoon cornstarch or potato starch

1/2 teaspoon vanilla extract

2 teaspoons dried egg whites

1 cup whole milk

Pumpkin Custard

This is the right holiday dessert for someone who wants traditional holiday flavors but also wants something easy to prepare. This custard is a rich and satisfying finish to the holiday meal. Served with a few cookies on the side would also be nice.

- Place all the ingredients in a large saucepan. Stir well. Cook, stirring often, over medium-low heat until the mixture thickens and just begins to boil. Pour into four individual serving cups and chill well, preferably overnight.

■ Makes 4 cups, serves 8 ■

1 1/2 cups milk

1 (15-ounce) can pumpkin (not pumpkin pie filling)

3/4 cup sugar

1/4 teaspoon salt

1/4 teaspoon ground cinnamon

3 eggs

1 tablespoon cornstarch or potato starch

1 teaspoon vanilla extract

> **NOTE:** You may notice that the spices in this custard are not nearly as bold as in a pumpkin pie. A richly spiced pumpkin pie filling is much too strong served this way. However, as with pumpkin pie, whipped cream is always nice on top.

Scalloped Apples

Some really good things you can order at a restaurant are just so easy to make at home. This is one of them.

- Combine all the ingredients in a medium-size glass bowl. Microwave on high for 3 to 4 minutes, stirring once or twice.

■ Serves 2 ■

2 apples, peeled, seeded, and chopped (see note)

2 tablespoons brown sugar

1/4 teaspoon vanilla extract

Large pinch of ground cinnamon

1 teaspoon cornstarch, potato starch, or rice flour

> **NOTE:** Gala apples will retain a little crispness whereas Yellow Delicious will be quite tender.

Soufflé, Chocolate ▪ *Corn-based*

I was looking for something delicious and chocolate to tempt you, and settled upon making a chocolate soufflé. There are a number of steps, but none are difficult. And the results will please any chocolate lover. This recipe was inspired by the Hershey's Deep Dark Chocolate Soufflé, but I must use different techniques as well as different flours to make the soufflé work.

- Preheat the oven to 350°F. Spray eight 1-cup ramekins with nonstick cooking spray, then dust insides of the ramekins with 1 tablespoon of the sugar.

- In a large, microwave-safe bowl, combine the cocoa, cornstarch, and milk. Stir well. Microwave this mixture on high for approximately 2 minutes, stirring periodically to better incorporate the ingredients, until quite thick. You may also cook the mixture in a saucepan over medium heat; stir constantly if using this method.

- To the same bowl, add the butter, vanilla, and $^1/_2$ cup of the sugar. Mix well. Beat in the egg yolks, one at a time. Set aside.

- In a separate bowl, with clean beaters, beat the egg whites to stiff peaks. Beat a small amount of the egg whites into the chocolate batter. Fold in the remaining egg whites.

- Pour into the prepared ramekins, filling to $^1/_2$ inch of top. Bake for approximately 30 to 35 minutes, until very puffed. Serve right away with your preferred topping. These soufflés will begin to fall minutes after removal from the oven. (Note, if they fall prior to serving, invert each on small serving plate, top with sauce, and enjoy anyway.)

▪ Serves 6 to 8 ▪

$^1/_2$ cup plus 1 tablespoon sugar

$^1/_2$ cup cocoa, 40 grams

2 tablespoons cornstarch, 15 grams

1 cup milk

4 tablespoons ($^1/_4$ cup) butter, softened

1 teaspoon vanilla extract

4 eggs, separated

Topping (optional):

Whipped cream

Fudge sauce

Ice cream

Soufflé, Vanilla ▪ *Corn-based*

A sophisticated dessert that is fun to prepare but even better to eat! When preparing the raspberry sauce for the topping, consider substituting another jam if your guests prefer other fruit flavors. You will notice that cornstarch is used twice in the ingredients, first to thicken, then as a flour base.

▪ Preheat the oven to 350°F. Spray eight 1-cup ramekins with nonstick spray, then dust the insides of the ramekins with 1 tablespoon of the sugar.

▪ In a large microwave-safe bowl, combine 2 tablespoons of the cornstarch and the milk. Stir well. Microwave this mixture on high for 1$^1\!/_2$ to 2 minutes, stirring periodically to better incorporate the ingredients until quite thick. You may also cook the mixture in a saucepan over medium heat; stir constantly if using this method.

▪ To the same bowl, add the butter, vanilla, and $^1\!/_2$ cup sugar. Mix well. Beat in the egg yolks, one at a time. Set aside.

▪ In a separate bowl, with clean beaters, beat the egg whites to stiff peaks. Beat a small amount of egg whites into the batter. Beat in the remaining $^1\!/_4$ cup of cornstarch (no lumps should remain). Fold in the remaining egg whites.

▪ Pour into the prepared ramekins, filling to $^1\!/_2$ inch of top. Bake for 30 to 35 minutes, until very puffed. Serve right away with the sauce. These soufflés will begin to fall minutes after removal from the oven. (Note, if they fall prior to serving, invert each on small serving plate, top with sauce, and enjoy anyway.)

▪ Serves 6 to 8 ▪

$^1\!/_2$ cup plus 1 tablespoon sugar

2 tablespoons cornstarch, 15 grams, plus $^1\!/_4$ cup, 30 grams

1 cup milk

4 tablespoons ($^1\!/_4$ cup) butter, softened

1 teaspoon vanilla extract

4 eggs, separated

Topping (optional):

Raspberry Sauce (page 447)

Streusel Topping ▪ *Corn-based*

Used in the Blueberry Crisp, this topping is terrific on ice cream or one of the pies!

- ▪ Preheat the oven to 375°F.
- ▪ Combine all the ingredients except the milk, and mix until powdery. Add the milk and mix until crumbly. Sprinkle on a baking sheet. Bake for 15 to 20 minutes, until lightly browned.

▪ Serves 4 ▪

4 tablespoons ($^1/_4$ cup) butter

1 cup cornstarch, 125 grams

$^1/_3$ cup sugar

$^1/_4$ teaspoon baking soda

$^1/_2$ teaspoon vanilla extract

$^1/_4$ teaspoon xanthan gum

2 tablespoons milk

Streusel Topping ▪ *Oat-based*

- ▪ Preheat the oven to 375°F.
- ▪ Combine all the ingredients except the milk, and mix until powdery. Add the milk and mix until crumbly. Sprinkle on a baking sheet. Bake for 15 to 20 minutes, until lightly browned.

▪ Serves 4 ▪

4 tablespoons ($^1/_4$ cup) butter

$^1/_4$ cup oat flour

$^1/_3$ cup oatmeal

$^1/_4$ cup packed brown sugar

1 teaspoon vanilla extract

Pinch of xanthan gum

Streusel Topping ▪ *Potato-based*

- Preheat the oven to 375°F.
- Combine all the ingredients except the milk, and mix until powdery. Add the milk and mix until crumbly. Sprinkle on a baking sheet. Bake for 15 to 20 minutes, until lightly browned.

▪ Serves 4 ▪

4 tablespoons ($^1/_4$ cup) butter

$^3/_4$ cup potato starch, 115 grams

$^1/_3$ cup sugar

$^1/_4$ teaspoon baking soda

$^1/_2$ teaspoon vanilla extract

$^1/_4$ teaspoon xanthan gum

1 teaspoon milk

Streusel Topping ▪ *Rice-based*

- Preheat the oven to 375°F.
- Combine all the ingredients except the milk, and mix until powdery. Add the milk and mix until crumbly. Sprinkle on a baking sheet. Bake for 15 to 20 minutes, until lightly browned.

▪ Serves 4 ▪

4 tablespoons ($^1/_4$ cup) butter

$^1/_2$ cup rice flour, 75 grams

$^1/_2$ teaspoon baking powder

$^1/_4$ cup packed brown sugar

1 teaspoon vanilla extract

$^1/_4$ teaspoon xanthan gum

Trifle, Chocolate and Then Some

Making a trifle is a delicious way to disguise a less-than-perfect outcome of a cake. Mine originated from a delicious chocolate pound cake that wasn't quite perfect in appearance. Okay, we could have eaten the cake just the way it was, but chocolate with more chocolate is pretty awesome.

4 slices chocolate pound cake, approximately $1/2$ cake

2 recipes Pudding, Instant Chocolate (page 427) (2 cups pudding)

2 plain chocolate Hershey bars, or 2 Butterfinger bars

■ Cut the pound cake into small cubes. Place half of the cubes in the bottom of four dessert dishes or one small casserole dish. Pour approximately $1/4$ cup of pudding into each cup, over the pound cake. Crush or chop one of the chocolate bars. Sprinkle over the top of the pudding. Repeat the layers of cake, pudding, and crushed chocolate bar.

■ Serves 4 ■

Trifle, Strawberry

Strawberries and Cool Whip can be dressed up as a special dessert. Make ahead of time so the flavors can blend. For a true strawberry shortcake trifle, substitute freshly whipped cream for the Cool Whip topping.

4 slices pound cake, approximately 1/2 loaf

1 (8-ounce) package Cool Whip topping, thawed

1 pound strawberries

3 tablespoons sugar

- Cut the pound cake into small cubes. Place half of the cubes in the bottom of four very large dessert dishes or one small casserole dish. Pour approximately 1 large tablespoon of Cool Whip into each cup over the pound cake. Set aside.

- Slice the berries and place in a medium-size bowl. Add the sugar and toss lightly until the sugar dissolves.

- Layer approximately one-eighth of the berries on top of the Cool Whip. Repeat the layers of cake, Cool Whip, and fruit. You will likely have Cool Whip topping left over for another use.

- Refrigerate for at least 1 hour if possible, for the flavors to blend.

■ Makes 4 very large servings that are better shared ■

Vanilla Crème with Strawberry Sauce

Here is a light vanilla custard topped with a fresh, flavorful sauce. Feel free to substitute frozen berries if fresh ones are out of season. Garnish with a little mint, if available.

- Combine all the custard ingredients except the egg whites, in a medium-size saucepan. Cook over medium head until thick. Remove from the heat. Let cool until barely warm.

- In a medium-size bowl, whisk the egg whites to stiff peaks (like meringue). Immediately add the cooled custard mixture and beat at high speed to blend. Pour into four cups.

- Combine all the sauce ingredients in a blender. Puree until the mixture is smooth and the sugar is fully dissolved. Pour over the custard. Chill. Garnish with extra berries.

■ Serves 4 ■

Custard:

1/4 cup sugar

2 cups milk

2 eggs, separated

1 teaspoon vanilla extract

Sauce:

1 cups strawberries, approximately 4 ounces

1 tablespoon Grand Marnier

2 tablespoons sugar

Zabaglione with Liqueur

I've never been a big fan of wine in my dessert sauces, as would be traditional in zabaglione. I've taken this classic foamy sauce and paired it with Grand Marnier. This is a lovely special-occasion dessert sauce for guests who cannot have dairy. Serve over fresh berries in wineglasses for an elegant presentation. Prepared, pasteurized, dried egg yolks may be used in place of the raw egg yolks, if preferred.

4 egg yolks

1/4 cup sugar

2 tablespoons Grand Marnier (or other gluten-free liqueur)

3 tablespoons water

- In a medium-size metal bowl, combine the egg yolks and sugar. Beat until thick and pale. Place the bowl over a saucepan of simmering water. The bowl should not touch the water. Blend on high speed with a handheld mixer until the mixture becomes soft and foamy, 4 minutes.

- Serve 1/4 to 1/3 cup of sauce over each serving of fresh berries. Serve this sauce within 30 minutes of making, for best volume.

■ Makes approximately 3 cups of sauce ■

> NOTE: Quite a few liqueurs are gluten-free. You must be cautious of "flavored" liqueurs and should confirm with the manufacturer if they are gluten-free. Kahlúa, Grand Marnier, crème de menthe, and numerous others are safe as of this writing. Visit the food lists at www.celiac.com and www.delphiforums.com/celiac for the latest on safe liqueurs.

22

SAUCES, SEASONING BLENDS, AND SALAD DRESSINGS

This chapter includes sauces, seasoning blends, and salad dressings. Some of these recipes appear for the first time in this chapter. Others are used elsewhere as part of other recipes.

It is my hope that grouping these recipes here will help you avoid the frustration of finding a recipe within a recipe. It is also my hope that you enjoy the recipes outside of their original presentation.

Asian Dipping Sauce

Very nice with Asian Meatballs (page 20).

- Combine all the ingredients in a small bowl. Stir.

■ Makes ¹/₄ cup sauce ■

2 tablespoons soy sauce

2 tablespoons distilled white vinegar

¹/₂ teaspoon sugar

Blackened Seasoning Blend

Although you may locate safe seasoning blends at your grocery store, I find blackened seasoning is often too salty. This blend has a few simple spices that will give you the kick that's needed.

- Combine all the ingredients in a small jar. Shake well to mix. Use as liberally as you dare!

■ Makes 8 to 12 servings ■

1 tablespoon salt

1 tablespoon paprika

1 ¹/₂ teaspoons ground cayenne

³/₄ teaspoon black pepper

Caesar Salad Dressing

Creamy and light, this dressing is hard to beat. It can be ready in moments, but the flavor will improve if permitted to sit for a few minutes. After you make this dressing, you may wonder why you ever bought dressing at the grocery store.

- Combine all the ingredients in a small bowl. Mix well.

■ Makes approximately 2/3 cup ■

2 tablespoons oil

1/4 cup mayonnaise

2 tablespoons apple cider vinegar

1/4 teaspoon garlic salt

Pinch of black pepper

1 teaspoon sugar

1 tablespoon grated Parmesan cheese (canned is fine)

Caramelized Onions

Served on top of a steak or pizza, these onions are a welcome change of pace. If you don't care for wine, substitute a little apple juice or water. Use wine that you enjoy drinking to ensure pleasing results.

- Put the butter and oil in a medium-size skillet, and place the pan over medium heat to start the melting of the butter. Add the onion, salt, and oregano. Cook until the onions collapse and begin to take on a golden color, approximately 10 minutes.
- Add the wine and stir until the onions are almost dry. Add the pepper.

■ Serves 2 ■

1 tablespoon butter

1/2 tablespoon oil

1 large onion, peeled and sliced thinly

Pinch of salt

1/2 teaspoon dried oregano

2 tablespoons dry white wine

Pinch of freshly ground black pepper

> **NOTE:** The pepper is necessary at the end to balance the sweetness of the dish.

Celery Seed Dressing

Don't let the name of this salad dressing scare you off. A little sweet and a little sour, it plays nicely with Fruit and Green Salad.

- Combine all the ingredients in a small bowl or jar. Mix well. Toss the dressing with the salad just before serving.

■ Makes $1/2$ cup dressing ■

2 tablespoons corn syrup or honey

2 tablespoons sugar

$1/4$ cup oil (not olive)

$1/4$ teaspoon salt

2 tablespoons vinegar

1 teaspoon celery seed

Pinch of black pepper

NOTE: The flavor of dressing improves if allowed to sit for a while.

Cheese Sauce

When you feel like some quick macaroni and cheese or want a nice sauce to pour over your broccoli, this is the recipe to use!

- In a large glass bowl, combine all the ingredients. Stir well. Microwave on high for 2 to 3 minutes, stirring at least once with a whisk.

■ Makes $1 1/2$ cups sauce ■

1 cup milk

1 tablespoon cornstarch, potato starch, or rice flour

4 ounces shredded cheddar cheese

$1/4$ teaspoon salt

Corn-Free Confectioners' Sugar

Many commercial brands of confectioners' sugar use cornstarch as an ingredient. You can special-order corn-free confectioners' sugar or perhaps find it in a health food store. Or, you can take just a minute to make some. I was successful when using a traditional blender, but failed when using a hand blender or food processor.

- Place the sugar and potato starch in a blender. Blend on the highest setting for approximately 1 minute, until the sugar is powdery. There will be a cloud of dust when you remove the lid from the blender, so you may want to allow it to rest for 10 or 15 seconds before removing the lid.

  - Makes just under $^1/_2$ cup confectioners' sugar ▪

$^1/_3$ cup granulated sugar
$^1/_2$ teaspoon potato starch

Egg Roll Dipping Sauce

This simple combination of ingredients makes for a special dipping sauce for egg rolls or Asian meatballs. It is fashioned after the sauce served at House of Kobe, our favorite Japanese restaurant in Hagerstown, Maryland.

- Combine all the ingredients in a small bowl. Whisk together to blend.

  ▪ Serves 2 ▪

1 $^1/_2$ tablespoons rice wine vinegar
1 tablespoon water
1 teaspoon sesame oil
$^1/_2$ teaspoon soy sauce (see note, page 449)
$^1/_8$ teaspoon hot sauce
$^1/_8$ teaspoon salt

Fudge Sauce

You can purchase perfectly delicious gluten-free fudge sauce right at your local grocery store, but it probably contains corn syrup as its sweetener. Because you (with multiple sensitivities) may need to avoid corn, I've included this much simpler yet equally delicious version that you can make in the microwave in just a few minutes. It will become quite crystallized after sitting for a while, so reheat any leftovers before using.

1 1/2 cups confectioners' sugar, 180 grams

3 tablespoons unsweetened cocoa powder, 15 grams

1 teaspoon vanilla extract

2 tablespoons butter

2 tablespoons heavy cream

■ In a large, microwave-safe container, combine all the ingredients. Stir to mix, although you will not be able to fully blend them yet. Microwave on high for 30 seconds. Stir again. Microwave for up to 1 more minute to bring to boil. Cool just a little before serving.

■ Makes approximately 3/4 cup ■

> NOTE: If you tolerate corn, add 1 tablespoon corn syrup to the mixture, to help prevent sugar crystallization.

Lemon Butter Sauce

This sauce is featured with our Steamed Salmon recipe. It would be delicious over poached eggs as well.

- In a small saucepan, melt the butter. Add the lemon juice and stir well. Add the heavy cream and cook over low heat until the sauce thickens slightly.

■ Makes almost $^1/_2$ cup sauce ■

4 tablespoons ($^1/_4$ cup) butter

Juice of 1 large lemon

$^1/_4$ cup heavy cream

Pinch of salt

Marinara Sauce

This light tomato sauce is bright with flavor. It doesn't overpower Asian rice sticks—or even spaghetti squash.

- Place the tomatoes in a small bowl and chop into smaller pieces.
- In a medium-size saucepan over medium heat, sauté the garlic in the olive oil until fragrant. Add the tomatoes and any juice, and the salt and pepper. Lower the heat to low.
- Once the tomato sauce is almost boiling, add the basil and stir well. Simmer for just a moment or two.

■ Serves 2 ■

1 (14.5-ounce) can diced tomatoes

1 tablespoon olive oil

1 clove garlic, minced

$^1/_4$–$^1/_2$ ounce fresh basil, stemmed and chopped finely

Pinch of salt

Small pinch of cayenne or black pepper

Onion Ring Dipping Sauce

This recipe is very much like the dipping sauce served with onion rings in a variety of restaurants. As always, I tend to go a little heavy on the spice, so lighten up the horseradish if you need to quiet the heat. Also good on sandwiches!

- In a small bowl, combine the mayonnaise, ketchup, and prepared horseradish. Mix well. Crush the dried parsley over the top.

■ Serves 4 ■

¼ cup mayonnaise
1 tablespoon ketchup
1 tablespoon prepared
  horseradish
pinch of dried parsley

Pizza Sauce

You will notice that this sauce has a rather strong flavor. It is perfect to elevate the flavor of homemade pizza or as a dipping sauce for bread sticks.

- In a medium-size saucepan over medium heat, sauté the olive oil and minced garlic, allowing the flavors to blend. Add all the other ingredients and mix well. Bring to almost a boil, then lower the heat to low and simmer for approximately 5 minutes. It takes a few minutes for the flavor of the dried spices to reawaken.

■ Makes approximately 15 ounces pizza sauce, ■
enough for two 12-inch pizzas

1 tablespoon olive oil
1 clove garlic, minced
1 (6-ounce) can tomato paste
9 ounces water
1 teaspoon dried oregano
1 teaspoon dried basil
½ teaspoon red pepper
  flakes
1 teaspoon salt

> NOTE: So, why not just use tomato sauce? I like to use tomato paste for two reasons. First, your finished sauce will be a better consistency. Tomato sauce is just too thin for topping a pizza. Second, certain tomato pastes (such as Contadina) contain just tomatoes—no other ingredients to analyze for possible hidden gluten.

Raspberry Sauce

I could go through a big process to achieve a nice raspberry sauce. But I don't need to. Smucker's makes several seedless jams that have all the fresh flavor you want. Just thin them with the right liqueur and you're ready. Be sure to double-check the gluten-free status of any liqueur—the distillation process and/or the underlying grain base makes it gluten-free, but added ingredients could introduce gluten.

3/4 cup seedless raspberry jam, 240 grams

1/2 teaspoon vanilla extract plus 1 1/2 tablespoons water, or 1 1/2 tablespoons vanilla liqueur

■ Stir the ingredients in a large cup until very well blended. If you are not serving the sauce within the next hour, microwave it on high for 1 minute (see note). Allow it to cool for several hours. If you are using the sauce right away, do not microwave it. It will still be delicious. Serve over soufflé, ice cream, or berries.

■ Makes approximately 1 cup ■

NOTE: Cooking the sauce in the microwave makes for a sauce that is slightly brighter in flavor and clearer in presentation. However, it takes well over an hour to regain some of its thickness.

Salsas

Good with corn tortilla chips, fish, or chicken.

■ For either salsa, combine all the ingredients in a small bowl. Allow it to sit for a few minutes for the flavors to meld.

■ Makes 1 1/4 to 1 1/2 cups ■

Pineapple salsa:

1 (8-ounce can) pineapple chunks in own juice

1/2 small onion, peeled and diced finely

Zest of 1 lime, chopped very finely

Juice of 1 lime

Mango salsa:

1/2 mango, pitted and peeled

1/2 small onion, peeled and diced finely

Zest of 1/2 lime, chopped very finely

Juice of 1 lime

1 teaspoon sugar (if mango is not fully ripe)

Sautéed Mushrooms

Presented with Mahimahi (page 234). This recipe would also be nice teamed with steak or placed in an omelet.

■ Place the mushrooms and butter in a saucepan. Cook over medium-low heat until the mushrooms are very soft.

■ Makes 1 cup ■

8 button mushrooms, sliced

2 tablespoons butter

Hint of salt

Sesame Salad Dressing

Although this dressing is presented with an Asian salad (page 263), it would be a refreshing on a green salad.

- Combine all the ingredients in a small bowl or jar. Stir or shake well to mix.

■ Serves 4 ■

$1/4$ cup sesame oil
  (no substitute)
$1/4$ cup mayonnaise
1 tablespoon plus
  1 teaspoon soy sauce
$1/4$ teaspoon salt

NOTE: Soy sauce is a risky condiment for individuals with gluten intolerance. Most major brands have wheat clearly included on the ingredient label, and caramel coloring can sometimes contain barley. La Choy is a major brand that is gluten-free at the time of publication, despite the fact that it contains caramel coloring. Many health food stores also carry gluten-free soy sauce.

If you venture out to eat, skip the soy sauce and any dish containing it. Or, bring your own!

Spicy Roadside Chicken/Pork Marinade/Sauce

- Combine all the ingredients. Mix well. This may be used as a marinade or baste for chicken or pork, or as a condiment to top fully cooked chicken or pork.

- Do not use sauce that has been used as a marinade or brushed on as a baste as a condiment for a finished dish. Contact with the raw meats will make the uncooked sauce unsafe for this use. If you wish to also use some as a condiment, set aside some portion to use later, before using the rest as a marinade or baste.

■ Makes 1 1/4 cups ■

$3/4$ cup apple cider vinegar
$1/2$ cup oil
1 tablespoon poultry seasoning
1 tablespoon black pepper
1 tablespoon cayenne
1 tablespoon paprika
$1 1/2$ tablespoons salt

Strawberry Sauce

Although this sauce is used with the Vanilla Crème recipe, it would also be ideal over pound cake, ice cream, and so on.

- Combine all the ingredients in a blender. Puree until quite smooth and the sugar is fully dissolved. Chill. Garnish with extra berries.

■ Makes approximately 1 cup ■

1 cup strawberries, approximately 4 ounces
1 tablespoon Grand Marnier
2 tablespoons sugar

Sweet-and-Sour Sauce

A great sauce for meatballs or sweet-and-sour pork.

- Drain but reserve the juice from the pineapple.
- In a small saucepan, combine the drained pineapple chunks, ¼ cup of the retained juice, and the chile sauce and sugar. Cook over medium heat until the flavors blend and the sugar is completely dissolved.
- Serve with any sweet-and-sour dish.

■ Serves 4 ■

1 (8-ounce) can pineapple chunks in own juice

1 (7.5-ounce) jar sweet chili sauce

4 teaspoons sugar

Teriyaki Sauce

Not all teriyaki sauces are gluten-free, but you can make a very nice version with a few simple ingredients. Using honey produces a light, bright-tasting sauce; using molasses creates a dark, earthy richness.

- In a small saucepan, combine all the ingredients. Bring to a boil. The sauce will thicken as it cools.

■ Makes 1 cup ■

²/₃ cup pineapple juice

¹/₃ cup molasses or dark honey

1 teaspoon apple cider vinegar

1 ½ teaspoons cornstarch or potato starch

Tomato and Olive Tapenade

Traditional salsa is great, but variety is the spice of life. This tapenade is good with traditional corn tortilla chips, but is also great on sandwiches, focaccia, and so on.

- ■ In a medium-size bowl, combine all the ingredients. Mix well.

■ Makes approximately 4 cups; serves 12 to 15 ■

1 pint cherry or grape tomatoes, diced finely

1 small yellow or orange bell pepper, seeded and diced finely (about 5 ounces)

1 small onion, diced finely

1 (5.75-ounce) jar green olives, drained and chopped finely

1 tablespoon olive oil

$^1/_2$ ounce fresh basil, chopped finely (optional)

Gluten-Free Resources

NATIONAL GLUTEN-FREE SUPPORT GROUPS

American Celiac Society
www.americanceliacsociety.org
PO Box 23455
New Orleans, LA 70183
504-737-3293

Celiac Sprue Association/USA Inc.
www.csaceliacs.org
PO Box 31700
Omaha, NE 68131
877-CSA-4CSA

Celiac Disease Foundation
www.celiac.org
13251 Ventura Boulevard, #1
Studio City, CA 91604
818-990-2354

The Gluten Intolerance Group of North America
www.gluten.net
31214 124th Ave SE
Seattle, WA 98092
253-833-6655

LOCAL CELIAC SUPPORT GROUPS

Celiac.com
www.celiac.com

Scroll down the home page to locate index, then click on support groups.

GLUTEN-FREE MAIL ORDER SUPPLIERS

We are fortunate that there are now numerous gluten-free food suppliers in the United States. Even better, most of what you need can be found at your local grocery store or health food store. A Web search of "gluten-free foods" will give you hundreds of options for high-quality gluten-free food suppliers, but you really only need a few. Here are several of the best:

Amazon.com
www.amazon.com

A surprising home to many gluten-free foods and baking supplies. You'll save if ordering in quantity, but be sure you like the item before you order in bulk. Many gluten-free books can be ordered quite reasonably there as well.

Breads from Anna by
Gluten Evolution, LLC
www.glutenevolution.com
Iowa City, Iowa
319-354-3886
877-354-3886

This small company has mixes for some very good breads. In my opinion, they made the best overall bread at the last conference I attended. And that is why they are listed here.

Celiac.com
www.celiac.com

Home to the "celiac mall," which includes numerous suppliers of gluten-free foods, books, and so on.

The Gluten-Free Pantry
www.glutenfree.com
PO Box 840
Glastonbury, CT 06033
860-633-3826

Ener-G Foods
www.energyfoods.com
PO Box 84487
5960 1st Avenue South
Seattle, WA 98124
800-331-5222

MANUFACTURERS OF SAFE OATS

Bob's Red Mill
www.bobsredmill.com
5209 S.E. International Way
Milwaukie, OR 97222
800-553-2258

Gifts of Nature, Inc.
www.giftsofnature.net
810 7th St. E, #17
Polson, MT 59860
888-275-0003

Cream Hill Estates
www.creamhillestates.com
9633 rue Clement
LaSalle, Quebec
Canada H8R 4B4
514-363-2066
1-866-727-3628

Gluten Free Oats
www.glutenfreeoats.com
578 Lane 9
Powell, WY 82435
307-754-2058

MANUFACTURER OF POTENTIALLY SAFE OATS

McCann's Irish Oatmeal
www.mccanns.ie
c/o New World Marketing Group
44 Post Road West
PO Box 71
Westport, CT 06881
203-221-8008

Available in grocery stores nationwide. Visit the Web site and click on FAQ to evaluate their manufacturing practices and the suitability of their oats for your diet.

MY FAVORITE GLUTEN-FREE BOOKS

Celiac Disease: A Hidden Epidemic by Dr. Peter Green. Dr. Green takes the reader through the sometimes complicated and intimidating world of gluten-free living. The serious medical content of this book is softened by Dr. Green's straightforward, down-to-earth writing style. The questions and struggles of real patients peppered throughout the work put a human face on the disease.

The Gluten-Free Kitchen by Roben Ryberg. I am naturally biased toward my first book. Several of my very favorite recipes reside there, including angel and chiffon cakes, breakfast gravies, raised doughnuts, and a number of main courses.

MY FAVORITE GLUTEN-FREE MAGAZINE

Living Without
www.livingwithout.com
PO Box 2126
Northbrook, IL 60065

ADDITIONAL RESOURCES FOR THE GLUTEN-FREE COMMUNITY

In addition to the national and local support groups, www.celiac.com is a wonderful resource for medical studies, recipes, diagnosis steps, and so on.

My favorite online discussion board is www.forums.delphi.com/celiac/start. Most important, they have adopted a "zero-tolerance" policy for inclusion of any gluten in the diet (i.e., simply picking croutons off a salad is not safe!). It is a great place to talk with other individuals who live the celiac diet every day. There is no fee for basic membership. You will sometimes find me there.

Another very good online discussion board is www.glutenfreeforum.com.

For vacation getaways without worry, visit www.bobandruths.com.

■ ■ ■ NOTE ■ ■ ■

Thousands of helpful organizations, companies, and Web sites are available to the gluten-free community. Mountains of information are readily available. After making your home safe, the next step should be joining a support group—whether national, local, or online—and learning more. And, if you're not the support-group type, learn more by visiting the Web sites included in this appendix.

Index

■ ■ ■